'The world of police and judicial cooperation in the EU is a highly complex one, filled with dilemmas. Whereas sovereignty remains the leading principle, internationalization of (organized) crime continuously calls for extensive information exchange and joint operations between enforcement agencies. This book presents an overview of legal and practical developments in both the EU and Norway. Anyone who is interested in cross-border law enforcement cooperation should read it!'

Toine Spapens, Tilburg University, Netherlands

'European police cooperation is a timely, yet often challenging, topic for lay and academic observers alike. This comprehensive, systematic and authoritative book is invaluable in helping readers gain an overview of this important field, and will be extremely useful to students, scholars and practitioners for years to come.'

Katja Franko, University of Oslo, Norway

'This book makes an important contribution to police literature by analyzing the impact of international and EU police cooperation on internal security and policy of a non-EU member state (Norway). The conclusion that EU police cooperation challenges Norwegian sovereignty and impacts on crime policy choices and priorities sheds a crucial new light on the consequences of cross-border policing.'

Antoinette Verhage, Ghent University, Belgium

Police Cooperation and Sovereignty in the EU

The State and the police are traditionally seen as closely connected phenomena. Today, however, rapid EU legal developments mean that European police forces are no longer tied to a specific national legal context or a specific territory in the way they used to be.

Norway is not a member of the EU. Or is it? This book shows that although it lacks formal membership status, Norway has become part of almost all of the major EU police cooperation measures and agreements. Not only does this mean that foreign police forces may operate on Norwegian territory and vice versa, but in addition, a wide range of EU regulations and cooperation instruments are incorporated directly into Norwegian law. With the increased focus on international and transnational police cooperation in mind, what does it mean to be a sovereign state in Europe today?

This book combines strong legal and theoretical analyses of a specific national system to show how this country is tied to and dependent on a wider international and supranational system of legal rules, technologies and concepts. This makes the book relevant not only for the Norwegian prosecution and police authorities, but also for readers outside Norway interested in exploring how and whether the police as a modern state function has changed through the implementation of international cross-border cooperation mechanisms.

Synnøve Ugelvik is Associate Professor at the Department of Public and International Law at the University of Oslo. She holds a PhD in Law from the University of Oslo and has previously worked as a deputy judge and public prosecutor at the Norwegian Director of Public Prosecutions Office. Her research interests include penal law, criminal procedural law, European police cooperation and police history. She is co-editor of *Justice and Security in the 21st Century: Rights, Risks and the Rule of Law*. Her research has appeared in international and Scandinavian journals such as the *European Journal of Criminology*, *European Journal of Policing Studies* and *Retfærd.*

Transnational Criminal Justice

The concept of 'transnational criminal justice' has frequently been interpreted in the academic literature as 'international criminal justice' or 'global criminal justice'. Many publications that use the term 'transnational' therefore discuss international criminal justice and international legal frameworks. Another form of studies that has developed under the umbrella of transnationality in the field of criminal law is comparative. There has hence been a move from the terminology of 'international', 'global' and 'comparative' criminal justice towards 'transnational' criminal justice.

This series considers these developments, but focuses primarily on publications that adhere to a more literal interpretation of the term 'transnational'. The aim of the series is to provide a forum for discussion of bilateral and multilateral relationships between nations in the field of criminal justice. International law influences these relationships, but is not the focus here. Equally, to explain transnational relationships, comparative analyses are required. While incorporating comparative studies in this series, their aim is the explanation of challenges to criminal justice cooperation in bilateral or multilateral relationships.

Series Editor
Saskia Hufnagel, Queen Mary University of London, UK

Titles in this series:

Police Cooperation and Sovereignty in the EU
Norway's Lessons for Europe
Synnøve Ugelvik

For more information about this series, please visit: www.routledge.com/Transnational-Criminal-Justice/book-series/TRANSCJ

Police Cooperation and Sovereignty in the EU

Norway's Lessons for Europe

Synnøve Ugelvik

Routledge
Taylor & Francis Group
LONDON AND NEW YORK

First published 2019
by Routledge
2 Park Square, Milton Park, Abingdon, Oxon OX14 4RN

and by Routledge
52 Vanderbilt Avenue, New York, NY 10017

First issued in paperback 2020

Routledge is an imprint of the Taylor & Francis Group, an informa business

Funded by University of Oslo.

British Library Cataloguing-in-Publication Data
A catalogue record for this book is available from the British Library

Library of Congress Cataloging-in-Publication Data
Names: Ugelvik, Synnove, 1978- author.
Title: Police cooperation and sovereignty in the EU: Norway's lessons for Europe / Synnove Ugelvik.
Description: Abingdon, Oxon ; New York, NY : Routledge, 2018. |
Series: Transnational criminal justice | Based on author's thesis (doctoral – Universitetet i Oslo. Juridiske fakultet, 2014) issued under title:
Inside on the outside : Norway and police cooperation in the EU. |
Includes bibliographical references and index.
Identifiers: LCCN 2018001981 | ISBN 9781472486776 (hardback)
Subjects: LCSH: Police—Norway—International cooperation. | Police—European Union countries—International cooperation. | Law enforcement—European Union countries—International cooperation. | Law enforcement—Norway—International cooperation. | International and municipal law—Norway. | European Union—Norway.
Classification: LCC KKN3000 .U34 2018 | DDC 344.48105/2—dc23LC record available at https://lccn.loc.gov/2018001981

ISBN 13: 978-0-367-58874-8 (pbk)
ISBN 13: 978-1-4724-8677-6 (hbk)

DOI: 10.4324/9780429503696

Contents

Author's preface xi
Frequently used abbreviations xiii

1 Introduction 1

1.1 Context and the issues at stake 4
1.2 Introducing the Norwegian police 6
1.2.1 The development of 'the police' 6
1.2.2 The history of the Norwegian state and its police 7
1.2.3 Modern police systems 12
1.3 On sovereignty 13
1.3.1 Territory and authority 14
1.4 Methods 16
1.4.1 Studying international police cooperation 17
1.4.2 The EU body of law and regulations 20
1.4.3 Limitations 20
1.5 Research questions and the way forward 22
1.5.1 A short guide to the book 22

PART I
Norway and the EU 25

2 The Police Act of 1995: the modern Norwegian police organisation 27

2.1 Police work in Norway: what should the police do, and how should they do it? 27
2.1.1 General measures 30
2.2 Police competences, including rules of conduct and procedure 33
2.3 Context and synthesis of the 1995 Police Act 35
2.4 The structure and units of the Norwegian police 36
2.4.1 The general structure 36
2.4.2 Organisational structure of the operational police 38
2.4.3 Everyone's responsibility and duty to police 40

3 The Nordic police cooperation outside of the EU system 42

4 The development of EU crime control policies and the Norwegian (non) membership 45

4.1 From World War II to Schengen 45
4.2 The EC via the Single Market to the Union 45
4.3 The Area of Freedom, Security and Justice, and the constitutional changes 47

5 The development of police cooperation within the EU 50

5.1 Council of Europe 50
5.2 TREVI – Europol 51
5.2.1 TREVI 51
5.2.2 EDU – Europol 52
5.2.3 Norway in Europol 55

6 Norway – inside or outside? 57

6.1 Norway and the EEA 57
6.2 The Schengen cooperation 58
6.3 From 'No' to 'Yes, please': what changed? 59

7 Internal sovereignty: the question of membership 62

7.1 Becoming a member 62
7.2 The obligation to justify 64
7.3 Two justifications: Nordic relations and cross-border crime 65
7.3.1 Sliding justifications 67
7.4 Moving in: From the EEA to the Schengen 69
7.5 Considering sovereignty infringements 71
7.5.1 The constitutional alternatives 72
7.5.2 The question of significant sovereignty 75

8 External sovereignty: Norway and EU institutions 79

8.1 The EU political institutions 79
8.2 The court of Justice of the European Union 81
8.2.1 Legislative procedure post-Lisbon 83
8.3 Influence and the Schengen Mixed Committee 84
8.4 Foreign courts with jurisdiction over Norwegian police activities 85
8.4.1 The ESA and the EFTA Court 85
8.4.2 CJEU and Norway 86
8.5 Jurisdiction and investigation 87
8.6 Effects for the state and state sovereignty 89
8.6.1 The social contract 92
8.6.2 The EU as a state? 92

PART II
EU police cooperation: the practical regulations and their impact on Norway 97

9 Information exchange and analysis 99

9.1 Informational police work in Norway 100
9.2 The Schengen information cooperation 101
9.2.1 The Schengen Information System (SIS) 103
9.2.2 SIS contents, access and processing rules 103
9.3 Other available databases 110
9.3.1 Prüm 111
9.3.2 Immigration data systems 112
9.3.3 Europol information databases 119
9.4 Eurojust 126
9.5 Differences and similarities between the systems 129

10 Actions following hits in the databases **134**

10.1 Requests for surveillance or specific checks 134
10.2 Arrest 135
10.2.1 Arrest after a SIS hit 135
10.2.2 Europol and Eurojust arrest 138

11 Liaison officers: between operational and non-operational cooperation 140

12 National law enforcement on foreign territory: operational cooperation 142

12.1 The development and content of the relevant Norwegian legal basis 143
12.2 Hot pursuit and cross-border surveillance 145
12.2.1 The grounds for crossing borders 145
12.2.2 General rules for hot pursuit and surveillance 152
12.3 Controlled deliveries and covert investigation 160
12.3.1 Controlled deliveries 160
12.3.2 Covert investigation 163
12.4 Considering the operational cooperation 169

13 Joint operations and investigations 171

13.1 Joint investigation teams 172
13.1.1 Requirements for JITs 173
13.1.2 Members, leadership and competences of seconded members 176
13.1.3 Finance and funding 178
13.1.4 The role of Europol and Eurojust 179
13.1.5 Use of information from JITs 181
13.1.6 The Nordic joint investigation teams 182
13.1.7 Discussing the legal changes of foreign police powers 183
13.1.8 The parallel investigations alternative 185

13.2 Joint operations 186
13.2.1 Overview 186
13.2.2 Regulations common in Articles 17 and 18 189
13.2.3 Joint patrolling 190
13.2.4 Public order assistance 191
13.2.5 A Nordic version 195
13.3 Managing investigation in Norway 198
13.4 Discussing the development of operational cooperation, joint operations and investigations 201

14 Impact on the Norwegian police 205

14.1 The wider effects of the Norwegian Schengen cooperation 206
14.1.1 Changes in the policing situation and crime focus 207
14.1.2 Examining a changed Norwegian police culture 212
14.2 Extraterritorial proximity policing 214
14.2.1 A skewed police focus? 215
14.2.2 Threat assessments and the Norwegian perception of reality 217
14.2.3 Security and order 220

15 Impact on Norwegian society 225

15.1 The public 226
15.1.1 Repressive effects 226
15.1.2 Policing, security and immigration control 230
15.2 The concepts of the Police Act section 1: what do 'state' and 'community' mean? 237
15.3 An EU sovereign? 240
15.4 Concept change in a post-Westphalian system 242
15.5 Outlook: A return to proximity policing 245

16 Bibliography 248

16.1 Norwegian legislation and public documents 263
16.1.1 Norwegian legislation 263
16.1.2 Norwegian administrative and parliamentary documents 264
16.1.3 Norwegian regulations, directives, circulars, instructions 266
16.2 Nordic legislation, agreements and other documents 267
16.3 European Union policy and legislative documents 268
16.4 International conventions 273
16.5 Court decisions 274
16.6 Reports, opinions, policy papers, etc. 275

Index 277

AUTHOR'S PREFACE

This book is a revised version of my PhD thesis, defended at the Faculty of Law, University of Oslo, in December 2014. Working outside of academia, and making a family, has somewhat delayed the revision process. This delay has turned out to be challenging, since both the Norwegian and EU bodies of laws, regulations and agreements change quite rapidly. Since 2014, Europol had its new Regulation, for example, and the Prüm Cooperation was *finally* (more or less) implemented in Norway. The book is updated as of December 2017 on all legal and regulatory matters.

I am indebted to several people for their important contribution to this book. I would like to thank Ragnhild Helene Hennum, Saskia Marie Hufnagel, Kimmo Nuotio, Inger Johanne Sand, Anine Kierulf, Christoffer Conrad Eriksen, Ingvild Bruce, Rune Utne Reitan, Geir Heivoll, Sverre Flaatten, Marius Stub, Thomas Frøberg, Erlend M. Leonhardsen, Kirsti Strøm Bull, Dag Egil Adamsen, Linn Elise Gjems-Onstad and Karin Maria Svånå for input at various stages of the process.

I would also like to thank my thesis examiners Valsamis Mitsilegas, Anna Jonsson Cornell and Vidar Halvorsen for their thorough, challenging and useful comments.

This research has mostly been carried out while I worked at the Department of Public and International Law at the University of Oslo. I returned to the department as an associate professor in 2016, and I am grateful for valuable support through all these years from the department librarians Karen Danbolt and Bård Tuseth, the Heads of Administration, Guro Frostestad and Øyvind Henden, IT engineer Kjetil Frantzen and Heads of Department Aslak Syse and Ulf Stridbeck.

The Department of Public and International Law is home to the criminal law and criminal procedure law research group in Oslo, which I consider myself lucky to be a part of. The annual Eskeland seminar at Finse represents the perfect mix of academic pursuits and fun. Thank you all for being good colleagues and friends.

I spent a year in England during the course of this research project, and I am indebted to the Centre for Criminology at the University of Oxford, and in particular to Ian Loader, and to Wolfson College at the University of Cambridge, for welcoming me into their inspiring research communities.

The research project was funded by the Research Council of Norway, for which I am obviously very grateful. My project has been a part of the wider Justice in the Risk Society research project, of which also Ragnhild Helene Hennum and Heidi Mork Lomell were members. They have both become dear friends in addition to being valuable colleagues.

Many thanks also to Tor-Aksel Busch and my former colleagues at the Director of Public Prosecution's Office, where I worked after the PhD defence. This experience was rewarding on many levels, and I am particularly grateful for the chance to bring these more practical insights with me into academia.

I am very thankful for having grown up in a wonderful family, where my parents always have cultivated a deliberative community, albeit not necessarily a democracy. I admire you both for your different kinds of enthusiasm, your kindness and wisdom. Thank you. My sisters and dear friends, Ellen and Ingrid, are of invaluable support, with their kindness and belief in me. Thank you.

One has done and been all of the above. Thomas Ugelvik is my best friend, husband and strongest critic. He believes in me more than anyone else, he cooks for me, reads to and for me and carries the load when I decide to throw my rifle over my shoulder and run after reindeer in the mountains. Thank you.

Thomas and I have always worked a lot. We have enjoyed late nights in the office, at seminars or elsewhere, all features of a traditional egocentric academic lifestyle. When our daughter, Eldbjørg, was born in February 2016, it altered everything. Who could have imagined how great that change could be? Eldbjørg: Thank you.

This book is for Eldbjørg and Thomas.

Frequently used abbreviations

AWF	Europol Analysis Work Files
CBO Manual	Cross Border Policing Manual CBO Manual 10505/3/09 (REV 3)
CFREU	EU Charter of Fundamental Rights
CJEU	Court of Justice of the European Union
CoE	Council of Europe
Commission	EU Commission
Council	EU Council
CPA	Norwegian Criminal Procedure Act
DPP	Norwegian Director of Public Prosecution (*Riksadvokaten*)
EAW	European Arrest Warrant
EC	European Community (law)
ECHR	European Convention for the Protection of Human Rights and Fundamental Freedoms (1950)
ECtHR	European Court of Human Rights
ED/EP CD	Europol Decision (EP CD when it might be confused with Eurojust Decision)
EEA	European Economic Agreement
EEC	European Economic Community
EGF	European Gendarmerie Force
EIO	European Investigation Order
EIS	Europol Information System
EJCD/EJD	Eurojust Council Decision
E–N	Europol–Norway Agreement
EP	European Parliament
EP–N	Norway and Iceland's agreement with Europol
ER	Europol Regulation
ETS	European Treaty Series
ETS no.182	Council of Europe Convention of 1959 2nd Protocol
EU	European Union
FD	Framework Decision
Forarbeid	White papers, consultation papers, and other Norwegian legislative preparatory works
GCPC	Norwegian General Civil Penal Code
JIT	Joint Investigation Team
LT	Lisbon Treaty

Ministry (MoJ)	Norwegian Ministry of Justice and Public Security (formerly 'Norwegian Ministry of Justice and the Police')
MLA/2000 Convention	EU Convention on Mutual Assistance in Criminal Matters
MS	Member State
NOU	*Norsk offentlig utredning (Official Norwegian Report)*
PA	Norwegian Police Act
PD	Norwegian Police Directive (*politiinstruksen)*
PRD	Norwegian Police Registration Directive
PWD	Police Weapons Directive (*våpenforskriften*)
SAA	Norwegian Schengen Association Agreement
SIRENE	Supplementary Information Request
SIS	Schengen Information System
SIU	Special Intervention Units
Stortinget	The Norwegian Parliament
TEU	Treaty on European Union
TFEU	Treaty on the Functioning of the European Union

1 INTRODUCTION

Section 1. Responsibility and purpose

The State shall provide the police service needed by the community. Police duties shall be performed by the police and *lensman* services.

The police shall, through preventive, enforcing and support activities contribute to society's overall effort to promote and consolidate the citizens' security under the law, and their safety and welfare in general.

The Norwegian Police Act, section 1[1]

A modern police force has a wide variety of tasks and obligations. The police are controllers and helpers. They are service providers and enforcers of legitimate violence. They are the factotums of modern societies. The police maintain social order, safety and (a perception of) security. A police force is charged with having an overview of what needs to be done, and where and when it should be done, in the community that has been made its responsibility. A core characteristic of the police is the link to the particular communities they work in.[2] The link may be relevant for several reasons. One is the necessity for intimate knowledge of the particular community's features to understand where the factotum's efforts are needed. Another is the fact that the police's attitudes and practices should be shaped by cultural values shared with the population they control and serve. A third reason concerns the legitimacy of the police role: the police force is responsible for citizens' needs and is accountable to the law.[3]

The theme of this book is Norway's situation as an insider and outsider of the EU. The police have traditionally had a monopoly on enforcing state violence. The state is composed of its citizens, so at least to some extent, they should decide what the police do. The international agreement, Schengen, was the start of a ground-breaking change of the possibilities for the Norwegian police and policing of Norway. What I argue in this book as being one of four challenges to Norwegian sovereignty, concerns the importance of the citizens understanding the state's action on their behalf.

Policing is generally acknowledged to be a central function of sovereign nation-states.[4] A state is often seen as fundamentally dependent on both its police force and its citizens to be a 'state'; one might say that, according to this view, a state without a police force is not a proper

1 Act of 04.08.1995 no.53 (Police Act [PA], unofficial translation by the Ministry of Justice and Police).

2 Bittner 1990:249.

3 Bayley and Shearing 2001.

4 Wallace 1999:509–510.

DOI: 10.4324/9780429503696-1

state. The last 20 years or so have, however, seen crime and mobility trends that have contributed to changes across nation-state borders, whereby national police forces are faced with new sorts of crimes and disorder and a greater number of non-citizens in their territories.

A range of cross-border police cooperation instruments has been established to target these new problems. The Norwegian Police Act sect. 1, quoted above, remains the same as it was before the changes following the implementation of Norwegian affiliation agreements to cross-border police cooperation. The legal and social context has, however, changed in many ways.

The state administration is directed by the government. It has at its disposal a large public organisation to administer laws and regulations as set out by the government itself, and scrutinised by the courts and parliament. The nation-state has these features, but is also defined by why a government controls this particular area, and why citizens accept this control. Schengen membership and other affiliations, I argue here, bring into question whether the state still has an ultimate responsibility for policing, crime control, and the general provision of security and welfare to its citizens. The main concepts in this book are closely related to each other. There is no community without individual citizens. Without citizens, there is no state. The borders within and surrounding Europe have changed with the broad cooperation entities such as the EU. The citizens referred to in the Police Act are not necessarily exclusively Norwegian citizens any longer. The kind of police service that is currently considered to be 'needed' may be something else than the desired police service of previous eras. Norway is the case examined in this study, but the findings are of general interest in today's Europe. The Brexit referendum and a seemingly general anxiety in Europe about national extremism, less EU loyalty, etc., make the case of Norway, an outsider state, pertinent at several levels.

A significant defining characteristic of the modern nation-state is *sovereignty*. My use of the concept will be explained in full in Chapter 1.3. For now, it is sufficient to remind readers that sovereignty refers both to the fact that a sovereign state has its territorial boundaries respected by other states (external sovereignty) and to its responsibility for protecting its subjects on that territory (internal sovereignty).[5] Further, a democratic state has its sovereignty constituted by the citizens of that state, which is often termed popular sovereignty. One point of departure is the Weberian notion that the police is the state's 'tool' of coercion within its territory and the only legitimate enforcer of violence against persons.[6] This legitimate force is made operational by and through the police. For Weber, this is a defining feature of the state. According to Manning, the police is "the institution formally charged by states to lawfully execute the monopoly over means of coercion".[7] In one view, the police constitute the state in a modern sense, because a state that cannot get anything done is not a state. The histories of the state and of the police are to a certain extent intertwined. The historical account of the police given in this book is therefore also the story of a changing state. There are significant variations both in the way societies have institutionalised the police function across socio-historic circumstances and the extent to which these police institutions have been monopolised and perceived to be legitimate.[8] It is, however, generally assumed in democratic states that the police act on behalf of a particular state (government)

5 In line with Hobbes 1998 [1651]:114, no.13, see also Walker 1993:37–38.

6 Weber 1958; Marenin 1982.

7 Manning 1977:105. E.g. Hobbes 1998 [1651]:7, also Luhmann, see Hagen 2010. Also, Neocleous 2003 and Ringmar 1996 on society as a body with different parts.

8 Deflem 2002; Deflem and Sutphin 2006.

within state territory, while military forces exert state power outside or on the borders of the territory. While these two entities may both use coercion or violence on behalf of the state,[9] the significant difference between them is that the armed forces are normally responsible for protecting the external borders and maintaining the security of a state, while the police are responsible for internal security and general order.[10] When a state's police exercise powers outside a certain territory, as in the case of international police cooperation in the general Schengen Area, the notion of state is challenged, so also the other central concepts in the Police Act sect. 1. The police's functions encompass more than the enforcement of state coercion. This aspect is highlighted, however, because the police *can* always resort to violence, legitimately, on behalf of the state. This aspect is also what is challenged when the police moves across the borders of its 'legitimating' state.

This book argues that the notion of the state's monopoly on legitimate violence on its territory is now, if not obsolete, then at least challenged. This might not be a new development: the increased use of private security guards and the building of private prisons in many jurisdictions may be seen to question the very notion of a state monopoly on violence.[11] Perhaps such a monopoly never actually existed in practice. In the Norwegian context, however, this monopoly is arguably the very foundation of the Police Act sect. 1, and in this book, the section is taken seriously.

There is not a great deal of research on the Norwegian police, and their role in cross-border European Union (EU) police cooperation. One reason for this may be the fact that Norway is not part of the EU. But as this book shows, Norway is definitely part of EU police cooperation. This book seeks to give a comprehensive account of the regulation of Norwegian participation in that cooperation. It does not, however, deal only with the legal state of affairs. Another aim is to analyse how the police force has developed, and to understand how the traditional relationship between the police, the state and citizens may be seen to be changing in modern European societies. This makes the book of relevance to readers outside Norway, who may be interested in an exploration of how the police as a function of the modern state has been affected by international cross-border cooperation mechanisms – those of the Schengen area and EU in particular.

There are three central findings. One is the challenge to the Norwegian sovereignty. The instruments of police cooperation imply, at least in a formal sense, that Norway has transferred some of its jurisdictional sovereignty to other countries. While it is frequently claimed that policing remains ultimately within Norwegian state competences, it can be argued that several aspects of police cooperation, at both the practitioners' and the political level, call this claim into question. The book also argues that aspects of international police cooperation may have effects other than the apparent, desirable goals. The other two findings concern the fact that, while the cooperation instruments of the EU, the European Economic Agreement (EEA) and the Schengen Agreement all have as a main purpose the increased circulation of people and 'freedoms', they also imply a shift in the state's focus on its internal security situation. This in turn implies, 1) an increased emphasis on policing crimes with

9 Walker emphasises, however, that the contemporary idea of an *independent* police power is also an important symbol of autonomous statehood (Walker 1993). This is not contradictory; my point is that the police do not have *complete* autonomy.

10 E.g. Bayley 1975:328–9. The military may also be considered to have been central in maintaining internal stability before the early 20th century Norwegian state was sufficiently established to maintain order based on a civil police force.

11 Harding 2012.

some kind of international aspect, including those simply involving police cooperation instruments, and 2) that police cooperation largely results in *limitation* of the circulation of many groups of individuals.

1.1 Context and the issues at stake

In the 21st century, societies are interconnected with and influenced by each other in ways unimaginable a hundred years ago, when each state (or community within a state) was responsible for policing its territory, or for stopping (or deporting) criminals (or potential criminals) at the border. While various forms of informal communication between police officers happened centuries ago, especially in border regions, *formalised* international cooperation across borders did not start to take substantial form before the late 19th century. Issues such as the white slave trade and counterfeiting were, however, mutual concerns of several governments even then. International cooperation gained momentum after the Second World War. The early regional European Community treaties of the 1950s were primarily intended to unite the European states in trade relations, and prevent acts of hostility. These early initiatives did not include measures on the police or crime control; policing remained a national preserve.[12] Terrorist attacks in the 1970s and '80s, however, encouraged initiatives on police and crime control cooperation. Internationalisation and globalisation increased throughout these decades, along with rapid technological development and the expectation that the law should be up-to-date and able to regulate these areas, as it did the more traditional normative areas of society.[13]

The EU is central to this book, both as an agreement, or collection of agreements, as an organisation and as a political entity. The EU is the single most significant actor for Norway in terms of international and transnational police cooperation. It is also central because of its status, and development as a – to some extent – supranational entity. The economic cooperation leading to the EC in the 1950s has developed radically, especially during the past three decades. There have been great changes since the early beginnings of informal cooperation in the 1960s and '70s in the area of justice and home affairs between member states, when there was no EC institutional direction, and only traditional public international law instruments to build on when drawing up contracts (most states did not regard such agreements as an essential part of their legal system[14]). During the 1990s, the role of human rights was strengthened, especially by the growth of the activity of the Court (ECtHR) based on the European Convention of Human Rights (ECHR). The development of the EU Area of Freedom, Security and Justice (AFSJ) may be seen as focussing on individual rights such as those sovereign states were commonly viewed as responsible for safeguarding. In addition to some degree of harmonisation of criminal law, the policing and security cooperation initiatives within, and linked to, the EU accelerated, as regards both the role of the European Police Office (Europol) and the legal grounds for such decentralised police cooperation as that occurring through the Schengen Convention[15], the Prüm

12 One explanation may be that the Cold War kept the security focus locked eastwards (Anderson *et al.* 1995:47).

13 Op. cit., see also Knepper 2011.

14 Peers 2011:9–10.

15 The Convention dates from 1985. The Schengen *Acquis* was implemented by the implementing convention (CISA) in the EU legal body by the Amsterdam Treaty of 1997 (1999). The term 'Schengen Convention' is used of the implementing convention, since this is the basis on which Norway entered into agreement with the EU.

Cooperation and the principles of mutual recognition, availability and data-exchange. To return to the mission statement of the Norwegian Police Act as quoted above – when the EU is supposedly the foremost area in which freedom, security and justice are to be experienced, the question may be raised as to how 'the state' can be the provider of the police service needed by the community.

While not a member of the EU, Norway has entered into, or is in the process of entering into, several EU police cooperation and other crime control agreements. Central measures and mechanisms described in part II of the book, include controlled deliveries across borders, covert investigations abroad, joint investigation teams consisting of police from several countries and joint patrols of police in territories beyond their home state.

In sum, there are a number of operational and information-related police cooperation instruments, designed to prevent crime and to uphold the wider public order. In other words, police cooperation mission statements very often appear to target core tasks of the Norwegian police. These international cooperation measures, then, seem to blur what is implied in section 1 of the Police Act. If police employed by one state do police work in other states, is 'the state' still the provider of the police service? Which state? Will foreign police officers have a different understanding than domestic officers of what it takes to maintain public order outside their territories and normal cultural contexts? How important is the traditionally strong link between a national police force and its state? These issues are included in the overarching question: Does the police still presuppose the state? In what way? And how will the answer to these questions impact on our understanding of the concept of 'sovereignty'?

Historically, it has been argued that the European state system made possible a "higher level of moral community within the territory of each single state" by offering each state a certain measure of safety from external interference from others; in other words, in the making of their domestic good order.[16] And under such conditions, a ruler was less likely to be overthrown by dissatisfied subjects. A recurring theme in this research project is the tension that arises when this distinction is blurred by police working outside the state territory, on tasks formerly reserved for the military.[17]

In this book 'police' refers to the police *force* – an organisational definition – i.e. the persons employed by the state to perform the activities the state finds necessary. This is meant to emphasise that it is a specific function organised in and by a state. The police do not always act with coercion, as already mentioned, but the coercive potential entrusted them by the state, is always present. The policing tasks performed by other actors, such as private security personnel etc., are not dealt with here. Outside the traditional police force, a functional definition of policing will include police activity performed by, for example, the coastguard, the coastal supervisory authorities, the armed forces, the customs authorities, and the state health authorities. The function of some of these bodies is discussed when they act as police as described in the Police Act.

The police are currently dependent on a specific government, both to be given tasks and competences, and for these tasks and competences to be legitimate – meaning that these are delegated by the citizens in a democratic society. Citizens need security, and are willing to give up certain aspects of freedom in order to achieve this; this is the core of classic social

16 Liang 1992:9.

17 Referring to what Brodeur has termed "high policing" tasks, i.e. those concerning the security of the state itself, not the internal territorial security or public order (Brodeur 1983).

contract theory. Citizens decide, when electing political leaders, which legislation is to be upheld and created, and consequently what limits there should be on their freedoms, and which actions constitute *crimes*. The state, and the concept of state legitimacy, only make sense in the context of a specific territory, a conceptual change often pinpointed as following the peace of Westphalia in 1648.[18] Although police organisations can be more or less attached to, influential for, and powerful within, various structures, there are no examples of police organisations acting completely independently of a state structure. Such an organisation might look like a police force, but would be something else entirely (where, for example, armed groups of state officials join in or carry out revolutionary activities outside state structures, they are military or paramilitary groups). Security guards, on the other hand, may have uniforms and tasks that make them look like police forces, but they have no legitimate authority or competence beyond that of ordinary civilians.

The EU over the past 60 years has developed many traits similar to those that developed in modern states from the 17th century onwards. These developments have consequences for the very concepts of citizen, nation-state and police, as I argue in the last chapter of this book. The relationship between state, territory and citizen should be seen as significantly changed when viewed through the lens of the changes in policing, and more specifically, through international, cross-border police cooperation in what may be seen as a regional 'community' of Europe: the Schengen Area. This is the subject matter of the book.

1.2 Introducing the Norwegian police

If one wants to understand the function of the police, and its organisation, an examination of its historical development may supply insights. The earliest police force was local, informal, and privately run. Today the police are a centralized force that is governed according to formal laws, rules and regulations on behalf of a state. From this perspective, the development of a modern police force can be said to be a form of statecraft: the police and the state have been mutually constitutive of each other. The development of police forces, as a more specific (and specifically modern) phenomenon, has been dependent on the political development of the nation-state. Different nation-states have different stories.

1.2.1 The development of 'the police'

The meaning of 'police' is often taken for granted, with an assumption that there is a common understanding. 'Police' and 'policing', however, are multifaceted concepts with complex meanings. Those performing what have been understood as police tasks, come in diverse forms throughout history and across geographical areas. This is necessary to understand if we want to comprehend how the present police force and its tasks became what it is. The term 'police' pre-dates the modern state. It derives from the Greek word *politeia*, denoting, among other things, good order and welfare within a community. Understood in such a broad sense, the police existed long before the modern state system, ever since early communities began to exercise some kind of control over their members.[19] The historic meaning of the term is, as seen above, still present in today's Norwegian Police Act.

18 Elden 2013; Stolleis 1988:366.
19 E.g. Bayley 1985:28; Anners 1997; Dubber 2005:ch.3; Neocleous 2000:1; Stevnsborg 2010:13.

The police organisation does not act on behalf of itself: it possesses certain competences delegated to it by someone. This dependence on a particular community is well formulated in Tilly's observation: "[T]he manner and form of policing register with extraordinary clarity the history of the interaction between the state makers and the people they seek to control".[20] It seems also to be commonly agreed that whoever performs policing activities, does so with specific aims. The ***aims and purposes*** of policing have to some extent also changed with the development of 'the police' in modern times.

In the 'politeia' sense, the police existed in very early communities, including in Norway. The modern police, however, have more narrow characteristics. Bayley characterises it as "public, specialized, and professional". Bayley's definition of 'public' is that police work is done on behalf of a collective community, and is also paid for by this collective (it is not privately funded).[21] Policing tasks, on the other hand, may be performed by private entities or individuals. The focus here is on the police force, as developed in relation to the state system and the citizens. This goes along with defining the police through their prerogative to employ coercive force against citizens on behalf of a government.[22] The limited territory of a king or feudal lord may not make up the 'community' that is necessary for the police to match this definition, one that is dependent on an authorisation in the name of a ***community***. Modern states (from the 17th century) grew out of communities that had evolved into towns and cities in the Medieval period. The 'invention' of the modern police is often seen to coincide with the birth of the modern state and thereafter with the ***nation*** state.[23]

The aim here is to provide the basis for an assessment of how the Norwegian police have turned out the way they have, the relevance of the changes to policing resulting from EU cooperation, and how these may impact the state and the Union in the future.

1.2.2 The history of the Norwegian state and its police

The Norwegian attitude to its relationship with the rest of Europe, is closely connected with the country's historic development as a state, outside and inside unions. During the last 600 years, Norway's history has been closely intertwined with that of its Nordic neighbours Denmark and Sweden. Norway and Sweden shared the same kings ('personal union') throughout the 14th century, and all three countries entered into the ***Kalmarunion***, a similar form of shared-monarch union, from 1397. While Sweden left in 1523, Norway remained, with various degrees of autonomy, in this 'personal union' with Denmark until 1814. From the 1660s, Norway to some extent had separate laws and institutions: it had, for example, its own army. Despite these elements of independence, however, Norway was ceded from Denmark to Sweden after the Napoleonic wars in 1814, and remained under Swedish rule in a forced personal union until 1905. The country nonetheless kept its constitution, drawn up in 1814, and separate parliamentary institutions, except for the Foreign Service, which was shared with Sweden.

Another point to be considered is whether one sees the state as a set of rules, policies and regulations – an ideal system made up of different agencies – or the various practices of state agents in 'the real world'. As stated by way of introduction, this book considers the state as

20 Tilly 1975:59.
21 Bayley 1985:24.
22 Op. cit.:7–11; Bittner 1970:36.
23 Op. cit.:18; Walker 2000:228.

a central government, whether run by a king or an elected body. But the 'state' is also taken to describe the nation-state, where a *people* possess the power over a certain territory. The history of the nation-state in the present chapter is relevant because it shows that a perception of Norway as a sovereign state flourished even while the country was part of various Nordic unions. This point will be taken up again later to elucidate why the present-day Norwegian state acts as it does in relation to international agreements and unions, in both general state areas and specifically police ones.

During the three centuries before the peace of Westphalia, the modern state was evolving, in that there was a continuous struggle to gain sovereign power over a certain area and to defend this area against other lords or kings. This did not involve the police while the struggle concerned the expansion or protection of borders: this task belonged to military forces. Until the Westphalian peace, there was a long series of wars in Europe.[24] As a result, much of the available resources went to the armed forces, either to arm soldiers to expand the realm, or to protect a community against attack. However, the development of the police resulted in a more permanent and stable state, as the general welfare and order of the community was given priority, instead of military defence, or increased imperialist expansion taking up most of the resources. No international treaty could be agreed upon unless all the signatories were reasonably secure at home. An official could not be trusted when entering into agreements on behalf of his state, if the internal hierarchies or power structures back home were not stable and trustworthy.[25] At the same time, the fact that states were able to allocate more resources to policing their internal territories, rather than just protecting or expanding external borders, contributed to the safety and security felt by a particular community within a particular state territory.[26]

The establishment of police forces proper is often seen as a new disciplining measure introduced by the newly reinforced absolutist sovereigns of European states in the 1660s. Stevnsborg, however, argues that strong, autonomous police authorities were created bottom-up, by municipal prime movers, as a response to local needs, and not as a result of monarchs' and lords' desire for control.[27] In the case of Norway, the police function in the form of the state's (then, the King in Copenhagen) control of its inhabitants had definitely been present since the 17th century. The bylaws may have been the most important form of control, however, and these were created locally. The mid-level positions in the steadily growing administrative apparatus in Norway were more often occupied by Norwegians.[28] Due to growing professionalisation, education was necessary, and the University of the Dano-Norwegian Union was located in Copenhagen. Similarly, the officers of the Norwegian army that developed from the mid-17th century were recruited via Copenhagen from Denmark, or elsewhere on the European continent. From one perspective, the Dano-Norwegian situation is characterised by the King's placing of strong (Danish) leaders in (Norwegian) administrative positions.[29]

One reason that local communities and citizens were not affected too heavily by the fact that the Danish occupied positions of power may be that there was a division between the tasks of the 'low' police and of higher administration. (A view that may be comparable to

24 E.g. Brett 2011:3; Kirchner and Sperling 2007:2.

25 Liang 1992:7–9.

26 E.g. Connolly 2002. This is further discussed in Part II.

27 Stevnsborg 2010:16; 18–19.

28 Rao and Supphellen 1996:87.

29 Op.cit.:87.

present-day perceptions of relations with the EU.) This was probably less important, however, than the fact that the *lensmen*, voluntary watchmen or other people performing police tasks closest to individuals, were locally connected. The police were part of the communities they policed. Especially in rural, undeveloped areas, small towns may have seemed far away from the wealthy elites. This may also pinpoint the difference between contrasting conceptions of the meaning of the police, who might be seen as an instrument of power employed from above, or a safety provider managed from below. According to Andenæs, the general Norwegian population were not resentful of Danish rule, as it was perceived as a protection from unfair rule by more local nobility and civil officials.[30]

The idea of the *nation*-state is often thought to have been born at the time of the French Revolution of 1789. In contrast to the *sovereign* state, which dates from the mid–17th century, the nation-state presupposes a common identity, a perception of being *Norwegian*, and experiencing belongingness and even love for one's country.[31] The sovereign state could easily be absolutist: those living there were mere subjects. The nation-state, however, is made far stronger and more stable when perceived as consisting of citizens who are self-identifying national subjects.

The police can be seen to have acted as a form of 'identity marker' in this situation. States by no means provided equal rights (or even equal obligations), and those regarded as citizens were only a small percentage of the population. One may, however, see a change from the use of the police to control the population, to its use for the common good of the population, now seen more as the state/ruler, under the inspiration, for example of the social contract theories of Rousseau and Locke that emerged in this period. One important element is the idea of people policing themselves. When citizens give up some of their freedoms to obtain security and protection from the sovereign, the coercive power wielded over them based on this delegation needs to be located not too far from them. Power wielded from too great a distance may prevent the sovereign from understanding what kind of security and protection citizens want. Such an understanding is necessary to keep citizens sufficiently satisfied that they will not revolt against the sovereign.

Seeing the traditional concept of 'police' in terms of the good order of a territory implied a conception of 'order' similar to what today constitutes general welfare state tasks, according to, for example, Foucault.[32] And a readiness to undertake welfare tasks implies that violence or lawlessness have given way to a more peaceful society where the authorities do not simply control, but also care for, subjects.[33] The growth of an expanding administrative state in these territories was characterised by the classic understanding of *politeia* – good governance and administration of the citizens in every area of life possible to regulate. Thus, the state administration had to concern itself with the well-being of everyone – in every way it could be ensured by control and regulation. In such a system, the police force represented the unlimited power of the sovereign.

Along with the rest of Europe, Denmark-Norway experienced more unstable and restless times from the late 18th century onwards. The establishment of the first Norwegian modern corps of constables in Kristiania (Oslo) in 1858, which replaced the watchmen that by then were deemed insufficient, exemplifies this general tendency.[34] When considering the impact

30 Andenæs 1998:35, see also Castberg 1961:14 ff.

31 Anderson 2006.

32 Foucault 2007:ch.12.

33 Brodeur 2010:49; 77.

34 Utseth 1947:34. The reorganisation took place throughout Norway in the following years.

of the police on the developing state and its internal affairs, there are two elements that seem to deserve attention. On the one hand, there are the coercive powers of any type of police (*lensman*, etc.) over offenders in the community, such as individuals committing offences like murder, theft, drunken and disorderly behaviour and failure to appear in church on Sunday. On the other hand, there are coercive powers given to the police to control the people *en masse*. During the 18th century, absolute monarchies sought to quell popular riots and anti-monarchist rebels, and this demanded a kind of police work quite different from what the police, either in rural or urban areas were equipped to do. The police were now tasked with protecting the state, which hitherto had been the job of the military, but against its citizens, rather than external forces.[35]

There are contemporary comments on the significance of the 'new' powers of the police, and debates about what kind of police force was *not* desirable. The police were obliged to be clearly identified by uniforms. The French semi-military *gendarmerie* was considered throughout the 17th and 18th centuries as a possible model in Denmark-Norway, especially following clashes between students and police in Copenhagen in the 1780s and '90s and other occasions when the military was called to assist the police.[36] This police model was, however, eventually rejected.[37]

At the end of the Napoleonic wars at the beginning of the 19th century, there were radical changes in Norwegian society. Embargoes and food shortages contributed to political and social unrest, and growing xenophobia. Various factors brought more migration from rural areas to the towns and cities. The organisation and nature of police work in urban areas is different from that in in rural areas, and a major increase in the population of cities all over Europe created new needs for urban police systems. New justice and police departments were established during the early 19th century, and a director police chief was made responsible for law and order enforcement for the entire Dano-Norwegian kingdom.[38] While the police could previously be seen as a tool for administering the affairs of the state, it was now turning into a more specifically preventive force defending the state against internal enemies.[39] An increasingly important police task was more thorough identity control, especially of foreigners.[40] In 1814, despite the move from Danish to Swedish 'partnership', the Norwegian capital achieved its own Norwegian government, in line with its own constitution. Norway resisted being ceded from Denmark to Sweden, preferring its independence in *partnership* with Denmark. Although the ceding went ahead, this only happened after a brief war, and the Norwegian government managed to obtain a large degree of sovereignty, that laid the foundation for the sovereign nation-state of Norway in years to come, and the final secession in 1905. The ceding in 1814 was made dependent on Norwegian approval. Norway claimed to be an independent kingdom – the Norwegian part of a separate nation – and that the principles of natural and international law prevented ceding.[41]

Before the liberal developments in the era of the Enlightenment, the division between the military and the police was largely functional: their aims could be similar and only their

35 As an example, the 1793 ordinance was amended to allow up to six years' incarceration for rioting or other disturbance of order and peace.

36 Stevnsborg 2010:30 ff.

37 Op. cit.:58–60.

38 Bonde 1994:27.

39 Axtmann 1992; Brodeur 2010:43.

40 Bonde 1994:27.

41 Andenæs 1998:35 ff.; Castberg 1961.

specific tasks differentiated them. In the Enlightenment era the concept of citizens' rights developed, and inspired constitutions, such as that of Norway, which generally prohibited the use of force by the army against citizens.[42] But all available forces in the service of the king would be deployed in cases of riots or public disorder threatening to overturn the state itself. The division of forces may be seen as being connected initially to the development of sovereignty as a manner of power division in the emerging nation-states, and later to democratic considerations.[43] When the use of coercive force is regulated, the possibility for the king's personal abuse of the armed forces is diminished, i.e. when Parliament controls the legislation regulating military intervention or assistance to the police.[44] Different policing systems within Europe have different histories. Different versions of military police forces, such as the French *gendarmerie*, also make the dividing lines between police and other coercive forces of the state less obvious when viewed in an international context. It has been argued that a police force presupposes a peaceful situation. The military and the police respectively take care of the external and internal security of a territory. Such dividing lines may be based on power division considerations, or simply on the division of tasks. More practically, however, as Brodeur argues, it may have been that the methods and weapons of the military were simply increasingly unsuited to narrow urban streets.[45]

The most important implication of 1814 the sovereignty change for Norway may have been increased respect from those beyond its territorial borders. Although Norway largely kept her own laws and traditions in the administrative field and elsewhere, and was thus never fully integrated into Denmark, sovereign rule in the uneven Dano-Norwegian Union had been firmly situated in Denmark since the late 14th century.[46] There was no Norwegian Council; the political leader was Danish and based in Copenhagen. Although the wealthy families of Norway were quite close to the Danish rulers, the chief administrative positions in Norway were occupied by Danish expats, be it in cities or the smaller towns.[47] Norway was in principle an independent kingdom in *union* with the more dominant Denmark until 1814, albeit subject to Danish political and economic rule.[48] The Danish-Norwegian chancellery had ultimate supervisory responsibility for the police until 1814, when the Norwegian Police Ministry took over.[49] According to Imsen, however, there are strong indications that local Norwegian communities were in practice relatively autonomous, and able to regulate themselves and their inhabitants.[50]

The regulations concerning police activity seem to have been largely independent of the sovereign, or the international legal position of the Norwegian state. While the 17th and 18th centuries saw a certain centralisation of control over the police across Denmark-Norway, the regional and local ordinances appeared to withstand, to some extent, 'governance at a distance'. One could perhaps expect significant consequences from Norway's move from being a subordinate in a 'union' with Denmark, to being a country in

42 Fleischer 1981.
43 Cf. e.g. Manning 2010:44; Fleischer *op cit.* The book is limited to Western developments, given the main theme is the EU context. In Western *colonies*, such as South Africa, policing and military were not necessarily distinct in the conventional way (Brogden 1989).
44 E.g. Frostad 2009.
45 Brodeur 2010:ch.2.
46 Even after 1536, when Denmark took the governing power of the union (Rao and Supphellen 1996:85).
47 Op.cit.:85–7.
48 Union at least after 1660. Andenæs 1998:34.
49 Utseth 1947:24.
50 Imsen 1997.

a personal union with Sweden. The highest administrative body for the police of Norway, which had been the Danish-Norwegian Cancelli, was not transferred into the Swedish union. Instead, this responsibility was given to the Norwegian Police Ministry.

1.2.3 Modern police systems

The history of neither the Norwegian state nor the Norwegian police should be seen in isolation: the history of the modern nation-states is a *European* history. Bayley argues that it is impossible to pinpoint the emergence of modern police at a specific moment in time. A modern police force does not appear simultaneously across Europe: rather, the features of modern police appear at different times in different countries.[51] Both the French and English pre-modern and modern police systems had local and regional, central and decentralised characteristics.[52] The 'modern police' in its general present-day form is considered to have been born in early 19th century England. The French model, which had some of modern traits, had roots in the 17th century, and Brodeur argues it was the first police force in the modern sense, having a particular focus on so-called 'high policing', i.e. 'state protecting' policing. This was *reinvented*, he argues, although in a less political way by the British 150 years later.[53] Either way, the Norwegian police share features with both models.[54] Nonetheless, the modern British police force more clearly bears the characteristics of today's modern police. The British model was an explicit inspiration for the 1912 Norwegian Police Committee that did the groundwork for the first Norwegian Police Act of 1927.

As in France and Britain, since the 19th century, the Norwegian state administration system and the police force have been divided into various agencies with specialised functions. These specialised police tasks seem to have developed in a similar way, independent of the categorisation of the various countries' police agencies.[55]

Criminal investigation at this time was a somewhat novel function of the police. Investigative police were not distinguished from 'normal' police or city guards before the 18th century. Policing primarily meant low policing; maintaining peace and order, and protecting people's life, health and property. The role of the police expanded, from upholding the king's peace and collecting the king's taxes, to include the enforcement of general order. The French police was sometimes infamous for achieving a very orderly society, but employing methods that did not necessarily ensure order was combined with security or safety. Comparison with the English model may be flawed because it inevitably involves the risk of anachronism: one is comparing very different periods of time. The English 'model' mainly evolved after the Enlightenment Era and is thus affected by a different view of the value of the individual. Either way, the English model was the inspiration for the first Norwegian national Police Act, especially in its discussions of the proximity and equality of police personnel vis-à-vis the people being 'policed'.

Irrespective of country, police tasks are characterised by the fact that they are seen as arising within a specific territory. Some tasks upheld the political order, for example the arrest of political opponents, the collection of taxes to finance the ruler, or the outlawing of people, to maintain control over the territory. Other types of task were those that to a lesser

51 Bayley 1975:340–1.

52 See e.g. op.cit.:348 ff. and further references; and Becker 1973.

53 Brodeur 2010:ch.2.

54 E.g. Furuhagen 2009:12.

55 Emsley 2001.

degree were for the benefit of the ruler.[56] The former, high policing, in a modern sense means protecting the security of the nation. Low policing thus turns the focus inward on the nation itself. It will be argued here that international police cooperation was originally a form of high policing, targeting crimes seen as threatening the security of the cooperating nations. However, in recent years, international policing may be seen to have 'turned low': the monarch's or sovereign state's security is not always the prime target of cooperation, which also focuses on the communities 'below' the nation, as in the case of public order policing.

In the context of this book, the important question is whether the understanding of what the police is and should be, is locally anchored.

1.3 On sovereignty

During the Schengen and EEA negotiations, it was frequently reiterated that Norway should maintain its sovereign status as an outsider to the EU. Norway is obviously still a sovereign and autonomous state in that the Government can veto any EU development, which, in only slightly different circumstances, according to both the Schengen and EEA agreements, would probably terminate Norway's membership.[57] As a member or associate member of these two agreements, Norway is bound to obey and implement Schengen-relevant and EEA measures decided by EU bodies. Among the agreement expansions concerning, for example, joint investigation teams, some are considered Schengen-relevant, some are not.[58] Although Norway's hybrid status means it has little influence and no decision-making competence, I will show in this book that Norway usually becomes, or tries to become, a member of any and all police cooperation instrument that is launched within the EU. This simple fact may call into question the claim that Norway has sovereign status as an EU outsider. Given a semi-constitutional binding, this has few legal consequences. One could ask, however, whether the developments discussed in this book may have *de facto* consequences for how the state acts as sovereign, and how the population can demonstrate its sovereignty, thereunder the factual effect of various police measures in the society and for the police.

Sovereignty is one of the concepts in political philosophy and the political and legal sciences that has received most scholarly attention. There are entire libraries devoted to discussions of various aspects of this concept. This is not a comprehensive theoretical treatise on sovereignty. This, rather, is a book about a specific political and legal development (European cross-border police cooperation) seen from a particular perspective (that of Norway). I am going to use this ongoing development to discuss certain aspects of sovereignty, understood as a practical phenomenon. 'Sovereignty' is used here as a 'sensitizing concept' which gives meaning to the phenomenon under study, and direction to the discussion. The treatment of the concept of 'sovereignty' is informed by this choice; I have chosen to highlight the aspects that I feel will be most useful in a discussion of the specific development under study.

56 Brodeur 1983; 2007.

57 EEA Agreement art.102. The termination is of the specific area of disagreement, not the agreement in its entirety (terminates the agreement for *all* EFTA states); in contrast to SAA art.11, which terminates the agreement. See more in Chapter 6 of this text.

58 The assessment seems to be that where *practical* problems need to be resolved, e.g. in relation to border control and crime trends, the inclusion is more relevant also to the EU (Bull 1997).

Sovereignty is a defining trait of the modern state. But the struggle to define sovereignty has been on-going for centuries. State sovereignty may imply national sovereignty, involve elements such as legal and political sovereignty, external and internal sovereignty, the notion – expressed in section 1 of the Norwegian Constitution – of *in*divisible sovereignty versus divisible sovereignty, and governmental and popular sovereignty.[59] Sovereignty is not the preserve of international law. It is central to many fields of social and historical research, to much of political science, including international relations, and, of course, to public law.[60] It hinges on issues such as the conditions for the existence and exercise of sovereignty, of *who* should exercise it and what forms these entities should take.[61] A traditional understanding of sovereignty is that it implies the full autonomy of rulers to act as they choose within a certain territory, without legal limitation by any superior entity.[62] It is thus important to the individual, because it determines who is in charge of her or him, positively and negatively, at any given time and in any given place. The question of sovereignty, then, fundamentally raises the issue of authority on a specific territory.

1.3.1 Territory and authority

Theories on the nation-state hold that the state derives its territorial rights from the prior collective right of a *nation* to that territory. Nations are groups defined by cultural characteristics that their members perceive themselves to share, such as language or a common culture, combined with an aspiration to political self-determination.[63] The concept of 'state' presupposes a territory limited by geographical borders. The *borders* are key to the definition. Within these borders, certain rules apply; beyond them other rules apply. The territories are never *given*, they are demarcated in the way they are, at any given time, because of human action. A territory is fixed because someone claims it – what Jessop calls the "territorialization of political power".[64]

After roughly the year 1500, the nation-state became the dominant structure in Europe; it had four particular features: "1) it controlled a well-defined, continuous territory; 2) it was relatively centralized; 3) it was differentiated from other organizations; and 4) it reinforced its claims through a tendency to acquire a monopoly over the concentrated means of physical coercion within its territory".[65] State boundaries were defined by international agreements, through which sovereign states acknowledged and guaranteed each other's existence.[66] Internally, state power enabled sovereigns "to define and enforce collectively binding decisions on the members of a society in the name of the common interest or general will".[67] The general will was less 'voluntary' or expressed before the 18th century,

59 Sarooshi 2004:1107, 1108–1109.

60 Our contemporary society is increasingly legally regulated; it is often spoken of a *juridification* of previously politicised areas. As Cananea argues, the growing number of transnational processes and intergovernmental negotiations gives rise to increased need for legal regimes, consequently giving rise to litigation (2010:997).

61 Sarooshi 2004:1107, 1109.

62 Chayes and Chayes 1995:26.

63 Miller 1995. Different nationalist theorists emphasise different formative ties, see Stilz 2011, and e.g. Chaims 2003 explaining statist and cultural nationalist theories.

64 Jessop 2009:416–421.

65 Tilly 1975:26–7.

66 Giddens 1987:171, Weber 1958.

67 Jessop 1990:341.

but the weight attached to the common interest and general will must have been one factor in a state's success: becoming and remaining an autonomous state relied upon a state's ability to homogenise its population.[68] This involved, for example, the adoption of state religions and the expulsion of minorities, and later, the institution of the police, which was one of the final building blocks in the structure of modern executive government.

Territorial border control is a clear sign of sovereignty. The EU Commission has established a new supranational EU border and coast guard service with a command and control centre that is independent of national authorities.[69] In some circumstances, the agency may operate on the borders of a Schengen member state regardless of its consent. The EU Frontex border guard system consists of national members, working outside national jurisdictions. I would argue that a supranational entity with control over who may cross the external borders of an area indicates both a decrease of the importance of the member states' demarcated borders, and an increased importance of the *European* area borders, controlled by the EU. I will return to the monopoly of violence *within* this territory below.

The state system contributed to establishing state sovereignty. Fast-forwarding to the 20th century, we could ask whether the contemporary 'state system' of Europe may *diminish* sovereignty. In the 20th century, trade-related agreements proliferated, both because of various modern developments, and because, at least in the western world, the state system enjoyed greater stability in its structure than ever before.

The concept of the state requires a ruler, someone who can take decisions, to protect a territory, and to allow or prohibit activity within it in order to maintain it in the way the ruler sees fit. Bartelson argues that the core of the concept of sovereign power moved from divine right in the medieval era, via the monarch in the renaissance, to *man* in the modern era; a final move often thought to have begun in 1789.[70] In the Enlightenment period, the figure of the 'citizen' came to the fore, implying that the subjects of the state were sovereign; this was later termed *popular* sovereignty. Contractarian theory had already been developed by Hobbes followed by Locke, but the strengthened position of *man* in social contract theory came in this period, with thinkers such as Rousseau.

In the Hobbesian and Bodinian sense, the principles of justice and order would be best provided by modern democratic states whose organising principles are antithetical to the idea that sovereignty means uncontrolled domestic power.[71] For Hobbes and Bodin, there should be *one* absolute authority as the sovereign. This fits poorly with the current system of modern democratic states in Europe. Krasner highlights four different facets of sovereignty: internal sovereignty, meaning domestic control; external sovereignty, in the sense that other states respect the sovereign's right to govern internal affairs; sovereignty as control over trans-border movements; and external sovereignty understood as the right to legitimately enter into international agreements.[72] In other words, it is unnecessary for a sovereign to claim to be the *one omnipotent* power on a territory. Trans-border sovereignty is important because of the difficulties arising from transnational trade and crime., which is central to our topic, and will be discussed shortly. What such contemporary theorists do, one may argue, is to replace the sovereign *absolute* with a *series* of contending, overlapping

68 Tilly 1975:43–45.
69 [2016] OJ L 251/1.
70 Bartelson 1995:236.
71 Krasner 2001:21.
72 Krasner 1999:9.

sovereignties.[73] There is nothing in this notion, then, that presupposes *one* nation state or government as sovereign. The question that we must turn to is how these other sovereignties may be established and how they may best be studied and understood.

1.4 Methods

An overarching purpose of this book is to question some of the terms, presuppositions and links in the purpose statement of the Police Act, section 1, quoted above. The research design is, briefly put, to analyse the recent developments in the field of police cooperation by exploring how important changes have impact on the content of central concepts in the Police Act, like 'police', 'state', 'citizen' and 'community'. I am going to discuss the meaning of these concepts and the dynamic relationship between them. The main framework for the analysis is based on changes in the Norwegian situation upon the country's participation in the Schengen cooperation and some subsequent or related international police cooperation instruments such as Europol. An important contribution of this book, is to give a thorough account of the police cooperation measures that are available (or may be available) to the Norwegian police today.

Methodologically, large parts of the book is an analysis of government policy documents; documents that may show what the state administration has intended the police to be. *Travaux préparatoires* or white papers are international terms for what in Norwegian is referred to as *forarbeid*. This broadly includes proposals, reports (*offentlige utredninger*), other debates and considerations forming the background to new or amended legislation.[74] The standard legal dogmatic methodology in Norway to analyse the current legal situation, implies placing heavy emphasis on these *forarbeid* documents. Such policy documents have a particularly strong position among Norwegian legal dogmatic sources, far more than in many other jurisdictions.[75] The quality of these works is also more even and thorough than in other countries, also compared with similar EU documents. To emphasise this, and to avoid confusion with similar sources in other jurisdictions, I have chosen to use the Norwegian word *forarbeid* throughout the book when referring to these documents. The specific references will obviously be to the type of *forarbeid* in question.

The term 'police' refers here to the institution and function of civilian public police forces that are formally legitimated within the context of national states with the tasks of crime control and order maintenance.[76] The aim is thus not to analyse what is immanent in the term; it is to comprehend how it has been *presented*, the way the state understands the link between itself and the police. The *forarbeid* are well-suited for this type of analysis.

When discussing intentions presented in policy documents, the 'state' is used alongside 'government' and 'Ministry'[77] to refer to the state administration of Norway. The state term in the book is, however, also, to some extent used in a more complex way to refer to a more abstract notion, implying also the limited territory and nation state of Norway; the general 'state concept'. Both usages are necessary to explain the link between the state and the

73 Ruback 2011:1.

74 Eckhoff and Helgesen 2001:65.

75 Bergo 2000.

76 E.g. Deflem and Sutphin 2006:266.

77 'Ministry' refers to the Ministry of Justice and Public Security throughout the thesis, when otherwise is not specified.

police. The 'state' implied in the Police Act might, then, conceivably both refer to the state as a specific administrative body, and to 'nation state' as an entity distinct from other similar entities.

At this point, that should suffice as working definitions of important concepts to get the book started. Given that a discussion of the dynamic meaning of these above-mentioned terms is in itself a purpose of this book, however, the definitory work will continue throughout the following 15 chapters.

1.4.1 Studying international police cooperation

In the 1997 *forarbeid* concerning the Norwegian Schengen Affiliation Agreement, the Ministry of Justice and Police[78] showed how broad and imprecise the term 'international police cooperation' can be. The term may refer to practical cooperation across borders, for example, in "the form of investigative cooperation; via the exchange of information and knowledge in various for a; cooperation through international or multi-national organisations like Interpol and the Schengen to international agreements such as the UN Drugs Convention; [. . .] directly between the police or authorities [. . .] or through an organisation or a forum like Interpol"; "[. . .] with the aim of crime fighting or criminal prosecution in an individual case; to uphold general public order or provide assistance to developing another country's police authorities".[79] A general division was and is made between the *operational* and the *overarching* police cooperation.[80] The former refers to the political and administrative agreements and negotiations, whereas the latter happens directly between the police or public prosecution services. After the entry into force of the Lisbon Treaty, the distinction between operational and non-operational police cooperation became very relevant. According to art.87 TFEU, there are different decision-making procedures depending on which type of measures is adopted. This book discusses both the operational and overarching cooperation.

Important contributions in research on the Norwegian situation related to EU police cooperation and crime control are especially Kvam 2014; Karanja 2008; Boucht 2012; Gammelgard 2001; Kleiven 2012b, 2013; Wold 2004; Larsson 2006; Ahnfelt and From 1996; and in Auglend, Røsandhaug and Mæland 2004 (2016)[81]. *Judicial* cooperation in criminal matters is less in focus here, see instead central authors such as Mathisen 2009, 2010; Ruud 2016; Suominen 2008; Tønnesen 1981; Tønnesen 1978. Some Nordic research is drawn upon, but the book is not comparative as such, *inter alia* because of the different positions as non-/members of EU. Because the lack of comprehensive literature in Norway (there are, for example, no Norwegian textbooks on EU criminal matters or policing), central contributions by Henricson 2010; Gade *et al.* 2005; and, for example, Cameron *et al.* 2011; Bergström and Cornell 2014 are applied. This book attempts to have significance also outside of Norway. I have not, however, made much use of 'third state' literature in general, as this goes beyond the scope of this particular study.

78 Hereinafter the Ministry.

79 St.prp.nr.42 (1996–1997):6.1.5, so also argued by Larsson 2006:457.

80 Similar to the macro, meso and micro levels of cooperation as discussed by Benyon 1993.

81 The second edition of Auglend *et al.* (2004) came in 2016 (Auglend and Røsandhaug 2016). The latest edition's chapter on internal police cooperation is shortened significantly, and in addition refers many places to the PhD this book is built on. There is thus quite a lot of information only available in the first edition, and Auglend *et al.* 2004 is therefore a frequent reference.

While Kvam (2014) and Karanja (2008) give comprehensive analyses of the Schengen Information and other EU police cooperation through information exchange, and Ruud (2016, in Norwegian) on cooperation in criminal matters abroad, there is no comprehensive research on the other types of EU police cooperation. This book attempts at providing that comprehensive research.

This book targets a substantial amount of policy documents.[82] The main emphasis is on the legal regulations and their creation. There is a vast body of historic research on Norwegian history in general, also related to related topics like the growth of the state and the role of the military and the church in maintaining order. Less, however, on *police* history. The general body of historic texts grows when the international level is included. Outside sources also provide insight into Norwegian history, especially since the European history is greatly intertwined, albeit with distinctive features and varying directions between the regions. The book draws only to a limited extent on these general historic accounts. Although a deeper historic analysis of the police as only a part of the societies before they became states, and the roles of other control and care instruments over the centuries would have made the present research better, a more systematic and thorough analysis has not been possible. Some Norwegian literature is explored, alongside the pertinent European police history literature.[83] The book has to no significant degree drawn on research in German and French languages.[84] While I aim to use the case of Norway to argue changes to the impact of the police function also outside of Norway, this does not include a comprehensive European police history. The following is limited to what is most relevant to understand the Norwegian situation.

I draw upon several studies that have been written on various aspects of transnational crime control,[85] contributing to the understanding of the historical background,[86] the legal basis of both bilateral and multilateral level, and the development thereof;[87] formal and informal cooperation;[88] the accountability of the various institutions,[89] and the relationship or struggle between the state sovereignty and transnational policing[90] (and all of the above intertwined).

The law has a cultural impact, and this book provides a discussion of the impact on the police, the individuals and the state following the expansion of police cooperation mechanisms post 1995.[91] The legal discussions on international police cooperation are often primarily human rights related, while police sociology often takes the police organisation as its subject. The area of intersection between the police function as being investigative, and administrative, performing both civil and criminal activities, is not as widely researched. And this intersection is what the book attempts to explore: the point where not only the criminal investigation function of the police 'goes international', but also the less regulated (and presumably more culturally dependent) order policing function.

82 For overviews over newer Nordic police research, see Høigård 2005; Valland 2011.

83 References are provided throughout. Central accounts follow for example from Marshall 1993; Emsley 1999a; 1996; 1999b; 2011; Davis 1991; Fosdick 1915; Becker 1973; Liang 1992; Axtmann 1992; Mosse 1975.

84 Honourable exceptions are Stolleis 1988, Ewald 1986 and Napoli 2003.

85 E.g. Deflem 2002; contributions in Mawby 1999; Bowling and Sheptycki 2012; Goldsmith and Sheptycki 2007; Sheptycki 2000; Andreas and Nadelmann 2006; Nadelmann 1993

86 E.g. Anderson *et al.* 1995; Apap and Anderson 2002; den Boer 1994; Gerspacher 2008.

87 E.g. Benyon 1994a; 1994b; 1996; Reiner 1992.

88 E.g. Gerspacher 2005

89 E.g. Walker 1993; Raab 1994; 2014; den Boer 2002b; 2010; Bruggeman 2002.

90 Loader and Walker 2007; Palombella and Walker 2009; Walker 2000; 2004a; Marenin 1982.

91 Contrasting jurisprudence to sociology of law: e.g. Timasheff 1937.

'Police sociology' is understood here as sociological research of areas such as police culture and organisations,[92] the occupational role and the police officers' perception of their role.[93] Police sociology also often discusses the political consequences of different styles of policing,[94] and the society's demands and perceptions of the police.[95] Also what may be termed 'security criminology',[96] concerning the topics of risk and security as they have penetrated mainstream criminology. Security criminology is typically conducted by both legal and criminological researchers (i.e. social scientists/sociologists). The target of this school of research is, for example, the legal currents and developments in criminal law, but also the question of a difficult balancing act between values like personal freedom and social security and safety. Human rights related research, (crim)immigration research,[97] surveillance studies,[98] research on the globalisation of crime control,[99] and research detailing increased punitiveness (i.e. increased sentencing frames) will also be drawn upon in the following.[100]

I take Norwegian legal sources, including the *forarbeid* and Norwegian legal literature, as a point of departure, because it is the Norwegian legal situation that I want to investigate. The book puts a particular focus on how and in what way the EU cooperation mechanisms and instruments apply to Norwegian police. To some extent some instruments that are currently unavailable may be made available in the future. These are also presented.

The focus is on the development in regulations, on what the police *may* apply and use in their work – not what they in practice make use of. This focus area is interesting because it shows how the state negotiates its possibilities within the Schengen/EU framework, but also with and within the national police. One of the book's contributions is to provide an independent and in-depth analysis of the relevant *forarbeid* in order to understand what the situation has been, and what it is becoming.

Parts of this project analyses the Police Act in Norwegian law in search for arguments in relation to the premises for international police work. The book concentrates on the debates and *forarbeid* prior to a selection of specific changes related to either a development of significance for the Norwegian situation (such as the Schengen and Europol cooperation agreements) or where there was debate in connection with a significant happening at the European level that could or may have led to changes in the (Norwegian) perception of the international situation.

The national Norwegian Police Acts were enacted in 1927, 1936 and 1995. Numerous amendments are made to the legislation without a complete replacement. Some of these changes brought about much *forarbeid* and political debate, others very little, depending on the significance the Government at the time ascribed to the amendment.

As is shown throughout part II of the book, despite its non-membership, Norway is member or associated member of many EU cooperation instruments. This implies that also EU policy documents and regulations are relevant legal sources. It is not, however, necessary

92 Such as Banton 2005; Loftus 2009; Reiner 1992; Loader and Mulcahy 2003.
93 Manning 1977.
94 Reiner 1992; Brodeur 2010; 1983; 2007.
95 Brogden 1982.
96 Bigo *et al.* 2008.
97 Stumpf 2006; Johansen *et al.* 2013.
98 Lomell 2007; Lomell *et al.* 2009; Ericson and Haggerty 1997
99 Aas 2007; Zureik and Salter 2005.
100 Such as Dubber 2005; Valverde and Dubber 2006; Sassen 2008; Marenin 1982; Sheptycki in general; Deflem 2002.

here to discuss methodology specifics of EU law, as it is not the application of these as such that are targeted. The EU regulations in the Justice and Home Affairs area have different impact in the Norwegian legal system than for the EU member states. The specifics are explained related to the various instruments in part II.

1.4.2 *The EU body of law and regulations*

EU law, regulations and policies are, to put it mildly, a dynamic research target. New developments arise and change in what is the current political focus. Whether or not one agrees with the argument that the European Union is *sui generis* a type of legal and even state entity, it is an indisputable fact that the EU law, including the EEA and Schengen, is another, and added legal system on top of or parallel to the member states' legal systems.[101] Doing research on the EU judicial and home affairs area has been described as aiming at a moving target in a crowded policy space.[102] It is challenging to follow the policy and legal development, not only at the national level but also at the EU level. EU documents are not translated to Norwegian given the non-membership, but the language is not a main issue. More problematic is the partial inaccessibility, at least experienced from the non-EU perspective. Not that various documents are restricted from non-member states' view, but the EU body of law and regulations is not 'standard legal sources' for Norwegian lawyers. A common challenge for all students of EU law is the quantity of documents produced, on various levels and within institutions. In most EU countries, the political discussions and the public debate on the police cooperation measures are continuous and vigorous. Norway seems to be an exception; there is, as is shown below, very little public or political attention directed at EU police matters. There may be several explanations for this, where the political system is one, and precisely the non-membership and thus the perception of 'full national autonomy' another. The relevant point here is, however, that the lack of UK-style debate makes the research object less obvious. Thousands of pages of Norwegian policy documents on the police have been written over the past thirty years or so. The documents and the debates relating to the international police cooperation measures have been far fewer. It is partly the case that various amendments have followed other laws than the Police or Criminal Procedure Acts, for example related to the police's access to immigration databases. Since this book has as a central aim to analyse what the Norwegian state has intended with its police regulations, much time has been spent on tracking the dynamic EU policies and the, where relevant, describe the resulting Norwegian policies, either because of Schengen relevance or affiliation or association agreements. The book attempts to be updated on both levels up until December 2017. The book is based on my PhD, defended in December 2017. It has not been possible to update also the literature review after that point in time.

1.4.3 *Limitations*

Assessing how EU cooperation mechanisms and instruments apply to Norwegian police in practice does not, in this study, refer to practical use of these mechanisms by the Norwegian police, but rather the available practical measures in the regulations in Norwegian law. The

101 See more on these challenges in relation to EU and international law in Cryer *et al.* 2011.
102 Raab 1994.

actual practice of working law enforcement officials would of course be very interesting data in an analysis of how the police cooperation actually works, but that would imply a different research outline and make for a completely different book.

The focus in the book is primarily on police measures, not judicial cooperation. This means that, for example, investigation measures involving a court order are mostly excluded. Cooperation involving legal assistance raises other issues – in addition, at least – as the 'proper' police cooperation.[103] These are typically concerning transfer of the criminal proceedings to another state,[104] extradition of a wanted suspect with the purpose of criminal proceedings,[105] and extradition with the purpose of execution of sentence.[106] The cooperation that involves a court decision or the public prosecutor has an extra 'safety valve' in that a lawyer checks the cooperating measures, whether they are legal, proportional, necessary, etc.

The police authority and competences are mainly regulated in the Police Act of 1995, which is the legislative basis for most foreign operational police cooperation.[107] The focus of this book is, however, the police cooperation outside of the court system – *policing* in terms of general security providing, such as maintaining order and preventing criminal acts.[108] Typical measures of cooperation, meaning which measures will be taken by the requested police, are search and seizure, interrogation of witnesses or suspects, declaration of subpoenas, giving access for foreign police in national information databases and systems for search and analysis, observation and wiretapping, and controlled deliveries.[109]

Intelligence and other forms of information-gathering, analysis and exchange is also subject for this book. There is, however, much research on police cooperation in the form of information exchange, particularly concerned with challenges such as human rights, and particularly data protection and the right to privacy.[110] Despite the relevance of the challenges to data protection and the individual's corresponding rights, the regulations of the individual's right to access, deletion and complaints will not be further developed here. The purpose is to provide good insight into the possibilities of the police and to some extent law enforcement more generally. The data protection field is at least as vast as the police cooperation itself, and opens an array of discussions and weighting of human rights such as the right to privacy. The body of literature on this is large, and reference is made to other authors for this.

To sum up: The book researches *forarbeid* to enactments and legal amendments of Norwegian police regulations. In the Part I, the *forarbeid* are researched with the purpose

103 St.prp.nr.98 (2000–2001):6. The Ministry of Justice and Police emphasised that the police cooperation and the public judicial law enforcement cooperation developed in different paces in Europe (St.prp.nr.42 (1996–1997):ch.6.1.5). Only in the past years have the two been combined in the same regulations, as traditional in the Nordic countries.

104 See e.g. 1972 Eur.Convention on the Transfer of Proceedings in Criminal Matters.

105 E.g. [2002] OJ L 190/1.

106 E.g. also the op.cit. and the Nordic Arrest Warrant of 15.12.2005, 2008 AA.
In addition to the multilateral EU or Nordic agreements, there are several bilateral agreements with countries outside of these. See e.g. Mathisen 2009.

107 Ot.prp.nr.56 (1998–1999):92. Excluding e.g. extradition and other judicial cooperation, and various information exchange.

108 This is the same limitation made by Auglend *et al.* 2004:5. For a general Norwegian overview of international legal cooperation in criminal matters, see e.g. the Rundskriv G 19/2001and St.meld.nr.18 (1999–2000).

109 Henricson 2010:168–72

110 See such as Prainsack and Toom 2013; Cameron 2000; Nouwt 2009; Karanja 2008 (in particular for Norway); Boehm 2012a; Cameron 2014.

of analysing the state's argumentation and justification when introducing new police cooperation measures or instruments. In Part II, the main research data is Norwegian legal regulations and the pertinent trans- or international police cooperation agreements and related documents. The research from central theorists on police cooperation are drawn upon to supply the primary sources.[111] Part II uses pertinent criminological and (legal) sociological research to discuss the *forarbeid* and the development as described in the two previous parts.

1.5 Research questions and the way forward

Sovereignty is an abstract concept that can be operationalised in many different ways. Structurally, the rest of the book, following this introductory chapter, is divided into two parts that each ask two separate sets of questions. These four questions all address different aspects of sovereignty. Broadly speaking, Part I (Chapters 2–8) will show how Norway entered into the EU police cooperation agreements, and her place as a sovereign state in this international hierarchy. Part II (Chapters 9–15) will focus on the way the EU police cooperation operationally is carried out with what consequences.

In the following, the book will be structured around the following four interconnected research questions:

Part I

1) Was the decision on the part of the Norwegian government to seek access to EU international police cooperation measures and instruments adequately founded on popular knowledge and sentiments (internal sovereignty)?
2) To what extent has the Norwegian government ceded decision-making competence to other agents on policing matters (external sovereignty)?

Part II

3) In what ways may the development of operational police cooperation regulations and measures impact on the Norwegian police?
4) In what ways may the development of operational police cooperation regulations and measures impact on Norwegian society and the Norwegian public?

These questions directly correspond to Chapters 7, 8, 14 and 15 below, respectively. The remaining Chapters (2–6 and 9–13) lay the groundwork for the discussions surrounding these research questions. They introduce the developments under study and describe the legal field they are part of. They thus provide the necessary context that makes it possible to address the research questions in an informed way. A short explanatory guide to this book structure is provided below.

1.5.1 A short guide to the book

In Part I of the book, I explain the development of Norway's relationship with the EU, alongside the development of the EU on the crime control area. In Part II, I give a comprehensive overview over Norway's position in and possibilities of police cooperation measures stemming from EU, including what is not available because of her outsider position. The

111 See ch.1.4.31 as detailed in the footnotes.

research data material, so to speak, in the first part, is thus the overarching agreements between Norway and EU, the political negotiations leading to these, and the legal and political hierarchies that Norway is placed in. The data material in the second part is the regulations of the specific measures in the EU police cooperation agreements, including, for example, information exchange in SIS and joint investigation teams. The two data sets combined provide a platform for analysing the consequence of the development of police cooperation for Norwegian sovereignty through a discussion of the four research questions introduced above.

Employing the first set of data as introduced and described in Chapters 2–6, I discuss the two aspects of external and internal sovereignty in Chapters 7 and 8. The first research question concerns internal sovereignty as related to popular sovereignty. This relates to *how* the state proceeded into the Schengen Cooperation and later EU association agreements, discussed from the perspective of the task of justifying these particular state actions in the eyes of the Norwegian public. Was the decision on the part of the Norwegian government to seek access to EU international police cooperation measures and instruments adequately founded on popular knowledge and sentiments (internal sovereignty)? This first research question is addressed in Chapter 7.

The question of external sovereignty is raised in Chapter 8. This chapter concerns the Norwegian state's (and Norwegian state institutions') positions in the EU hierarchy. It raises the second research question: To what extent has the Norwegian government ceded decision-making competence to other agents on policing matters (external sovereignty)?

Part II of the book concerns the *practical* measures of the agreements and their consequences. Regardless of whether sovereignty is maintained on paper because of procedurally correct negotiations, for example (an issue discussed in Part I), Part II asks whether the practical outcomes of the agreements are consistent with what was presented to the Norwegian public.

Chapter 14 concerns the changes to the Norwegian police following the practical police cooperation developments described in Chapters 9–13. Pertinent issues are whether it still is the state that enforces the monopoly of violence within its territory, if foreign police officers act as the practical enforcers. Here, I address the third of my research questions: In what ways may the development of operational police cooperation regulations and measures impact on the Norwegian police?

The fourth and final research question concerns the relationship between the state and the police in relation to wider Norwegian society. The forms and intensity of policing in a society may have effects on the perception of belongingness, of risk, of safety, and of trust – trust in the state, and in other fellow citizens or individuals in society. Norwegian society is changing, not least through the police cooperation mechanisms, in what is becoming an increasingly interconnected world. In what ways may the development of operational police cooperation regulations and measures impact on Norwegian society and the Norwegian public? This issue is discussed in Chapter 15.

PART I

NORWAY AND THE EU

The 19th century saw the birth of truly global policing. The germinal phase primarily dealt with political terrorism, anarchists and opponents of the established regimes in general.[1] The cooperation between national police forces was more or less informal until the early 20th century. According to Deflem, there was a shift from political policing to policing of distinct crimes on the global level during the 19th century.[2] Also two later decades have shown politically motivated crimes becoming impetus for increased police cooperation; the terrorist activities of the 1970s (Baader Meinhof, Rote Armee Fraktion, etc.)[3] and the first decade of the new millennium after the 9/11 attacks in the USA. Politically motivated crimes such as terrorism challenge the traditional boundaries between crime and acts of war, both at the national and the international level. The 1990s is also the decade when the Norwegian government took international police cooperation – in particular the EU related forms of cooperation – to a new level. In Part II, I map the landscape of currently available police cooperation measures and instruments, but always from a Norwegian point of view, and always as these instruments relate to the 1995 Police Act context. This is why Part I starts off with a chapter devoted to this Act, explaining the Norwegian regulations of the national police work. The change in focus further in Part I does not mean that the Norwegian context is left behind. Second, however, in this Part I, the point is to elucidate the process of Norway's way into the EU via the Schengen Agreement. This requires showing briefly the development of the EU in this field, and the Norwegian position in the various forums and agreements. I then use the facts from those chapters to discuss the two first research questions described above. The first concerns a form of *popular sovereignty*; I ask how and to what extent the Norwegian state involved its citizens when entering into the Schengen Cooperation and subsequent police cooperation agreement. The second concerns a form of *external sovereignty*. By this, I refer to the Norwegian state's level of autonomy as a partner in the EU, and the extent to which the EU's regulations or institution's decisions may be seen to override Norwegian internal/national decisions, etc.

The situation in Norway around 1995 is taken as a main point of departure. That point in time is not chosen just because it is the year the current Police Act entered into force, but also because this is approximately the start of the Schengen negotiations between Norway and the EU. The policing situation that the current Norwegian legislation and the pertinent international agreements imply when seen together, may be said, in effect, to represent a

1 E.g. Deflem 2002; Nadelmann 1993; Knepper 2011.
2 Deflem 2002.
3 Ahnfelt and From 1996:23 ff.

DOI: 10.4324/9780429503696-2

major change from the situation up until the mid-1990s. The Schengen cooperation was the first police cooperation agreement to be assessed in depth at the political level. The cooperation was, in many ways the starting point for the rapid and dynamic evolution of many other measures and agreements on the area of crime control and public order maintenance, such as the widening and deepening of the Europol, the Eurojust, the Prüm, Frontex, and so on. This is the reason why the Schengen Agreement will get by far the closest focus in the book.

Norway is, I argue, in a dual position, both inside and outside of the full-fledged EU cooperation proper.

2 The Police Act of 1995

The modern Norwegian police organisation

For purposes of comparison, it is necessary to provide an overview of the current state of the Norwegian police, before delving into international developments and subsequent/ potential changes.

The most radical development in terms of international cooperation in Norwegian law took place in the early and mid–1990s. This coincided with the implementation of the Police Act of 1995. The *forarbeid* for the 1995 Act will be assessed to the extent these are relevant to the issues at stake. The aim is to explain what was considered significant, both in terms of important innovations, and how risks and benefits were weighed, and to discuss what the amendments and arguments may imply for issues such as the closeness between the state, the police, and the citizens, and the importance of territorial jurisdiction, risks and security perception.

Less than ten years passed between the first two Norwegian national Police Acts of 1927 and 1936. Almost 60 years passed between the second and the third. Major social and technological developments took place during that period, and one would expect similarly radical changes in the policing situation. Comprehensive *forarbeid* and debates on the development of the new police act began to appear as early as the 1960s.[1] Several police reform committees (with varying mandates) were appointed. Their suggestions were debated exhaustively. The public debate on what the police should be like was lively, especially during the 1970s.

In the following, the focus is the present-day police regulations, i.e. the 1995 Police Act with Directives. These will be the basis for the analysis of the international police cooperation measures in subsequent chapters. The presentation contains a description of the context of and justifications for the new Police Act, but it also gives a description of the purposes, organisation and structure of the present-day police. An understanding of the structure of the police organisation, together with the relevant institutions and actors of the Norwegian police is necessary to understand the role of the police in relation to the state.[2] As a whole, this chapter supplies a brief overview of the police of Norway today.

2.1 Police work in Norway: what should the police do, and how should they do it?

To identify the tasks and purpose of the police is in a way to define 'order'. The police must establish and maintain public order. *In practice*, the creation of order is probably mostly

1 Ot.prp.nr.22 (1994–1995):8.

2 It is not, however, the intention here to provide an in-depth account of the detailed structural development of the police organisation.

DOI: 10.4324/9780429503696-3

unproblematic from the perspective of the individual police officer, who *knows* when a situation is becoming disorderly, and when it is time to intervene. This practical and often tacit knowledge is part of what being a police officer is all about.[3] This fact may, however, be seen as a challenge for the principle of legality: individuals should be informed what boundaries the state puts on their scope of action.[4] International police cooperation, especially as regards order policing, may challenge this.

Previous Norwegian police legislation identified no clear purpose for the police, or limits to their powers. The general power of attorney (*generalfullmakten*), based in customary law, was the primary source of police powers before the 1995 Act. The police had a wide general authority, without any legal basis, to intervene in individuals' lives, in order to maintain public peace and order, and prevent criminal activities.[5] In 1995, the customary gateway section was considered to breach the principle of legality, because all state interference in the individual's personal sphere must be based in law. Both the general purpose of police work (sects.1–2) and some specific tasks were finally fixed in the 1995 Act. The PA sect.7 describes the situations where the police may intervene, and the purposes of such intervention. Although intentionally non-exhaustive, it was deemed that, *in lieu* of more casuistic legislation, there was a need for each individual police officer to have a clear value-based rule of thumb when executing discretion as part of his or her general duties.[6] Some core concepts need explaining, since they will be revisited later when discussing foreign police influence. Since the rules on what the police should do, and how, are relatively open-ended, the purpose of the Norwegian police, and the rules of their conduct, are relevant to examine.

The general purpose for all police work was fixed in sect.1 of the 1995 Act. It should be remembered that sect.1 lays down that the State shall provide the necessary police, and that the police have a responsibility to provide security under the law, and welfare and safety in general.

'Security under the law', translates *rettssikkerhet* in the 1995 Police Act, which is a somewhat vague term.[7] Preparing for the 1995 Act, such terms were suggested formalised. Procedural rule of law guarantees are definitely included, but a 'thicker' understanding is also implied. The Police Role Committee (I) explains it as a 'legal safeguard' (*rettsvern*), which is a service citizens receive in return for being law-abiding.[8] The core of the term, they argue, is the protection of personal safety, which suggests the classical liberal rights: security for one's person and property. The police were also seen as carrying out the state's responsibility to ensure that citizens enjoy the rights bestowed upon them by law, such as freedom of speech, civil rights, and freedom of movement. A perfect society cannot exist, however, since people inevitably have different ideas of perfection. Society requires that everyone must accept some restrictions, depending on the prevailing ideas in the specific social context. The important link between the rights of individuals and the social order is visible here. In more recent policy documents on the police role (in contrast to the documents from the 1980s and earlier), the Ministry narrowed the understanding of the rule of law. 'Efficiency' was considered to be less important than the respect for the individual's

3 See in depth Heivoll 2017.

4 Op.cit.:54–5.

5 E.g. NOU 1988:39 p.48; NOU 1981:35 e.g. pp.45–7; Castberg 1955:71–2

6 Op.cit.:13; 16–7.

7 On rule diverging theories on the contents of 'rule of law'; e.g. Tamanaha 2004. The aim here is to assess the legislator's version – which is broader.

8 NOU 1981:35 p.67.

rettssikkerhet and privacy in police work.[9] In the mid–2000s, the Ministry argued that *collective* safety had become more important since the 1970s' focus on the ***individual***, because of an increasingly complex society, new technologies and new forms of crime.[10] This seems based both in the development of crime, and on the development of international courts' adjudication related to privacy and procedural justice in general.[11] At any given time the values of collective security and individual freedom are being balanced in practical police work. The balance seems to have tilted in the direction of the former value in the early 21st century, in contrast to "the currents of legal policy in the 1970s".[12] The fact that the meaning of *rettssikkerhet changes*, demonstrate the importance that a clear purpose should be specified in the Police Act, giving interpretation guidelines for when the terms themselves seem unclear and inadequate.

Investigation is a central police task. The concept of 'investigation' refers, according to the Criminal Procedure Act (CPA) sect.226 to such police work that has as purpose to retrieve the necessary information to determine a question of indictment, criminal liability, and/or the stopping or deterring of criminal activities.[13] The distinction between investigation, intelligence and preventive work has consequences for this thesis. On a national level, the distinction determines the hierarchical police leadership in the specific case or work. Moreover, police investigation has its legal basis in the Criminal Procedure Act, whilst other police activities are regulated in the Police Act, the Public Administration Act and other specific legislation.

In addition to the definition of the purpose of the police, and of what this involves, the 1995 PA contains several rules of conduct for police officers. In the *forarbeid* to the Act, ten basic principles for the structure of the police force, and for its, activities and role in the community were set out by the Police Role Commission and later approved by the Government. These principles are the basis for the current Police Act, and have been reiterated so many times,[14] that they are arguably fundamental to Norwegian policing. These principles may be seen as describing the traditional Norwegian police. They are:

- The police force reflects the ideals of society
- The police force has civilian characteristics
- The police force constitutes one unified force ("*enhetspoliti*")
- The police force is decentralised
- The police officer is generalist
- The police force interacts with the public
- The police force is integrated in the local community
- The police force recruits officers from all levels of society
- The police prioritise their tasks, placing emphasis on preventive activities
- The police force is subject to effective control by society

9 Op.cit.:174–5.

10 St.meld.nr.17 (2001–2002); St.meld.nr.42 (2004–2005):66–7.

11 St.meld.nr.42 (2004–2005):65–7.

12 Op.cit.:65.

13 Police work related to crime is either tactical or strategic. Tactical investigation of a committed crime is normally an investigation with the purpose, for example, of determining criminal guilt. Strategic investigation targets prevention or unravelling of possible future crime. See Hov 2007:43; RA 99–238. The purpose determines the categorisation, according to Myhrer 2001:10.

14 NOU 1981:35; NOU 1987:27, Ot.prp.nr.22 (1994–1995):13; Innst.S.nr.192 (1991–1992), etc.

These constitute the "essential needs of the community", as stated in sect.1.[15] The tasks of the police are formulated in the 1995 Police Act sect.2, on the basis of these ten principles. The 1995 Police Act (PA) and the relevant version of the Police Directive (1990) include regulations on the measures available to the police, but say little about *which* measure should be used *when*, and under what circumstances. Still, a number of guidelines are laid down in the legal regulations. The PA sect.6 and PD sect.2–1(2) emphasise the prime importance of preventive measures. This obviously does not mean that the police should not intervene in ongoing criminal action, but that they should take preventive measures before actions turn into crime or disorder. This is reflected in the requirement that a stronger measure should not be taken before a less drastic one has been shown to be futile.[16]

The police are thus responsible for enforcing both what may be called particular order, and general order in a community.[17] While maintaining particular order means preventing, stopping or deterring specific criminal acts, maintaining general order helps ensure a general sense of security in society. Of course, general and particular order maintenance will be closely related in practice: the mere presence of the police in local communities may be seen as important, both to prevent crime, and to create a feeling of safety and security among citizens.[18] Much police work is non-coercive, and therefore the principle of legality does not arise.[19] This may, as discussed below, be changing with the increase in international police cooperation. Policing 'order', presupposes a relatively clear understanding of the content of the term, and this may depend on context and time.

2.1.1 General measures

All police activities must be in accordance with the purpose and general guidelines of PA sects.1 and 2; briefly summed up: they must be part of the state responsibility for the provision of welfare, safety and security under the law. The police objectives should as far as possible be achieved by non-coercive measures, i.e. through the gathering of "information, advice, order or warning or by taking regulatory or preventive action".[20] Coercion is defined as forced physical interference towards a person or property.[21] The Act relating to legal procedure in criminal cases (CPA) part IV contains the regulations of coercive measures (*tvangsmidler*) in Norway. It is common to all coercive measures regulated in Part IV that they are intermediary steps in a criminal procedure. When a case is closed, coercive measures are replaced either with dropping of the charges, a conviction or a return of the seized object to its owner.[22] There are, however, several types of coercive measures available to the police that do not fall within the Part IV category. The police have legal bases to intervene

15 According to NOU 1981:35 ch.5.

16 PA sect.6(2), PD sect.3(2).

17 Loader and Walker 2007:95; Marenin 1982.

18 See e.g. Tuffin, Morris and Poole 2006.

19 For example, passive observation requires no legal basis.

20 PA sect.6(1), PD sect.3–1.

21 PD sect.3–2. Coercive measure could arguably mean the same as any measure similar to those requiring legal bases, thus those interfering in the individual's private sphere. With such a definition, measures of intelligence exchange for analysis reasons would fall within the ambit. The wording seems as such less appropriate, since there is no doubt that, for example, wiretapping of a telephone or a room is a coercive measure, although it does not actually *physically* deal with the person or property.

22 Andenæs and Myhrer 2009:278.

in various ways to maintain public peace and order. According to sect.7(1) PA, such intervention is legitimate when the purpose is:

1 to halt disturbances of public peace and order or when the circumstances give reason to fear such disturbances;
2 to protect the safety of individuals or the general public; or
3 to avert or halt violations of law.

The primary available measures are listed in the same section, second paragraph, establishing that the police in such cases may *inter alia* "regulate the traffic, prohibit loitering in certain areas, turn away, render harmless or impound dangerous objects, turn away, remove or apprehend persons, order activities to be halted or modified, enter private property or area or order areas to be evacuated". The purposes and measures thus coincide greatly with the 'general authority', signifying the non-casuistic characteristic both of the Act and of the police tasks in customary law. Outside the three purposes of 7(1), the police may also take action on behalf of other public bodies if the "circumstances entail or threaten serious breaches of the peace, if the public authority in question is not available or intervention by such authority is presumed to be impossible, futile or cannot take place in time". In case of a lack of compliance with a decree given with basis in 7(1), the police may see to it that necessary action is taken to prevent the negligence from causing damage, injury or from endangering the general public, at the expense of the negligent party (7[2]).

The police may use force if there is legal basis for this, and coercion is 1) clearly necessary and 2) defensible in light of the seriousness of the situation, the potential consequences of the enforcement and the general circumstances.[23] The relevant coercive measures available to the Norwegian police outside the Criminal Procedure Act are examined in the following.

2.1.1.1 Apprehension and detention

Being apprehended by the police and involuntarily removed from any premises is an intrusive measure in the individual's private sphere. The coercive measures regulated in the CPA have different implications for whether the measure must be based on a court order, but also on which status the apprehended receives. Apprehension and detention based in the Police Act do not, contrary to following the CPA procedure, result in the status as charged, with the subsequent due process rights following this status (sect.82[2]). This is because the measure has a public order purpose, not one of criminal procedure. Where the aim of the coercive measure is unclear or not decided, the rules according to the CPA should be applied.[24] The police can legitimately bring individuals to the police station or other police premises for up to four hours, under certain conditions.[25] Suspicion of criminal activity is not a necessary requirement for the police to apprehend someone with basis in the Police Act. The detention must initially and continuously be necessary pursuant to sect.8, which gives bases to take in anyone 1) guilty of disturbing the peace and order or lawful traffic in a public place, 2) failing to comply with a police order to remove their person from a public space, when the circumstances gives reasonable grounds for fear of disturbance of public peace and order

23 PA sect.6.
24 Ot.prp.nr.22 (1994–1995):20.
25 CPA sects.171–173, 175–176.

or of lawful traffic, 3) failing to give their name, date or year of birth, position and residence upon demand by the police, or who supplies details whose accuracy there is reason to doubt, or 4) encountered at or near a place where a crime must be presumed to have been committed immediately beforehand.

The individual's rights in case of apprehension, arrest and detention follow from ECHR art.5. The first paragraph guarantees "the right to liberty and security of person", and forbids deprivation of liberty except in certain cases mentioned in *litri* a–f, in addition to a requirement of a legally prescribed procedure. *Litra* a concerns detention after a court conviction, but *litri* b-f are all relevant in the present context. The competences of the Norwegian police to apprehend and detain according to the Police Act are all in accordance with the ECHR. Lawful arrest or detention of a person is legitimate when it is b) in order to secure the fulfilment of any obligation prescribed by law or c) when the action is taken to bring him before a competent legal authority on reasonable suspicion of having committed an offence or when it is reasonable considered necessary to prevent his committing an offence or fleeing after having done so. Detention is further legitimate outside of criminal cases when d) it is of a minor, by lawful order, and for the purpose of educational supervision or of bringing him before the competent legal authority (in the Norwegian case this would also include the welfare authority custody), or e) it is of a person with the purpose of preventing the spreading of infectious diseases, or of persons of unsound mind, alcoholics or drug addicts or vagrants. The final ground is that of arrest or detention of foreigners who are to be prevented from entering the country or with the view to deport or extradite (*litra* f).[26]

Several important procedural rights are required in such situations (paras.2 and 4). The rights vary slightly, whether it is a case of arrest or detention, which corresponds with the Norwegian division between actions taken within the ambit of criminal law or administrative law. In the former situations, there are requirements of prompt information of the grounds of the arrest and any charge, and for the information to be in a language the arrestee understands. For both arrest and detention, anyone must be given the opportunity to issue proceedings as regards to the lawfulness of his detention, which must be speedily decided by a court of law. In case of a ruling of unlawfulness, immediate release must occur. This does not imply a right to bail. Bail is legally based in CPA sect.188(1), but generally not used in Norwegian legal practice. Unlawful arrest or detention further implies a right to compensation (para.5).

2.1.1.2 Search

Search implies an external observation of the individual's body, in addition to an examination of clothing and luggage. This police search is not equivalent to the kind of search requiring judicial decision in the CPA. It is strictly limited from for example undressing the individual.[27] The general sect.7 allows search in public places if it is necessary to maintain

26 Case law from the ECtHR on this matter includes the prominent Saadi v UK 13229/03 Grand Chamber 28 January 2009 which requires the detention of asylum seekers to be arbitrary, carried out in good faith closely connected to the ground relied upon and in a place and under conditions that are appropriate. Importantly also that the length of the detention does not exceed that reasonably required according to the purpose. As to the necessity in the length of detention, the court in the M and others v Bulgaria 41416/08 26.07.2011 ruled that two years and eight months was too long, even though the detainee was 'unreturnable' due to technical difficulties in securing deportation.

27 Ot.prp.nr.22 (1994–1995):62.

the public peace and order. Section 7a is a new legal basis for the measure of search of body or vehicle when there is reason to believe someone is in possession of, or stores, guns. Being relatively intrusive, this measure can only be used if the purpose is to prevent criminal acts endangering someone's life, health or freedom. This in contrast to, for example, a search related to *any* gun, such as hunting weapons, when there is no suspicion of illegitimate use. There are two additional alternative requirements; either that the search happens in situations or places where a) such criminal activities tend to take place, or b) where there is reason to believe that such criminal activities are planned or prepared. As such, even though the requirements are strict and according to the principle of legality, there is a wide margin of appreciation for the enforcing police officers.

Search subsequent to arrest may be performed if there are difficulties establishing the identity of the apprehended. Any objects capable of harming the detained or others may be removed and retained by the police. Any person removed, detained or apprehended may be searched to locate weapons or dangerous objects in general.

2.2 Police competences, including rules of conduct and procedure

In the context of international police cooperation, a question of the utmost importance is whether Norwegian police can be confident that the principles and values they are governed by, also are respected when foreign police take action either on their home territory, following a request from Norwegian police, or on Norwegian territory, for example, as part of a joint investigation team. What foreign police do in their own jurisdiction is beyond the Norwegian authorities' responsibility; concern about 'foul play' according to Norwegian standards would thus only be significant from a moral point of view.[28] When such concerns are voiced concerning police work within Norway, it is commonly said that foreign police must in all cases abide by Norwegian law. This is necessary to ensure sovereign control of the territory. Nevertheless, it seems clear that it has never been the intention to fix police competences and limitations fully in law. There has never been a desire to regulate police tasks by legal means. Instead there is a reliance on training and guidance of police officers to guarantee they behave appropriately when applying their wide discretion.[29] The education provided by the Norwegian police college is seen as an important governance tool for society to maintain the civil machinery of power "according to the standard that society at any time wishes".[30] Changes in the training and education of cadets are important, since discretion and wide scope of action are bestowed upon them on the assumption that they have the requisite integrity.

The state's overall responsibility for the police was further emphasised in 1995 by clarifications to the voluntary and/or private police function (1995 Act sect.26).[31] The revision was made to signify that the public peace and order function of the police, as well as that of criminal investigation, belonged at the state level. Neither private nor municipal actors should be responsible for such activities. Private parties are allowed to protect themselves and others in immediate danger, and certain security functions related to specific events or nature conservation may be carried out, within the limits set by the General Penal Code.

28 With the caveat of breaches of human rights, which may be targeted outside and over national jurisdictions.
29 NOU 1981:35 p.84; Ot.prp.nr.22 (1994–1995):10.
30 Ot.prp.nr.22 (1994–1995):33.
31 Op.cit.:53–4.

One distinguishing characteristic is that private 'policing' *must* be defensive in character: to control, observe, and if necessary report to the police. Another characteristic is its purpose: if only private, and not public, interests are concerned, private policing may be accepted.[32]

The 1995 Act brought only minor *changes* from the previous Police Act of 1936 to police powers (aside from fixing them in law), but also set out more closely the criteria for holding police authority. Who 'the police' are in the 1995 Act sect.1 is relevant to is closely related to the characteristics of the state. The police are the enforcers of state power on the state's territory. The state, by fixing in law the requirements for obtaining police powers, emphasises its core competence to decide who shall exercise them on Norwegian territory. For prospective officers to be given police powers, the 1995 Act sect.20 (cf.18) requires that they have no criminal record, and are Norwegian citizens. Both requirements were seen in the *forarbeid* as necessary to ensure public trust in police officers.[33] As to citizenship, the Ministry considered it vital that those enforcing power *in persona*, as the persons who embody the state and *are* the state when exercising their legal competences towards individuals, should have strong ties both to the state they embody and the fellow citizens they relate to. Such bonds of loyalty were considered be formed by shared citizenship. There should be absolutely no doubt, when acute situations arise, that police officers share Norwegian values and the traditions inherent in the Norwegian police's *modus operandi*.[34] The 1995 Act sect.20(1) emphasises the validity of the police powers within the realm. This makes plain both the territorial delimitation of state jurisdiction, and that national police territory extends across all internal borders.

There are requirements regarding how police activities should be carried out. The PD sect.3–1 emphasises the obvious: action taken must be *legal*. Furthermore, it should be deemed *necessary* and *proportionate*, in view of 1) the seriousness of the situation, 2) the nature and purpose of the police service in question, and 3) circumstances in general. Furthermore, police officers must be truthful, unbiased and impartial in their personal behaviour, and must act as effectively as possible within budgetary and legal frameworks. Particular emphasis is placed on human rights. Action taken must respect human rights, especially in relation to privacy and dignity as set out in human rights law.[35] Arrests and other interventions should be executed in such a way as to minimise public humiliation for those arrested. As for all public use of authority, the principle of equality applies, meaning that all equal situations should be treated equally. Applying this principle to day-to-day activities may seem considered, since the situations the police deal with are so different that the officer's discretion and the need for rapid decision-making will often prevent a full "equality assessment".[36]

The 1995 Act makes it a legal obligation for officers to live in the district where they are employed, so that they can fulfil their duty to serve as police officers even when off duty (sects.22–23). This was considered vital, both because police officers could be immediately available in serious situations, and that they could be part of the social network in all police

32 Op.cit.:53 and Ot.prp.nr.54 (1999–2000):ch.7.4 concerning the need for clear demarcations between security guard work and police functions and tasks.

33 Ot.prp.nr.22 (1994–1995):36.

34 Op.cit.:36.

35 PA sect.6(3–4) and PD sect.3(4–6). The PA sect.3 limits the Act and interpretation of the Act by international law or by agreements with other states. In addition, the Human Rights Act sect.3 establishes that the ECHR and certain other human rights protection conventions with protocols should prevail in cases not in accordance with Norwegian legislation. This also follows from the Norwegian Constitution from 2014.

36 See Ot.prp.nr.22 (1994–1995):18.

districts, by connecting to their local community.[37] In other words; a police close to the people they serve.

2.3 Context and synthesis of the 1995 Police Act

Christie argued that crime and crime control must be understood in the context of a particular social order, and that changes in this order have significant consequences for it.[38] Norway was not a wealthy state in the years following the Second World War. In the 1950s and through the next couple of decades, there was significant economic growth and, as in the other Nordic countries and Western Europe, industrial growth was at an all-time high.[39] Norway's wealth increased significantly after the oil industry began to develop in the 1970s. Economic prosperity may be one of several reasons for Norway's indecisive stance in ongoing public and political debates on how the police should be organised and employed. Christie's arguments have been criticised, for underestimating the informal social control present in urban areas, and misunderstanding the 'subsidiarity' of public control functions such as the police.[40] However, a few characteristics of the Norwegian situation at the time when the revision work on the early 20th century acts commenced may clarify which points were emphasised in the policy documents.

Two police reform committees were appointed in 1966 and 1974 (the Aulie and the Ekanger Committees, Police Role Committees I and II respectively), because the policing situation was seen as increasingly complex and the police organisational structure as outdated. The first recommended a "police directorate" model, the second a police department within the Ministry of Justice and Police. Both reports led to debate. In the case of the Aulie report, this was because it was seen as suggesting political control over the central police administration should be weakened (in that moving the administration to a directorate outside the Ministry would lead to less direct political control) and also because of the reasoning behind the suggested changes. Should the police be more or less centrally controlled and managed? And why should the system change? Some critics argued that the suggestions implied centralisation of the organisation of the police, in a direction that would lead to a policing situation not in keeping with Norwegian traditions.[41] In his explicitly political book of 1978, Mathiesen gave an analysis of what he terms the "war of the police" (*politikrigen*) during the 1970s, discussing various sides of the debates around what the police should be like in the future. Despite its lack of balance, his account gives an insight into the contemporary debates in the media and in the wider public. Newspaper headlines claimed that the police were powerless in the face of enormous problems of violence, and that the nature and structure of the police stopped them preventing crime and disorder; they just reacted after the fact.[42] The Aulie Report claimed that an "epidemic" of unrest was spreading throughout the world, probably because the mass media described events all over the world, and communication between countries was rapidly increasing. The police were faced with massive social problems that were expected to get worse.[43] Police professionals

37 Op.cit.:39–40.
38 Christie 1995:3.
39 Helle *et al.* 2013:330–3, Sejersted 2013.
40 Johansen 2008; Olaussen 2007.
41 Lorentzen 1981:206.
42 Referred in op.cit.:209–11; Mathiesen 1979:20.
43 Aulie-innstillingen 1970:20.

(*embetsmenn*) argued that an increase in the number of police officers was necessary to ensure that people felt secure. The opposition, on the other hand, claimed that the increase in crime was caused by changes in the social structure, such as a general weakening of *primary* social control among citizens. Both Lorentzen and Mathiesen criticised the media coverage of the police and police requirements in this period, arguing that a few well-placed headlines (by conservative forces in society) were steering public opinion into 'understanding' that the policing situation in Norway was untenable.[44] This is, of course, only one side of the story, but it is indicative of the intensity of the disagreements at the time, concerning in which direction the Norwegian police should develop.

There were two concurrent developments in this period. On the one hand, a number of special police units were established or formalised, and the 1970s saw the start of a general reform of the Norwegian police organisation.[45] On the other hand, perhaps as a response to the first development, there was a vigorous debate around the unity and proximity police tradition in (local) society.

The Police Role Committee (I) showed that there had been a significant increase in order policing assignments in the larger cities during the 1960s and '70s. It emphasised that, unlike in earlier times, order policing did not mainly consist of 'on the beat' presence, but meant increased numbers of tactical call-outs.[46] As such, it was not seen as being 'proximity policing'.

This is the same period at which the international police cooperation instruments within the EU (EEC) were gaining momentum. Thus, elsewhere, there were similar concerns over insufficient police, even at non-state levels. The Norwegian adaptation to European development is the focus of Part II.

2.4 The structure and units of the Norwegian police

It follows from the 1995 Police Act (PA) sects.1;15–16 that the police service is a *national* service, provided by the state, and headed by whatever ministry the King may decide (currently the Ministry of Justice and Public Security). This means that other private or public bodies cannot intervene in the core area of police duties, but does not in itself limit the state's power to establish more than one branch of the police.[47] The police force is united and nationwide, although several specialised units exist. Some of these have particular international police cooperation functions, such as the National Criminal Investigation Service (*Kripos*). Other ways police competence may be enforced outside of the ordinary forces is presented, to show how police authority can be enforced within Norwegian territory outside normal situations, and to provide an idea of potential obstacles for non-national police force powers preparatory to, or outside international police cooperation.

2.4.1 The general structure

The Norwegian police consists of approximately 13,000 employees, in 12 police districts, each answerable to a local chief of police, and to the centralised bodies.[48] Every district is

44 Op.cit.

45 The special units are described below in the account of the structural hierarchy and organisation of the police.

46 Op.cit. p.98.

47 Op.cit.:12, see also Frostad 2008:272.

48 There were 54 districts until 2002; the number was reduced to 12 in 2015.

divided into local and rural police stations, at the discretion of the king. These are subordinate units managed by chief superintendents. According to the Ministry, police work should normally be managed and carried out locally, and this is ensured by this relatively decentralised organisational structure.[49] Nonetheless, centralised and specialised departments are considered necessary to carry out criminal investigation policing in particular. These departments both assist the local districts, and sometimes concern themselves with more complicated police activities.

The Norwegian police are, broadly defined, organised in a hierarchical three-level structure: the Ministry, Directorate and local districts. The PA sect.16(1) regulates the management structure: the Ministry and Police Directorate constitute central management, which takes responsibility for professional and administrative matters. Operational responsibility belongs to the lower levels. Governance and administration are the preserve of the state, but the state-level responsibility is for bigger issues: general planning and prioritisation, and overall control of the police function. The management of day-to-day policing activities is to be kept local. It is emphasised that "democratic control" is important, both over the central leadership and the police in the areas where they operate.[50] The Ministry of Justice and Public Security (the Ministry) is head of the police service, but the governing power of the Ministry since 2001 has been delegated (1995 Act sect.15) to the National Police Directorate (POD).[51] Some special units, such as The Norwegian Police Security Service (PST), are on the same hierarchical level as the Directorate.

The Norwegian prosecution and police authorities are partly. The chiefs of police and the police officers with law degrees (police prosecutors) are employed in the lower prosecuting authority within the police. The higher levels of public prosecution, encompassing the public prosecutors (*statsadvokatene*) and the (Office of the) Director of Public Prosecution, are separate from the police, and are responsible for prosecuting more serious crimes. While the chief of police is head of the prosecution section of his staff, he is not superior to it in *prosecutorial* matters: these come within the remit of the Public Prosecution of the district or the Director.

This arrangement is not common in other European jurisdictions. In Europe, only Sweden and Denmark were found in the *forarbeid* to have comparable systems.[52] While the police initiate and carry out investigations, the police prosecutors are usually in charge of the operations, and take some of the decisions on coercive measures. An example is the decision to arrest a person in Norway on the strength of a hit in the Schengen Information System (SIS).[53] This more intertwined structure may facilitate international judicial police cooperation, since the prosecutorial authorities have other competences, such as the power to request that measures be taken abroad.

49 E.g. Ot.prp.nr.22 (1994–1995):28.

50 Op.cit.:26–7.

51 Such a directorate had been suggested repeatedly ever since the 1912 Committee, but was considered, also in relation to the 2001 amendment, a cost- inducing intermediary part between the local police function and the (police department of) the Ministry. The Ministry in 1995 *did*, however, acknowledge that there was a steadily increasing need for a strengthened leadership function of the police, because of "increased mobility and a need for international cooperation" (my translation). (Op.cit.:26; Innst.S.nr.192 (1991–1992). The historic debates on the state level organisation appear in the forarbeid 1935 Politikomiteens innstilling:21–22; Innst.O.I. (1936):4. See also Auglend *et al.* 2004:121–123; Johansen 2006; Johansen 1989.)

52 Op.cit.

53 Utleveringsloven 1975 sect.20. On the general prosecution authority rules and the relation in investigation, see CPA sects. 55; 67; 225, cf. chapters 6–7. See more in Andenæs and Myhrer 2009 ch.7; 32; Rieber-Mohn 1996.

2.4.2 Organisational structure of the operational police

Police officers have a considerable amount of discretion over how tasks are performed in day-to-day work aimed at preventing public disorder and crime. The regulations are broad and general: officers should, for example, direct their attention to everything is endangering, or might endanger, the public or obstructing general traffic; he must interfere to protect anyone in distress or is in danger of getting involved in a fight or something else that will disturb the public peace.[54]

One of the ten basic principles is that officers should be generalists. Nevertheless, it is argued that increased social complexity and changes in crime are, as seen above, make special police competences necessary. A brief overview is given here to illustrate which tasks ordinary police will typically *not* perform. The special units are subordinate to either the Police Directorate (like ordinary police when performing police functions), or partly (when performing prosecutorial functions) to the Director of Public Prosecution.[55] Several special units are located in the Oslo police district.

The structure of the police is determined by the need to organise the police force in the way best suited to achieve the purposes set out in the PA sect.1, in accordance with the various principles described above, such as having a decentralised police in close proximity to individuals. Close cooperation with other public authorities on preventive work is also a main priority.[56]

As part of the decentralisation principle, police forces are administered and managed *locally*.[57] Despite the fact that districts are autonomous, the way resources are allocated means that some tools or skills may not exist everywhere. This was supposed to be remedied by the 2015 police reform, which reduced the number of police districts from 27 to 12. Seven special units provide in addition services directly to the districts.[58]

Another core value of the Norwegian police is the united nature of the force. While a central aim of this book is to look at possible divergence from this principle in *international* cooperation, there are also internal issues that challenge the governing principles. The Crown may allow the setting up of separate police agencies for one or more particular areas of police work (sect.16(2)). According to the *forarbeid*, this allows more flexible organisational solutions.[59] Given the wording ("one or more particular areas"), it would not be possible to set up a new general police force. A chief of police is responsible for the force in his district, and its head (sect.16[1]). He may, however, seek assistance from neighbouring districts or from special units.[60] The district usually retains responsibility for police operations.

A distinction may, as mentioned above, be made between what can be called the provision of particular and general order.[61] Most forms of international police cooperation in Norway involve special police units, primarily the National Criminal Investigation Service (Kripos). The role of Kripos will be revisited in the presentation of police cooperation measures. Since this book discusses the police's role in both particular and general order, the following provides a general overview of the special units concerned with this.

54 1995 PA sect.2; PD sects.8–2 and 8–3.
55 The Police in Norway 2010.
56 Ot.prp.nr.22 (1994–1995):25.
57 Op.cit.:28.
58 Op.cit.
59 Ot.prp.nr.22 (1994–1995):66.
60 PD sect.7–4.
61 Loader and Walker 2007:95; Marenin 1982.

The special terrorist police were established within the Oslo police district in the 1970s. Gradually, the Ministry established other such units in all the major police districts. Crimes related to terrorism are often considered to border on political crimes, and it was discussed whether this function should be subject to military control. It was not taken for granted that anti-terror policing could reflect the values of the civilian Norwegian police force.[62]

The most pertinent special units are the National Authority for Investigation and Prosecution of Economic and Environmental Crime (Økokrim), Kripos (the National Unit for Combating Organised and Other Serious Crimes) and the Norwegian Police Security Service (PST).[63] These units are particularly involved in international policing, either in tasks and responsibilities and/or as contact points for foreign law enforcement. Even if they are often located in Oslo, all these special units have national responsibilities.[64] In the police reform of 2015, currently being implemented, the expertise of the special units is intended to be more broadly available locally.

Økokrim is a centralised unit tasked with investigating, prosecuting and creating analyses in the area of serious economic and environmental crime. It is subordinate to the Police Directorate and to the Office of the Director of Public Prosecutions (in prosecutorial matters), but decides independently which cases to investigate. The fact that it is centralised implies national authority, but also an obligation to train and advise other public prosecutors and police. Several forms of police cooperation are carried out by Økokrim. Cooperation includes operations, and information exchange: according to the Police Directorate, Økokrim is a major participant in knowledge and best practice exchange in various international fora.[65] It may thus be considered to participate in informal network cooperation outside more formalised channels.

The Norwegian Police Security Service (PST) is a secret service branch of the police. PST responsibilities include the prevention and investigation of crimes against the security and independence of the state, illegal surveillance, the spreading of weapons of mass destruction, sabotage and politically motivated violence and terrorist-related crimes (PA 1995 chapter IIIa). The PST has ongoing contact with ordinary police authorities and foreign security services (PA sect.17c).

The PST, the police and other special services cooperate in several ways. In some situations (e.g. in terrorist-related crimes), the PST will perform the covert investigations, while the ordinary police do overt work, such as interrogation and seizure.[66] The PST is a part of

62 The issue was controversial, and the Police Role Committee considered dismantling the special police force (Lorentzen 1981:217).

63 The full list includes The national anti-terrorism unit and *Emergency Response Unit* (Contingency Platoon) is the police force's special deployment unit for hostage, terror and sabotage situations. The *Crisis and Hostage Negotiation Service* has a specialized team for terror, hostage and kidnapping situations. These are part of the *civilian* police force, they generally have no military or paramilitary characteristics, links or competences, as is more common in other countries. The *Norwegian Police's Bomb Squad* is organized under the police dog patrol (K–9) service in Oslo. The *Mobile Deployment Concept* is responsible for the coordination of joint efforts in case of massive disturbances of general order, e.g. in the form of violent demonstrations. In other extreme situations, the *Police Negotiation Unit* may be advisor to the Royal Ministry of Foreign Affairs (MFA) on effective siege management and negotiation strategy and tactics. The *Norwegian Police's Helicopter Service* and the responsibility for a *Royal Police Escort* are localized in Oslo Police District

64 Ot.prp.nr.22 (1994–1995):33–4.

65 For overview of Økokrim's various non-EU cooperation instruments, see http://www.okokrim.no/about-oekokrim [29.05.17].

66 http://www.pst.no/oppgaver/samarbeid/ [29.05.17].

the police, but their ambit has similarities with that of the military. Part of its legislative framework is the Security Act,[67] enabling "effective countering of threats to the independence and security of the realm and other vital national security interests" and "safeguarding the constitutional rights of individuals" (sect.1).

The PST cooperates with the police of other states, within their area of responsibility. Security and surveillance related activities, and the preventive work done by the PST are seen as crucial to international communication.[68] In such serious cases the PST increasingly takes advantage of cross-border communication to cooperate with police and security authorities throughout the world, as well as through NATO and other international organisations. Cooperation consists of exchanging information, which was a consideration for the PST threat assessments of international effects on Norwegian society. Despite the autonomous role of the PST, cooperation channels with new countries and services must be established in agreement with the Ministry of Justice.

The *Military* Intelligence Service (*E-tjenesten*) maps and counteracts *external* threats to national security, and reports to the Ministry of Defence.[69] The *E-tjeneste* may not, unlike the PST, keep Norwegian citizens under overt or covert surveillance on Norwegian territory.[70] Exceptions apply for Norwegian citizens suspected of providing intelligence to foreign powers. In such cases, military surveillance may be initiated after conferral with the PST. The *E-tjeneste* has a legal basis for cooperation with the PST, for example, in information exchange. The *E-tjeneste* may also pass on to other public authorities information they themselves are not entitled to make use of. As an example, the PST has its own high-security communications system. It was stated early on that they would not employ SIS, since the system is too insecure for the kind of sensitive information the PST deals with.[71]

PST international cooperation involves an interesting body of regulations and procedures.[72] This book is generally limited to secret policing and concentrates on 'ordinary' international police work and cooperation. A central task of the PST is to create and publish open and covert threat analyses, both of threats against Norwegian society and Norwegian relations with foreign cooperating bodies and agencies. These threat assessments are revisited in Chapter 14.2.

The discussion of whether the particular order changes because of police work across borders is returned to in Chapter 15. International police work and the Norwegian regulations relating to it will be explored in Chapter 4 onwards.

2.4.3 Everyone's responsibility and duty to police

The main rule of police work in Norway is that only the police do it. Before later looking at the international cooperation measures departing from this principle, an exception to the rule is examined, to show that the purpose of policing may be more important than who carries it out.

To some extent, the Norwegian society as a whole, and each member individually, are responsible for 'policing' in terms of PA sect.1: together they constitute the state and

67 Lov 20.03. no.10 1998.

68 St.meld.nr.18 (1999–2000):23–24.

69 ISA sects.1 and 2, see also E-tjenesteinstruksen sect.5.

70 ISA sect.4.

71 E-tjenesteinstruksen sect.5(3); ch.4.

72 St.prp.nr.42 (1996–1997). On the use of secretive coercive measures in Norway, see Bruce and Haugland 2014.

society.[73] Two types of legitimate physical force exist in addition to the police monopoly, and ordinary rules of procedure: citizen's arrest, and the police officer's right to act outside the regular decision-making hierarchy in emergency situations. It follows from the Penal Code (GCPC) sects.17 and 18 that anyone is entitled to use force, i.e. to commit otherwise illegal acts, to prevent or stop an attack or threat against themselves, or against someone else's person or property. The action must be necessary, justified and ethically reasonable.

Arrest of individuals should generally be performed by police authorities (CPA sect.175 cf. PA sect.20) acting on a decision by the prosecution authority.[74] Exceptions arise when delay means the offence might not be stopped or the offender might escape. In such cases, an officer may make an arrest without a decision from the prosecution authorities. In addition, any individual may, under the CPA, seize a person caught in the act, or on trailing someone on 'fresh clues', or seize stolen goods, when delay entails any form of risk (CPA sects.176; 206). These regulations give private security companies the right to apprehend offenders caught in the act. Until recently, they were also interpreted as giving a legal basis for foreign police officers to exercise such powers in Norway. The regulations demand that the person or things apprehended should immediately be surrendered to the police. Seizure must follow the ordinary l requirements for apprehension set out in the Act: CPA sect.174 rules that anyone caught in the act may be arrested by police authority (cf. sect.175) no matter what the minimum sanctions are. This corresponds to sect.176. Regarding apprehension after trailing 'fresh clues', citizen's arrest is only permissible if someone is caught in the act of committing a crime punishable by six months or more in prison (sect.171). This excludes shoplifting, for example.

After this introduction to some rules, regulations of principles of central importance for the Norwegian police, we now move to the Norwegian relationship with external actors and agencies. I will first briefly consider police cooperation outside of the EU system (Chapter 3), before I go into the various available forms of EU police cooperation in detail (Chapters 4–6).

73 See e.g. Reiner 1992:8 on moral obligations to use force.

74 Which is part of the police, e.g. the police deputies (CPA sect.55), but normally not part of the operational police who actually carry out arrests. Note the difference between police detaining someone for a short period of time, cf. PA sect.8 and arrest with a legal basis in the CPA. In principle, procedural safeguards automatically take effect at the point of arrest, but are not applicable to short-term police detention. This is returned to in Chapter 13.1.2.4.

3 The Nordic police cooperation outside of the EU system

Maintaining the Nordic relationship was one of two main justifications from the Norwegian government in the 1990s to join the Schengen cooperation. In order to later consider that justification, this section gives an introduction to the Nordic cooperation outside of the EU system.

Even before the Schengen Agreement, Norway was party to several formal international agreements on crime control; bilaterally and multilaterally. These have primarily regulated cooperation on the legal level, requiring court decisions. As a general rule, the international police cooperation avenues involving Norway prior to Schengen participation concerned specific cases, and took place according to the regulations in the Criminal Procedure Act and the Police Directive (PD), alongside guidelines of the international judicial cooperation that Norway was a member of. The most prominent agreements up until the 1990s were those of the UN and the Council of Europe. The subject matters were extradition procedures, and to some extent harmonisation of legal systems in order to facilitate extradition, for example the early agreement on drugs, terrorists and white slavery conventions.

On the Nordic level, the cooperation, including the formalised parts, is based on close ties and is in many ways as deep (meaning topical breadth and geographical width) as the EU instruments. The particularities of the applicable practical cooperation measures are accounted for in greater detail below. Operationally, the Nordic cooperation contains the same measures that were made available over the first ten years or so of EU and Schengen cooperation. Two prominent types are explained here, the passport-freedom/open border development, and the police/customs cooperation (PTN).

The Nordic cooperation has a long tradition, also informally, either through knowledge exchange and best-practices seminars, etc., or simply via direct contacts between personnel, typically in border districts.[1] The cooperation in the justice and home affairs areas was formalised to some extent in the 1950s with the passport and free-travel agreements between the Nordic countries, and with the Nordic Council: the Inter-Parliamentary Committee of 1952. The Nordic Passport Union has since 1954 been the international legal basis for the Nordic countries as a 'free travel' area. The removal of passport requirements came alongside the agreement giving these Nordic citizens the same right as national citizens to reside and work in the other member states. A 1957 agreement, dissolving the passport control at the internal borders, also based the control measures on the external borders of the Nordic countries. This led to a close cooperation on both immigration control and on police and customs control.[2] A governmental aim was that the general public should see and

1 Similar in Spapens 2008 and Sheptycki 1998:216–217.
2 St.prp.no. 42 (1996–1997):2.

DOI: 10.4324/9780429503696-4

experience a common control practice irrespective of the national borders between the Nordic countries. And the police of the border regions are reported to generally have regular direct contact and exchange information with colleagues across the border.[3] The Nordic chiefs of the national police forces (*rikspoliti*) have annual meetings to discuss coordination of the police activities in the Nordic countries.[4] In addition, there are frequent meetings between various state instances in the Nordic countries to better the cooperation; from police education meetings, the international secretariats of the heads of the countries' police, and also more recently meetings on defence cooperation, and crisis and emergency cooperation.

The cooperation further deepened with the first Nordic Police Cooperation Agreement in 1972.[5] At the same time, Nordic agreements on judicial cooperation in criminal matters, for example, concerning extradition, were formalised. The policiary agreements and cooperation have primarily been agreed upon between the chiefs of police; not legally formalised, and thus not been politically or publically debated.

The first thorough governmental international crime control assessment in Norway (1997) concluded that the Schengen cooperation was important to complement and fill the gaps between bilateral and overarching agreements, the Nordic, and the Interpol cooperation, concerning operational and intelligence police cooperation.[6] At the time of the relatively new EEA cooperation, it seems probable that the Schengen cooperation was perceived as necessary to follow up the intensified cooperation on economic matters: A higher level of freedom necessitated a higher degree of control.

The purpose of the Nordic agreements has been the same all along: to facilitate and improve expediency and communication processes between the relevant authorities, removing all 'unnecessary' bureaucratic procedures.[7] The Agreement gives no independent legal basis; it is more of a simplifying guideline for practitioners on how to apply existing treaties and provisions under the national law of the different states.[8] The current Nordic Police Cooperation Agreement, replacing the revisions of 2002 and 2012, entered into force in 2016.

Further, the Police and Customs Cooperation (PTN) was also central for the cooperation in the Norwegian border regions prior to the Schengen Agreement. The PTN was established in 1982 and given a permanent board from 1987.[9] The main purpose of the cooperation was the improved efficiency of the fight against drug-related and organised cross-border crime. The focus shifted already in 1997 from primarily drug-related crime to cross-border 'organised crime' in general.[10] The PTN also produces an annual joint Nordic Organised Crime Threat Assessment. A liaison officer secondment arrangement give legal basis for secondments on behalf of all the Nordic countries together, in countries where drug-related or other serious cross-border crime takes place. The liaison officer, independent of country of origin, would report back to *all* Nordic countries. In addition, an intelligence system was established for obtaining and exchanging information, with access

3 Op.cit.:24.
4 St.prp.nr.42 (1996–1997):ch.6.2.3.
5 1972 Nordisk politisamarbeidsavtale.
6 St.prp.nr.42 (1996–1997):6.9.
7 St.prp.nr.42 (1996–1997):ch.6.2.2, 2012 Agreement no.1. See also Kleiven 2012 and Kleiven 2013 (on Nordic liaison officers).
8 2012 Agreement no.1; Bull 1997:145; see also Boucht 2012:254.
9 The current regulatory basis was established by the Nordic chiefs of police in 2009.
10 St.prp.nr.42 (1996–1997):ch.6.2.5.

for all the Nordic countries' relevant authorities. The member states allot the intelligence work in the various other countries between themselves, and subsequently share the results. The *Kripos* is responsible for the Norwegian part of the PTN, including the professional and administrative responsibility for the Norwegian police liaison officers, and the contact with the Nordic liaison officers stationed around the world.[11]

The primary purpose of the liaison officer arrangement is to establish contact and cooperation with the host state's authorities on fighting crime that is significant to the Nordic countries.[12] Cooperation should only be initiated in the case of crimes that affect two or more member states. One target area has from the mid–1990s onwards been motorcycle crime, where cooperation and information exchange of information between the police and customs were considered vital. A 'Nordic task force' was set up, consisting of a pool of experts from the countries' police within specific crime areas, mapping the motorcycle criminals of Europe, and creating a joint weapon register.[13] Nordic cooperation also includes the Nordic Arrest Warrant agreement, which is discussed later.

The newer instruments, as discussed below, take things a step further, when the wider *European* operational cooperation measures enter the scene. Knowledge and information exchange is facilitated through similar languages in the Nordic regions. The technological development and extended access to far more countries' information through the EU instruments may, however, side-line the more regionally limited alternatives. Trust is a keyword also in the EU context in order to make the area of justice, freedom and security a reality.[14] In the next two chapters, the construction of the practical EU police cooperation of the Europol and Schengen instruments is presented, before a consideration of Norway's seemingly ambiguous – simultaneously both hesitant and eager – accession to *parts* of these cooperation instruments.

11 St.meld.nr.18 (1999–2000):ch.3.2.2.
12 St.prp.nr.42 (1996–1997):ch.6.2.5.
13 Op.cit.:pt.6.2.6.
14 Fijnaut 1995; den Boer *et al.* (2008); Larsson 2006.

4 The development of EU crime control policies and the Norwegian (non) membership

4.1 From World War II to Schengen

After each of the two world wars of the 20th century, the European countries faced the same chaotic conditions with large numbers of displaced people, thriving black markets, and much general anxiety and despair.

Cooperation between the European states has traditionally not had a police focus. The cooperation on security matters on an international level has focused on peace, not crime control. After the devastating Second World War, there was a clear need to maintain peace and economic prosperity in Europe. In 1949, the Council of Europe (CoE) was established by ten states as a common European forum for cooperation. The European Convention of Human Rights (ECHR) was created the year after, an instrument that has had great impact on the national human rights regulations. Based on the idea that trade agreements would create closer contact between countries, and at the same time enhance a Western European cooperation that would strengthen the resistance against the Eastern Block, a trade and economic community including six states started taking shape from around the same time. One of the principal instruments of the trade cooperation was the removal of import and export tax between the member states, and the joint regulations would lower the level of competition and enhance cooperation. Another important development was supranational bodies, including a court, that could steer the common policy development and settle disputes between member states. The first police and crime control frameworks were of UN origin, for example, on combating international drugs and drug trafficking. The UN frameworks are, however, less binding. The EU and the Council of Europe frameworks were, and have steadily become in practice, more compulsory.

The EU has undergone great changes since its post-war beginnings, from being an international cooperation to its current status as an international organisation with supranational, federal characteristics. Pelinka has described this as an ongoing process, steadily moving towards a federal system. In this federal system, more or less intended policy and agreement developments follow each other as a continuing spill-over effect.[1] The question of who or what drives the developments, and for which reasons, is discussed in Chapter 8.9.

4.2 The EC via the single market to the union

The three EC initial treaty bases were the Treaty on the European Coal and Steel Community (ECSC),[2] in force in 1952; the Treaty on the European Atomic Energy Community (EURATOM); and the Treaty on the European Economic Community (TEC), both in

1 Pelinka 2011.
2 The ECSC was abolished 23.07.2002, cf. the Treaty of Paris, art.97.

DOI: 10.4324/9780429503696-5

force from 1958.[3] In 1967, the three treaties were merged into the EEC, but remained independent legal instruments until 2002. Where the trade community agreements (ECSC and EURATOM) concerned specific policy areas, the EEC had a wider focus. The purpose of the EEC was generally to facilitate internal trade between the member states, increasingly moving in the direction of an open internal market. While the EURATOM and the ECSC regulated only the specific applicable trade measures, the EEC Treaty constituted a broader framework agreement for the general economic cooperation.

The Treaty on the European Economic Area contained the regulation of the entire institutional composition of the Community and is still the primary source of EEC law. The institution of the European Court of Justice (now Court of Justice of the European Union [CJEU]) and the European Parliament (EP) had competence over all three Treaty bases.

The economic challenge to the Community changed during the 1980s, due *inter alia* to the global recession affecting the member states' economies in this period. A white book was drafted and agreed upon in 1985 to improve the joint internal market. Simultaneously, the work on the Single European Act (SEA) had started.[4] The SEA entered into force in 1987, leading to significantly closer cooperation in the international market between the member states. It also led to stricter requirements of harmonisation of the national regulations, and to an increased number of community regulations. The SEA changed the decision mechanisms in the EEC: the qualified majority result, instead of unanimity, was introduced in voting processes in many of the community policy areas. The requirement of unanimity was previously considered to be an obstacle to swiftness in the regulation processes. Police and justice cooperation, however, still fell under the unanimity decision-making process.

The intentions of the 1985 white book were not considered to be sufficient from an integration perspective. The Maastricht Treaty, known as the Treaty on the European Union (TEU), was signed in 1992 and entered into force in March 1993.[5] The focus was on creating an economic and monetary union with more common policies and policies of integration.[6] It was no longer talk of simply an economic community; a stronger economic and political *Union* was in the making. The Treaty did not contain the rules on the economic community, only the *changes* of the EC Treaty, which by the TEU was a Union Treaty (art.8). An important novelty in the TEU was the so-called pillar system. There important differences between the pillars when it came to interaction between the member states and the Union, and to what degree the member states could influence the legislative processes. The first pillar consisted of the economic community (EC; economic, environmental and social policies). Common foreign and security policies were collected in the second pillar, while justice and home affairs policies (police and judicial cooperation in criminal matters) constituted the third pillar. Of major significance was the governance of the different policy areas: On cooperation on first pillar issues was supranational, implying that regulation concerning these matters could be decided with qualified majority voting. Even if a member state (MS) was opposed to a proposition, it would be bound by the majority. In the supranational policy areas, the doctrine of direct effect was applicable, implying that regulations are immediately binding within the member states, and not dependant on implementation

3 Sejersted 2004:26; Fichera 2009.
4 Sejersted 2004:27.
5 TEU.
6 Peers 2011:5 ff.

by the state. The second and third pillars were more intergovernmental – and thus international – in nature. In these matters, Union decisions were made with unanimity. Especially the third pillar including policing and crime control cooperation was characterised by a high level of nation-state sovereignty and less supranational activity. Although the Maastricht Treaty clearly signified a more integrated union, member states still resisted the inclusion of policing and crime control into EU law.[7]

4.3 The area of freedom, security and justice, and the constitutional changes

The history of the EU treaty developments shows leaps in the integration or 'proximisation' of the EU cooperation. While the treaty changes of the early 2000s were less progressive, the *policy programmes* in the crime control areas in these years also demonstrated great initiative from the EU to deepen the cooperation.[8] The policy programmes have different characteristics, suggesting the general direction of the Union and the interpretation that should be used on the treaties. The Tampere Programme was characterised by a normative and legislative focus of the Union, reinforcing the institutionalisation of police cooperation, giving EU institutional anchorage to such agencies as Europol and Eurojust.[9] As for internal security, mutual recognition, especially in the field of justice, was emphasised. The Hague Programme, however, was less normative and more practical in its focus, centring on consolidation and, for example, coordination of the police cooperation. The Stockholm Programme, goes further in a normative direction, emphasising more (obligatory) trust between the member states. The so-called principle of availability was the major internal security focus, but there was also an increased investment in practical cooperation such as the strengthening of Europol's operational role. The major expectations were of a better overall structure and strategy for internal security, interacting with the strategy for information exchange and a greater emphasis on harmonisation as an integration tool. The *efficiency* of the police cooperation measures was emphasised, in addition to more dynamic legal tools, such as the Europol Regulation, described in Chapter 5.2.[10] The Stockholm was the last of the police programmes, as a "more political and strategic approach" was considered appropriate after the "EU justice and home affairs policies [. . .] have become 'mature' policy areas".[11] Nevertheless, a European Agenda on Security was adopted by the Commission on 25 April 2015 to set out the main actions to ensure an effective EU response to terrorism and security threats in the European Union over the period 2015–2020. Target areas have been on firearms and explosives, border security and fighting terrorist financing, including an expansion of categories in the Schengen Information System II (SIS II is returned to in detail in Chapter 9.2). As stated in a 2016 Commission

7 Fijnaut 1993. The EC law regulated only the first pillar matters, since these with the Maastricht Treaty change still only regulated *community* law – the other two pillars consisting of *union* 'law'. Another significant difference was the difference in the legal instruments used: The EC law in the first pillar applied via directives, regulations and decisions; with other instruments in the third pillar such as conventions, framework decisions and recommendations (Peers 2011:25).

8 Also the standing committee on internal security, COSI, was emphasised as an important new body (TFEU art.71), with the purpose of ensuring promotion and reinforcement on internal security. See e.g. Cornell 2014.

9 den Boer and Bruggeman 2011:137.

10 Op.cit.:138.

11 http://europa.eu/rapid/press-release_MEMO-14-174_en.htm [30.05.17].

press release: "transnational threats such as terrorism cannot be addressed effectively without a common European approach".[12] A main aim is to more efficiently conquer terrorism in the EU, and the recent and, unfortunately, on-going terrorist attacks thus continue to spark intensified cross-border police cooperation.

Two EU treaties have had significant impact for the Norwegian relation to the EU system. The Treaty revision of the Amsterdam Treaty (1997, in force 1999) altered the pillar system.[13] The purpose of creating "an Area of Freedom, Security and Justice" (AFSJ) within the EU was first explicitly formulated here (art.29). The AFSJ included increased cooperation precisely on issues concerning crime control and policing. Enhanced AFSJ cooperation implied, for example, the implementation of the previously 'independent' international cooperation of Schengen into the EU *Acquis*, because the purpose of 'free flow' across the Union was the same as the Schengen cooperation. The two institutions also had several legal, functional and institutional links. The policy content of the three pillars was shifted, and immigration, asylum and civil law issues were transferred from the third to the first pillar, making them EC law. This implied *inter alia* that the Schengen *Acquis*, consisting of both immigration and police regulations, was split and implemented in separate pillars, both EC and EU legal orders. This had implications for Norway as a Schengen member outside the EU, changing the mechanisms of decision shaping and making, to more excluding towards non-EU members.

Initially known as 'the reform Treaty', the Lisbon Treaty (LT) made significant amendments to the EU Treaty bases. The Lisbon Treaty reiterated and emphasised that the Union should aim to constitute an Area of Freedom, Security and Justice (Title V). The pillar system from the Maastricht Treaty of 1992 was also abolished, turning all EU matters into EC matters. These changes to the majority vote had significant consequences for the supranational aspects of the Union.

As a AFSJ policy development, a view that all police authority of all member states should have access to the data of all other member states (the principle of availability)[14] was suggested, making the 'competition' between national police forces fair and equal. The principle of availability implies that all police officers in the Union, when they require, shall have access to information in the other member states, if this information is available to a national police officer of that state. The information may not be withheld, except where ongoing investigations so require. As Kvam argues, while the principle of mutual recognition primarily targets the cooperation between or involving criminal procedural/judicial cooperation, the availability principle obliges police authorities on request to supply information such as reports, analysis, etc.[15] Due to sovereignty challenges, the principle of mutual recognition was established as a middle way.

On the EU level, the distinction between operational and intelligence or other non-operational work has consequences for the decision mechanisms in the EU institutions. The Lisbon Treaty introduced different decision-making procedures for these two areas of police regulation.[16]

12 http://europa.eu/rapid/press-release_IP-16-1445_en.htm [22.08.17]

13 [1997] OJ C 340/1.

14 Proposal for a Council Framework Decision on the exchange of information under the principle of availability for a framework decision on information exchange under the principle of availability suggested in the Hague policy programme of 2004.

15 Kvam 2008:142–3; also Henricson 2010:175–6. See also Chapter 9.3.1 this text.

16 Art.87 TFEU, cf. art.84, is the general governing article of police cooperation within the EU.

Another Lisbon Treaty change was the EU's Charter of Fundamental Rights of the European Union (CFREU).[17] The Charter was made a legal tool in the Union, with the same status as the two general treaty bases (TEU and TFEU) and a binding instrument in the interpretation and creation of the Union's legal documents. This implies that in cases concerning application of EU law, the charter is directly enforceable in national courts of member states (art.51 no.1 TEU). The aim of the charter is not to establish new rights, but to collect existing rights previously scattered over a range of sources including the ECHR and United Nations (UN).[18] The Charter also contains economic, social and cultural rights, and new rights such as the right to a clean environment, and broader non-discrimination provisions regarding elderly people, disabled people and so on.

The Lisbon Treaty implied several quite radical changes compared to the former treaty bases. Since these changes are now the present situation, the regulations concerning police and police cooperation in a broad sense are given substantial attention in Chapters 9–13. These chapters deal with the competences of the police in the various legal systems.

It was not until the EEA and the Schengen cooperation agreement became realities that Norway had a formal role vis-à-vis the Union. I will return later to the way the EU policies and regulations are shaped and decided upon, and how Norway as a state has and has no access to these processes and institutions.

The EU forms of police cooperation that have surfaced in the past 15–20 years are by far the most binding and dynamic in the Union's history. They impact the current Norwegian policing situation to a significant degree. It is necessary to have an understanding of the EU as a system to be able evaluate the position of Norway as a non-EU member. The institutional composition of the Union is therefore introduced in the following, followed by the Norwegian relationship to these institutions.

17 [2012] OJ C 326/2.

18 The charter confirms some safeguards developed in ECtHR case law, for example the right of an individual access to information about him or herself (Xanthaki 2008). On the development of EU fundamental rights, see Walter 2007.

5 The development of police cooperation within the EU

The point of the book is to elucidate the changing policing zoom, from a focus on the local, via a centralisation and nationalisation process, and towards the more supranational current situation, that may first be seen in the Norwegian context as of the Schengen negotiations, and to consider how and to which extent this change has affected Norwegian sovereignty in different perspectives. To understand the Union's move towards more 'integrated' policing instruments, it is necessary to give an overview of the cooperation development in the Union. There have been two main trajectories of the development of police cooperation within the EU proper: the TREVI cooperation, leading to Europol, and the Schengen police cooperation, leading to the Schengen Convention that was later incorporated into EU law. Both are elaborated on in depth below, including the different available police measures, included those that have been developed in later agreements. Prior to that, the way these two first cooperation mechanisms were evolved, needs some explanation. The Europol track is the main focus in this chapter, while Schengen is developed together with the Norwegian relationship to it, in Chapter 6.

5.1 Council of Europe

First, however, a fundamental convention for international legal cooperation in Europe must be introduced; the Council of Europe's 1959 Convention on Mutual Assistance in Criminal Matters (MLA).[1] Norway is affiliated to the Convention and both protocols. The Convention established the obligation to give such assistance as far as possible within the jurisdiction of the law enforcement authorities in the relevant state (art.1 no.1).[2]

Since the establishment in 1949, the Council of Europe (CoE) has developed into a very influential international organisation with the purpose of furthering and safeguarding the ideals of democracy and human rights, and economic and social security.[3] The The European Convention for the Protection of Human Rights and Fundamental Freedoms (ECHR) has perhaps been the most important legal instrument, with the Court enforcing complaints on breaches of the Convention. The CoE does not involve police officials or any operative

1 ETS 30 (1959). The Convention was supplemented with additional protocols 17.03.1978 and 08.11.2001 (ETS 182).

2 Although the Convention entered into force in the early 1960s, the large majority of Council of Europe MS ratified much later. Denmark, Greece, Italy and Norway were the first to ratify the Convention in 1962 (http://conventions.coe.int/Treaty/Commun/ChercheSig.asp?NT=030&CM=&DF=&CL=ENG [08.06.2014]).

3 See, for example, Schutte 1995 and Anderson *et al.* 1995:220–222.

DOI: 10.4324/9780429503696-6

personnel in any way. Its work takes place directly between governments, and in various committees consisting either of ministers or high officials and civil servants. To Norway, it was emphasised in 2000, the most relevant development in policing matters is the establishment and development of conventions in the criminal and criminal procedural legal area. The CoE Conventions on Mutual Legal Assistance and Extradition was considered to be most important in the context of EU police cooperation. The CoE Pompidou Group (Co-operation Group to Combat Drug Abuse and Illicit Trafficking in Drugs), established in 1971, was also emphasised as a successful forum for an integrated and overall approach to the fight against drug-related crime.[4] Some of the international conventions of the EU and the CoE overlap, but since the members of the organisations differ, they have – partly – different impact areas. The Council of Europe Convention has a total of 50 ratifications/accessions.[5] EU countries are also CoE members. Potential Norwegian challenges related to non-EU membership is thus to some extent remedied by, for example, the 1959 Convention with protocols concerning mutual assistance in criminal matters.

5.2 TREVI – Europol

5.2.1 TREVI

Most EU countries are members of Interpol. The EU (then EC) countries started work in the 1970s on establishing a specific community police cooperation mechanism for various reasons. One reason was that Interpol was perceived to be inefficient due to its global range and involvement, with many different and partly conflicting interests to take into account. Another was the delimitation Interpol has towards police cooperation on crimes of religious, racial or political character (except terrorist crimes [art.3 Interpol]).[6] One should also consider the incentive from the EU point of view to employ police cooperation to strengthen and/or protect the EU single market, and the crimes committed towards EU-related interests specifically (this seems at least to be a point in retrospect).[7]

The TREVI cooperation was established between the member states in 1975. Originally a consultative forum for discussion on the minister level to strengthen the work against terrorism, TREVI had no common institutions.[8] The cooperation was purely intergovernmental, and separated from the EU institutions. The Commission had no observatory status in the TREVI meetings; the Parliament was given only limited access. The access for the Commission was denied up until 1990, because the member states emphasised the importance of the pure intergovernmentality of the organisation.[9] The TREVI forum had varying influence in the development of political attitudes and level of commitment within the police cooperation.[10] From the mid–1980s, the traditional TREVI police cooperation was increasingly integrated into the general justice and home affairs area, and was seen as important to the development of the Union; the closer the market cooperation, the closer

4 St.meld.nr.18 (1999–2000):38–40.

5 http://conventions.coe.int/Treaty/Commun/ChercheSig.asp?NT=030&CM=&DF=&CL=ENG [31.05.2017].

6 Occhipinti 2003:31.

7 Ahnfelt and From 1996:19–20.

8 Op.cit.:19; 61; Benyon 1993. The TREVI abbreviation has come to stand for 'terrorism, radicalism, extremism and violence international' (Occhipinti 2003:31).

9 Anderson *et al.* 1995:56; Benyon 1993:168.

10 Benyon 1993:157.

the police cooperation, so to speak. Up until the Union Treaty (1993), TREVI was the most important police cooperation forum in the EU, and the competence was gradually extended.[11] There has been four main working groups throughout its existence: on terrorism; policing, policing techniques and police education; on international crime in a broader sense; and, finally, the so-called TREVI 1992 working group, dealing with a wider security policy program in relation to the removal of internal border controls following the Single European Act.[12] Although the TREVI cooperation was dissolved *per se* when it was incorporated into the Union bodies, the working group structure was continued. The history of the organisation may thus be relevant to understand the present state of affairs.[13]

5.2.2 EDU – Europol

The Maastricht Treaty's Title VI established provisions on cooperation in the fields of justice and home affairs, including a Declaration on Police Cooperation. As such, this was formal start of the inclusion of policing cooperation as a 'common interest' in the Union. It was also the start of the European Police Office (Europol) (art.K.1 (9)).

The Europol Drugs Unit (EDU) was a predecessor and in a way the first stage of Europol. The work of the EDU was concentrated around the collection and sharing of intelligence regarding the smuggling of illegal drugs and related crimes such as money laundering.[14] After a Council Joint Action of 1995, the role of the EDU was expanded. It now also covered trafficking in nuclear and radioactive substances, "crimes involving clandestine immigration networks" and "illicit vehicle trafficking", and, later, also included trafficking in human beings.[15]

The latter amendment was made to give the agency a broader field of competence, and – one may infer from the text – also because the Council was aware of the difficulties in the process of getting the Europol Convention into force. Lacking a central database, the EDU information exchange and transfer was dependant strictly on the member states liaison officers placed in the EDU headquarters, and on each country's national data protection laws. Europol, with greater competences both in operative and information exchange capacities, was founded already one month after the EDU. But even though the Europol Convention was signed in 1995, it did not enter into force before 1998, after all the required supplementary measures were in force.[16] The cooperation between states directed through Europol started in July 1999.

The initial legal basis was the Europol Convention of 1995,[17] later amended and supplemented with five protocols concerning jurisdictional issues,[18] immunity privileges of Europol staff,[19] and changes to competences both regarding substantial crimes and operational

11 Ahnfelt and From 1996:61.
12 Benyon 1993:154 ff. Another ad hoc group was also responsible for developing Europol in 1991, expanding on the work of the TREVI 3 group on international crime and planned national drug investigation units.
13 Ahnfelt and From 1996:53.
14 Peers 2011:931.
15 [1995] OJ L 62/1; [1996] OJ L 342/4.
16 Peers 2011:931.
17 [1995] OJ C 316/1.
18 [1996] OJ C 299/1, giving national courts the jurisdiction to refer questions on the Europol Convention to the Court of Justice.
19 [1997] OJ C 221/1.

competences.[20] In addition to the protocols, a series of legislative acts were introduced (primarily Council Decisions[21] and acts implementing the Europol Convention).[22] Interestingly, there were great challenges in the final phase before the parties could agree to take the Convention into force in the first place, but very soon after the entry, substantial amendments were implemented to enhance the efficacy and competence areas of the organisation. It was still a general reluctance at the state level to move towards a common European police force, implying perhaps supranationalism within the sovereignty core of policing.[23]

The lengthy ratification processes that all the Europol amendments went through prompted a major change to the Europol legal basis.[24] The Convention was replaced by a Council Decision (the Europol Decision, ED),[25] in force from 1 January 2010; a legal instrument that could be changed much more effectively. The Decision established Europol as a Union agency. This implies that it is funded over the budget of the EU, and thus is under the budgetary control of the European Parliament. The wording also changed so that Europol was assigned more of a partnership role instead of merely supporting, facilitating and requesting action from the national authorities.[26] Art.88 TFEU allows the Council to expand the powers of Europol. Four such major points were proposed for improvement: the member states' obligation to comply with Europol's requests for data should be strengthened; the Europol data system should be restructured to improve the interlinking of data on various levels; the UK-based CEPOL should be merged into Europol's training hub (it was moved to Budapest, Hungary in 2014), strengthening the common approach and increasing coherence, efficiency, transparency, etc.; and finally the Parliamentary scrutiny of Europol should be strengthened by strengthening its duty to report to both the EP and the national parliaments.[27]

The new Europol Regulation of 2016 (in force 1 May 2017) was introduced in The Lisbon Treaty (art.88; 87[2b] TFEU). This implied a mechanism for control over Europol's activities by the European Parliament, together with national Parliaments.[28] The new Regulation is meant to contribute to an overall enhanced coherence of the governance of EU agencies. This includes the weakening of the autonomy of Europol as an agency, for example, making the Commission, instead of Europol itself, competent to negotiate international information-sharing agreements. The change reduced the member states' rights to refuse to supply data to Europol, implying that not even national security or on-going investigations could justify refusing to deliver information. This was considered to be too radical an infringement into national sovereignty for some states.[29]

20 [2000] OJ C 358/1 on money laundering, [2002] OJ C 312/1 on Europol's participation in JITs and prompting member states' investigation, and [2004] OJ C 2/3 on extension on competences.

21 [2002] OJ C 26/21); Terrorism [1999] OJ C 26/6); Forgery of money and means of payment ([1999] OJ C 149/2) and on dealing with the forms of serious crime listed in the Annex of the Europol Convention ([2001] OJ C 362/1).

22 E.g. on rules of procedure (Mitsilegas 2009:164).

23 Occhipinti 2003:42–3; den Boer and Walker 1993:9. Sheptycki concluded that these transnational policing infrastructures consisted partly of *already* existing institutions, and novelties such as the Europol only added administrative complications (1995:43).

24 [2009] OJ L 121/37 in the preamble (2).

25 Op.cit.

26 Peers 2011:873.

27 [2016] OJ L 135/53. Critique from e.g. den Boer and Wallace 2000:505; den Boer 1998:71).

28 2013/0091 (COD) pt.3.

29 UK opted out, because it saw the extensions in the Regulation as threatening the "operational independence" of national police autonomy (https://www.gov.uk/government/speeches/the-european-commissions-proposal-for-a-europol-regulation) [31.03.2017]. See also den Boer and Bruggeman 2011:137.

The Europol organisation is growing. It had over 1000 employees in 2017, compared with 323 in 2001. Included in this number are around 200 liaison officers who are seconded to the organisation. Three officers of the total Europol force (including liaison officers) are Norwegian.[30] Although still without coercive powers on its own *per se*, the increased powers to 'force' member states' police to give data of sufficient quality, within certain time limits, increases the impression that Europol truly has powers to decide over member state police forces.

5.2.2.1 Objectives and measures

The objective of Europol is to

> support and strengthen action by the competent authorities of the Member States and their mutual cooperation in preventing and combating serious crime affecting two or more Member States, terrorism and forms of crime which affect a common interest covered by a Union policy (art. 3 no.1)

The mandate also includes "related criminal offences" (no.2). These are listed (a–c) as those committed in order either to procure he means of perpetrating acts, to facilitate or perpetrate acts, or ensure the impunity of those committing acts, all of which Europol is competent. There have been many changes in the competences of Europol. The requirement of the crime is that it is "serious" and affects more than one state, while the demand for "factual indications" and an organised criminal structure are taken out. The threshold for Europol involvement has through these changes steadily been lowered. Nevertheless, the tasks and objectives are still limited. The crime must be serious, and not only affecting relations within one country. This, for example, excludes violent crime restricted to domestic or personal relations (meaning crime that is not in any way, for example, drug-related, which one could often interpret as having trans- or international links *per se*), or property crimes such as burglaries (provided the offenders were not taking advantage of the Schengen benefits concerning the lack of border controls, and are travelling between countries on a 'raid'). The 'serious offences' are listed in an annex to the Decision, currently consisting of 24 crimes.[31] Certain specified 'related offences', such as facilitating or trying to cover an example of up one of the 24 types, are also within competence.[32] Note that in contrast, the Schengen cooperation is comprised of basically all kinds of crime.

The tasks of Europol are presented in art.5, with the aim to "collect, store, process, analyse and exchange information and intelligence", to inform national authorities of information about criminal activities, aid national authorities to begin or coordinate investigations, provide intelligence and support as regards major events; and draw up the threat assessments and strategic analyses. Europol has also been given other tasks by the Council, and a role as the body supervising the transfers of financial data to the US.[33]

30 https://www.europol.europa.eu/content/page/staff-statistics–159 [31.05.2017].

31 Corresponding with the offences for which dual criminality has been abolished under the European Arrest Warrant, cf. art.2(2) of the EAW FD.

32 Art.4 (1) and (3).

33 Art.4 of the Swift Treaty ([2010] OJ L 195/1).

5.2.2.2 Accountability of Europol

Although Europol is within the jurisdiction of the CJEU, and of the EU Justice and Home Affairs Council (JHA), and each Minister that take parts in the Council is accountable to his own national parliaments, the organisation has been criticised for its democratic deficits. Briefings from the JHA Council have often restricted or received late, diminishing the democratic transparency,[34] and the Europol structure of being an informal 'old boys' network', based on informal contacts outside of transparent, formal structures.[35] Several accountability measures are in place, though. In operative work through JITs, the Europol officers are legally accountable to the Court, and may testify in criminal proceedings in the member states. The European Parliament has budgetary powers over Europol (art.51), and the Management Board, etc. must appear before the Parliament when requested (art.58), implying more binding and broader information rights. The control formerly done by the Joint Supervisory Body (JSB) was replaced by the European Data Protection Supervisor (EDPS), and oversees the information gathering and analyses of Europol (art.43), in addition to supervision by national authorities (art.42). A new Joint Parliamentary Scrutiny Group (JPSG) was constructed to to "politically monitor Europol's activities in fulfilling its mission, including as regards the impact of those activities on the fundamental rights and freedoms of natural persons" (art.51). The general changes do not imply any changes for Norway. Given Norway's non-membership, the country does not either way have any influence in the parliamentary control. The EFTA Countries submitted a resolution where enhanced parliamentary scrutiny should include parliamentarians of the EFTA states, at least as "observers to inter-parliamentary meetings where the scrutiny of Eurojust and Europol activities will take place", to ensure that "the democratic legitimacy and accountability extend to the entire area of Eurojust and Europol cooperation and activities".[36] Europol's role in the focus shift of the Norwegian policing situation will be returned to in ch.15.4.

5.2.3 Norway in Europol

As part of the 'friends of TREVI' group, Norway was a part of the development of police cooperation from the very beginning in the 1970s. Cooperation outside the Schengen does not 'automatically' include Norwegian participation, as detailed below. In the late 1990s, the Norwegian government clearly expressed that Norway wanted to participate not only in the development of the Schengen cooperation, but also police and judicial cooperation outside of this framework.[37] Only EU members may be members of Europol. The Agency can, however, establish and maintain relations with third countries and third bodies (art.23). After Europol and Eurojust became autonomous legal agencies within the EU system, the agreements with third parties are made directly between that party and Europol and Eurojust, not, as before, with the EU as a whole. This means that the agencies' activity is autonomous within the legal framework.

In addition to the expected benefits of Europol related to measures that would compensate for the dismantling of the internal borders, the Norwegian government expressed in the

34 McLoughlin 1992, Loader 2002b.
35 McLoughlin 1992, den Boer 2002b.
36 Resolution CMP Ref. 1123117.
37 St.meld.nr.18 (1999–2000):61–63.

forarbeid to the Norwegian Europol Agreement another reason for wanting to take part in Europol.[38] The *forarbeid* underscored that Norway needed to take part in the evolving "new unifying political concept" in the EU concerning the area of freedom, security and justice. Europol was expected to play a major role in the future cooperation on international, organised crime fighting, both between the EU countries and internationally.[39]

The international legal basis for Europol has changed since Norway entered into the cooperation agreement. From the more traditional Convention via the Decision, to an EU Regulation. The Norwegian government's attitude has, from the early appreciation of its outsider role, been that each new development of Europol should be discussed specifically in *Stortinget* and though consultative papers by the concerned Norwegian institutions.[40] This was considered to be important precisely because the Europol cooperation was not of the traditional regulatory type, but a more dynamically evolving cooperation on a knowledge and experience exchange basis.[41]

Having gained some insight into the Europol cooperation, and in general specifically into Norway's generally enthusiastic attitude to the European police cooperation instruments, the following gives a more thorough account of the process of the Norwegian membership in or affiliations with the various EU cooperation agreements. This process signifies what may be argued to be a change in the Norwegian policing situation, exemplified by the focus change in the relevant policy documents and *forarbeid*. The role of Norway in the Schengen cooperation is different than the Europol relationship. In contrast to the Schengen cooperation, there is no Norwegian participation in the financing of Europol or influencing Europol's decisions.[42] Norway is *less* of a 'third country' in the Schengen cooperation. In the following, the brief history of the Norwegian relation to the EU via the EEA agreement is presented, and subsequently the contestations and justifications that were made during the 1990s. In this period, Norway rejected EU membership, but became a party to the EEA and Schengen.

38 St.meld.nr.18 (1999–2000):61, my translation.
39 Op.cit.:63–64.
40 Op.cit.:2.
41 Op.cit.:66.
42 Kvam 2008:136 fn.326.

6 Norway – inside or outside?

6.1 Norway and the EEA

The Norwegian people have twice in referenda – in 1972 and 1994 – voted against membership in the European Union. Norway has, however, been a member of the European Free Trade Association (EFTA) since 1961, which aim "to provide a framework for the liberalisation of trade in goods amongst its Member States", without the political cooperation EEC membership implied.[1] The Agreement on the European Economic Area (EEA), which expanded the economic market to include some European non-EU states, was signed in 1992, and entered into force on 1 January 1994. The Agreement was implemented in Norwegian law by a specific Act.[2]

The EEA Agreement aligns Norway with the EU member states on the single market, implying free trade, and the applicability of the four freedoms of goods, persons, services and capital. The EFTA states participate in the legislation process by shaping and providing input, but not in the decision-making. They are, however, obliged to comply with all EU regulations concerning the EEA, and contribute substantial funds to the EU. Compliance is controlled by the EFTA court and the surveillance body ESA. The EEA Agreement does not regulate police or other forms of crime control, but there are several regulations that require criminalisation of certain activities.[3]

The political cooperation in the EU was expanded beyond the strictly economic area to include both to some extent common foreign and defence policies, and also the social and home affairs areas. Police and justice cooperation also became a prominent cooperation area, including immigration, asylum, criminal law and police cooperation issues. That being said, the EEA Agreement was, however also dynamic, still only an economic agreement. In the mid–1990s, Norway began negotiating an affiliation to the Schengen cooperation. An agreement was in place in 1996, the final agreement signed in 1999. The following outlines the *forarbeid* and debates taking place in connection with the developments in the police area related to this affiliation agreement, not, generally, the discussions in juridical theory. First, however, an introduction to the Schengen cooperation is given.

1 http://www.efta.int/about-efta/european-free-trade-association [06.06.17]. See more on this e.g. in Sejersted 2011; Fredriksen and Mathisen 2012.
2 Lov 27. november 1992 nr. 109.
3 E.g. related to illegal breach of competition rules, and thereby police control.

DOI: 10.4324/9780429503696-7

6.2 The Schengen cooperation

The intention of the Schengen Agreement was to achieve a "gradual abolition of controls at the common frontiers" between the members. An "increasingly closer union of the peoples [. . .] should be manifested through freedom to cross internal frontiers for all nationals of the member states and in the free movement of goods and services". This could in turn affirm the solidarity between these peoples.[4] Built on the model of the Nordic free travel area cooperation (the Nordic Passport Union), as described above, the membership and affiliation were built on reciprocal obligations and a high level of confidence between the parties.

The Agreement was signed by five EU member states[5] (but outside the EU framework) in the town of Schengen in 1985. It had two main purposes. The first was the facilitation of the least well-functioning of the EC's four freedoms: the freedom of movement of people. The Schengen cooperation resulted in the abolition of border controls between the Schengen members, exempt exceptional situations.[6] It also entailed uniform regulations and common standards for external border control, and to some extent common regulations on asylum and visa processes.

The second purpose was the introduction of the so-called compensatory measures to a Schengen Area without physical checks on the internal borders. The measures in the cooperation were partly concerned with immigration control, and partly security and law enforcement measures. The former implied coordination measures of border control and surveillance, harmonisation of border control instructions and harmonisation measures related to illegal immigration. The latter were measures of cross-border police cooperation, mutual legal assistance, for example, concerning extradition, customs cooperation, direct information exchange, and connected privacy rules.

In 1990, the Convention Implementing the Schengen Agreement (CISA) was signed, and throughout the years since the 1985 Agreement, the focus had shifted to advancing the police cooperation following strong compensatory measures in the CISA. The articles concerning security and compensatory measures ended up outnumbering the articles regulating free flow.[7] The cooperation entered into force in 1995, and in 1997 the Schengen *Acquis*[8] was incorporated into the EU legal framework. The implementation implied that Schengen membership became compulsory for all EU member states, although opt-outs were permitted. Norway became 'partner' in the Schengen cooperation in 2001. The Lisbon Treaty's removal of the pillar system dissolved the differing legislation procedures in the EU in the Area of Justice and Home Affairs. This at least to some extent made the Union activity also on the law enforcement area more supranational.

The removal of border control between the Schengen member states was fundamental to the cooperation. This idea was no novelty in the Nordic context. While the abolition of

4 CISA preamble.

5 Germany, France and the BeNeLux countries.

6 Temporary border controls may be introduced in situations "where public policy or national security so require" (CISA) art.2(2). Examples are in Norway after the 22/7 2011 terrorist action, and in several member states, including Norway, because of recent terror attacks in Europe during 2017.

7 Karanja 2008:50.

8 The Schengen *Acquis* consists of the Schengen Agreement of 1985, the Schengen Implementation Convention of 1990, the protocols and agreements on accession of Italy (1990), Spain and Portugal (1991), Austria (1995) and Denmark, Finland and Sweden (1996), the association agreements with Norway Iceland and Switzerland, and the decisions and declarations of the Schengen Executive Committee (den Boer and Bruggeman 2011:137).

internal border controls would lead to somewhat less control in Norwegian ports and airports, the Ministry considered that the general level of control of persons would increase, and, in total, a need would arise for new and increased control arrangements.[9] Several police districts saw it as positive that the Schengen required *departure* control on the *external* Schengen borders (CISA art.6), in other words, on airports, ports, and the land border towards Russia.[10] This in fact constituted a reinstatement of borders control in Norway, after the abolition in 1986, and as such implied *a higher* control level on the borders than before.

While the border control of persons between the Schengen member states was abolished, the customs control still applied. The Schengen cooperation did not contain regulations on customs, nor did or does Norway have customs agreements with EU countries. This implied that customs control of goods imported to Norway was to continue, but the persons control was removed from the border areas. The police in some police districts expressed concern about these changes related to the ordinary border control.[11] Abolition of border controls required enhanced possibilities to prevent and defeat illegal immigration and cross-border crime.[12] In other words, although crime control was not very often performed in connection with border control in Norway prior to the Schengen cooperation, the formal abolition of such border controls still had to be compensated.

In addition to the general duty in the Schengen Agreement to cooperate, the perhaps most significant measure (at least in practical application) is the Schengen Information System (SIS, SISII). In addition to the SIS, the member state police agencies have access to databases such as the Visa Information System (VIS), the Eurodac, and the information systems of Interpol and the EU's police body Europol. Seen in total, these systems include vast numbers of various different kinds of data on individuals and objects, in connection with suspects, missing people, immigration cases, analysis and investigative information, photos, etc. The police may, to various degrees, search and register in these databases. They may also request that foreign police take certain actions on the basis of registrations. Typical examples are arrest or searches. The details on these measures are given in Chapter 10. The process of the Norwegian membership to the Schengen cooperation is first discussed in the next two subchapters.

6.3 From 'No' to 'Yes, please': what changed?

For Norway, the Schengen Agreement implied a generally lowered threshold for police cooperation and fewer restrictions related to requests for assistance between Norway and other Schengen members. Before Schengen, the letters rogatory (*rettsanmodning*) could in general only be sent via the Ministries; so also in Norway outside of the Nordic cooperation.[13]

Before the Schengen cooperation, there was no formal connection between Norway and Europol or the EU cooperation on justice and home affairs. According to the Norwegian

9 Ot.prp.nr.56 (1998–1999):20; 99.

10 Op.cit.:18–20. It was emphasised by the Ministry that the preparatory discussions in 1998 were *not* on the material contents of the Schengen cooperation, since these had already been debated in *Stortinget* a couple of years before. This was, however, the first occasion for the practitioners across the country to express their opinion on the consequences.

11 Op.cit.:19.

12 Ot.prp.nr.56 (1998–1999).

13 St.prp.nr.42 (1996–1997):ch.5.7.1.

Ministry of Justice (MoJ), several negative developments in the mid–1990s necessitated a focus on international, cross-border police measures.[14] Several concerns were underscored in the official documents. International crimes were reported to have become increasingly serious, especially various types of organised crime. Their numbers were also increasing.[15] A government committee (*Sikkerhetsutvalget*) was appointed in 1990 to evaluate the Norwegian security situation with a particular focus on crimes and threats related to terrorism. The Committee's considerations related to the changes to 'old-fashioned' criminal acts show the awareness of an increasingly vulnerable Norwegian situation. Norway was considered to, "[c]ommunication-wise as well as economically and culturally, [be] drawn into a process of increasingly strong international integration", which also would subject the country to negative characteristics of international developments.[16]

International influences and stronger international integration made Norway more vulnerable. While this conclusion concerned terrorism, the argument was the same when the Committee discussed the international crime situation. Reported crime increased six-fold in Norway from 1960 to 1990. Similar increases in crime rates could be found around Europe.[17] While the majority of crimes within Norway were still committed by Norwegian citizens, a "not insignificant share" of certain types of crime was committed by foreigners or Norwegian citizens of foreign origin, according to the Committee.[18] The police's investigation into international criminal groups could sometimes be more difficult because of linguistic or cultural differences. Such challenges warranted new interaction with foreign police, in addition to the development of new policing methods. The development was traced to the 1989 dissolution of the strong border control that was the Iron Curtain, which functioned, according to the Ministry, as an efficient block against crime and immigration from Eastern to Western Europe. Combined with political unrest in the former Eastern bloc countries, this led to a "radically new crime threat from the east".[19] Such tendencies were increasingly present in Norway as far back as the 1970s, especially in connection with motorcycle gang-related crime. Organised crime groups with international connections gained in strength, the use of firearms increased and Norway saw an "explosive increase" in the seizure of heroin from 1994 to 1996.[20] Other cross-border crimes that were emphasised were drug trafficking, the export of stolen vehicles, human trafficking, certain types of economic crimes and crimes related to prostitution.[21] The European market after the Single European Act had improved access and openness for legal and illegal 'business' alike.

A more open and internationalised society, and, especially for the western European countries, the fact that less 'frightening' sentencing frameworks and prison conditions,

14 The following refers to the statements of the Ministry of Justice in chapter 6 of op.cit.

15 NOU 1997:15:28–29.

16 NOU 1993:3, my translation.

17 NOU 1997:15 pp.24; 28–9. See e.g. generally den Boer 2002a.

18 NOU 1997:15 p.23.

19 St.prp.nr.42 (1996–1997):6.7.

20 From 26 kg; 49 kg; 75 kg. Op.cit.:ch.6.1.2, similar in St.meld.nr.18 (1999–2000):2. According to the Customs Norway, the two singular all-time largest seizures of heroin occurred in 1997 (18kg) and in 2006 (46.9 kg) (http://www.toll.no/templates_TAD/Article.aspx?id=148863&epslanguage=no [10.06.2013]). According to a later government document, there was a 57% decrease in the seizure of heroin in Norway from 1998–2007 (Meld.St.7 (2010–2011) pt.4.1.2). Drug-related crime stagnated at the turn of the 20th century (op.cit. pt.4).

21 St.meld.nr.18 (1999–2000):8–9; NOU 1997:15 ch.3.

made criminals migrate westward.[22] Since Norway was part of this new, open market, the 'free movement of criminals' was considered "an increasing [. . .] threat to the stability of [Norwegian] society". The concept of 'internal security' was developed, referring not to each respective member state, but to the common, borderless European area, which Norway wanted to be a part of, albeit not completely.[23]

The growing Norwegian economy (in the late 1990s), in contrast to many other countries, was also expected to generate unwanted interest from criminals dealing in international economic crime.[24] In short: There was a lot to worry about.

An increasing awareness of international influence on the Norwegian 'justice and home affairs' situation is visible, an influence that makes the country more vulnerable. As seen in the previous chapter, the situation was similar within the EU in this period of time. Broadened and deepened cooperation appeared necessary, both in and outside of the Union.

Is Norway inside or outside the Union? This is a fundamental question in this book. Norway should be considered as *both* inside and outside, given its position in the Schengen cooperation. It seems, based on the statements and considerations in the policy documents concerning Schengen that *nothing* really changed between the negative referendum decision and the Schengen accession. The state's perception, as presented in the various *forarbeid*, was that due to the increase in international crime such as smuggling of narcotics, Norway had to join. Other forms of smuggling and organised cross-border crime in general were also seen to increase quite rapidly. The only way to counter this development was to cooperate more, and more deeply on the international level. Several events on a global and regional level were also mentioned as part of the argument for accession, in particular the change of the political scene in post-Soviet Europe, and the general economic and communicative changes. These traits and currents formed the backdrop of the Norwegian application to participate in the strong EU/Schengen cooperation. The changing international security situation, in connection with the new availability of cooperation measures, simply did not leave Norway a choice in the matter.

To consider the changes that the Schengen Cooperation Agreement and subsequent agreements have brought to the Norwegian police and for the Norwegian state, part II focuses on the actual available policing measures resulting from the international cooperation instruments. In the following, the process of the Norwegian membership into the Schengen will be delved deeper into.

22 St.prp.nr.42 (1996–1997): pt.6.1.1, also e.g. Anderson *et al.* 1995:21 ff. Den Boer and Doelle 2002:8–9 argue, however, that the presence of borders is advantageous to criminals, who may take advantage of heteronomous legislation – irrespective of border controls.

23 St.prp.nr.42 (1996–1997) pt.6.1.2–6.1.4.

24 Op.cit.:12–14.

7 Internal sovereignty

The question of membership

Recall from Chapter 1.3.1 that internal sovereignty implies that the sovereign rule is established – on an on-going basis – by the people in the community ruled by this particular sovereign. This chapter targets whether the state did sufficiently alert and inform the Norwegian population of the process and contents of Norway entering into the Schengen Cooperation. The lack of quality of the state justifications, in particular, may be seen as inadequate for the people of Norway to make informed decisions on government rule, which is central to enforcing popular sovereignty. My first research question is:

> *Was the decision on the part of the Norwegian government to seek access to international police cooperation measures and instruments adequately founded on popular knowledge and sentiments?*

Declining levels of crime may imply that cross-border policing *works*. What works in policing, however, is notoriously hard to determine.[1] Even presupposing that increased targeting of international, cross-border crime (partly) lowers the crime level, it may be difficult to assess whether the way forward should be more of the same, or something else. Nevertheless, the justifications in policy documents preparing legal amendments should, at least to some extent, reflect what is known to work. Not just what a committee or the Ministry 'want to change'. The influence EU may have on these 'wants' is explored below. First, an explanation of why justifications are important, before I present the relevant justifications. The analysis of sovereignty infringement for this section follows in ch.7.5.

7.1 Becoming a member

The Norwegian Police Act sect.1 underlines that the state shall supply the police service needed for the community. This link is, however, reciprocal or dialectic: the police contribute to shaping the citizens' needs, they do not just react to what is expressed 'bottom-up'. The national, trans- and international police cooperation mechanisms are developed simultaneously to meet the challenges of more cross-border crime. In a more globalised world, the changes occur more rapidly than in the past, and legislation is constantly under pressure to keep pace.

It is particularly important that policing, a form of state action that always contains the possibility of coercive force, is founded in law. The contemporary international situation

1 Maguire 2012.

DOI: 10.4324/9780429503696-8

challenges the legitimacy of the police. The Westphalian sovereign state can no longer be easily demarcated and defined. Bowling and Sheptycki argue that the nation state system has turned into a transnational one.[2] In its wide array of crimes and variety of governance and crime control measures, the global neo-liberal market – including the 'regionally global' market within the Schengen Area, is more complex than what Weber reacted to when he constructed his classic definition of the state. It is challenging to consider the legitimacy of anything, when the notions traditionally used to assess it are old, and to some extent under siege. Following authorities such as Hobbes, Locke and Rousseau, the people give up parts of the right to positive freedom (freedom to self-govern) to the sovereign, in exchange for security and negative freedom.[3] The deal struck is 'the social contract'. In the context of the EU, who make up 'the people', that is so vital to the production of legitimacy? When rulers adhere to supplying security, this may thus be seen as legitimate governance. Defining 'security' or 'necessary police', however, may vary greatly according to geographical or temporal differences.[4]

The question here is whether it is possible to achieve *security* for citizens, when the legitimacy they confer plays out beyond the traditional nation state level, in the (supranational) EU. It might not be possible to give EU citizens security without pan-European cooperation in crime control. The dilemma is that, equally, it might not be possible to properly legitimate such pan-European cooperation in a democratic (or any other) way, because true European democracy is difficult to achieve without a common sense of European peoplehood.[5] Procedural legitimacy may be achieved through nation-state politicians being able to vote at the EU level (excluding, of course, Norwegian politicians), but another form of legitimacy may be equally important, namely that resulting from a common deliberative society. There is a lack of deliberative legitimacy because, for example there are no viable channels for citizens to express their agreement or disagreement.[6] The European states have very different historical and cultural backgrounds, and face different economic and geographical situations. Their experiences of wars, brutality, crime, more or less friendly relationships with neighbouring states, and access to different natural resources, and so on, are factors that make it unlikely that EU citizens experience *security* in exactly the same way. Questions about how far some people's freedoms should be limited, to ensure a feeling of security for others, may have many different answers. Norway has a varying degree of influence on EU police and crime control developments. Hence procedural legitimacy is weak, from the Norwegian point of view. There may, however, be output legitimacy: the results of police cooperation, or the justifications for implementing the relevant agreements are so good that they outweigh the lack of direct influence by the Norwegian people. I do not contest that the Norwegian people delegate, so to speak, their sovereignty to their politicians, thus also making international sovereignty-transferring agreements procedurally legitimate. Again, this underscores the importance of justifications, and, also the effects of the various measures.

2 Bowling and Sheptycki 2012:35 ff.

3 Berlin 1969.

4 Beetham 1991; Beetham and Lord 1998.

5 Mine is one of many different perspectives on the controversial issue of European identity. Another, perfectly valid claim is that there is a common European mentality emanating from the Enlightenment. But the aim here is to highlight a particular feature.

6 Habermas 1996.

The first two proper Norwegian debates on international police cooperation took place in 1997, as a direct consequence of the Schengen cooperation, and in 2000, in preparation for Europol affiliation. These two debates may signal a new political awareness of the fact that these police cooperation agreements introduced a new era, for the Norwegian police, and perhaps also for Norwegian society.[7] While freedom of movement was a vital issue in the Schengen negotiations, the emphasis was almost completely on crime control measures. The focus may thus be said to have shifted from being mainly on *freedom* to being mainly on *security*. This development can be seen in both EU and Norwegian policy t. It may also suggest that justifications are indeed necessary, but that their nature is less important.

There were several debates, concerning among others sovereignty issues, in connection with the early Norwegian EU agreements in the mid–1990s. These debates primarily took place in the general context of the question of EU membership, but it also had ties to the Schengen and later Europol agreements. The contestations and the justifications given in the government documents are important because in one understanding of the concept of sovereignty, the *citizens' right to decide* on developments influencing on their lives is necessary to legitimise the sovereign's rule over them. In a procedural legitimacy perspective, justice is guaranteed by the particular process by which it comes about.[8] A democratic polity is dependent on the ability to contest political leadership and policy development.[9] These justifications are described and discussed in the following chapters. Citizens' acceptance of the criminal justice system may have several foundations: either that they have 'decided themselves', through elections, so-called input legitimacy or procedural legitimacy, or the *output* of the measures simply seem *good*. Legitimacy-wise, this may suggest that if the EU limitations on the member states give better results in terms of less crime and more security, so-called output legitimacy, it doesn't matter if they are not deliberated much on the national level.

In the current European security climate, the question is whether security policies, more specifically on police cooperation and punishment, are actually based on the wishes of the citizens of the member state in question. In this perspective, popular sovereignty is discussed as undermined if the citizens are not made sufficiently aware of current matters they should – or should not – consent to.

7.2 The obligation to justify

Justifications have particular significance in the area of interference into the individual's private sphere. The state must give positive justifications for the use of violence or threat of violence; the kind of force that only the police legitimately embody in modern societies.[10] This follows from the Norwegian Constitution's principle of legality, and from the notion of the democratic state's legitimacy: The police are put to work on behalf of the people *and* the government. Whether police work concerns the special or general order, or is to do with investigation or maintaining order, the presence of the police always imply a *potential* for the use of coercive measures and general interference with individuals' privacy. It is in the

7 St.meld.nr.18 (1999–2000):ch.1.
8 More on normative legitimacy with further references in Eriksen 2009.
9 Føllesdal and Hix 2006.
10 E.g. Schmitt 1996.

nature of the police, at the core of their function, that they can legitimately interfere in a situation. Equally important is the power to select, define or ignore particular situations, depending on whether they are considered within or outside their remit. For the potential to intervene to be considered legitimate in the abovementioned understanding, I argue that it requires the justification of underlying priorities and strategies.[11]

During the last 20 years, the development in the EU policy area of 'freedom, security and justice' has been rapid and dynamic. In 2010, Norway's Office of the Auditor General presented a critical report assessing the police effort to fight organised crime: It showed that while the police constantly argued the need for more resources and for adopting the 'international', extraordinary investigative measures such as covert search, surveillance and communication control, the actual use of such methods was ***declining***. In the so-called Police Analysis,[12] the recent Norwegian police reform was suggested, on the basis *inter alia* of the Audit General report. Although the level of reported crime both in Europe and in Norway had declined during the previous decade, according to the Police Analysis, the crimes committed were more complex, dangerous, and organised, and frequently crossed borders. The analysis was widely criticised for not considering relevant research, including that showing that increased centralisation and specialisation do not necessarily work as intended.[13]

The justification for staying outside of the Union was based on a set of assumptions, both of a positive and negative nature. Norway is to a large extent in fact taking part in the police cooperation mechanisms that are based in the EU regulations. In the following, the Government's justifications that even (seem to have) convinced the former opposing minority are presented.

In the following, we move from general concerns to how the security-scene changed in the 1990s and subsequent years.

7.3 Two justifications: Nordic relations and cross-border crime

Initially, free travel and maintaining Nordic relations were the main issues at stake in the Government's view. Fighting cross-border crime soon after completely took over as the reason for joining the Schengen cooperation.

As with all historical developments, it is impossible to have knowledge of the counterfactual history; whether Norway would have been left on the outside of the Nordic relations in general, and whether e.g. Finland would have had to carry out a tough third-country border-control regime at the Finno-Norwegian border, is anyone's guess. Some other solution would probably have been found, but this is mere speculation. It is of course noteworthy that both Sweden and Finland soon after became full EU members. The domestic political importance of *Nordic* cooperation may have decreased significantly.

There has, however, been a steady maintenance and development of the Nordic relations in the crime control area. The latest Nordic Police Cooperation Agreement was revised as recently as in 2017, and the Nordic Arrest Warrant (NAW) has continued the close Nordic cooperation on extradition. Norway may be somewhat more excluded from the 'deepest'

11 See also Barker 2001.
12 NOU 2013:9.
13 Høringssvar fra Riksadvokaten 2013; PHS Høringssvar 2013.

EU cooperation mechanisms that are heavily built on principles of mutual recognition and availability, typically including the European Arrest Warrant (EAW) and facilitated exchange of evidence. Non-Schengen membership could, of course, have excluded also association agreements to such instruments. Nevertheless, it seems fair to suggest that the Norwegian situation in the Nordic fraternity looks unchanged through the lens of t the revisions and renewals of the Nordic cooperation instruments. Agreements that do *not* exist, e.g. between Finland and Norway or Sweden and Norway on limitations of hot pursuit into each other's territories, also tell an interesting story about Nordic cooperation. These neighbouring countries continue their tradition of high level of mutual trust, to the extent, I would suggest, that fewer formal legal texts are needed.

With the Nordic example in mind, the success of police cooperation measures in general may depend on close relationships between the cooperating countries and police officers in question, both geographically and culturally. This is of course what the EU project may be changing: an expansion of the area where the police forces and governments shall enjoy trust and cooperation previously reserved for close neighbours. The conclusion in the Nordic case, however, is that this regional cooperation *also* is alive and well. While it is impossible to know what had happened, had Norway stayed outside of the Schengen cooperation, it is probable that the Nordic cooperation on police and judicial affairs would have continued. This justification was thus not valid in this sense.

When police competences have been developed and/or expanded, the emphasised issues are historically largely the same: The risks and lack of control related to 'strangers', people believed to lack a social commitment to the local community, have been stressed repeatedly. The *description* of the problems is somewhat different in the 1912 Police Committee documents, preparing the first national Norwegian Police Act, compared to, for example, *forarbeid* to the amendments in 2005. But the challenges mentioned are largely the same.[14] In the 1912 Report, increased police presence was considered necessary in areas where the population was composed of a high degree of seasonal workers and migrants.[15] The policing of other 'races' and foreigners was more challenging because of their weak relationship with the local community. The connections with the neighbouring Russia were steadily increasing, leading to new and intensified challenges.[16] A police presence should give the foreign states an impression that Norway was 'in control' of its internal state territory, being a powerful and well-functioning state.[17] These are typical problems that, as seen in the *forarbeid* during the past hundred years, have been targeted in various laws and regulations. The Schengen cooperation gave new grounds for policing foreigners in an administrative law sense, but also at least combined with crime control policing.

Increased focus on police cooperation through the Schengen Cooperation was considered imperative due to the growing mobility, open borders, and the consequential crime. International influence, however, is nothing new. Norway has only been a non-union member, a completely independent nation for 112 years. *All* legal systems, perhaps particularly in the 'Western world', are influenced by each other. And the same kinds of issues and

14 E.g. Ot.prp.nr.60 (2004–2005).

15 1912 Politilovinnstilling:8.

16 Op.cit.:8; 13.

17 Op.cit.:9. Another benefit of the Norwegian Schengen association 80 years later was the curbing of what was popularly called the 'Russian whore traffic' and tourists without a credible reason for staying in Norway. *Storting* meeting 08.06.1999:5.

problems will arise in several jurisdictions, especially in regions with close geographical and cultural proximity.

And there were also alternatives. As an example of *formal* policy influence, where Schengen to some extent is intertwined or building on UN cooperation, is the CISA requiring member states to take certain measures to prevent their liberal politics on certain areas of drugs, such as the Dutch policy in regards to marihuana, from spreading into the borderless area of the Schengen.[18] CISA art.70 establishes a duty for the member states to "set up a permanent working party" to develop joint measures and techniques for fighting drug-related crime, and propose e.g. practical cooperative projects, crime and criminal procedure legislation, in this area. Art.71 requires the member states to among others adopt "all necessary measures to prevent and punish the illicit trafficking in narcotic drugs and psychotropic substances" (no.1). If taken seriously, these two articles should mean that this international working party quite significantly influences the national developments in drug-related crimes. It was argued in the proposal that these provisions on drug-related control are limited in form and scope, and that this was due to the more thorough regulation in other international instruments such as the UN conventions.[19] Art.71 also explicitly gives the UN conventions on drugs and psychotropic substances as bases for the Schengen member states' 'target area', to which Norway already was signatory.[20]

Norway has a tradition for low crime levels. If the same kind of concerns periodically resurfaces and the Norwegian police and crime control situation is perceived as broadly a success, it is not obvious that the police situation needed changing. The state response has been that a completely new situation is developing in the borderless Schengen Area.

7.3.1 Sliding justifications

In 1997, the Nordic free travel arrangements and the fear of an 'outsider position' were the primary justifications for Norwegian affiliation with the Schengen cooperation. In 1999, when the present Association Agreement was negotiated in *Stortinget*, the former secondary argument had replaced the primary; the need for enhanced police cooperation. It was imperative to be part of the Schengen police cooperation. This was considered the *only* way to stop an international crime wave that was gaining momentum. Police cooperation was seen as necessary to compensate for the problems that would result from the free movement of people. On the other hand, opening the borders was itself considered a measure to enhance closer cooperation in the "fight against international, cross-border crime, which is an increasing challenge in Europe".[21] It is notable that when the Foreign Committee of *Stortinget* asked the Minister of Justice whether enhanced police cooperation could be strengthened *without* a weakening of the border control, the Minister simply responded that the "Schengen countries' effort to strengthen the police cooperation builds on a condition of removing control of persons at the borders".[22] And it could not be documented that

18 GA's opinion of 15 July 2010 in Case C–137/09 *Josemans*, in particular 113–123, cited in Vries (2013), also CISA art.87.

19 St.prp.nr.42 (1996–1997): ch.5.5.10; UN Convention against illicit traffic in narcotic drugs etc. (1988); UN Convention on psychotropic substances (1971); UN Convention on Narcotic Drugs (1961, 1972).

20 St.prp.nr.42 (1996–1997) op.cit.

21 St.prp.nr.42 (1996–1997), my translation.

22 Innst.S.nr.229 (1996–1997):68.

the level of crime generally had increased since the dissolving of the border control.[23] It was also emphasised that security and stability include the enhancement of safety for the individual, hereunder protection against crime, and that this crime was becoming increasingly international and organised.[24]

To some extent, the Ministry thus employed a dual and – perhaps – paradoxical reasoning: Dissolving border controls would create a need for more police cooperation. Simultaneously, the police cooperation was an autonomous reason for dissolving the border controls. In other words: Was the enhanced security a *purpose* of dissolving border control, or a *consequence*? Or both? This is important if the reasoning is used 'illegitimately'. Continuous expansion of cross-border police measures may be necessary on the grounds that the open borders make crime flow much more freely across borders. It should be acknowledged, however, that the police cooperation was already a justification for the borderless Schengen Area in the first place.

Considering the validity of justifications: Had there actually been a critical rise in numbers, justifying the cooperation needs? A presentation of the national crime and policing situation was given in the *forarbeid* concerning general police methods in 1997. It emphasised that the clear majority of the crime committed in Norway was committed by Norwegian citizens.[25] For s*ome* categories of crimes, however, a "not insignificant share" was committed by foreign citizens or Norwegians with foreign origin. The police investigation into these criminal groups was particularly challenging due to the international aspects. Statistics Norway could show that the crime level rose almost continuously from 1960 to 1990 – with almost six times as many investigated crimes in 1990,[26] similarly to in Europe in general.[27] The changes were explained with several factors: typically characteristics associated with 'globalisation' and/or modernity traits like increased communication, travel, new markets, etc. Nevertheless, the numbers applied to assess the level of crime and the analysis presented in NOU 1993:3 were criticised from researchers for being weak and simplistic. The connection between registered and actual crime had not been considered, for example disregarding the fact that the crime-reporting rate had risen, and that increased police control leads to higher registered crime numbers, nor the changes to the statistical database. Another major critique was the Committee's failing to take into account the fact that the rise in crime primarily consisted of petty property crime, not the types of crime that the Committee claimed required new investigation methods. The Ministry concluded, however, that the crime level (in numbers) was of less importance, and placed major weight on the apparently general agreement that crime was changing in character.[28] While this consideration concerned investigation methods, the numbers were generally applied also in considering the need for international police cooperation.

The first ever Norwegian 'working committee' to *Stortinget* concerning international police cooperation was appointed because of the Schengen cooperation. The second such *forarbeid* came already in 2000, concerning the Norwegian Europol association and around the same time as the second round of legislative amendments following the Norwegian

23 Op.cit.:69; 78.
24 St.meld.nr.18 (1999–2000):2.
25 NOU 1997:15 p.24 (my translation).
26 Op.cit. p.24. The statistics of reported (not investigated) crimes were not registered before 1990.
27 Op.cit.:28–29.
28 Ot.prp.nr.64 (1998–1999):ch.6.1. The 1993 numbers were built on in the NOU 1997:15:28–29.

entrance into Schengen.[29] It was now simply stated that Norway would want to participate in future EU developments. Cooperation not building on the Schengen *Acquis* would in principle exclude Norwegian participation, and other agreements should thus be pursued.[30] The Nordic free-travel argument was no longer in focus. Intensified police and criminal procedure cooperation within the EU was partly the same as the motivation for the police cooperation in the Schengen relations, i.e. compensatory measures to the dismantling of the internal border controls. Partly it was, since the early 1990s, the general establishment of an "Area of freedom, security and justice" within the Union, "a new unifying political concept in the EU relations".[31] And Norway wanted to be a part, albeit to no greater extent than before.

These two reasons were reiterated in the 1999 *forarbeid* and through subsequent legal amendments to the Schengen cooperation, the expansion of these and other international police cooperation measures, and even the later 2013 changes. General social changes were considered in the *forarbeid* to result in new general trends in crime, and the positive effects of the Schengen and EEA cooperation – free movement of people, goods, services and capital over unchecked borders, and the resulting increased profits – would inevitably also make crime more international.[32] The benefits of free travel and an open market bring negative effects that require even more of the compensatory measures, and the emphasis on these measures became increasingly important as primary purposes of cooperation.[33] There was, in other words, an imperative need for more cooperation, and more resources and measures should be made available to the police.

The majority voted 'yes' to Schengen membership because it would continue and expand the Nordic Passport Union, according to the concluding debates. The enhanced European police cooperation, improving the fight against drug-related and other international crime, was, however, considered the primary advantage.[34] In other words, the reasons had already in the early debates altered somewhat.[35]

7.4 Moving in: from the EEA to the Schengen

The Norwegian population decided against EU membership in a consultative referendum in 1994 (52.2% v. 47.7%). State sovereignty and national autonomy were among the most frequently voiced reasons to vote against membership.[36] Norway was already a member of

29 St.meld.nr.18 (1999–2000):2; Innst.O. nr.89 (1998–1999).
30 St.meld.nr.18 (1999–2000):61–63.
31 Op.cit.:61, my translation.
32 Op.cit.:8.
33 Op.cit.:8–9.
34 Innst.S.nr.229 (1996–1997):3.
35 Kvam 2008 argues that the Schengen cooperation in which Norway participates, constitutes a weakened cooperation in the fight against crime. As long as the intention is read such that the only sufficiently effective cooperation against crime necessitates full-fledged membership of the EU, this might be right. If understanding the Schengen cooperation as containing primarily or only compensatory measures to the actions taken within the Schengen Agreement, this may indeed be argued as shortcoming *when the target area also is that of the EEA*, which includes the free movement of more than simply the persons-control in the Schengen.
36 There were also other justifications, e.g. regarding resources, especially regulation of the fish industry. Neumann argues that the sovereignty emphasis is a part of the Norwegian *mythos* (2001). The notions of a 'national identity' and how this plays into the Norwegian-Europe politics have been discussed by several theorists, e.g. Wæver 2002; Tanil 2012.

the European Free Trade Association (EFTA) since the 1960s. From being an *alternative* to the EU, the EFTA states negotiated an agreement with the EU. The agreement made the EFTA countries part of the European Economic Area (EEA) and gave the EFTA states comprehensive access to the internal market of the Union. Briefly put, the four freedoms and the EU competition regulations were now also applied to the EFTA states. The Schengen Cooperation Agreement signed soon thereafter was explicitly described as a "replacement" for the "losses" resulting from staying outside the Union in terms of the lack of border controls. Norway wanted to stay outside and remain independent, but was also weary of the dangers and risks that independence entailed. The country wanted to remain fully sovereign, but at the same time, it wanted access to the benefits of EU membership. The EU debate in Norway in the early 1990s was massive. A separate EEA debate was, however, almost non-existent. It was, as is seen immediately below, uncontroversial that some measure of sovereignty had been lost with the EEA Agreement, although not as much as would be the result of full EU membership.

Entering into the EEA Agreement in 1994 implied a transfer of sovereignty from Norway to supranational surveillance and adjudicating bodies of the ESA and the EFTA Court. Both opponents and many of the supporters of the EU were critical to the EEA Agreement since it implied either too little or too much cooperation with the EU. Both sides agreed that the EEA Agreement would imply too great a loss of sovereignty with not enough actual influence. The applicable constitutional process shall ensure agreements being subject to the highest procedural legitimacy possible to attain in Norwegian law. This legitimacy is important both for creating procedural legitimacy in itself, and more specifically legitimacy for transferring sovereignty. The debates concerning which constitutional process are therefore targeted particularly the next sub-chapters.

The EEA Agreement does not regulate police or criminal law. Member states may, though, be obliged to criminalise certain acts that jeopardise the four freedoms.[37] The EEA concerns *trade*, and may thus be seen to infringe on the individual's personal sphere to a lesser extent. This was the immediate context for the Schengen negotiations shortly afterwards. The Schengen Accession Agreement was decided with simple majority. Interestingly, the debates around sovereignty that had raged so fiercely prior to the 1994 referendum had already silenced.

Norway participates in all Schengen bodies alongside and on equal footing with all EU Schengen members, with one important exception: the decision-making process. After the Amsterdam Treaty, the decisions related to the Schengen *Acquis* lay with the EU Council. For the EU members, the agreement implied a transfer of decision-making competences and direct effect, alongside many other EU community competence issues. It was considered a major challenge to transfer and 're-create' an agreement between Norway and the EU where Norway was supposed to end up with both an insider and an outsider position. The agreement had to be international, without any supranational consequences for Norway. At the same time, it should ensure Norwegian participation in the development of the EU framework whenever Schengen relevant acts would be created.[38] The minority fraction's arguments concerning *inter alia* that the abolition of border controls at the internal Schengen borders would lead to an augmented risk of international crime such as drug

37 An example was the discussion of the controversial Data Retention Directive. It was considered as a telecommunications directive – not a police measure of crime control – and thus placed within the EEA policy area, and therefore not seen as Schengen relevant.

38 St.prp.nr.50 (1998–99):4.

smuggling, reduced freedom to decide the directions of refugee and asylum policies at the national level, fear of lessened data protection and procedural rule of law guarantees, and that there would be an increased pressure on *Stortinget* to approve new acts from the Schengen steering body, the Mixed Committee.[39]

7.5 Considering sovereignty infringements

The question is whether lack of sufficiently good information from the government constitutes an infringement on sovereignty. To consider this, necessitates an account of the government's deliberation of the case at hand; entering into the Schengen cooperation. This also includes the Government's assessment of whether the agreement as such constituted a transfer of sovereignty. When the legislative changes in connection with the Schengen Agreement were prepared in 1998 and 1999, a general governmental view was that the substantial matters of the Schengen measures were agreed upon. In retrospect, Norway's accession to the Schengen cooperation was the start of a rapidly and dynamically growing body of regulations to which Norway became member. The justifications and reasoning in the following amendments and new agreements often built upon the legal basis and *forarbeid* of the initial Schengen association. Emphasis is on the initial proceedings because it seems particularly problematic that the first building block, so to speak, was placed on sand. This non-legislative process of the SAA was met with much non-political and political critique, because *Stortinget* had to take a stand on the matters without the relevant consultative hearings regarding the consequences of the agreement.[40] Some politicians *wanted to* discuss the (potential) consequences of membership, even though this was not the theme for the later process. Many similar issues were debated simultaneously. An example is the second round of negotiating the Norwegian Schengen Agreement, after the moving of the Schengen *Acquis* into the EU *Acquis*. This happened in the same period as the legislative changes from the initial Norway-Schengen Agreement.[41]

There was a change in government three times between the Norwegian Schengen application and the finalisation of necessary legislation amendments subsequent to the agreement. The presiding government during the first consultative rounds voted *against* the Norwegian Schengen Association Agreement in *Stortinget*, but were, nevertheless, loyal to the majority. The *substantial* issues were considered agreed upon and set. Nevertheless, since this ratification voting of 1997 happened before the Amsterdam Treaty was finalised, a new consultative round took place, also with regard to re-evaluation of the constitutional questions that could arise from the roles of the EEC Court, the EU Parliament and Commission in the Schengen, and as such, the new cooperation agreement would have procedural and institutional implications in the agreement.[42] Eventually, there was general consensus on the

39 Innst.S.nr.147 (1998–1999):5; Innst.S.nr.229 (1996–1997).

40 *Storting* meeting 08.06.1999, statement from Valle, SV. It shall be noted, however, that the open hearing that took place before the voting in *Stortinget* went on over two days, resulting in a 200-page document in which the debate was evident, including commentary from and questions to experts in this area. The document also contains a substantial body of written questions and answers from the justice and the foreign committee of *Stortinget* to the Government, showing that such preparations not only happened 'spontaneously' in the hearings. (Innst.S.nr.229 (1996–1997); in total around 250 written Q & As).

41 I.e. Innst.S.nr.147 (1998–1999) and Innst.O.nr.89 (1998–1999) and their underlying preparations and recommendations.

42 Innst.S.nr.229 (1996–1997); St.prp.nr.50 (1998–99): pt.1.1–3; Ot.prp.nr.56 (1998–1999).

proposed legislative amendments. Irrespective of the later changes in Norway's position in the 'contractual relationship': The debate concerned simply inevitable consequences.[43]

To shine light on what was considered to be at stake in the political processes towards Schengen membership, and the arguments made related to influence and impact of these new international memberships, the following targets the applicable constitutional rules when Norway enters into treaties, the considerations made through challenging process leading up to the final ratification, and finally the assessment of what encompassed 'significant sovereignty' related to the Schengen cooperation.

7.5.1 The constitutional alternatives

From the Norwegian point of view, the implementation of the Schengen cooperation into the EU *Acquis* implied less influence on the Schengen matters. Although "the EU member states [. . .] acknowledge that no one has the complete overview of the results of a closer connection between the Schengen and the EU *Acquis*",[44] the Norwegian Government considered that it was a major benefit if the Norwegian agreement was established *before* this implementation was finalised. Already being party to the cooperation before having to deal with the EU as a whole, would, the Government felt, give Norway a better ability to maintain political and constitutional interests,[45] *Stortinget* agreed on ratification on 09.06.1997. On 16–17 June 1997, the Amsterdam Treaty was agreed upon in the EU, deciding that the Schengen *Acquis* would be implemented into the EU as a result. The formal ratification of the Norwegian agreement took place on 30.07.1997.

While the Norwegian kingdom is indivisible (the Norwegian Constitution [NC] sect.1), sect.93[46] establishes exceptions. A specified transfer of sovereignty may take place to an "international organisation" when the purpose is "to safeguard international peace and security or to promote the international rule of law and cooperation". Such a treaty may only be agreed upon by the Government after *Stortinget* has agreed with a ¾ majority. The second paragraph, however, states that sect.93 does not apply "in cases of membership in an international organisation whose decisions only have application for Norway exclusively under international law". This would typically be the UN. The EU and Schengen apply also towards individuals and intra-state level, thus more far-reaching in some respects. Whether or not the Norwegian affiliation to the Schengen cooperation entailed transfer of sovereign powers from Norway to an international organisation determined which section was applicable.[47]

Two other constitutional alternatives regulate foreign agreements. Sect.26(1) and (2) entitles the Government to enter into international agreements without consent from *Stortinget*. The second paragraph makes an exception in cases of "treaties on matters of special importance" but also states that "in all cases, treaties whose implementation, according to the Constitution, necessitates a new law or a decision by *Stortinget*, are not binding until *Stortinget* has given its consent thereto". Simple majority is sufficient after this

43 E.g. Innst.O.nr.89 (1998–1999):chs.3 and 8.

44 St.prp.nr.42 (1996–1997):2, my translation.

45 Op.cit. ch.8.

46 The NC was revised 17.05.2014, and the procedure in sect.93 is now in sect.115. This change had no material or procedural consequences.

47 On the Norwegian debate on the constitutional question; e.g. Boe and Sejersted 1999, Holmøyvik 2013.

vote. The Schengen Agreement was considered by the Government to be *unquestionably* of special importance.[48] The Agreement also caused the enacting of the new SIS Act

Section 93 was not considered to be appropriate procedure, as the Government meant that the Schengen membership and association would not have any other *implications* than those of international law, i.e. no sovereignty infringements. This was not, as seen below, uncontroversial.

The constitutional regulations on international agreements did not fit well with neither the Schengen Agreement, nor the later police cooperation agreements and amendments. Traditional international law treaties would adhere to principles commonly agreed upon concerning mutual respect for sovereign decisions, albeit within agreed upon limitations like human rights. The membership in the North Atlantic Treaty Organisation (NATO) implies commitments that limit future Norwegian state action; as does the EEA.[49] The challenge of the police cooperation measures, however, was that they do not place the commitments and permissions on institutions, but on other states' authorities. The discussion was therefore whether sovereignty was *actually* transferred, or whether Norwegian authorities still ultimately were in charge of all police activity following the Schengen Agreement and subsequent police cooperation instruments. Such transfer was not considered covered by sect.93.

Enforcing police power has so-called direct effect for the citizens. Enforcing foreign police powers on Norwegian territory did not in itself infringe on Norwegian sovereignty. If the agreement implied, however, that Norwegian authority pre-approved that foreign authority could be used, before knowing the results or potential actions, this *would* imply partial transfer of sovereignty.[50] If sanctions more or less explicitly loomed in case of 'non-compliance', the international agreement would be in breach with the NC sect.1.[51] The Government emphasised the importance of decisions and considerations being *de facto* freely and autonomously taken.

The controversial question was whether the police cooperation measures implied 'significant' (*inngripende*) changes to the Norwegian sovereign power of the government. These measures' impact decided the *simple* constitutional procedure of entering into the Schengen cooperation. Enforcement of coercive powers by foreign police on Norwegian territory, i.e. the provisions on hot-pursuit and cross-border surveillance (CISA arts.40 and 41), *were* considered infringing on Norwegian sovereignty.[52] However, the degree of transferred authority was seen as a very small part of the Schengen cooperation. The enforcement of these foreign powers was also subject to strict legal limitations, making the infringements on Norwegian sovereignty in practice insignificant.[53] Foreign police would not be permitted to autonomously enforce their national jurisdiction on Norwegian territory, and no autonomous right to make arrests abroad was encompassed.[54] This is only partly true: arrest

48 Op.cit.:ch.4.1.1.

49 St.prp.nr.50 (1998–99):ch.4.3.1.

50 Op.cit.:ch.4.3.3.

51 Op.cit.:ch.4.3.4.

52 Op.cit.:ch.4.4.2. Both Swedish and Finnish authorities deemed these articles of the CISA to be transferring a certain degree of sovereignty, in contrast to Denmark's assessment. The Norwegian government considered this applicable to variations in the *wordings* of the different Constitutions – not different considerations of the actual 'infringement' of sovereignty.

53 St.prp.nr.50 (1998–1999):ch.4.4.2.

54 St.prp.nr.42 (1996–1997).

was and *is* allowed by foreign police officers, but only following Norwegian legislation (CPA sect.176). Further, there had also previously been customary-based hot pursuit and observation between the Nordic countries.[55] And the continuation and expansion of the cooperation included in the area of Schengen police cooperation, was simply a mutual cooperation between equal states, 'giving and taking' with similar interests, and with equal sovereignty 'risks'.

If Norway disagrees with a new Schengen measure, the SAA art.8 no.4 regulates political negotiations. The SAA has rules on consistent application of the Agreement, and Norway has committed to implement new Schengen-relevant regulations to ensure coherence and unity. This in practice implies that the dynamic development of EU regulations has great impact on what Norwegian future regulations would become and entail. In the potential situation that Norway acted or enacted in breach with the applicable regulations, the effect would be the potential termination of the agreement (SAA arts.11 no.3 cf. 10 no.2). This was, the Government argued, not a *de facto* significant transfer of legislative authority because of two circumstances diminishing the practical effects.[56] These were 1) that it was unlikely that the extent of the Schengen cooperation in the *qualitative* sense would develop much. This view was also ensured by the rules of SAA art.8 no.1 cf. art.2 no.3, that decide that only new regulations 'amending' or 'building upon' existing provisions shall be implemented by (the non-EU members) Norway and Iceland. The *quantitative* development of the Schengen regulations was expected to be steadily growing, but in both cases, the Norwegian government expected no substantial amendments to take place through the Schengen cooperation. Such changes would normally happen through treaty replacement.[57] 2) The other 'safeguard' against the EU overruling the Norwegian legislator was the degree of Norwegian influence on the processes within the EU regarding Schengen development. Although decision competence was out of the question, there would be decision-shaping through the negotiations in the Mixed Committee (SAA arts.4no.1;3 no.1; and 8no.2[a]).

The worst-case scenario of Norway's refusing a measure, thus the Agreement potentially being terminated (SAA art.8 nos.2 and 4), was seen as an unlikely scenario. Norwegian interests would in most cases be the same as the interests of the other Nordic countries, and that these, being EU members, would (more or less implicitly) maintain Norwegian interests within the EU, the Government argued. Measures would hardly be introduced or assistance requested that would be in breach with Norwegian interests or values.

As seen above, the Schengen *Acquis* was implemented into the EU legal framework almost the very instant that Norway signed the Schengen Cooperation Agreement in 1997. Norway could no longer be an associated member, and a new affiliation agreement had to be negotiated. Norway's influence on the further Schengen development was radically diminished. These processes were in practice intertwined. This is an important point related to this current sovereignty discussion. In 1997, the Ministry argued that few *de facto* changes would follow from the Schengen police measures. These measures were in reality not new, but already in place via the Nordic cooperation agreements. In 1999, the necessary legal changes post-Schengen were seen as *imperative* given the new levels of increasingly serious crime. A core question was whether the enforcement of foreign jurisdictions' police powers on Norwegian territory was compatible with the principle that the state alone shall wield the

55 Ibid.
56 Op.cit.:ch.4.4.4.
57 Op.cit.:ch.4.4.4.

power of police. The matter was 'solved' in defining and justifying the police cooperation as bound to Norwegian legislation, and thus within the state's ultimate competences. EU policies and regulations on justice and home affairs matters, including policing, are dynamically and continuously developing. And this has been an important recurring justification for all new police cooperation measures. The possibility for citizens to consider the state potential for coercion (as inherent in the police) must be seen as particular significant when the policies are developed outside of the Norwegian society and largely disconnected from Norwegian public debate. The 'foundational' debates and the subsequent justifications for the *forarbeid* concerning the developments transferred to the Norwegian policing situation, are thus significant for the later agreements.

So far, we have seen that a steady governmental view was that the Schengen cooperation was not sovereignty infringing, and even if they were, other aspects were more important.

The political debates did not concern challenges related to the police function ***outside*** nation state borders. At the same time, the 1995 Police Act *forarbeid* were less preoccupied with international cooperation, and definitely not to the degree in the *forarbeid* subsequent to the Schengen Cooperation. Because the SAA did not lead to a specific new Act in Norway, the proposition to,[58] and the negotiations in, *Stortinget*[59] are the only *forarbeid* to the Agreement. There were no non-political consultative hearings. The substantial content has – arguably – thus never been properly debated in consultative hearings because of the two rounds of Norwegian Schengen negotiations. The only debates were connected to, the actually required legislative amendments to Norwegian law on the basis of the 1996 Agreement.[60]

It is somewhat troubling that the debates and processes concerning what should be considered the first and most fundamental police cooperation agreement that Norway entered into, may be seen to be less than thorough, not subject to the most 'solid' constitutional process, and generally based on vicarious arguments.[61] The final conclusion, that international police cooperation meant, in general, an only insignificant degree of sovereignty transfer, has become a foundation for the subsequent twenty years of police cooperation development. The arguments of those opposed to these political processes are presented in the following.

7.5.2 The question of significant sovereignty

In a representative democracy like Norway, the political parties are an integrated part of the influence citizens may exert. The constitutional process of either simple or qualified majority,

58 St.prp.nr.42 (1996–1997).

59 Innst.S.nr.229 (1996–1997). For a quite comprehensive bibliography of both Norwegian and EU documents of the Schengen agreement and processes, see Glasser 2006.

60 There were several Schengen provisions adopted in the Schengen cooperation, but none necessitated amendments in Norwegian law, according to St.meld.nr.33 (1998–99): pt.1.3.

61 Another example of a rapidly evolving and undebated cooperation instrument was the implementation of the Norwegian Eurojust cooperation. Neither Eurojust nor Europol have practical operational powers, and the allegations of sovereignty infringement were not applicable in the same way as with Schengen. As seen in Part II, there may, however, be significant influence through these bodies on national operational policing. But what is also interesting from these parliamentary debates (and public debates in general) is that they do not separate to any significant degree between the various international police instruments. Efjestad argues that whenever the Eurojust cooperation has been touched upon in *Stortinget* debates, this has almost only been just as a 'hang on' to the Schengen and Europol discussions (Efjestad 2009:16; 41).

and the opportunity to contribute to the debate in consultative hearings, are vital in this relation. For this reason, the Norwegian Schengen debates are explored in this subchapter. This may also shed light on why there were hardly any debates in the new millennium.

The constitutional procedural issues at stake, and the political process during the 1990s, relate to the fundamental relationship between the state, the police, the citizens and the wider community, both because of the argument that the state chose to put forward, and also the lack of influence Norwegian citizens have been given to decide what sort of police service that may be said to be 'needed' (Police Act sect.1). Since 2001, there has not been *any* dissent in *Stortinget* against any of the more than 20 new propositions that has required political majority.[62] This is an interesting and almost unprecedented level of consent. On the one hand, the new police cooperation measures may clearly have led to increased efficiency. On the other, however, the efficiency seemed less important for the abolition of border controls in the first place: the police and the media showed that Schengen membership had challenges and increased crime as consequence. In other words; once the membership was a reality, most politicians may have seen the new development with closer ties to the EU as a necessity.

The issue considered here is the question of significant sovereignty transfer in the agreement, when Norway lost much influence vis-à-vis the EU/Schengen cooperation, during the period between 1996–1999.[63] Since the agreement Norway already had made in 1996, no new amendments were considered requiring legal changes. Nor did the administrative and economic consequences diverge from the presuppositions in the original agreement.[64] The major practical change, however, happened between the 1996 Norwegian Schengen Cooperation Agreement and the 1999 Schengen Association Agreement.[65]

The Government's assessment of the constitutional issues was criticised for being superficial, and not giving *Stortinget* sufficient understanding of the issues at stake.[66] It was also argued to be constitutional challenges in the significant body of guidelines that the Schengen Agreement gave legal basis to, for example, in terms of the many guidelines from the Executive Committee. Many of these were exempt from the general public and the detailed control of the procedural guidelines, which was seen as taking a significant piece of authority from the Norwegian government and other authorities in decisions that would impact the Norwegian policing situation.[67] Eventually, some changes were made after the consultative rounds of the initial legislative proposals. A major change was that more of the Schengen Convention text was incorporated in legal text, especially in the SIS Act related to the legal purposes of registration in the information system.

Although the police measures in CISA art.40 and 41 would directly affect the citizens, and therefore required legal basis, it was argued that in contrast to the EEA Agreement, the Schengen measures were less *materially* encompassing in the Norwegian society. Norway

62 E.g. NOU 2012:2 ch.22.1.

63 See the extensive proposition from the Government and the recommendation from the Committee of Foreign Affairs for an overview of the debates (Innst.S.nr.147 (1998–1999)).

64 Op.cit.:4; St.prp.nr.50 (1998–99).

65 St.prp.nr.50 (1998–1999):5. An expected deficit for Norwegian influence was that EU member states would discuss Schengen relevant matters in the EU Council, regardless of the emphasis on that Schengen matters were to be brought up *also* in the Mixed Committee (SAA art.4).

66 St.prp.nr.50 (1998–1999):ch.4.1.2

67 Innst.S.nr.229 (1996–1997):7.

had in the latter agreement *more* right to influence than in the EEA system.[68] Given that the EFTA Court can overrule national decisions, entering into the EEA Agreement involved some transfer of sovereign competence from the Norwegian state. The decision of EEA membership therefore followed the qualified majority procedure of the Norwegian Constitution sect.93, and the EEA Agreement was implemented in Norwegian law by the EEA Act. The Schengen Agreement was, in contrast, eventually considered a hybrid, and the emphasis put on the, although perhaps fictive, freedom inherent in the potential to refuse decisions taken by a supranational body.[69] The totality assessment should be decisive for the procedure (NC sect.93[2]).[70]

The procedure was criticised because the measures direct effecting Norwegian citizens from non-national bodies in terms of legislative, executive or judicial authority, formally or in practice, should be sufficiently politically assessed. Whether foreign bodies would enforce coercion *without* basis in Norwegian law was an important question. This would entail a breach of the principle of legality, but not infringe sovereignty.[71] In other words, if the *initial* Norwegian Schengen Cooperation Agreement (1996) had been considered *together* with the later Association Agreement (1998), a NC sect.93 voting in *Stortinget* would probably have been required.

In conclusion, while the general assessment was that the cooperation entailed some transfer of sovereignty, these aspects were both expected to be negligible, and subject to reciprocity, Norway would not give any sovereignty away that was not 'traded in' for the same 'sovereignty gain' abroad. This is controversial, seen in light of all available police cooperation measures (as presented below in part II). This does of course not mean that all subsequent agreements are illegitimate or flawed *per se*, but it may raise questions concerning the need for and/or requirement of justification vis-à-vis the general public. In the context of the later amendments, that made the Police Act sect.20a more of an 'open-ended' section, these arguments seem less convincing. The governmental argument that these issues were not uncertain in any way, are unconvincing, at least in retrospect.[72] It seems unfortunate not to have used the qualified majority voting process when this was such a contested result. The perceived legitimacy of the Schengen preparation and subsequent ratification would have been strengthened.

As argued above, the legal procedures had some initial flaws. I would even argue that the flaws were transferred to subsequent agreements. The Government shall consult *Stortinget* if a matter that has been dealt with before, has changed its character.[73] This might be said to be the case with, for example, Eurojust after the new Council Decision.[74] Whether a measure or instrument has changed fundamentally in character, or has just undergone 'minor' changes, may be difficult to gauge. A cooperation instrument or measure may not necessarily *formally* change for the resulting practice involving quite broad discretionary competences to have changed. As long as the original agreement is submitted to *Stortinget*, a natural interpretation is that it has accepted the 'leeway' as such. If the cooperation

68 St.prp.nr.50 (1998–1999):ch.7.4.3.3;7.4.4.2.

69 Ibid.:ch.7.3.

70 Ibid.:ch.7.5.

71 Ch.7.4.2.4.

72 Innst.S.nr.229 (1996–1997):114–145.

73 *Stortingets forretningsorden* art.13 and 13a; Sejersted 2002.

74 [2008] OJ L 138/14.

measure changes are dealt with superfluously, however, the acceptance may be seen as less informed. It seems that the duty to consult *Stortinget* primarily applies when the Government itself is the urging party to expand cooperation. If the initiative originates more bottom-up, or changes simply take place at the 'bottom', such a duty, seems relevant only if the Government itself is sufficiently notified.

It is hard to say whether Norway and the Norwegian police would have developed the same way had it not been for the Schengen membership. The recent trend in the field of EU police cooperation has been to create instruments outside of Schengen; instruments Norway seem to want to be included in. From this perspective, the procedure of entering into the initial Schengen/EU police cooperation might be said to be of diminishing importance. The debate around a possible transfer of sovereignty resulting from the Schengen Agreement is consequently less interesting. The most important consequence has perhaps not yet appeared: the direction and the dynamic character of the cooperation may, it seems, certainly lead to police and crime control issues that surpass national borders. The lack of a real possibility to refuse to implement EU development in practice could be argued to render the NC sect.26 procedure inapplicable. As the final conclusion was based on a 'totality assessment', it was possible to disregard these objections.[75]

This chapter has addressed the issue of internal sovereignty. More specifically, I asked the following question: Was the decision on the part of the Norwegian government to seek access to international police cooperation measures and instruments adequately founded on popular knowledge and sentiments? In conclusion, many minor changes may individually not change the character of the cooperation, but the result may, over time, amount to substantial transformation. It seems fair to say that the assessment and subsequent information and justifications given to the Norwegian citizens, were inadequate.

75 St.prp.nr.50 (1998–99):ch.7.4.3.4.

8 External sovereignty

Norway and EU institutions

Relevant rules and regulations building upon the Schengen *Acquis* apply to Norway as a result of the Association Agreement. The EU Court of Justice has ruled in a way that implicitly assumes jurisdiction over the Association Treaty.[1] A treaty between the EU, Norway and Iceland has also been signed, committing the parties to implement all provisions on the EU mutual assistance and its protocol that do *not* fall within the scope of the Schengen *Acquis*.[2] The structure and institutions of the EU to some extent constitute a supranational entity, and this thus also affects Norway. Some has argued its turn towards a federal state.[3] An introduction to the Union institutions is relevant to comprehend Norway's sovereignty in the context of the EU non-membership, but also, at the same time, membership in *some* of the EU police cooperation instruments.

The term 'external sovereignty' refers to non-subordination of state power to a foreign will, to the extent that self-determination is diminished.[4] As shown above, the international agreements are not as such sovereignty-infringing in the sense that Norway cannot withdraw from these, if the cooperation is no longer wanted. The same applies, obviously, as regards the role of Norway in, or her subjection to, the EU institutions that are presented in the following. My point is, though, to underline how Norway is involved or affected by EU institutions *despite of* the country's non-EU membership, and ask whether her external sovereignty may be seen as diminished as a result. This brings us to the second of my research questions:

> *To what extent has the Norwegian government ceded decision-making competence to other agents on policing matters?*

This question cuts to the core of a traditional notion of sovereignty: Is the state still free to make its own decisions? The point in the following is to briefly describe how the Union works, and what part Norway has and does not have in and with that system.

8.1 The EU political institutions

The EU has three central political institutions: the European Parliament (Parliament/EP), the European Council (Council), and the European Commission (Commission).

1 Case C–436/03 Van Esbroek.
2 [2004] OJ L 26/1 (preamble no.6).
3 Pelinka 2011.
4 E.g. Grimm (2015): Chapter B, III.

DOI: 10.4324/9780429503696-9

According to the 2012 official report on the Norwegian agreements with the EU, the Parliament has traditionally not been an important contact point for Norway. After the Lisbon Treaty, however, there has been increased work also in the Norwegian Parliament (*Stortinget*) to influence the EP and debate with EP politicians, since this is perceived as a more open forum, also for the Norwegian 'outsiders', than the Council and Commission.[5]

The role of the European Parliament has become increasingly more important. A major shift occurred with the Lisbon Treaty, from the EP being a mostly consultative body to having rights of legislative initiative and decisions alongside the Council on most of the Union policy areas.[6] The Council and Parliament also have the budgetary authority (art.16 TFEU, arts.294;225;314;312 TFEU), and the powers of scrutiny and overseeing powers over the other EU bodies (arts.233;290;291 TFEU). The Parliament must also be consulted on common foreign and security policies (art.36 TEU).[7]

As a non-member of the Union, Norway is not a participant in the Council (or member of the European Council). The Council is made up of Minister Representatives of the member states, and as such represents the national interests to some extent. Further, Norway's intake in this work is either through meetings alongside other third countries, subject to Council invitation; through informal meetings and dialogues; and through formal contact points in the EEA context or bilaterally with various EU countries. Norway has access to the Council structure, however, when Schengen-relevant matters are discussed. When the Council is addressing such matters, the meetings take place within the Mixed Committee (SAA arts.3–5). This implies that Norwegian officials participate in the primary preparation for legislative proposals; on the first committee level of the Council preparation; and within the ambassadors' meetings within Coreper II. The right to participation entails *being present,* not a right to vote. Norway may suggest proposals (art.4 no.4) and express opinions on any matters (no.2). The Mixed Committee shall ensure that Norwegian (and Icelandic) concerns are duly considered (no.1). Representatives of the Ministry of Justice, the Police Directorate and other justice authorities participate each week in Council meetings in Brussels. This participation, according to the 2012 Committee, ensures that Council documents with relevance for Norwegian policy areas linked to Schengen are thoroughly prepared and politically assessed also by non-EU member states.[8] The Committee also informed that although Norway had been invited to 98 of 143 informal ministry meetings in the Council in the period 2007–2011, the cabinet ministers do not as a general rule prioritise to attend these meetings.[9] There may be several explanations to this; a lack of time, a lack of priority, or a lack of perceived influence. Without empirical studies, this is mere speculations.

The voting of new EU actions in the Council is done according to qualified majority (art.16 nos.3–5). The Council is also in charge of coordination of the economic politics of the Union; the negotiation with third countries and international organisations (arts.218 TFEU;37 TEU); development of common foreign and security policies (art.22 TEU); and

5 NOU 2012:2 pp.181–182.
6 The Commission may also *propose* laws for adoption by the Council or Parliament. As of 2012, ordinary citizens may petition the Commission to propose laws on their behalf, if the proposal is backed by one million people (art.11[4] TEU; 24[1] op.cit.).
7 The EU Ombudsman is employed by the Parliament, who reports back to the Parliament on mistakes committed by the EU bodies (art.228 op.cit.).
8 NOU 2012:2 pp.180–182.
9 NOU 2012:2 p.178–179.

the coordination of the cooperation on the criminal procedural areas of courts and police cooperation (e.g. chapter 4 of Title V, TFEU). A legislative 'emergency brake' can be pulled if members of the Council consider that a draft directive will affect fundamental aspects of their criminal law; they can demand that the directive be referred to the European Council, and the legislative procedure is suspended and subject to further *forarbeid*.[10]

The main task of the Commission is to carry out the decisions made by the Parliament and the Council (arts.17 TEU;249–250 TFEU). The Commission also supervises the member states' compliance with the treaty regulations. The Commission may start proceedings before the CJEU, where it believes a member state is not fulfilling its obligations (TFEU art.228). In the other EU governmental bodies, members may promote their own national interests and issues, but the Commission acts independently of the member states. It shall solely ensure and forward the interests of the EU itself (art.17 TEU). This national 'disinterest' makes the Commission the negotiator of international agreements on behalf of the EU (Council), for example, with Norway. The competence to negotiate international agreements, arguably, emphasises the supranational 'government character' of the EU.[11]

Despite the non-EU member status, Norway does have, because of the European Economic Area agreement (EEA, see Chapter 6.1), so-called 'national experts' working both in the Commission and in other agencies of the EU.[12] The job of the national experts is to aid in the work of the various General Directorates of the Commission (DGs), with the same responsibilities as the permanent employees of the Commission. The Norwegian state pays the salaries of the national experts, but has no instruction competence over them. They are, however, from a Norwegian Ministry of Foreign Affairs point of view, considered useful to gain insight in and first-hand knowledge of – and even some influence over – the political processes of the EU.[13] The Norwegian EU ambassador stated in 2009 that the growing number of EU bodies and bureaus is a challenge to the Norwegian possibilities to influence EU policy development, since Norway rarely may claim any position in these bodies when similar institutions are not created on the EFTA side.[14] The EFTA states are also entitled to participate in the working groups that process the legislative proposals from the Commission, and in the comitology procedures when the Commission has delegated legislative competence.[15]

8.2 The Court of Justice of the European Union

Since Norway is not an EU member, it is not, as a point of departure, subject to the Court of Justice of the European Union (CJEU) jurisdiction. Given the requirement of uniform application of the agreements' measures, however, CJEU court practice concerning the application of Schengen or EEA-relevant measures may have significant impact on how the Norwegian courts may adjudicate, the Government legislate, and the Public Administration Act. In the police and police cooperation matters, this is – for now – of less importance, since the Court does not have jurisdiction over such activities. This also follows in SAA art.9, as for national court practice. A differentiated interpretation or application may lead

10 In that case, the ordinary procedure is suspended (Art.20[2] TEU, Art.329[1] TFEU).
11 Gundersen 2010 ch.3.
12 Declaration to art.100 of the Agreement.
13 Difi Rapport 2012:1.
14 Quoted in NOU 2012:2 p.177. See also generally Fossum and Eriksen 2014.
15 NOU 2012:2 p.180.

to the termination of the Schengen Agreement for Norway (SAA arts.10–11). The influence on and jurisdiction over Norway is discussed further below in ch.8.5–6.

According to the principle of subsidiarity (art.5[3] TEU), the EU institutions should not intervene when the member states may take satisfactory action on their own. The principle does not apply when the EU has exclusive competence. The EU *may* take action, however, when the objectives of an action are not fulfilled by the member state. This principle is included in the treaties to ensure that power is exercised as close to the citizen as possible. To make the Union function homogenously, it has since the beginning been considered necessary to have a centralised court adjudicating disputes between the member states, and between member states and the Union on application and fulfilment of the EU law. The Court also gives preliminary rulings and advice when requested by the national courts, and may give verdicts in cases where subjects of EU law (individuals, companies or organisations)[16] claim 'direct action' for some damage inflicted by the Community. The CJEU's judgements are binding for the national courts and member states' governments in general.[17]

EU law may be adjudicated both in national legal systems and in the CJEU, but the latter has the responsibility of making sure EU law is applied in the same way in all member states. The competence of the Court was originally limited to EC law, but the Lisbon Treaty extended the Court's jurisdiction to include the entire body of EU law.

At 1 December 2014, the transition period ended of the most far-reaching innovation in the criminal justice area stemming from the Lisbon Treaty. This is the extension of scrutiny power by the EU Commission and Court of Justice over the member states' implementation of EU criminal justice law.[18] There are, in other words, supranational institutions in the international entity the states have established and joined into, that now may overrule these member states' legal system. Both EU and member state legislation concerning the EU justice and home affairs area, such as police cooperation and security measures, are subject to judicial review. All member state national penal legislation enacted to comply with EU regulations can now also be reviewed before the CJEU. Examples of EU regulations with a criminal justice subject matter are e.g. those concerning money laundering.[19] The Court cannot, however, try the validity or proportionality of actions by the law enforcement agencies whilst maintaining law and order or safeguarding of internal security, i.e. the operational activities as such.[20] Legality can also be reviewed when it concerns some restrictive measures against natural or legal persons, e.g. the freezing of accounts of suspected terrorists.

The CJEU also has jurisdiction over acts of the Commission, the Council, the European Council, the European Parliament, and institutions and other agencies of the Union.[21] This is not directly relevant primarily for the police cooperation measures, given the above-mentioned delimitations to operational police activity. It does, however, signal the increase in EU power in the supranational area, and thus generally the Court's influence on former 'absolutist' state sovereign areas. The extension in 1999 of the Court's jurisdiction implied, I would argue, quite a big step on an integration scale. And this may serve to show how the

16 Art.263(4) TFEU.

17 The general regulations on the Court are laid out in TFEU section V.

18 [2012] OJ C 326/1; Mitsilegas *et al.* 2014.

19 Framework Decision on money laundering and confiscation of 5 July 2001 2001/500/JHA (2001). The general trend has been that criminalisation can be imposed to a certain degree when the actions may affect other interests within the ambit of EU legislation.

20 Art.276 TFEU.

21 Arts.263 and 267 op.cit.

Schengen cooperation that Norway entered into in the late 1990s has become something rather different than it was at the time of the association.

8.2.1 Legislative procedure post-Lisbon

The removal of the pillar system introduced the ordinary legislative procedure (qualified majority voting [QMV])[22] also to the area of policing. Art.87 sets up important divisions between the different legal bases and procedures for EU policing law, where some are still subject to what is termed a 'special legislative procedure'. Art.87(3) opens up for a fast-tracking procedure in case of non-unanimity on issues *not* affecting the Schengen Acquis. The procedure in 87(3), similar to that of 86(1) is to some extent identical to the process of the emergency brake rules, except in contrast to the latter, fast tracking involves MS requesting, not vetoing, to invoke the special procedure. There are two distinct issues regarding this 'pseudo-veto':[23] One is that the Treaty rules do not regulate a potential failure to reach an agreement in the Council. This is unlikely, given that the nine MS who have suggested the enhanced cooperation legislation should be inclined to accept the terms suggested. The other issue is the possibility for those desiring 'enhanced cooperation' to change the decision-making regulations from unanimity to QMV, and a special legislative procedure into an ordinary legislative procedure.[24] This form of enhanced cooperation among some MS is considered by the EU to be "a last resort, when it has established that the objectives of such cooperation cannot be attained within a reasonable period by the Union as a whole".[25] The special and to some extent secluded cooperation must be furthering to the Union's objectives, protect its interests and reinforce its integration process, etc., and not be disrespective of non-participating MS' competences, rights and obligations.[26] There is no reference to enhanced cooperation agreements outside of the EU legal framework such as the Schengen cooperation.[27] The European Public Prosecutors Office (EPPO) may *become* an example, as it so far follows the same pattern as the Schengen Agreement; it is in function within some countries as a 'laboratory' before a prospective later implementation into the EU proper.[28]

While the decision-making process remains unanimous voting in the Council and consultation of the EP as regards to legislation in the operational police cooperative area,[29] QMV is accepted on non-operational legislation.[30] This means that all police cooperation measures regarding intelligence work and information systems and exchange may be legislated with

22 Art.294 TFEU.
23 Peers 2011:70.
24 Art.333 TFEU.
25 Art.20(2) TEU.
26 Art.20(1) TEU and Arts.326–27 TFEU.
27 Peers 2011:93. Although such a statement seems to emphasise more the commercial aspects, and not the FSJ aspects, this might be a good consideration of applicable values.
28 More on EPPO Chapter 10.2.2.
29 This legislation procedure is now termed the 'special legislative procedure' in art.289(2). These procedures concern approximately 30 legal bases in the Treaty. The Council and EP are still involved in the adoption of legislation in these processes, but they are subject to somewhat different rules than those governing the ordinary legislative procedure. Contrary to the special procedure as regards police cooperation (art.89), concerning e.g. the enhanced powers to the European Public Prosecutor, it involves unanimity and consent of the EP (art.86, see Peers 2009).
30 Art.87(2) TFEU.

qualified majority. Operational – and as such potentially coercive – police work is thus still placed within the remit of member states' sovereignty. There is, though, a very strong link between the gathering of and analysis of information and operational activities taking place as a consequence of shared information.[31]

8.3 Influence and the Schengen Mixed Committee

Norway has no say in decision-making on Schengen-related acts. Each act must, however, be implemented specifically in Norwegian law; they do not have so-called 'direct effect' (art.8 [2]).[32] Norway could influence and cooperate in the decision-making procedures ("decision-shaping"), but not in the decision-making itself (CISA art.140). This would take place through the so-called Mixed Committee (*fellesorganet*), with meetings at expert, civil servant and ministerial levels. While Norway and Iceland could not participate in the decision-making process, they had proposal competence, and the same rights as the member states to discuss the propositions. Decisions that were made in the EU that would have implications for the Schengen cooperation, have to pass the consultative mechanism in the cooperation agreement (art.2.3 cf. art.3.[a]). All new Schengen relevant regulations should, as a general rule, be implemented simultaneously and equally within all Schengen member countries (art.8[3]). If Norway and Iceland were to not implement at the same speed, or at all, the agreement would be abolished within three months. Such abolition could be decided by any party to the agreement without any further justification, and this was a vital part of the sovereignty discussion: There was no mechanism to force Norwegian authorities to act or implement against their will.[33] Norway has not employed the right to veto up to this date. It has been argued that Norway in reality has a 'veto by proxy' in EU matters concerning Schengen, since Sweden in particular would go far to avoid guarding a border towards a 'third country' Norway.[34]

The final proposal to *Stortinget* briefly repudiated supranational concerns as to the changes to police measures with the Schengen cooperation. Norwegian police will (and have) access to the Schengen Information System, but there would not to be any centralised authority that would have decisive influence over the Norwegian authorities on any level.[35]

As a member or associated member of the EEA and the Schengen Agreements, Norway is bound to obey and implement Schengen-relevant or EEA measures decided in the EU.[36] Norway has in many ways less political influence in the EEA Agreement (see Chapter 6.1) than it has in the Schengen cooperation within the EU. The EFTA experts have access and take part in some of the working parties and committees chaired by the Commission, but none of those chaired by the Council or in the Council itself. The Schengen Agreement gives Norway access to all levels of decision *shaping*, but no saying in the final decision *making*.[37]

31 Peers 2011:906.

32 1999 Schengen association agreement (SAA).

33 Innst.S.nr.147 (1998–1999):2–3.

34 Bull 1997:151.

35 St.prp.nr.42 (1996–1997) ch.3.

36 Bull argues that since Norway and Iceland share all obligations of the Schengen cooperation, it could be a natural consequence that they also had a part in the decision-making (op.cit.:151).

37 The justification seems to be that where there are *practical* problems to be solved, e.g. in relation to border control and crime tendencies, the inclusion is more relevant also to the EU (Bull 1997).

There have been two main challenges to Norwegian Schengen influence. Although the Schengen agreement is clear on the matter – the associated members shall be consulted in the same manner as the EU member states on the applicable planned measures – the division between Schengen-relevant and non-relevant may be hard to maintain in practice. Further, the Norwegian agreements that must be negotiated separately may be outdated, and that they are not automatically updated when new instruments are established in the EU. This was the case with the Cooperation Agreement between Norway and Eurojust (see Chapter 9.4). This may also entail that Norway finds herself part of a cooperation that is different than the one they negotiated membership in (on the terms at the moment); another, the exclusion that could result from negotiations that are not unsuccessful due to EU member states' unwillingness. Notable, however, is that both Eurojust and Europol have gained legal status of their own, meaning that the EU does not, as a whole, need to ratify new agreements or amendments such as where a few countries are blocking Norway's entry into the EAW.

The abolition of the pillar system in the Lisbon Treaty, and thereby the transfer of the justice and home affairs matters, such as police cooperation matters, into EU law, was another challenge for Norway. This implied the removal of the more 'natural' separation of issues that could and could not be considered Schengen-relevant. This has led to situations where Norway has claimed issues to be Schengen-relevant, because of a desire to join and/or influence the EU, but where the EU has refused. Prominent examples are Europol, Eurojust and the European Arrest Warrant.[38] Dissolving the pillar system also had benefits, related to what has arguably been too strong a focus on the EU crime control instruments. The pillar system kept Norway completely outside of the first pillar issues, such as social strategies that could be promoted in addition to, and balancing of, the introduced crime control instruments.

8.4 Foreign courts with jurisdiction over Norwegian police activities

The question is whether this state of affairs challenges Norway and EU or Schengen member states' ultimate decision competence over their police forces and their crime control or public order strategies. Two issues are relevant here. One is the jurisdiction of national courts in 'each other's' cases, in other words, whether in, for example, a joint operation consisting of several countries' law enforcement authorities, the participants may decide for themselves which country shall prosecute the other issue, which is discussed first, concerns whether the supranational courts may rule or advise in ways that overrule Norwegian authorities, and thus sovereign competence; starting with the EFTA Court, followed by the EU Court of Justice.[39]

8.4.1 The ESA and the EFTA Court

Any criminal law provisions or policing procedures, that may affect the internal market regulations of the EU (e.g. provisions or procedures that may be in breach of one of the

38 Tanil 2012.

39 The European Court of Human Rights (ECtHR) undoubtedly has this competence, although the extent may be disputed.

four freedoms), may be subject to an EFTA Court ruling. All new relevant EU legislation is also introduced through the EEA Agreement. Judicial control of the EEA takes place through the EFTA Surveillance Authority (ESA) and the EFTA Court.

The ESA monitors compliance with EEA rules, ensuring that these internal market rules are applied homogenously in the EU and the EEA. The surveillance system has two pillars: EU member states are supervised by the European Commission; while the participating EFTA states are supervised by the EFTA Surveillance Authority.[40] Norwegian compliance with the EU/EEA law is generally subject to four levels of controls; through Norwegian public administration; through Norwegian courts of law; by the ESA (with responsibilities similar to the Commission); and by the EFTA Court (similar to the EU Court).[41] The ESA and the EFTA Court only have jurisdiction over the EEA Agreement, and not any other Norwegian agreement with the EU, such as the Schengen Agreement. The Committee that prepared the 2012 report on Norway's relationship with EU emphasised that the opportunities for Norwegian participation and influence were far better in the original Schengen Cooperation Agreement (i.e. before the *Association* Agreement) than in the later EEA development.[42] The Data Retention Directive[43] was initially seen as one of the few controversial Schengen-relevant measures that Norway should, many believed, consider to veto. Instead, the Directive was re-interpreted as EEA relevant since it was deemed to be a regulation of the telecommunications market. The Directive was thereby implemented in Norway, only to be rejected by the CJEU.[44] This may be seen as a symbol of the Norwegian 'over-accomplishment' of EU policing and police relevant measures. Norway is a full-fledged EEA member and thus subject to these internal market regulations. The Norwegian government may of course withdraw from the agreements if it disagrees with a ruling or recommendation, but these international influences do surely affect the way the state of affairs is conducted internally. The over-accomplishment is arguably a symbol of not exercising the sovereign right – duty? – to debate and individually assess the currents from the EU.

8.4.2 CJEU and Norway

The CJEU does not have direct jurisdiction over Norway, as a non-EU member. Its decisions and recommendations will, however, have strong implications for Norwegian law, and for Norwegian policing, since Norway, through the Schengen Agreement, is bound to develop and maintain a homogenous development of Schengen-relevant practice and regulations as decided by the EU. Norway will thus, regardless of its non-membership, be bound by the interpretations given by the Court to EU member states. In other words: the decisions from the CJEU are in reality binding for Norwegian authorities, including the political government, the Norwegian courts, and to some extent also Norwegian police officers and their work in practice.

Before the Lisbon Treaty entered into force in 2009, the EU Court of Justice did not have jurisdiction over matters of policing and police cooperation. For Norway, this implied

40 [1994]OJ L 344/1, with amendments up to September 2013.

41 NOU 2012:2 p.198.

42 Op.cit. p.696.

43 [2006] OJ L 105/54.

44 http://curia.europa.eu/jcms/upload/docs/application/pdf/2014-04/cp140054en.pdf [09.04.14].

that the Schengen-relevant matters in this field were outside the ambit of the supranational court of the EU. Non-compliance with Schengen-relevant measures would previously lead to discussion in the Executive Committee (now the Mixed Committee), and could and can lead to termination of the Norwegian Schengen Association Agreement. An evaluation committee subjected to the Council is responsible for overseeing the states' compliance with the Schengen regulations; this applies both the EU states and the non-EU Schengen states such as Norway. There is, however, no continuous oversight and court control of the Norwegian compliance. This may change after the Court's increased jurisdiction over the Schengen/criminal law/policing matters as well.[45]

The jurisdiction implies that the Court have given rulings on *inter alia* what the member states may and may not do in terms of policing in the border areas. While the actual operational activity is excluded from their jurisdiction, the Court may see, for example, the setting up of a police patrol for temporary border control, which turns out to have the character of more constant control, as illegal. A specific example, and one that limits both the Norwegian legislator and the Norwegian police's more or less unofficial guidelines and practices, may be that in accordance with the so-called Schengen Borders Code,[46] member states may exercise their police powers within all their territories; also border zones. Nonetheless, since border checks of persons are absolutely prohibited, the enforcing of such police power must not in any way be equivalent to a border check.[47] The Schengen Borders Code has set out guidelines on the basis of the Court's rulings, which Norway thus should follow in order to ensure equal practice throughout the Schengen Area.[48]

8.5 Jurisdiction and investigation

While the CJEU may influence the state's allocation of police personnel and resources, and to some extent the regulation of crime control measures, another jurisdictional question is relevant in the governing of police operations, namely that of prosecutorial jurisdiction. There is no single international specific principle determining which state has jurisdiction over a criminal investigation when several states are affected by the crime/s in question. There are far more specific rules regarding civil jurisdiction and several principles governing the jurisdiction concerning the trial itself. It has been argued that it is harder to find a state with no jurisdictional claim, than figuring out which state actually has jurisdiction.[49] The result is frequent conflicts of jurisdiction, since too many states may be in the position to start prosecution.[50]

The mandate is governed by the jurisdictional rules of the state; in the case of Norway, the question is whether the crime in question is subject to territorial jurisdiction; to active (by Norwegians abroad) or passive (against Norwegians abroad) nationality jurisdiction; or to the so-called universal jurisdiction principle implying that *all* states have jurisdiction over

45 NOU 2012:2 p.697.
46 [2006] OJ L 105/1.
47 See also on control inside the Schengen area in Karanja 2008:384–393.
48 C–278/12 PPU Atiquallah Adil v. Minister voor Immigratie, Inegratie en Asiel; C–188/10 and C–189/10 Aziz Melki and Sélim Abdeli.
49 Steyerlynck and Thomaes 2002:10–11. See their study for presentation and discussion of the various jurisdictional principles. Although the study was performed over ten years ago, there do not seem to be any clear solution(s) to these challenges yet.
50 See practical suggestions for solutions from a Norwegian point of view in Ruud 2016.

some particularly heinous crimes such as genocide.[51] To some extent, national jurisdictional principles may overlap, leading to potential lacunas, or to double criminality. Chapter 3 of the Schengen Convention regulates the application of the *ne bis in idem* principle; that no one, as a general rule, shall be prosecuted for the same acts more than once in any member state. Again, this only points at the actual prosecution, not investigation. But any conclusive finalisation from the prosecution; anything that prevents further prosecution in *one* state, falls within this scope. *Ne bis in idem* is also regulated in the ECHR seventh additional protocol 4 and the UN CIVPOL Convention art.14 no.7, but these both regulated the principle within *one* state.[52] The problem with the basic territoriality principle in the context of this book – the principle that any state has jurisdiction over crimes committed wholly or partly on their territory – is that the crimes (or, in the case of order policing 'disorderly elements') in question will almost *always* to some extent be committed in more than one state, given the cross-border element. There are several international regulations of such questions, and some have been set out in the EU *Acquis*. Several measures have required EU member states to criminalise certain acts. This does not in principle imply a prioritisation of the police's work; it is still the public prosecutor that decides independently whether or not criminal investigations shall be initiated when a crime is reported to them or made apparent in other ways.[53] The *failure* to investigate certain crimes that affects the international commitments that Norway has through the EEA, Schengen or other agreements, however, may have serious implications. Art.4(3) TEU states that the member states must "take any appropriate measure, general or particular, to ensure fulfilment of the obligations arising out of the Treaties or resulting from the acts of the institutions of the Union". The Commission oversees the application of Union law, cf. TEU art.17 no.2, and may bring a potential breach before the Court, cf. TFEU art.258(2). The Court may require the member state to comply with its verdict, and even in some cases impose economic sanctions on that state, cf. TFEU art.260(2) and (3). While individuals may not in person bring a case to the Court, they may, when directly affected by an EU measure (e.g. when it is not fulfilled, or such), make a member state or the Commission aware of the issue, and request their assistance.[54] Perhaps more important is the effect the Court's case law and EU regulations have within national law, which the individual may argue in *national* courts.[55] In the Lisbon Treaty, the Council gained the authority to draw up "strategic guidelines for legislating an operational planning", and a standing committee was designated to following up the promotion and strengthening of the operational cooperation on internal security (arts.71;240 TFEU).[56] The European Public Prosecutor's office may be a solution; so also recommendations of Eurojust (see Chapter 10.2).

The lack of clear procedural rules concerning investigative 'leadership'. This may imply a possibility for 'forum shopping' in the choice of the appropriate state to lead an investigation. The lack of such clear rules are not directly infringing on the individuals' rights to foreseeability of their legal situation. Unpredictability concerning which state leads the investigation of a crime is not problematic as long as the act in question is criminalised in

51 Peers 2011:823–4.

52 See more as regards the *ne bis in idem* limitations to prosecution and extradition in Rui 2009; Mathisen 2009.

53 Extensively and in depth of the development in Norway of the right and duty for the police and prosecution to investigate and prosecute in Kjelby 2013.

54 Gundersen 2010:119.

55 Emphasised for example in the extensive *Europautredning*, NOU 2012:2, pp.198 ff.

56 [2010] OJ L 52/50.

the countries concerned, and the rules on guilt and exemptions from punishment are the same. This is by and large the situation in the cooperating EU countries (including Norway).

Still, there is something not quite right about a level of arbitrariness concerning leadership of investigations. The decisions could favour the states with the most eager prosecutorial or political authorities and disfavour the others. There may be various reasons for wanting and not wanting to take on cases with cross-border elements, such as the economic burdens for the police, a resulting decrease in 'easy, rapidly solved cases', corrupt police systems and even repercussions for local police from mafia-like groups in some countries. Either way one looks at it, it implies that the monopoly on investigation and prosecution decisions – integral parts of the state monopoly on violence – is challenged to some extent. It could also affect the level of punitiveness across the states, since some law enforcement authorities may be more or less punitive or lenient in their approach to indictments, etc.[57]

This chapter has argued that the impact of the EU bodies and institutions on the Norwegian policing situation has been greater than anticipated 20 years ago. The Norwegian policing situation needed change, according to the Government in the 1990s. Although the change would imply a shift of Norway's sovereign police monopoly, this was worth it, for two reasons in particular: the maintenance of the traditional Nordic cooperation relationships, and the efficient policing of the expected increase in border-crossing crime and migration. As for the managing and steering of investigation operations within Norway, the *de jure* competence is still squarely placed with the Norwegian police and prosecution authorities. In practice, however, there may be a certain degree of external influence and even pressure present. The number of provisions regulating autonomous foreign police activities has grown, but is not necessarily part of the Norwegian legislation (yet). The legislation is, however, becoming increasingly open-ended). It is no longer only serious border-crossing crime that may warrant the crossing of borders by foreign police: 'ordinary' policing (order policing) is also increasingly being performed irrespective of borders and nationalities.

The EFTA Court and the EU Court of Justice both have a certain level of influence on Norwegian legislation, also in the criminal law and policing area. The jurisdictional rules are underdeveloped. While investigation operations must always adhere to the relevant national law, the increased cross-border cooperating and internationalisation of police and prosecution agencies may, for example lead to investigation efforts (e.g. through Eurojust) being moved from the administrative level of the home state to another state. This development may, as such, be seen as a weakening of the link between the state and the police.

Norway is obviously a sovereign and autonomous state, considering that the Government has a veto right, which according to both agreements (following only slightly different processes), generally will terminate Norway's membership.[58] There are no other direct consequences apart from the termination itself, although there would obviously be political and financial costs.

In the following, the effects of these impacts and changes are discussed.

8.6 Effects for the state and state sovereignty

The dynamic and quite radical development from the early economic cooperation within the European community, to the present full-fledged Union encompassing more and less binding cooperative instruments on all kinds of policy areas. Several very important

57 See in this line also Snacken 2012.

58 EEA Agreement art.102 (terminates the agreement for *all* EFTA states); SAA art.8 no.4.

developments happened through the 1990s, including the creation of the EU's goal of establishing and maintaining an *Area* of Freedom, Security and Justice on 'its' territory.[59] The Union area is surrounded by one common, external border towards the non-Union area. As mentioned already, police and crime control, which is within the core of the area of freedom, security and justice, are generally also considered core aspects of national sovereignty. *International cooperation on* such issues is not in itself infringing on national sovereignty. The question is whether the cooperation has evolved into something outside of national 'control', so that the nation states' sovereignty is weakened in a manner that they do not want or realise.

It has been claimed by several scholars that after the very rapid development the past twenty years or so in the criminal justice area on European level, states are no longer exclusive holders of sovereign power. There are two significant changes in more old-fashioned cooperation between states. One is that the cooperation increasingly involves *individuals*. The other is that the international entities, meaning non-state actors, are growing in autonomy and importance. States are still the main subjects of international law. However, the states do not any longer have the monopoly of *production* of the inter- or transnational law.[60] The international organisations have gradually transformed – or are being transformed – into global governance institutions. And these institutions no longer only regulate states, like international law traditionally did, but increasingly also individuals, including the way states treat their own citizens. This may be seen as redefining traditional state sovereignty: As a result, states are bound by rules and regulations that make the old images of international society and the consent-based production of international law appear anachronistic.[61]

While community law always had "led to the erosion of national sovereignty through granting rights to citizens", the EU criminal law development can be seen as reversing this paradigm.[62] The emphasis in EU criminal law instruments was firmly in facilitating the exercise of state powers rather than bestowing rights upon individuals. This is not uncontested: the very point of the AFSJ was an aim of providing the European citizens with an adequate protection against the threats of crime.[63] Before the Lisbon Treaty entered into force in 2009, a large part of the 'justice and home affairs' were *outside* of the communitarian sphere, mostly safely lodged in the third pillar out of reach of a supranational touch.

Connolly argued that terrorism as a form of *non-state* 'war', rather a war against a network instead of another state, has challenged the notion of the 'inherent' sovereign state power.[64] The joint fight against terrorism has called attention to the fragility of territorial order, and thus offers a manner for states to reaffirm the state system, quashing the network of non-state power anomaly. The question is whether the same logic may be used in the 'European area of criminal justice'. While there is not necessarily an anomaly to quash, I would argue that the EU and Schengen cooperation in criminal justice and border control is a way of fortifying the European nation states. There are undoubtedly some serious transnational crime problems in the contemporary world. The nation states may well be unable to sufficiently fight these alone, at home. In addition, participating in international agreements

59 Ref. Amsterdam Treaty.

60 Cohen 2012 (1985) ch.1.

61 Op.cit.

62 Trinidas in the foreword in Mitsilegas 2009:v.

63 Nuotio 2004:177.

64 Connolly 2002:207.

such as criminal justice fora may, as mentioned above, in itself be a sign of vital sovereignty. The authority of the ruler has been funded on perhaps first violent power, then God, the king or queen, and then to a greater degree *man*, and then man *postmodern*. In contemporary states, this is closely related to the population and its rights.

Although the state monopoly of violence is challenged, or at least different from before, it is equally clear that no other entity has taken over the monopoly. The Norwegian government argues with no less vigour that it is an independent state with ultimate control over the policing measures performed within its territory. Part II of the book shows the expansion of police cooperation measures and instruments that Norway is or will be part of. The expansion is to a limited degree initiated or even influenced by the Norwegian state itself. This sub-chapter discusses the large distance between the initiator of these measures and instruments at the EU level, and the citizens of Norway, from a social contract perspective. A discussion of the development of EU into a state-like entity follows.

In 2013, the Norwegian Government aimed to clarify their current political priorities related to the European cooperation in a Working Program for EU and EEA matters.[65] The Working Program is not a binding legal document. It does, however, give significant signals about how the state, meaning the supreme governing authorities, perceives the relevant situation, current challenges and at least an explanation as to how the resources of the state should be allocated.

The document provides an interesting viewpoint on the lack of independence the Government perceived that Norway has in some areas. Three main policy fields related to police and policing were prioritised: issues of societal security as part of the EEA framework; justice and home affairs cooperation; and security issues related to foreign affairs. The Government emphasised the EU as an important actor for Norwegian societal security in general and the state of (emergency) preparedness in particular.[66] Further, although the 'Area of freedom, security and justice' is limited to the EU, both the causes of the challenges to such an area, and the dealing with such causes, were to a large extent shared with Norway, and closer cooperation should be attempted whenever possible. Sovereignty was considered of paramount importance, though; national enforcement of jurisdiction shall not be impaired: The existing Schengen cooperation is the applicable framework.[67] With a view to the steady expansion of the Schengen cooperation; this seems then as quite a flexible limitation.

The state thus argued on the one hand that it is sovereign, on the other hand that it is placed in a position of interdependence vis-à-vis the international community and the EU in particular. The Government suggested that Norway is more attentive than the EU when it comes to 'root causes' and long-term peacekeeping work.[68] Although Norway apparently agrees with the EU on most crime control issues, it did not accept the EU terrorist list.[69] So the state has not capitulated. It may still be argued, though, that there have been changes to the traditional concept of 'the state' through the development as showed in Part II of this book.

65 Working program for EU/EEC matters 2013. The tendencies are similar in the working program for EU matters 2017.

66 Op.cit.:44.

67 Op.cit.:56.

68 Op.cit.:77 ff.

69 Council Decision 2009/1004/CFSP of 22 December 2009 updating the list of persons, groups and entities subject to Articles 2, 3 and 4 of Common Position 2001/931/CFSP on the application of specific measures to combat terrorism (2009).

8.6.1 The social contract

The social contract implies that citizens give up parts of their freedom to the state to achieve the security they need to enjoy the freedom that remains. The police are thus part of the state's work to secure everyone's freedom.[70] The issue at hand is whether the police cooperation instruments or any changed national measures should be considered illegitimate when they originate at another level than state citizens. Does the legality of the international agreement that is *basing* the international 'legislator', suffice as an alternative?[71]

The production of *security* in the Union Area requires the curtailment of citizens' freedom; to some extent, positive as well as negative freedom. When freedom is curtailed on a supranational level, it becomes even more important that the citizens of member states have a democratic arena to influence or decide *how* they should be controlled and by whom. Being a full-fledged member of the EU would not solve the 'problems' of the dissolved monopoly of violence, or the sovereignty issues that have been discussed. There are clearly similar challenges for the EU members, for examples of trust and efficiency in the implementation on the various developed police cooperation instruments. But this is, of course, particularly challenging for Norway. Even though the international agreements are correctly entered into, the lack of direct influence may be said to have loosened the tie or connection between the citizens and their relevant contract partners.[72]

This tie may be seen as especially important in relation to policing. Not only because of the associated constant potential of violence or intrusions into the private sphere, but also because the *need* of police services that the PA sect.1 is concerned with. I argue that this need may be easy to lose sight of from the perspective of the supranational level. If the lack of political debates in Norway surrounding the implementation of new measures and instruments is anything to go by, it seems that the international level is simply considered the appropriate one to understand the Norwegian situation as well. While this might be correct, it is hard be absolutely sure, given the lack of debates and discussion.

In the following, the question is whether the EU may be seen to be taking over state functions, which could impact whether the 'state' in the Police Act sect.1 is still the same entity, given the development the past 20 years or so.

8.6.2 The EU as a state?

The EU has competences only as conferred by the member states, and when conferred, only to the extent that the competences are in accordance with the principles of subsidiarity and proportionality.[73] Constraining the execution of EU powers, the principle of subsidiarity delimits the EU from taking action instead of the member states, if the actions could be performed at the national level. Furthermore, the EU involvement must not be of greater

70 Berlin *et al.* 2002; Hobbes 1998 [1651]; Rousseau 1958 [1762]; Locke: book II. Others have claimed that this is a faulty understanding of the state-consequences following the Westphalian peace; that the states are such understood because they are constantly at a terror-balance or war – not respecting territorial borders. The territorial state delimitation is still applicable, one may argue, regardless the process.

71 The 'democracy deficit' of the EU is not this thesis' primary research object. See for example Moravcsik 2002; Føllesdal and Hix 2006; a body of research from the Norwegian ARENA Centre, e.g. Eriksen 2008; Eriksen and Fossum 2001.

72 E.g. Lavenex 2010:473–5.

73 Arts.4 no.1 cf. 5 no.1 TEU.

extent than necessary to achieve the objectives of the EU treaties. The member states and the Union have *shared competences* in the principal Area of freedom, security and justice.[74] This implies that the member states have the right to legislate in the relevant area of law, but if the EU legislates on the same matter, the EU law prevails.

Security enactment in the development of an *area of security* is subsidiary, e.g. in relation to the development of police cooperation at an EU level. The question here is whether what may be looked at as dissolution of the monopoly of violence is in accordance with the principles of subsidiarity and proportionality? While Norway is not an EU member state, the question is relevant to Norway, because Norway in many ways is *acting* like a member state; most EU instruments are quickly incorporated, or association agreements drafted. A growing supranational state-like entity that Norway has increasingly broader and deeper policing cooperation agreements with, may be said to impact the sovereignty (or perception thereof) also of Norway.

The described developments described may be said to challenge the Weberian notion of state monopoly on legitimate violence. A twist on this notion could be suggested: A state is a state only when it is capable of monopolising legitimate violence within a certain area; in other words, is not contested unduly by other security providers (private, other states, other entities). This is clearly a controversial suggestion. The international police cooperation instruments are described and defended on political and practical levels, are within the ultimate control of Norwegian laws, and thus within sovereign rule. It is *violent force* that is supposed to be monopolised, not any other part of the field of policing. In many countries, the traditional police service and duties are spread out among several agencies, including state, municipal and civilian entities. In Norway, however, there has been strong resistance to dissolving the 'unity police model'. The ten principles of policing, stating *inter alia* that the Norwegian police is *one*, are still frequently reiterated.

It has been reiterated in Norwegian policy documents during the last 100 years that it is among the core tasks of the *state* to ensure order, peace and tranquillity on its territory. Offering citizens security and safety is one way to maintain this order, peace and tranquillity. The globalisation of trade, and similarly, of crime, especially within the internal borderless Schengen Area, has created a common perception that no EU member state has the ability to control borderless crime by itself. Facing these challenges, the states are to some extent unable to provide security and safety on their own. The founding idea of the various systems, practices and policies of police cooperation is that the more than 1.2 million policemen and women working within the member states of the EU will be far more efficient in their work of preventing cross-border crime if they work together.

The increasing fragmentation of bodies and processes within the EU through which the JHA cooperation takes place may suggest that there is a persistent tricky balancing challenge also between what Lavenex calls "looser trans-governmental coordination" and the increase in security cooperation on internal state matters.[75] There are several legal instruments that have been made Norwegian law after being shaped and decided upon outside Norwegian territory, both politically and geographically speaking (the processes were described above; the practical regulations follow in part II). According to Lipset,[76] fledgling states are faced with two related problems: legitimating the use of political power and establishing a national

74 Art.4 no.2 (j) TFEU. This happened after the Lisbon Treaty. See also Cornell 2014.
75 Lavenex 2010:409.
76 Lipset 1963:21.

identity. Following such an understanding, the EU seems to be adding to the sense of European *peoplehood*, and thus, one may argue, legitimising itself further. With the growth particularly of the EU police bodies such as Europol and Eurojust, one may ask whether, or to which degree, there is a *struggle* between the individual nation state and the EU. Defending an idea of a *monopoly* of legitimate violence is getting harder. By providing a common area of freedom, security and justice, the Union is in fact making the citizens face risks, dangers and challenges that the Union in turn tries to provide security from. There would be no need for yet another form of police cooperation framework decision, one could argue, were all the states capable of dealing with their problems autonomously.

Before a democratic state becomes democratic, it must be constituted in an undemocratic fashion. Somebody must decide that *we decide* that this is the time to constitute a state, that these people are its subjects, etc.[77] Following such a reason, one may say that *the* creation of a public prosecutor and a stronger and more closely-knit police force, in itself *constitutes* a community. Citizens demand from their sovereign that he shall protect his people. This virtual contract is agreed upon between the citizen and the nation state government. If another actor, the EU, later shows the citizens that other risks and dangers are looming, other sources of insecurity, that the nation state supplier of security cannot protect the citizen by himself, one may perhaps expect citizens to want to change their contract partner and involve another sovereign.[78]

It has been a common criticism that new forms of police cooperation instruments have been initiated before the instrument they are replacing have even entered into force.[79] According to evaluations, the Swedish Initiative did *not* facilitate the exchange of information it envisaged, because only a few member states used it. The Prüm Decision, however, had proved to be very efficient in identifying criminals and solving crimes.[80] While it may be hard to know whether or not a police measure or new instrument will work or is working, this does not exempt the Government from trying to find out. Other reasons for the impressive tempo the new, often partly overlapping cooperation instruments in the EU have been drafted and implemented, may also be that the production of new instruments demonstrates what may be called 'political vigour'.[81]

The body of *forarbeid* in general is enormous in Norwegian law, and it has been, it seems, growing increasingly faster during the past few decades. The Norwegian society is in many ways far more complex than it used to be. But one could also argue that the increased regulation may heighten the complexity. Bigo discusses how politicians were not historically all that interested in crime, at least not in the context of individual security.[82] The growing state administration in the policing and police cooperation area may be a sign of increased focus on self-legitimation. Mitsilegas argues that the state may be seen as *strengthened*, not weakened, in the era of globalisation.[83] It has extended its reach through *inter alia* and internationalisation of its substantive criminal law, and through securitisation tendencies

77 See e.g. Walker 2004.
78 More in this line in Aas 2007 chapter 6.
79 E.g. Block 2012:99–101; Spapens 2011.
80 Report from the International Centre for Migration Policy Development (ICMPD) (Saloven *et al.* 2010).
81 Also the development of penal law and harmonisation thereof may be discussed as Union activity with a 'nation state' appearance (Nuotio 2005). It acts on what traditionally is within the sovereign competence of the nation states. For discussion on this issue, see e.g. Elholm 2009; Ugelvik 2012.
82 Bigo 2000a.
83 Mitsilegas 2012.

moving immigration control aspects into the increased more general surveillance of all individuals on state territory. The following up on various initiatives by the EU bodies is a way for the state to achieve a type of target objectives proposed to it. The implementation of new EU police instruments and measures may be seen as an easy way to show political vigour also on the national level. It is, further, far easier to show the increased numbers of measures, agreements and instruments, than the actual results at the level of crime rates and statistics.

This chapter has addressed the issue of external sovereignty. To what extent has the Norwegian government ceded decision-making competence to other agents on policing matters? The development described may be said to signal a state that is at least as active in the crime control and policing area as it used to be, but that there are, in addition, more players on the field. Recall the focus of the Norwegian Police Act's purpose: the police service shall be the police service that is needed by the community. It is an open question whether the increased internationalisation, is a suited gauge for what the best, 'needed' crime control and/or policing strategies should be. Viewed together with Norway's *de facto* place in the hierarchy vis-a-vis the EU, there are, arguably, challenges to Norway's external sovereignty.

PART II

EU POLICE COOPERATION

THE PRACTICAL REGULATIONS AND THEIR IMPACT ON NORWAY

Norwegian police are the police of Norway, and 'the police' means those employed in the Norwegian police force. There are, however, complicating factors. The following concerns the practical cooperation with the police of other countries.

There are two main types of cooperation. The first, in criminal matters, primarily consists of mutual judicial assistance, including transmission of cases between the courts in different countries, extradition for prosecution or execution of punishment, including arrest decisions, confiscation and fines, and to some extent the harmonisation of criminal law.[1] The second, in police work, may take the form of joint investigation, joint patrolling or liaison officer cooperation. The two types are, however, not completely distinct. In Norway, the judicial authorities are the courts, the public prosecutor and the chiefs of police. This may not be the same in the legal systems of other countries: Norway, unlike most other European countries, has its prosecution authorities partly intertwined with its police. Police cooperation thus probably involves cooperation with countries where also the judicial authorities are not involved. This division may become blurred when the police's ability to make requests more directly outside the judicial authorities, is increased (e.g. from the previous formal requests for access to data on criminals, to the Prüm cooperation giving direct access to other national systems). It is not blurred in the sense 'hard to determine', but because it may reduce the amount of material that is off limits. The state may, of course, change the areas of responsibility and duties of state organs as it pleases. This may, however, have implications for persons on whom data is exchanged, as regards – for example – when they will get the procedural safeguards connected to being criminally charged.

Most police work is not coercive or operational, but some form of information exchange, between police and individuals, or between police (sometimes across borders). This is therefore the first type of police cooperation dealt with in this part of the book. It is followed by police cooperation through liaison officers follows, before the more operational cooperation is discussed. As in Part I, in Part II I will address two specific research questions (in Chapters 14 and 15 respectively) this factual presentation and discussion.

Among the few legislative changes considered necessary following the Schengen Cooperation, were 1) regulating foreign police authority, which in Norwegian territory was unregulated in the Norwegian Police Act prior to 2001, and 2) removing the regulations concerning Norwegian border control, as the Schengen Cooperation prohibits such control (art.5 [1]). Immigration control was still a vital concern, but then to a greater extent had to be carried out in urban areas (1988 Immigration Act sect.44). External border control

1 E.g. Henricson 2010:33.

DOI: 10.4324/9780429503696-10

competence was also changed, as the CISA rules that only police personnel may perform such control. Such competence had to be delegated to the military personnel guarding the borders.[2] The arrangement on the partial police authority delegated to the military forces on the Norwegian-Russian border was insufficient according to the relevant Schengen evaluation, and necessitated a new paragraph in the 1995 Police Act sect.20. Also, the SIS Act with its personal data rules applying to the pertinent databases, was enacted. The Ministry argued, however, that the legislative change was not necessary because of the Schengen membership, but primarily because the requirements of legal bases of public action had become stricter around the turn of the millennium than in the 1950s when the border-arrangements were made.[3] A few amendments took place subsequently, such as one in 2012 on delegating Norwegian police power to foreign police (PA sect.20a). This will be dealt with below.

2 Some years later, the legislation concerning control of the border with Russia was amended significantly, and resulted in the 2005 Directive (05.08.2005 no.852).

3 Ot.prp.nr.31 (2000–2001):8.

9 Information exchange and analysis

The purpose of police work in the Police Act sect. 1 is unchanged in cross-border operations: it aims to safeguard citizens' security under the law, and their safety and welfare in general. To achieve this, the police have various preventive and operational resources at their disposal.

In Part I, the agreements, and the process of entering into them, were introduced. Some details on how these measures developed will now be given, to show how they have changed since the initial agreements Norway signed. This chapter explores police cooperation through information exchange and analysis. Chapter 10 deals with the actions that may follow a hit in the information databases. Chapter 11 analyses which actions may or must be taken regarding information exchange databases. Chapter 12 gives an account of the liaison officer arrangement, which is an 'in between' form of cooperation. Chapter 13 deals with foreign law enforcement on the territory of other states, i.e. operational cooperation such as hot pursuit and controlled deliveries. Chapter 14 examines joint operations and special intervention units.

Informal international police cooperation such as sharing wanted notices by means such as mail or phone has been taking place for a long time.[1] The exchange of information –by simply talking to another police officer at an international seminar or on the phone, or discussing people, trends, impressions, etc. – may happen without any legal basis, as long as the conversation does not involve breaches of professional secrecy. Confidentiality will often be waived in the interests of investigating, preventing or averting a criminal offence.[2] The main changes brought by the international cooperation mechanisms and instruments may be said to be technical systems (technical solutions, expedience, etc.); accessibility; and the political will or pressure to use the systems.

While Norwegian Schengen membership did not necessarily imply new forms of cooperation measures for the police, it did imply formalisation. Perhaps at least as important as the cooperation, were the data protection regulations concerning such work, and cooperation that had previously taken place informally. Informal cooperation lacked transparency, data protection and oversight, either from the state political authorities, data protection bodies, or the public. Police cooperation involving information registration, and exchange between various crime control actors, will raise issues concerning individual rights. There are an increasing number of databases containing personal data on a wide range of people. Many different police and prosecution actors, from many countries, have access to these systems.

1 E.g. Joubert and Bevers 1996:27–9.

2 PA sect.24(1) with reference to the CPA sects.61a–61e; PRA sect.22–29; Public Adm. Act sect.13–13f.

DOI: 10.4324/9780429503696-11

Swifter information exchange between the police of several countries may challenge the ability of individuals to access personal data, and, as we will see, the increasing number of databases, makes it more difficult for individuals to know whether and/or where information may be stored about them. Data protection, access to data, retention periods and deletion of data are governed by several sets of rules,[3] both nationally,[4] within the various instruments themselves,[5] within general regional 'frameworks',[6] or at the EU level (e.g. the Data Protection Framework Decision).[7]

The objectives of Norwegian police work should as far as possible be achieved through "information, advice, order or warning or by taking regulatory or preventive action" (Police Act sect.6(1), Police Directive sect.3-1). This means as far as possible without coercive measures, understood as physical interference with a person or property (PD sect.3-2). The focus of EU measures on policing has also been on facilitating the gathering, transfer, analysis and exchange of information. There is, however, a close connection between information-related and operational police work: if a Norwegian police officer gets a hit on a wanted person in the Schengen Information System (SIS) when searching for a stolen vehicle this person is in possession of, this 'informational' police activity will probably lead to an arrest. There may be several situations where sharing and comparing data between law enforcement authorities are relevant or necessary. Examples would include solving cases by identifying persons in the DNA or AFIS database of another member state (MS), linking unsolved crimes to other unsolved crimes in different MS and to the same (as yet unidentified) person, etc.

9.1 Informational police work in Norway

The point of departure is the Norwegian legal basis for information gathering and exchange. Police information-gathering does not need a legal basis unless such gathering means invading a person's privacy, according to the principle of legality, which protects individuals from illegitimate governmental interference.[8] This principle, based in Norway on the Constitution (sect.96). ECHR art.8,[9] requires public authorities interfering with an individual's private and family life to have a legal basis, in addition to the action being "necessary in a democratic society" with regard to e.g. prevention of crime or the protection of the rights and freedoms of others (art.8[2]).[10] The 'necessary in a democratic society' criterion recurs in the legal instruments giving the EU or national law enforcement agencies access to information systems, as a limitation on their involvement in cross-border crime-fighting. All the European police cooperation instruments adhere to the ECHR. The ECtHR has established that "necessary" indicates that there is "a pressing social need". This does not mean 'indispensable', but neither does it mean something weaker, such as 'admissible',

3 Now PDA and The Police Registration Act (Prop.114 L (2012–2013)).
4 Such as in the SIS Act, the Personal Data Act and the Criminal Register Act.
5 E.g. within the Europol Regulation, and in the CISA, etc.
6 Such as the Convention for the Protection of Individuals with regard to Automatic Processing of Personal Data (Innst.S.nr.229 (1996–1997):41; 43).
7 de Moor and Vermeulen 2010a:106; [2008] OJ L 350/60.
8 See e.g. Andenæs 1998:176–180; Lund 1996:72–3; 302–304; Eckhoff and Smith 2006:ch.23.
9 The Convention is Norwegian law, prevailing over other Norwegian legislation (Human Rights Act 1999, sect.3).
10 See e.g. Arai 2006; Heringa and Zwaak 2006.

'ordinary', 'useful', 'reasonable' or 'desirable'.[11] There are several legal bases for such encroachments, even when the Norwegian police do things that otherwise would be illegal. The Criminal Procedure Act allows searches (ch.15); concealed video surveillance and technological tracking (ch.15a); seizure (ch.16); communication control (ch.16a) and other audio surveillance of conversations by technological means (ch.16b). In some situations, these measures can be used preventively (ch.17b). The Police Act also gives legitimates such coercive measures as physical searches to establish identity (sect.10).

Perhaps the most important legal regulations, especially as regards international police information exchange, concern the collection and storing of information. Information can be stored by the police, but when computerised and registered, strict limitations apply.[12] The regulations governing the exchange of information involving judicial measures, and that of information exchanged by other law enforcement authorities, followed in a 2013 Directive.[13] The general legal basis for the exchange of information with foreign authorities is in the Act concerning police registering (Police Register Act, PRA)[14], where section 22 regulates all such information exchange outside the SIS Act.[15] PRA sect.22 allows the distribution of information to foreign authorities when necessary in a specific criminal case (at the investigative, preparatory, procedural, execution, follow-up or controlling stage, cf. sect.26), or to prevent crime (sect.22[1]).

Part 12 of the wide-ranging Directive on Police Registers covers information exchange under foreign legal Acts, cf. PRA chapter.[16] The Directive's chapters 70–73 concern the main police information exchange instruments (Eurodac; the 'Swedish Initiative'; the Prüm regulations; and the VIS).[17] All the cooperation mechanisms, except chapter 72 (Prüm) and the DNA regulations have been in force per 01.07.2014. Note that the Act does not apply to the Schengen information exchange regulated by the SIS Act. An in-depth analysis of the Norwegian regulations, including the Police Registration Act, as concerns the police's ability to share data with foreign law enforcement authorities (and the relevant limitations) has been made by Kvam.[18] Compared to his work on this subject, the following is more concerned with the international possibilities for the Norwegian police. The focus here is therefore on foreign or international regulations; the Norwegian regulations will only be referred to when necessary. The Norwegian discussions on who in the police may carry out international information exchange are also analysed.

9.2 The Schengen information cooperation

The Schengen Information System II (SIS) is a database available to the police and immigration authorities of Schengen member states. It is designed "to maintain public policy and public security, including national security, in the territories of the Contracting Parties" (CISA art.93). This purpose should be seen in context with art.39 when the SIS is employed for

11 E.g. Handyside v. UK (1976 1 737)§ 48; Karanja 2008:114.

12 See Wold 2004 ch.6.2.

13 Forskrift om internasjonalt samarbeid i straffesaker (2012).

14 Lov 28.05.2010 no.16.

15 Prop.97 LS (2011–2012).

16 See also the *forarbeid* Ot.prp.nr.108 (2008–2009).

17 Ch.70:(Eurodac) [2008] OJ L 350/60; Ch.71: [2006] OJ L 386/89; Ch.72:(Prüm cooperation) [2010] OJ L 238/1:ch.73: [2008] OJ L 218/129.

18 Kvam 2014.

police purposes, underlining the obligation to assist the other Schengen member states in the prevention and detection of criminal offences, i.e. what may be termed general police work.

The SIS was perceived as necessary for common external border control, and to maintain efficient police cooperation in the Schengen Area.[19] It served the additional purpose of giving the controlling authorities the tools to carry out investigations and crime control, provided certain requirements were met.

Schengen information and intelligence gathering cooperation meant nothing qualitatively new in Norway, as shown above. The legal basis for such international exchanges existed in the Act Relating to Criminal Registration (*strafferegistreringsloven*). International police requests for information would go via Interpol; it would often take several weeks to get an answer.[20]

The SIS is much like an ordinary Norwegian police register. Like the Norwegian Police Registration Act (sect.4), the Convention contains clear requirements as to the purposes for registration (arts.94, 95–100) (I return to these immediately in the next paragraph). Registration must also be in accordance with the general purpose of the Convention, in other words, art.94: "to maintain public policy and public security, including national security".[21] The latter article also gives an exhaustive list of the personal details that may be registered.

The Swedish Initiative Decision of 2006 amended the Convention (art.39 nos.1–3 and art.46). The Decision was Schengen-relevant, and thus applied to Norway. From July 2014, it was regulated in Norwegian law by the Police Register Directive (ch.71). A new development was that the member states were to exchange information using all existing channels, and share information spontaneously with competent authorities in other member states when "there are factual reasons to believe" that this may "assist in the detection, prevention or investigation" of crimes listed in art.2 of the European Arrest Warrant (EAW).[22] A further proviso was that the exchange should accord with the law of the providing state, and "with what is deemed relevant and necessary for the successful detection, prevention or investigation of the crime or criminal activity in question" (art.7[1–2]). There are also regulations to expedite response times.

The Decision clearly states that it does not impose any obligation on member states to gather or store information to assist the law enforcement or judicial authorities of other member states, or on ag state receiving a request for information to carry out coercive measures because of it.[23] As an agreement between member states, this is quite a straightforward international instrument, promising a heightened level of information and intelligence obligation. It is less intrusive (sovereignty-wise) than the mechanisms involving 'supranational hubs' such as Europol. The Decision repeals the provisions of CISA art.39(1–3) relating to exchange of information for the purpose of conducting criminal investigations or intelligence operations.

In the early 2000s, a new generation SIS was planned, both to meet technical difficulties arising from the expected EU expansions of 2004, and the need for more SIS functionality, such as the inclusion of biometric data like photos and fingerprints, and the interlinking of alerts (e.g. a stolen car linked to a missing firearm used in a robbery). In 2005, the Prüm Treaty was signed. Increased operationalisation of police competences, and the start-up of

19 Ot.prp.nr.56 (1998–1999):52.
20 Fijnaut 2010:116.
21 Ot.prp.nr.56 (1998–1999):59–60.
22 [2006] OJ L 386/89 art.6(1); 7(1).
23 Op.cit. preamble (3–5).

SIS II took place in 2007. Before that, because of anticipated delays in SIS II, the intermediate SISone4all was adopted.[24]

The Norwegian SIS Act concerns police cooperation within the SIS system 'in Norway', and applies only to Norwegian use of this information. It involves, however, both information registered by Norwegian authorities, and the use of foreign data by them.[25] The Schengen system is based on mutual trust between the states, and hence the police, on every level. A precondition for Norwegian 'surrender' of authority has been that the control of all police measures ultimately remains Norwegian; this ensures that no action is in breach with Norwegian legislation. This is most important in the case of requests for coercive action from foreign police, which would be prohibited by the principle of legality in Norwegian law. This also follows from the SIS Act sect.5(3), implementing CISA art.95(2), that makes Kripos responsible for examining the legal basis of the requesting state. It also follows from the CISA art.95(2), but not from the SIS Act, that Kripos or the national agency responsible shall, when in doubt, consult the other states involved, to make sure the requirements of legality are met in the requesting state.[26]

9.2.1 The Schengen Information System (SIS)

The Schengen Information System consists of one central reference database (C.SIS) situated in Strasbourg, which is run and maintained by a common support function. Each Schengen member state also has a national SIS database (the N.SIS databases) operated and controlled by the national SIRENE office; in Norway, it is located within Kripos. Searches take place directly in the C.SIS database, but the N.SIS exists both to communicate technically with the central database, and to maintain control over all information registered by national authorities.[27]

The data and information procedure is decentralised in the SIS, meaning that, an officer in any police district may register an alert in the system, regarding, for example a missing person or stolen firearm. The alert must, however, be checked by the SIRENE office before it is transmitted to the C.SIS in Strasbourg. Data may only be registered by an official who has had such a competence in the national system. In Norway, only police officers with public prosecutorial competence may register an alert on an arrest (the SIS Directive sect.1–2). SIS is implemented as part of the national search register ELYS, and the Norwegian police structure. This means that any search in ELYS will generate an alert, if relevant information is contained in the SIS database.

9.2.2 SIS contents, access and processing rules

SIS is primarily a search register. Originally, this was its only function: it allowed competent authorities to register and search in vast numbers of hits on people and things.[28] SISII has developed into a more investigative database, including more diverse data – more like traditional national police databases.

24 Council Document No. 15801/06, pp.14–16.

25 Op.cit.:119.

26 This should have been regulated in the Norwegian SIS Directive, but this never happened (Berg 2011 note 19 to sect.5).

27 St.prp.nr.44 (2007–2008):2.

28 According to a press release from the EU Commission, there were approximately 45 million hits in the system during spring of 2013 (http://europa.eu/rapid/press-release_MEMO-13-309_en.htm [06.01.14]).

The rules of registration and search in the database are strict, and limited to particular purposes, which are listed. Data referred to in art.94 no.2 (persons for whom an alert has been issued; objects referred to in art.100; and vehicles in art.99), may be registered for the purposes specified in articles 95–100 (the Norwegian SIS Act, sects.5, cf. 6–9). These involve: wanted persons for arrest or extradition; third country nationals who have been refused re-entry into Schengen; missing persons or persons who should be placed in police custody; people who are to be summonsed, or are required as witnesses in connection with criminal proceedings; data on vehicles or persons for purposes of surveillance; data on things subject to seizure or needed for use as evidence in criminal procedures. These purposes are accompanied by additional requirements, concurrent in Norwegian law in the SIS Act sects.7–10, as regards the actions requiring to be taken by foreign police, or by Norwegian police. Norwegian police are encouraged to check SIS whenever, for instance, they stop and check someone on the street. Personal data (name, date and year of birth, address or place of work) may be requested from Norwegian citizens if there a need to do so (CPA sect.333 and Police Act sect.8). If people seem foreign and "the time, place and situation give grounds for such a check", police officers also have a responsibility to carry out the state's (border) control of immigrants and foreigners on the territory, which may include a search in SIS.[29]

9.2.2.1 Access and control

One of the innovations resulting from Schengen cooperation was the move from mostly centralised contact between national police authorities to direct communication between officials on local levels (through information exchange and databases searches). Nevertheless, only a limited number of individuals have access to information in the SIS when they perform certain police tasks. The group consists (in Norway) solely of certain Norwegian authorities, and Kripos is still the general national contact point for Norwegian police in their dealings with foreign countries. If a foreign request concerns registry information, Kripos must handle the request; this rule applies to all other foreign requests for police cooperation. Requests from Norwegian police to Interpol or national Interpol agencies also have to be sent through Kripos. The ordinary police may, however, exchange information directly with foreign police when such exchange is unobjectionable.[30] Special rules apply between the Nordic countries.[31]

National authorities have ownership only of data they themselves have registered, even when there are obvious errors, such as incorrect registration of someone's gender (SIS Act sects.2, 5 and 24). Such limitation of both registration and access was insisted on by the Ministry as an important safeguard during the consultative rounds on the SIS Act.[32]

29 Art.21 of [2006] OJ L 105/1.

30 Forskrift om internasjonalt samarbeid i straffesaker (2012) sects. 32–33.

31 Nordic Agreement on Mutual Legal Assistance (Nordic MLA 1974) and Nordic Police Cooperation Agreement (2016 ANPC). Nordic police relations are to a far greater degree built on direct contact outside international channels (Kleiven 2012b).

32 The request from the Customs authorities to have direct access was refused at the time. It is notable that this was changed some ten years later by a legislative decision in 2010 (Prop.94 L (2009–2010), Innst.310 L (2009–2010), Lovvedtak 61 (2009–2010)), but the change has not yet entered into force (June 2014). The custom officers' access is delegated to them both because the Customs Norway and the Ministry of Finance argued that many other Schengen member states had direct access to customs authorities, and because Customs plays an important role in the controlling of the borders (especially immigration control). Delegating 'border control'

The general rules of access follow from the CISA itself, but the structures and arrangements of member states' legal and administrative systems regulate access nationally. Norwegian access rules follow in the SIS Act. While the ordinary police have direct access to searches in the SIS (sect.12), this only applies to authorised officials, when performing border control or "other control" functions ([1]a and [2]). The exhaustive list in sect.12(1) includes such officials; the public prosecutors; parts of the immigration authorities; and authorities responsible for vehicle registration.

Other police authorities may request information from the register when carrying out forms of control other than border control (sect.13[1]b).[33] The principle of necessity is embedded in both sections: information may only be accessed when it is necessary to carry out a specific task. This means, for example, that a police officer cannot search for or use information for unrelated purposes: SIS should not be randomly searched to see if something interesting turns up. The national SIRENE office with the central responsibility for registering and controlling the Norwegian data entries into SIS is in Kripos headquarters.

International organisations also have access, either directly, or via national authorities as in the case of liaison officers, based for example on CISA art.47 and on the EU Framework Decision of 2003.[34] A national police officer accesses data following the normal, national procedures, but the information retrieved may be used in an international forum or mechanism. Europol also has access to the SIS (CISA art.101A).[35] Access is search-only, is purpose-limited, and restricted to certain types of data. This implies registrations based on CISA arts.95, 99 and 100, which are strictly police resources, not administrative resources such as immigration registries. Only authorised Europol and Eurojust staff may perform searches. Europol may not use information from the SIS without the consent of the member state involved. The use itself, given consent, is subject to Europol regulations alone, and not dependent on any national rules (art.101A nos.3;4). Europol may make use of the information within their competences (art.88 TEU), although sharing information with third countries or organisations is also subject to member state consent (no.4).

Eurojust's access to the SIS (art.101B)is even more restricted: it is limited to national members of Eurojust – in other words, staff employed at Eurojust are excluded – and to fewer types of information than Europol can access – only information registered on the basis of arts.95 and 98 (persons wanted for arrest for extradition purposes, for prosecution, or as witnesses). Use of the retrieved data is governed by Eurojust regulations.

As a control measure enabling transparency, all searches in the SIS must be electronically registered; this applies to national searches and those of Europol and Eurojust (art.103).[36] One

functions to the customs officers because of the police's 'inability' to perform international borders control, brings a somewhat odd blurring of competences. The differences between the two offices become less clear, and challenging when the customs officers, to a greater and greater degree, also in Norway, become armed. The change seems to have been suggested as a result of the long-term failure of implementation of the SIS II, see Prop.94 L (2009–2010) ch.2. SIS II entered into force in April 2013, many years after the insufficiencies of SIS I were clear.

33 The list in sect.13(1) includes a) the police and customs authorities and the Coast Guard when performing border control: b) police and customs authorities when performing control other than border control, and the Coast Guard when performing tasks otherwise done by police and customs authorities; c) the public prosecutors; d) immigration authorities in cases as mentioned in sect.12(1) c; road management authorities in cases as mentioned in sect.12(1) d; f) the Ministry and the Police Directorate when exercising superior authority.

34 [2003] OJ L 67/27.

35 An extension by Council Decision 2005/211/JHA ([2006] OJ L 256/18).

36 Other control measures include the obligation to ensure data and access protection cf. art 118; and allowing the Joint Supervisory Body control (JSB [101A]).

issue raised regarding these organisations' use of the SIS, is the possibility that the initial restrictions might be sidestepped. Europol and Eurojust might cooperate with third parties and apply their own regulations, using information retrieved from SIS, in ways not originally intended.[37] This could even lead to 'illegitimate coupling' of information from the SIS to other information databases (e.g. Europol's own information and analysis databases) or forums these agencies have access to – unlike the 'primary' users (i.e. the member states' police). This problem is acknowledged, and a solution is sought to it, in articles (101A [6b] and B [4]), which prohibit connecting or transferring data from the SIS to any other computer system, unless, in the case of Europol, such use is allowed according to paragraphs 4 and 5 of the same article.

While the SIS is primarily is a traditional police information database, the EU police and prosecution bodies also have access to a large body of information from the police and immigration authorities of the Schengen member states. The easier access and exchange that now exists within the same data system indicate a major change from the old slow international processes. While there may have been informal exchanges, which were possibly more efficient, the notoriety is better. The new systems may make access more equal because it is less dependent on police officers knowing each other.

9.2.2.2 Registration of data on persons and objects

I will now examine the police's use of the SIS to obtain evidence, or information in investigation or intelligence work. Immigration control is an important part of SIS information exchange, and partly a police task. The interoperability between immigration related data and police use is discussed in ch.9.3.2. The measures that may be applied and requested are explored in depth after an overview of the kinds of data that may be registered.

Information on persons (alerts) may in certain situations be registered in the SIS *to achieve the aims* detailed in the CISA arts.94(1) cf. 100/the SIS Act sects.5 cf. 7. Such cases are when individuals:

- (CISA art.94 no.1, SIS Act sect.7 no.1) are wanted for arrest and extradition;
- (no.2/no.2) are to be refused entry, in accordance with the Immigration Act sects.66 (a–c;e–f);67–68;
- (no.3/no.3) are missing, or should be taken into custody because they constitute a threat to themselves or others;
- (no.4/no.4) are the object of administrative tasks which make it necessary to find out where they live, serve them with subpoenas, or require them to stand trial;
- need to have a verdict pronounced against them;
- are wanted in relation to a custodial sentence.

It is voluntary for each state to decide whether to register a person on these terms, depending how important the case is. Registrations must be in accordance with national legislation.

The only data that can be registered in the SIS on a person, cf. SIS Act sect.6(1) and CISA art.94 no.3 (in the SIS Act's succession) is:

a) surname and given names, with any aliases entered separately;
b) place and date of birth;

37 See e.g. Boehm 2012b:162 ff.

c) any permanent physical characteristics ;
d) sex;
e–f) photos and fingerprints;
g) citizenship;
h) whether the person concerned may be armed, violent or have escaped;
i) reason for the alert;
j) the authority that has registered the alert;
k) the decision motivating the alert;
l) action to be taken, i.e. arrest or protective custody;
m) links to other alerts registered in the SIS in accordance with SIS Act sect.9a;
n) the type of offence in question, when applicable (e.g. robbery).

Unlike Norwegian law, CISA art. 94 no.3 (last paragraph) allows registration of sensitive personal data, such as criminal convictions or sexual orientation. Such data must be carefully protected if it will be processed automatically. The CISA art.92 no.3 formulation was not included in Norwegian law, to exclude the possible interpretation that other information not particularly mentioned could be registered.[38]

Data on objects may have alerts registered on them in the SIS when the object is sought for seizure or use as evidence in criminal proceedings, cf. SIS Act sect.9 and CISA art.100 no.1. These data "shall" be registered in the SIS, although this is not an obligation for the Norwegian authorities. The SIS Act. sect.6(2) states that data "may" be registered in the case of the following:

a) motor vehicles with a cylinder capacity exceeding 50 cc, boats and aircraft;
b) trailers with an unladen weight exceeding 750 kg, caravans, industrial equipment, outboard motors and containers;
c) firearms;
d, e, f, h) blank official documents, identity papers, vehicle registration documents or number plates, bearer bonds or credit cards which have been stolen, misappropriated or lost;
g) banknotes with their registered numbers (in the CISA *litra* f, the banknotes should be suspect);

The SIS Act does not, in the categories in *litri* a–c, contain the phrase "which have been stolen, misappropriated or lost". This implies that such vehicles or firearms may be registered only if the alert accords with the requirement concerning purpose (for seizure or use as evidence) and if the case calls for registration (necessity, SIS Act sect.5[1]).

The list of categories, the data within the categories, and the access restrictions have been amended several times since the initial Schengen Convention. It has been extended to include, for example, boats, aircraft, industrial equipment, credit cards and licence plates. The most significant amendment was perhaps when biometric data – photos and fingerprints – were included in SIS.[39] Although such information, as seen above, has long been included in Norwegian police databases, there have been data protection concerns about its inclusion in the SIS, because of possible mismatches due to possible errors, and also because

38 Ot.prp.nr.56 (1998–1999) pt.6.4.3.4.
39 See further discussions on the SIS II in immigration relations in Peers 2011:203–8.

it may lead to the registration in police databases of people, such as immigrants or witnesses, who are not suspected or convicted of crime. One restriction is that photos and fingerprints can only be used to confirm the identity of a person who has already led to a hit based on other information; thus the police cannot, for example, use a fingerprint as the only search 'word'. There are, however, plans to make photos and fingerprints 'first-hand' identifiers, to make identification more precise.[40]

The SIS II Regulation also changed MS obligations regarding the registration of immigrants. Where someone is considered a threat to public policy, or public or national security, it is mandatory to issue an alert in the SIS, in other words, this "shall", rather than "may" be done, the latter remaining an option for registration for other policing purposes (art.24[2]). The threshold of suspicion regarding intention to commit serious crimes has also been lowered, from "clear evidence" to "clear indications" (2[b]).

Schengen cooperation implied, as we have seen, a formalisation of existing police cooperation measures, including information exchange. This may also be seen in the long-standing Nordic police relations: it continues in ch.12.2 of the Nordic Police Cooperation Agreement of 2012 that all wanted notices sent between the Nordic police shall be exchanged in accordance with the Schengen cooperation, the EAW or/and the EAW Association Agreements with Norway and Iceland when these are in place. Wanted notices shall also accord with the Nordic Arrest Warrant. The requirements are the same for these instruments as in the Schengen cooperation.

9.2.2.3 Interlinking of alerts

Interlinking of alerts was initially prohibited in the SIS. If, for example, a police officer got a hit indicating a person was wanted for an armed robbery, it was not permitted to have links from the 'wanted' hit to missing bank notes and stolen travel documents from the robbery, although these would have separate alerts in the system. Such interlinking is common practice in Norwegian police registers.[41] Linking may only take place if there is a clear operational need for it. Interlinking does not affect access competence, the measures that are requested taken for each hit, or the limitations on deletion.[42] Data may not be stored for longer than the specific case requires because a piece of interlinked data could still be useful. If, for example, a missing person is found, but the stolen vehicle used for the kidnapping is still missing, the data on the person must be deleted (CISA art.112). There is no clear definition in the Norwegian *forarbeid* of what "a clear operational need" means, although this requirement is said to be stricter than the ordinary requirement of necessity. The Ministry of Government Administration and Reform argued that there should be clear guidelines for when there was such an operational need. The Government agreed, but considered it would suffice to give such guidelines in an instruction. Such an instruction, or amendment to the present SIS Directive, has not been made.[43] Since the vehicle registration authorities and the customs authorities, for example, have partial access to the SIS, it was important to make clear their competences had not widened, despite the possibilities for interlinking. One could imagine a scenario in which the vehicle registration authorities

40 St.prp.nr.44 (2007–2008):2; Article 22 of the [2006] OJ L 381/4.
41 Kvam 2008:142.
42 [2006] OJ L 381/4 art.37; SIS Act sect.9a.
43 Ot.prp.nr.38 (2007–2008):14.

(VRA) did a search for a vehicle when registering it on the national database, and got a hit on the car as stolen, wanted for evidence because it had been used in a robbery, and linked to several suspects. The VRA are only allowed access to information about the vehicle, to check whether it is stolen or missing (SIS Act sect.12[1]d;[2]). It is up to the member states to create links in accordance with the SIS Regulation and their national legislation. This means that, for example, the Maltese police could have created links between a car, a stolen firearm, and a doctor wanted for arrest for performing abortions (which is illegal in Malta). Performing abortions is legal in Norway, so the Maltese link is incompatible with Norwegian law. It would then be up to the Norwegian authorities (Kripos's SIRENE) to ensure, (by flagging it as unaccomplishable) that Norwegian SIS users did not access this link.

9.2.2.4 Transmitting additional information

These are the basic rules concerning data registration, searches and access. There are, however, various kinds of information that is relevant during an investigation.

Although SIS contains more information than a simple hit/no-hit system, additional information cannot be registered in the database. There are, however, rules on transferring such information, with specific limitations. Such types of additional information are listed in CISA art.95 no.2a–e and art.99 no.4a–g, including data on persons or objects involved in crime (which authority issued the alert; the nature and classification of the offence; the circumstances of the crime; etc.). Transmission of such information is subject to two requirements: 1) supplementary information must only be used for the purpose the information was given for, and 2) such transmission must be necessary to achieve that purpose. The SIS Act (sect.11) only partly regulates transmission of supplementary information, while referring to the limits set out in the CISA. Since the transmission is of information that cannot be transferred directly under Schengen regulations, in Norwegian law it is subject to the regulations in the Acts relating to criminal registration and to personal data.[44] Only Kripos can transmit such additional information. Since SISII, both Nordic and European Arrest Warrants (EAWs) may be registered in the SIS after SIS II.[45] Such information would previously have needed to be exchanged bilaterally between member states.

One reason for not allowing such additional information in the SIS is that it partly consists of data from the police's working registers. Rules on individuals' access differed between the various registers: individuals may not claim access to police working registers, but they are entitled to such SIS-access according to SIS regulations. Data protection and other rules regarding such information are regulated outside the Schengen cooperation, by national legislation; in the case of Norway, in the Act concerning the registration of data in criminal cases.[46] This means, of course, that there may also be different rules on professional confidentiality and data protection within the cooperating member states.

Several police districts and entities initially questioned how far they would need to check, say, the grounds for suspicion that would justify a registered alert for purposes of discreet surveillance or specific checks. The Ministry, however, ruled that the SIS should not be considered an ordinary police working register, precisely because registration of 'ordinary'

44 Respectively CRA and PDA.

45 [2002] OJ L 190/1. Norway has an association agreement with the EAW, in addition to the Nordic Arrest Warrant (NAW) which has long facilitated extradition between Nordic countries (Arrestordreloven 2012 [only in force for Nordic arrest warrants]; NAW 2005).

46 Strafferegistreringsloven of 1975; but the PRA from July 2014.

police intelligence was not permitted.[47] The additional information that such police data would constitute, would only be transmitted the SIS. This meant that such communication would need to satisfy national procedural and material requirements. Therefore, the existence of reasonable grounds for suspicion, in the case of an alert for the purposes of a coercive measure such as seizure or arrest, would be checked, in accordance with national law, before an international transmit.

The restrictions on content and access, and the processing rules means there are national and international requirements for data protection and safeguarding people's private lives. Those suspected or convicted of criminal activity, and others, such as witnesses and others not registered for crime-related purposes, all have these rights. The rules also ensure some national control over the registered information. This helps maintain the notion that no police action should be outside the ultimate control of the state, and thus outside sovereign competence. The intertwining of SIS and national police registers, however, may be seen to significantly expand the geographical scope of Norwegian police information. It also tends to blur the investigative and immigration control tasks of the police. While the restrictions mentioned above clearly limit what may and may not be done to protect the interests of individuals and the state, it is notable that these restrictions changed during subsequent years, removing many barriers, and this could be 'greasing' a slippery slope.

As a very large database with information on persons and objects, the SIS was an important new tool for the Norwegian police. It made information more accessible, and replaced much slower formal exchange channels. This significantly improved the access to information of local police. As we have seen, it has been argued that SIS formalises previous informal contacts outside letters rogatory and Interpol channels. Much of the Norwegian police did not, presumably, have the same informal contact network as those working in Kripos, Økokrim or with officers in border regions. Thus, database access meant, that many officers 'on the beat' throughout Norway could check identity and potential alerts when stopping people in their local towns.

Searches and their results could provide information of relevance for a criminal investigation. Since the SIS is designed to assist in both crime control and immigration control, hits might have nothing to do with a criminal investigation. The SIS thus arguably serves to further the police role in immigration control. Databases that may contribute to the blurring between crime and immigration control in various databases are dealt with in what follows.

9.3 Other available databases

Soon after the Madrid bombings, and other terrorist attacks in the early 2000s, the 2004 EU policy programme – the Hague Progamme – identified a clear link between movement, migration and terrorism, and emphasised the need for a coherent approach to registering data in these areas.[48] One of the measures introduced was the provision of access for law enforcement authorities to immigration databases, on the grounds that "[i]mproved border controls and document security play an important role in combating terrorism".[49] Also crucial was interoperability between data systems, this being the "ability of IT systems and

47 Ot.prp.nr.56 (1998–1999):62.

48 The Hague programme:1.7.2; Mitsilegas 2009:245–6.

49 EU Council Declaration on Combating Terrorism.

of the business processes they support to exchange data and to enable the sharing of information and knowledge".[50] Interoperability was suggested as a solution to various shortcomings of SIS (II), VIS and Eurodac, databases that were seen as under-exploited. This was because there were too many limitations on alphanumeric searches, insufficient benefits for frequent *bona fide* travellers, the identification of illegal immigrants was too difficult, entry and exit monitoring of third-country nationals was incomplete, and EU citizens were not registered at the European level. Existing asylum, immigration and visa data could not be used for internal security purposes, i.e. policing.[51] Mitsilegas criticises the Commission for treating interoperability merely as a technical, a not political, issue, which, he argues, may be seen as an attempt to depoliticise issues that may have far-reaching consequences. According to Mitsilegas, the 'war on terror' has justified especially two main data system synergies at the EU level; the enhancement of 'interoperability' between the various EU databases; and possibility for law enforcement agents to gain access into immigration databases.[52]

Some police databases are tools for national police within their territory. Others are international databases, available to national police. Others are national or international, with non-policiary purposes, but access for the police. The development of these databases has, over the past couple of decades, significantly expanded the resources of the Norwegian police. This chapter sets out to give an account of the police information exchange databases, and the mechanisms that are, or will be accessible, to the Norwegian police outside these, in the Schengen *Acquis*. It also seeks to show how the police have increasingly gained access to administrative information databases, particularly those of immigration control. A comparative analysis of the databases and systems is provided in ch.9.4.

9.3.1 Prüm

The Prüm furthered the principle of mutual availability established by the Hague Programme, which provides for data to be readily available to law enforcement authorities across borders.[53] This cooperation became binding EU law in August 2008 (Council Decision and the Implementing Decision).[54] The Decision comprises only "essential parts" of the original Prüm Convention, meaning the information exchange provisions. Three databases for law enforcement authorities expanded information exchange through Prüm: a DNA Database network (with DNA profiles; a hit/no hit-system, meaning that, if there is a hit, the registering country must be contacted for information); an Automated Fingerprint Identification System (AFIS) database network (fingerprint data, hit/no hit); and a Vehicle Registration data network (direct access to alpha data).[55] The EU did not consider the Prüm cooperation to be Schengen-relevant. Thus, for Norway to be included, an association agreement was negotiated with the EU in 2009.[56] It did not come into force before 2017 because of technical issues. The relevant

50 COM(2005) 597 final:3.
51 COM(2005) 597 final:4–7.
52 Mitsilegas 2009:245–7
53 Hufnagel 2013:77.
54 [2008] OJ L 210/12.
55 Another database, the European Car and Driving Licence Information System (EUCARIS) facilitates the exchange of vehicle or driving licence registration data, and obliges MS to make their national registers available. Law enforcement agencies have access to it. Norway has been party to the Treaty since 2012.
56 [2008] OJ L 210/12 For the Norwegian role in Prüm and other information exchange, see Kvam 2008; 2014.

legal regulation, chapter 72 in the Police Registration Directive (PRD), has still not come into force (September 2017).[57]

When Prüm Decisions do not give the Norwegian police access to other information than what is already available through the Schengen cooperation, they can now make direct searches in the DNA and fingerprint registration systems of the member states. Furthermore, the Prüm Decision obliges member states to set up DNA databases, if none exist.[58] The police may search directly in other Prüm member states' (online) DNA registers to investigate specific criminal offences. In Norway, such searches are regulated in the PRD (sect.72–12), which had not come into force by November 2016. On the basis of Prüm, in the meantime Norway and Sweden can make bilateral 'mutual availability' searches in DNA registers.[59]

The cooperation mechanisms of the Prüm are explored in Chapter 13.2, since they are particularly interesting as regards the Joint Investigation Teams (JITs).

Another database Norway is not currently party to is the EU Criminal Records Information System (ECRIS). Established in April 2012, it is designed to improve the exchange of criminal conviction information between EU countries.[60] The ECRIS connects national criminal records databases, giving judges and prosecutors easier access to the criminal records of all EU citizens, thus helping support verdicts or indictments. The system is decentralised: when a MS convicts a non-national, it must to send information on the case to the offender's home state, since this state holds all such data. If the convicting state needs information on the criminal record of the indicted person, this must be requested from the home state. In 2016, the Commission adopted a proposal for a Directive amending the Decision, to include information on third country nationals. So far, there are no documents confirming Norwegian participation in the ECRIS (September 2017), although the Government has expressed interest.[61] A new EU agency for the management of large-scale IT-systems – EU-Lisa – operationally runs SIS II, VIS and Eurodac. Since 2017, there have been plans for a centralised ECRIS third country national system including interoperability features. Time will tell how this affects third country Norway's access to these data.

9.3.2 Immigration data systems

Hitherto police access to administrative databases such as immigration registers has been very restricted, and the two types of databases have been clearly separated. One reason for this is the principle of purpose limitation, whereby information shall only be used for the purpose for which it was gathered.[62] A key concern is that this blurring of boundaries between databases containing information on 'the innocent' and on suspected/convicted people may decrease the scrutiny and democratic control of the use made of data.[63] In other words, when giving information, say, the Directorate of Immigration, people must be

57 See Prop. 54 S (2015–2016).

58 Mitsilegas 2009:261; Bellanova 2008. See also Bigo *et al.* on the issue of the principle of mutual availability drawing the subsidiarity of the EU towards lowered civil liberties for citizens (Bigo *et al.* 2007).

59 http://kriminalteknik.nu/bilateralt-utbyte-och-sokning-av-dna-profiler-fran-brottmal-i-sverige-och-norge/ [10.09.2017].

60 [2009] OJ L 93/33.

61 Meld.St. 7 (2010–2011):24. See Stefanou and Xanthaki 2008; Mitsilegas 2009:250–2; Kvam 2014.

62 See in depth on the purpose of the limitation principle in crime control measures in Norway in Kvam 2014:ch.10.

63 E.g. Mitsilegas 2009:246; and EDPS Opinion 29.04.13, with reference to previous Opinions with similar concerns of 2005; 2006; 2009 (fn.27).

confident that it will only be used for the purpose they were informed of, such as an asylum decision. This seems particularly problematic when foreign police officers are allowed access, if seen in connection with the issue of national police control on national territory.

The gradual abolition of internal border controls and reinforcement of the external, joint border control instated by the Schengen cooperation brought mutual responsibility for immigration control. In the absence of checks on those travelling between Schengen member states, these states had to trust each other's s ability to control crime within their jurisdictions, and will to cooperate in fighting cross-border crime. It also required confidence in the ability of each state to carry out external border control, since the right of free movement also involved third country nationals, not just Schengen citizens. The Schengen Information System (SIS), as we have seen, contains information on immigrants who have been refused entry to the Schengen Area (CISA art.96 cf. 94). The regulations on access to this data for national police are the same as for that on criminal cases. There has also been a substantial development of common databases for immigration purposes, which are not related to those containing e.g. information given in visa or asylum applications.

In Norway, all asylum or visa applicants have their photos and fingerprints taken and stored.[64] Fingerprints are digitalised and held in the Foreign Registry at Kripos. Until 2003, Norwegian police could not access these registers when investigating crimes committed in Norway. Access was allowed only when information requests were submitted by Interpol or foreign law enforcement authorities concerning serious crimes.[65] The Norwegian Immigration Register is a separate fingerprint database within Kripos, established in 1992. The Ministry argued for access because statistics showed that immigrants were responsible for much of the cross-border crime in Norway, and it was necessary to prevent foreign criminals and international crime taking root in Norway. Myhrer argues that the previous limitation was plainly misguided, since it meant the police demanded unnecessary resources when a simple search in the register could settle a case. In addition, the police could not target a whole immigrant community when they suspected someone within it.[66] Since the legislative change, national police have access to the database when investigating one or more criminal acts that may lead to imprisonment for more than six months.[67] The Foreign Register and the Fingerprint Register are within the same register, which means that, if an asylum seeker is also a convicted criminal, his fingerprints are only registered once. The information is, however, separated, taken out and access granted under separate sets of regulations.[68]

Norway is a member of the Dublin and Eurodac cooperations.[69] The Dublin Convention replaced the Schengen provisions on asylum, because some member states feared that the absence of border controls would increase not only cross-border crime, but also the number of those applying for asylum in several Schengen countries ('asylum shopping').[70] The VIS cooperation is Schengen-relevant (VIS preamble no.27), and thus also includes Norway. VIS was implemented in Norwegian law in the 2008 Immigration Act (IA) sects.32,

64 IMD 2009 sects.18–1; 18–2.

65 Act of 04.07. no.81 2003, abolishing IMD 1990 sect.130.

66 Ot.prp.nr.49 (2002–2003):ct.2.1.3; Myhrer 2004a:90–1.

67 Immigration Act 2008 sect.100(3).

68 Myhrer 2004b:540.

69 [2001] OJ L 93/40.

70 Peers 2011:358. See p.357–368 for more details on the asylum aspects and the concurrent data protection regulations within these regulations.

101–102. In accordance with the NC sect.26(2) and the Norwegian Schengen Association Agreement (SAA) art.8(2)c, *Stortinget* had to approve the amendments. There was no debate on them.[71] These agreements gave foreign law enforcement authorities access to the Norwegian foreigner register, which formerly was only possible under specific extradition agreements or after a special assessment.[72] The Dublin Convention replaced the Nordic passport cooperation that regulated asylum applications. The Agreement also opens the possibility for Norwegian affiliation with future Dublin amendments, and Norwegian access to the 2003 Council Decision.[73]

9.3.2.1 Visa Information System (VIS)

Based on CISA art.9 (1), the Visa Information System (VIS) was established in 2004 to improve visa information exchange between the Schengen member states, thus facilitating the processing of visa application and implementation of the joint Schengen visa policies. VIS came into force in 2011, including in in Norway. In contrast to the Schengen Information System, where the registration of data is to the responsibility of the member state (MS), the VIS implies a more stringent common policy and stricter regulations. The open, borderless area is open to all, which means that all MS may be affected by how fellow states handle visas. Just as the Dublin cooperation seeks to prevent 'asylum shopping', VIS targets 'visa shopping' (IA sect.102a[f]). However, member states' internal policies on extending three months visas are, however, their responsibility alone.[74] The Eurodac Fingerprint System was an EU immigration resource, but law enforcement authorities gained access to it through the Framework Decision of 2013. The purpose of the database was originally to facilitate the implementation of the Dublin cooperation, ensuring applications are only assessed once, in the first member state the applicant arrives in (art.3[1]).[75]

VIS was established as an immigration control tool with the special purpose of "contribut[ing] towards internal security and combating terrorism"; it was accessible to national police departments.[76] The police do, however, also have access to immigration

71 http://www.stortinget.no/no/Saker-og-publikasjoner/Saker/Sak/?p=42405 [21.11.13].

72 Ot.prp.nr.36 (2008–2009) ch.4.1; Immigration Act 2008 sect.100 cf. IMD 2009 sect.18–3. The other national data systems that the police have access to when investigating crimes are: SSP ('The central crime and personal data register', consisting of the criminal records database; the main person database; the Modus database [known offenders]; the nickname database; parts of the person photo database, and register of who are filed with fingerprints, photo and DNA); the BOT (containing all tickets, on-the-spot fines, ordinary fines, etc.); FREG (the Central Register of Residents); ELYS (II) (the national register for police's [internal] wanted notices. ELYS II (the central register consisting of the ELYS, the SIS and Interpol's Automatic Search Facility [ASF]); DUF (the Immigration database); and the DNA database (established in 2008, containing an investigation database, an identity database and a track register. Police registers are generally regulated in the Police Registration Act. See more in Kvam 2014.

73 Pedersen 2004:420. The Dublin III Decision ([2013] OJ L 180/31) was implemented in Norway in December 2013.

74 Ot.prp.nr.36 (2008–2009):pt.2.2.

75 The Dublin Regulation is also revised (from 2014) ([2013] OJ L 180/60), but the reference here is to the current [2003] OJ L 50/1. Dublin is part of the Common European Asylum System (CEAS) with a general treaty basis in art.78 TFEU.

76 According to the EU Justice and Home Affairs (JHA) Council in their preliminary conclusions (referred to by Mitsilegas 2009:247).

databases that have no crime control purpose. This is particularly interesting because it may be seen as blurring of police work and crime control onto other administrative fields of law

The VIS is built up in the same way as SIS. The system consists of a central unit for all visa information (Central-VIS), national units for every Schengen member (Norway has NORVIS), and a communication structure between these levels (Immigration Act [IA] sect.102). The member states must register and transfer information in the form of alphanumeric data on the applicant, whether a visa has been obtained or refused; photos; fingerprints; references to previous applications; and fellow travellers of the immigrant (IA sect.102 a–b).[77] Fingerprints are the search key, when a crime is being investigated. As mentioned above, through NORVIS, the national police may have access to more information than the foreign police or Europol. The information available, in addition to fingerprints, when the conditions mentioned above are met, matches the following search terms: VIS, cf. IA sect.102e[2–3]): name, sex, date and place of birth; nationality; travel documents; journey details; place of residence; fingerprints; visa data (type, number), I.D. inviting or guaranteeing the application. If there is a hit, some additional information may be supplied: photos or other information on the visa application; and any comments noted in the application process.

The authorities responsible for visa applications may register and amend information in the VIS (IA sect.102c[2];VIS art.6). In 2008, although originally an immigration resource, VIS was opened, under certain conditions, to investigative searches by police. The police cannot register a wanted-notice in VIS or link one to a person register. This function does not exist in VIS (the Norwegian police would employ SIS or Interpol, or contact particular people or liaison officers via the PTN or Eurojust, or use the national ELYS).[78] If visa authorities suspect criminal offences are being committed, they must alert national police.

Police access is subject to several requirements (IA sect.102e[1]). The crimes should be terrorist offences or other serious criminal offences. This means "offences under national law which correspond to or are equivalent to" the offences in the EU Terrorist Combating Decision art.1–4, and the European Arrest Warrant (EAW) art.2(2).[79] The police may not 'randomly' or for risk-assessment purposes search more widely: the search must be limited to a specific case, "necessary" in that the police (MS police and Europol) have "reasonable grounds to consider that consultation of VIS data will substantially contribute to" achieving their tasks as allowed in the VIS.[80] The wording has been controversial. Some have

77 The Norwegian Data Protection Agency expressed concern about taking fingerprints of children (Ot.prp.nr.36 (2008–2009) pt.6). The minimum age for registration of children's fingerprints is 12. In the Eurodac fingerprint system, children over 14 shall be registered (Immigration Act 2008 sect.101; Immigration Directive 2008 sect. 18–5).

78 [2008] OJ L 218/60 art.3(4); in Norwegian law generally Forvaltningsloven sect.13(1)b no.6; in case of more imminent danger GCPC sect.139 (but see Myhrer 2004a:95 arguing that the threshold is too high for the immigrations authorities' obligation to notify the police).

79 [2008] OJ L 218/129 art.2(1) c–d cf. [2002] OJ L 164/3 (amended in 2008) and [2002] OJ L 190/1. 'Serious crimes' are those listed in the EAW article that are also punishable under national law with a custodial or detention order for at least three years, e.g. participating in a criminal organisation; rape, forgery, racism and grievous bodily injury. 'Terrorist offences' are "intentional acts" which in "nature or context, may seriously damage a country or an international organisation where committed with" certain listed aims, e.g. destabilising or intimidating peoples or governments. The 2008 amendments added recruitment to and training for terrorist activities ([2008] OJ L 330/23 art.4).

80 IA sect.102e(1); [2008] OJ L 218/60 art.3(1); [2008] OJ L 218/129 arts.4; 5(1).

claimed that the threshold for access should be made higher, by requiring evidence of the reasonable grounds.[81] In the Norwegian Immigration Act sect.102e, requirement is for "reasonable grounds" for presuming that the information will, to a significant degree, contribute to the police task in question. The criterion for 'reasonable grounds' is similar to that governing when the police may start a criminal investigation, under the Criminal Procedure Act sect.224 (1). The criterion has three elements: 1) the decision to investigate must be factually justified; 2) circumstances must indicate that a criminal offence has probably been committed; and 3) it must be proportional, considering all the elements in the situation, to subject the suspected person to investigation, and to employ investigative resources on the matter.[82]

Access to VIS is limited to police (and Europol) personnel responsible for control of the crimes in question. In practice, the Norwegian Police Security Service (PST) and Kripos.[83] Kripos and the PST keep a list of those in their units who have access to VIS, and strict procedures must be followed (Police Register Directive sect.73–14; 73–15): when all criteria in IA sect.102e are met, the competent police and prosecutorial authorities may forward a reasoned request for access to VIS via Kripos or PST (sect.73–5) as the national contact point, which checks the legality of the request before processing it. In urgent cases, however, the authorised police or public prosecution entities may request information from Kripos verbally, electronically or in writing, and Kripos must comply immediately (sects.73–15). Purpose-limited access is available to ordinary police performing border control tasks, such as. checking the identity of a foreign-looking person.[84] As a rule, then, the police may not search in *the* VIS; searches are limited by purpose and necessity, and are performed via centralised authorities that, if there is a hit, pass back the information requested. Additional data, such as notes on a visa application, may also be sent when an initial search has led to a hit.[85]

Europol's access to VIS is limited to the central database, and does not include the national versions (e.g. NORVIS).[86] Its access is otherwise delimited by its mandate, and like that of MS police, by the requirement for specific purposes. Europol processing of retrieved data must be authorised by the MS that has registered it.[87] Europol access is understandably not mentioned in the Norwegian legislation concerning VIS, since only access to the central, not the national, database was in question. Police access was not debated separately; the legislative changes were treated solely as part of the immigration authority changes. This was seen as unsatisfactory by, among others, the Norwegian Data Protection Authority.[88]

VIS has many of the functions the Dublin system was designed to serve, namely to establish whether an asylum seeker has previously had, or applied for a visa (or other permit) in a particular country.[89] Eurodac, another immigration control resource related to the Dublin cooperation has police access rules quite similar to those of VIS.

81 Mitsilegas 2009:245. This was not problematised in the Norwegian *forarbeid* to the implementation.
82 Myhrer 2001; RA 99–238.
83 Ot.prp.nr.36 (2008–2009):pt.7.
84 IA sect.102c.
85 IA sect.102e(3).
86 [2008] OJ L 218/60 art.3.
87 [2008] OJ L 218/129 art.7(1) and (4).
88 http://www.nytid.no/arkiv/artikler/20071220/politiet_far_soke_i_visumbase/ [26.11.13].
89 Peers 2011:361.

9.3.2.2 Eurodac

Under Eurodac, all asylum seekers aged 14 years and over and every non-EU citizen or citizen of a non-Eurodac member state who crosses borders illegally, or who is found inside them illegally, shall have his or her fingerprints taken.[90] These are then sent to the Central Eurodac System and checked against ones sent by other member states to see whether and where the person has applied for asylum before and whether they should therefore be dealt with in accordance with the Dublin Agreement (arts.3–10). The final identification – the linking of the fingerprints to the individual – is the responsibility of the member state alone (art.4[6]); thus it is a hit/no-hit system. Before Eurodac prints were registered in 2003, all searches for fingerprints took place via Interpol or bilateral agreements.[91]

Eurodac was only accessible for asylum purposes. The new Regulation of 2015 permits, in criminal investigations, member states' police, and Europol, to compare fingerprints with those registered in Eurodac.[92] Only designated authorities, either national or from Europol (art.7), are authorised to request such comparisons, when there is "substantial suspicion" that someone has committed or will commit a crime, and the likelihood that information in Eurodac is necessary for the "prevention, detection and investigation of serious crimes and terrorism".[93] The Norwegian authority with responsibility for Eurodac used for immigration control is Kripos, which will thus also be the National Access Point, if Norway gets an association agreement with the recast Eurodac FD. As of August 2017, this has not happened. Law enforcement competences are divided between the designated law enforcement authorities and the verifying authorities. These act independently, without the former having power to instruct the latter (art.6[1]),[94] as with VIS access. There is a strict two-instance access system, meaning there is an extra barrier between administrative and policing searches. Only the verifying authority may request access to Eurodac via the National Access Point, which establishes that all conditions for comparison in art.20 or 21 are met (art.6 no.2 cf. art.19). There are emergency procedures allowing the conditions to be checked ex-post, but not outside the verifying authorities' channel (art.19[3]).

Safeguards are provided by the conditions of use. In contrast to VIS, Eurodac access requires law enforcement authorities to have exhausted all available criminal records resources, including the Prüm and VIS databases (art.20[1]).[95] Searches may only concern individual cases, and must be the last resort (art.20 [1]a and b). Searches should involve only those suspected of very serious crimes, such as murder and terrorism, since these "mean [. . .] that there is an overriding public security concern", which makes police access to the database proportionate (a). Finally, there must be "reasonable grounds" to believe that such a comparison will "substantially contribute" to the prevention, detection or investigation of

90 [2003] OJ L 50/1 art.4, IA sect.101.

91 Vandvik 2004:230.

92 [2013] OJ L 180/1.

93 Op.cit. arts.5–7 cf. art.1(2); quote from the preamble (13). The crimes are those listed in the European Arrest Warrant ([2002] OJ L 190/1) and the Council FD on combating terrorism ([2002] OJ L 164/3), if they are punishable under national law with three years' imprisonment or more, cf. art.2(1)j; cf. PRD sect.73–4. The authorities with exclusive responsibility for "intelligence relating to national security" (the EOS in Norway) have no access (art.5[1]).

94 It may be within the same unit, but act independently (art.6[1]).

95 The Prüm search may be refused if there are "reasonable grounds to believe" that such a search would fail to establish identity (art.20[1]).

the offences in question (op.cit. c). The reasonable grounds are described as "substantiated suspicion" that a search may lead to relevant findings in a category of the Regulation.

The conditions for Europol's access to Eurodac are set out in art.21. They are only slightly different from those of the member states.[96] No.1 *litri* b and c are equivalent to art.20 no.1 b and c, but the necessity requirement in (a) concerns the member states' law enforcement action. The crime in question must fall within the mandate of Europol, which obviously includes terrorist or other serious offences (the requirement for member states' action). Processing data from Eurodac for Europol requires the member state of origin's authorisation (art.21[3]). This may be seen as emphasising the 'non-supranationality' of Europol: it has no 'autonomous' interest and is merely a resource for its members.

Norway is bound by the Eurodac Regulation, which was implemented directly into the Immigration Act sect.101, except for the articles concerning police access. These fall outside the scope of the present Norwegian affiliation agreement,[97] although the new regulation is applicable in every other respect, and Norway is party to the Dublin (now III) cooperation. Negotiations are underway on the Norwegian side (August 2017).[98] This non-applicability means that, according to the new regulation, the Norwegian police cannot search in the Eurodac register, while their implementation of the Regulation in full, makes it possible for other member states' law enforcement authorities, and Europol, to search Norwegian Eurodac information, without 'reciprocity', until Prüm cooperation is a reality in Norway. The Ministry argues that foreign law enforcement access is nonetheless a good thing, since this will contribute to the fight against serious crime and terrorism.[99] However, this lack of reciprocity, as we have seen, appear problematic as regards maintaining external sovereignty.

9.3.2.3 The challenges of interoperability and police access

The preamble to the regulation recognises that the purpose of Eurodac has changed in a manner that "interferes with the fundamental right to respect for the private life of individuals whose personal data are processed in Eurodac". The standard EU requirement is that measures should accord with laws that are sufficiently clear and have foreseeable outcomes; at the same time, any interference has to be "necessary in a democratic society to protect a legitimate and proportionate interest and proportionate to the legitimate objective it aims to achieve".[100] The seriousness of the crimes in question satisfies the requirement for proportionality (Eurodac 2013 preamble [10]). It is underlined that safeguards are particularly important, because law enforcement authorities are searching in registers containing information about people with no criminal record (13) and people not suspected of serious offences (15),. Personal data is safeguarded by art.22(1–2), which requires all communication to be secure and electronic (so phone contact is not permitted), thus preserving a record of the procedure, for control purposes.[101]

Much of the basic information is the same as that held in the databases the police initially have access to, and in the immigration control databases. The latter may include, however,

96 New access from 2015 ([2013] OJ L 180/1).

97 [2013) OJ L] 180/1 arts.5, 6, 19–22, 33, 36, 39(3), 40(7) and 43 Prop. 62 L (2014–2015).

98 Prop.25 S (2013–2014) pt.4.

99 [2009] OJ L 138/14.

100 Peers criticises Eurodac for already being in breach of the purpose limitation principle of data protection law, because it holds data too long (2011:366).

101 There are specific data processing and protecting measures in ch.VII of the Regulation.

alternative or more extensive information, such as remarks made in visa interviews. Giving police access to this information extends police competence into the civil administrative immigration control area. This may give Norwegian police access to interview material collected 'extraterritorially', for example as part of a visa interview in a European border country – information that, prior to the new VIS access rules, would have been unavailable.

VIS and Eurodac both have a strict division between local and central levels. All searches must go through a national control entity. Thus, they are both centralised police resources, while they work as decentralised immigration control tools, since immigration does not need to go via Kripos. Police access is contingent on its necessity, and its importance for purposes of controlling serious crime, in contrast to SIS access, for which more ordinary police tasks (public order, etc.) are sufficient.

The next chapter focuses on the international police cooperation databases of Europol and Interpol in contrast to the i systems designed to assist immigration control, and whose sole purpose is policing. We will now see if, and to what extent, Norwegian police get access to (and return the compliment) 'foreign' police information. The structures and purposes of these entities in relation to Norway's position is also relevant – for example, the question of its non-EU membership status vis-à-vis Europol cooperation.

9.3.3 Europol information databases

Europol has, then, access to some of the data in the SIS, VIS and Eurodac, but cannot register data in them. The Europol Programming Document for the period 2017–2019 stated that EU MS "should use Europol as their channel of choice for law enforcement information sharing across the EU". It is acknowledged that there are a multitude of relevant information exchange systems in the Union, which makes information management complex. Europol needs to "have a clear overview of the existing information flows, [. . .] especially in regard to SISII, PNR and the Smart border package".[102] Europol has its own system, and serves as an operational hub for data exchange between the member states, itself and third parties. Apart from information "clearly obtained in obvious violation of human rights" (art.23 [9]), most information may be held in and processed through theEIS, albeit with various requirements regarding purpose and necessity.

In May 2017, the Europol Regulation (ER) came into force and the European Information System (EIS) became a single large database – an Integrated Data Management Concept.[103] This is a novelty for EU information exchange systems, and has been viewed as a step towards an EU database of criminal data and intelligence.[104] The former system (TECS) was considered outdated, because it could not identify links between different investigations within and across the three databases. TECS had three components: an information system (EIS); working registers for analytical purposes (AWFs); and an index function. In contrast to the previous version, there are now no references to access regulations for the specific databases and instead there is a list of legitimate purposes for which Europol can process the data collected (Art. 18). The new legal instrument changes Norway's access to data, and while presenting the Regulation rules arising from it, I will keep this fact in mind.

102 Europol Programming Document 2017–2019 17.01.2017, p.4.
103 E.g. Europol Programming Document 2017–2019 ch.1.1.
104 Coudert 2017.

Access for the MS and third countries such as Norway previously varied between the different TECS databases, but access rules are now dependent on the purpose for which information is processed (ER art.18) – a purpose-limitation principle. The purposes are the same as those served by the existing databases. The data supplier decides the purpose it may be used for (art.19).

The change has several advantages, according to the Europol Working Programme. The rules for information processing are related to the data itself, rather than to systems or databases.[105] Processing all data in a single database improves searches, facilitates the identification of links, and ensures better analytical support for the MS. A single system means less duplication of data, and fewer systems that different people may have access to – or lose track of. It may also improve data protection. In contrast, the Europol Convention initially set many restrictions on full access by the MS, with only general information being directly accessible. This was cumbersome, and changed in the 2009 Decision.[106] Access is now even easier.

While Norwegian access to EIS is, in principle, the same as under the 2001 Agreement, the way it differs from MS access has changed. Art.20 regulates access by MS and Europol staff. In accordance with national law and ER art. 7(5), these have direct access to searches in all personal data provided for cross-checking to identify links between analyses of a strategic or thematic nature, and information on persons who, for example, are suspected or convicted of crimes within Europol competence, or who there are "factual indications or reasonable grounds" to believe will commit such offences (art.20 [1]; 18 [2]a–b). Indirect access, i.e. hit/no hit, applies to operational analyses (art.20 [2]; 18 [2]c). Strategic and operational analysis mean "all methods and techniques by which information is collected, stored, processed and assessed" either with the aim of 1) "supporting and developing a criminal policy that contributes to the efficient and effective prevention of, and the fight against, crime" or 2) "supporting criminal investigations" (ER art.2 b–c).

Further processing of accessed data may only take place for the purpose of "preventing and combating" crimes within Europol's competence, or other forms of serious crimes as listed in the EAW (art.20 [3]a–b). Europol staff have access to all information to the extent required for their duties [4]. Eurojust and OLAF has hit/no hit access to all three types of data, without prejudice to restrictions on MS access (art.21 [1]; art.19[2]).

Direct search is not allowed for third countries and third parties. There are provisions allowing the exchange and transfer of data to them; for Norway the most significant of these are art.23 and art. 25. Actual searches require Europol staff to search in EIS for Norway. There is clearly a risk that requests from non-MS may not be priorities for Europol.

The information accessible to MS and Europol under art.20 [1–2] may only be accessed and further processed [3] for the purpose of "preventing and combating" either "a) forms of crime in respect of which Europol is competent; or b) other forms of serious crime", as set out in the EAW.

The objectives of Europol are, as set out in art.3, to "support and strengthen action" by the member states' law enforcement authorities and their mutual cooperation "in preventing and combating organised crime, terrorism and other forms of serious crime affecting two or more Member States". Like member states, Europol must adhere to its own set of rules.

105 Op.cit.

106 The change was criticised by the EDPS, who recommended more – not less – restrictions on data concerning people not (yet) convicted of crime [2007] OJ C 255/13 pt.25, and by the Europol JSB, that emphasised that access should be delimited when the nature of the data so required (see de Moor and Vermeulen 2010a:1101).

Nevertheless, the objectives stated signify that Europol is a resource for the MS. This is also shown by art.22, which makes Europol responsible for promptly informing member states when it is aware of information concerning them. If there is "imminent threat to life", access restrictions imposed by the data originator are disregarded [2]. Along with this responsibility, one also sees that Europol must decide what information or crime link is relevant. This shows that Europol has some autonomy regarding the police information systems, and may have some influence on which criminal investigations are linked to which member states' police forces (and third countries and bodies).[107]

Apart from publicly available data, Europol may only access data submitted to them by sources in one of three categories (art.17). There are a number of regulations, cross-referenced in a rather complex manner. Member States may give Europol information when this is accordance with national law and art.7, which is a long article regulating the national units of Europol MS (art.17 [1] a). The MS shall, for example, "supply Europol with the information necessary for it to fulfil its objectives, including information relating to forms of crime the prevention or combating of which is considered a priority by the Union" (art.7 [6] a). How it is supplied must be in accordance with national law (d), and not interfere with national law enforcement or security (para.7). There is no obligation to supply certain types of information (para.7 a–c), f such as information on national security.

The second and third category of legitimate Europol sources of information (art.17 [1b–c) are a) EU bodies, third countries and international organisations (which applies to Norway), and b) private persons and parties. These may supply information in accordance with Chapter V, which regulates Europol's relations with partners: section 1 contains common provisions on whom Europol may cooperate with (art.23), ("in so far as necessary for the performance of its tasks", and general rules for the processing of data for these partners.[108] Information may be freely shared (para.2), although the sharing of personal data must be "proportionate for the legitimate performance of [Europol's] tasks" (para.5). Nothing is said on who will assess proportionality, but the principle of ownership is strong throughout the Regulation and can probably be assumed to apply here too (e.g. preamble paras.24–27). Art.23 [6] sets out the important innovation that the data provider has the prerogative of deciding how the processed data should be used. If photos of a wanted man are forwarded from Germany to Europol to check if he is the same person as an arrested drug-smuggler in Sweden, Europol cannot release them for other purposes, or to other parties – unless Germany consents.

Section 2 covers the transfer and exchange of personal data. The general requirement is that this should be purpose-limited, in accordance with art.19(2)–(3), and without prejudice to art.67 (see fn.108). Transfer to third states and international organisations must also be based (see art.25 [1]) on a) a Commission Decision that the recipient can offer adequate data protection (an 'adequacy decision'), b) an international agreement (pursuant to art.218 TFEU) on adequate safeguards on privacy and fundamental rights, or c) a cooperation agreement made before 1 May 2017, allowing such data exchange, under art.23 of the ED. The latter applies to Norway's 2001 Association Agreement.

To safeguard data protection, there are limits on further use of the data (decided by the data supplier, art.19), on which data may be supplied (art.23, art.28, art.30), and on access – only to be available when absolutely necessary (e.g. art.30).

107 See also for third states in this relation: Hufnagel 2016.

108 The data originator may indicate restrictions on access or use (art.19 [2]), and in some cases so may Europol [3]. Europol must apply rules on discretion, confidentiality and protection of sensitive data (art. 67).

Unlike SIS entries, there are no limits on what data may be stored and processed, except for data obviously obtained in breach of human rights. However, as in the ED, there is a requirement that the registration should be necessary to perform Europol's tasks: essential, for example, to. prevent a drug-smuggling operation involving two or more countries. Purpose limitation is assumed to be ensured if, for example, personal data is transferred to third countries "only if necessary for preventing and combating crime that falls within Europol's objectives" (preamble para.34). Another safeguard is the requirement that "Europol should not store personal data for longer than is necessary for the performance of its tasks" (para.41; art.31).

As in the SIS, when there is other relevant information, the MS or Europol should exchange it upon request (Annex II [4]). The Europol Regulation does not oblige member states to offer information spontaneously. Such an obligation does follow from the Swedish Initiative art.7, to which Europol, Eurojust and their member states adhere. The Swedish Initiative does not, however, impose an obligation to gather and store information for the specific purpose of passing it on to other parties (Decision art.1[3]). The Decision is Schengen-relevant and thus applicable to Norway.[109]

Before 2009, Europol was not permitted to receive information from private parties and persons. The Europol Decision changed this, and Europol can register and process such data under certain conditions (ER arts.26–27). The ability to get information from elsewhere than designated police authorities, broadens Europol's competence: it signals a change from being merely a central hub, to having tasks similar to those of national police on the beat, – the ones ordinary people normally have contact with. This raises the question whether Europol should function as a 'higher instance' – or simply another instance – when citizens of a member state (or third state) are unhappy with the way their national police are responding to crime. As information from private sources must be lawfully collected and processed in accordance with national legislation before it reaches Europol, the Decision was criticised for not being an adequate legal basis for processing such data.[110] This may be seen as being remedied by a strict requirement that national law shall be adhered to, or that, at least it transmits to or communicates with national contact points following art.25 [1]. Information from private parties outside certain categories is prohibited, unless the MS, or third state that Europol forwards such data to, has concluded such an agreement (art.26 [4]). Europol's transfer of personal data is also limited: it must be based on case-by-case assessment, strictly necessary, and be one of the following: a) undoubtedly in the data subject's interest, (who consents or can be presumed to consent to the transfer; b) "absolutely necessary" to prevent imminent crime within Europol's competence; or c) publicly available data whose transfer is essential to support MS fighting internet crime, which concerns an individual case, and where no fundamental rights or freedoms override the public interest of the transfer. There are thus detailed regulations, and they seem reasonable. The data transfers in question are not between Europol and the police of any state, but between Europol and private parties. These may use such data differently from the police – for example, for commercial purposes such as banking or insurance.[111] The Decision (art.25[3–5]) ruled that information from private parties or persons may only be transferred through the national contact points, if the data comes from parties in third states with which

109 [2006] OJ L 386/89.
110 [1995] OJ L 281/31 (e.g. art.6); de Moor and Vermeulen 2010a:1108.
111 de Moor and Vermeulen 2010a:1108.

Europol has no cooperation agreement (3[c]). This may seem a limitation on the autonomous operational activity of Europol. Another restriction is that Europol cannot contact private parties or persons directly to obtain information (Art.26 [9];27 [4]). The same rules apply to receiving and processing information from private parties as partners. Personal data, however, can under no circumstances be transferred to private persons [5].

9.3.3.1 Operational analyses

Analysis Work Files (AWFs) were, according to Europol, the "only existing legal tool[s] at the European level to simultaneously store, process and analyse factual information (hard data) as well as intelligence (or soft data)".[112] AWFs no longer exist, but art.18 [2]c and [3]a–c regulate the processing of information in "operational analyses", a concept that appears similar. The term refers to "all methods and techniques by which information is collected, stored, processed and assessed with the aim of supporting criminal investigations" (in contrast to the strategic use of data to support and develop criminal policies) (art.2 b–c). Operational analyses are parts of projects, i.e. not data available for searches in the overarching system. The Europol Executive Director must define their purpose, and decide on the categories of personal data, subjects, and participants that should be involved, and on the conditions for access, and inform both the Management Board and the EDPS (a). The use of personal data for anything other than the purpose of the specific analysis project is prohibited unless it is "necessary and proportionate", and compatible with the project for which the data will be processed.

The categories of people about whom data may be registered follow in Annex II. In addition to suspects and convicted persons (cf. also art.18 [2]a), they include those who might be called to testify in investigations or criminal proceedings; victims or potential victims of an offence; contacts and associates; people who can provide information – in connection with offences for which Europol has competence under art.3. Art.30 regulates the processing of "special categories of personal data". This includes data on non-offenders (and non-suspects), such as witnesses, and minors; or sensitive data concerning racial or ethnic origin, political opinions, religious beliefs, health or sexuality. Processing these categories of data is subject to stricter requirements of necessity and proportionality for fulfilling tasks within Europol's competence. The sensitive data must also supplement data already processed. Collection of such sensitive data in isolation is prohibited. Europol alone has direct access to these data, and they may not be transmitted outside Europol unless this is "strictly necessary and proportionate in individual cases concerning crime" within Europol's objectives. Like the old AWFs, operational analysis projects (OAPs) may function as frameworks within which the analytical cooperative work between Europol analysts, various organised crime and terrorism specialists, and the member states is carried on. They are, thus, more like internal police work files. Only authorised Europol staff may access the data, but there are no restrictions on the participants the Executive Director may include in the OAPs. As with the AWFs, this probably means that Norwegians can still take part as third state expert investigative associates, share their data, and participate in larger operations.[113]

In the past, as a third country, Norway could not be a member of the AWF groups. This exclusion led to widespread use of less formal sub-groups within the Europol structure in

112 AWF 2012:4–5.
113 Op.cit.:23–41.

which entities other than member states could participate.[114] This has changed, and currently, the same requirements apply for existing agreements with the entity, providing sufficient data protection and confidentiality exist (ER art.30 [3]). What has changed, is that the Executive Director now decides the framework and contents of OAPs, rather than the MS in cooperation with Europol. In practice, this probably makes little difference, since consensus is key to successful cooperation.

OAPs have some similarities with the joint investigation teams (JITs), which are open to Europol participation. Europol may "assist in all activities, and, for example, provide members and seconded members of the JITs with any information within the EIS (ER art.4 [1] c–d; art.5 [1];cf. art.18). Since Europol may propose a MS to establish a JIT, analysis from OAPs may influence such investigatory groups.

'Focal points' are long-term, high-budget projects arising from strategic or operational priorities. They may have a commodity-based, thematic or regional angle, thus, they could involve Drugs Trafficking (commodity), Albanian organised-crime groups (thematic), or the Baltic (geographic). Operational projects may be set up inside or outside such points. Norway is currently participating in 14 focal points.[115]

9.3.3.2 Access to EIS and AWFs

Member states access EIS via the national contact points (in particular art.7). Access is subject to the regulations of the ER, and to the rules and procedure of the accessing party. Member states' police may thus not gain access to information they would not be entitled to in their own country. The MS appoint certain competent authorities who may perform restricted searches in the EIS, receiving only hit/no hit information, not the full range of data, as in art.12 (art.13[6]). "Competent authorities" are defined in art.2(a) as

> all police authorities and other law enforcement services existing in the Member States which are responsible under national law for preventing and combating criminal offences. The competent authorities shall also comprise other public authorities existing in the Member States which are responsible under national law for preventing and combating criminal offences in respect of which Europol is competent.

The member states are responsible for how their authorities use the system, and this use must be electronically traceable. This is one of the safeguards facilitating control of the legality of data processing.[116] Europol has competence only in cases of serious crime that are within its mandate (art.3). The MS, however, may use the data retrieved from Europol databases to combat all forms of serious crime, albeit within any restrictions noted on the 'hit' by the registering state (art.20 [3] cf. [1–2]). For example: if a Norwegian police officer registers personal data and the circumstances around a seizure and arrest in Bergen, but notes that one of those arrested is a 15-year-old boy, the data may be flagged with a warning that the boy should not be extradited to any country where the age of criminal responsibility is less than 15, and that information registered on him should not be made available to such a state.

114 Wold 2004:50.

115 POD 2016.

116 Such checks shall be performed by the member states' designated authorities when the data is in the MS, whilst Europol is responsible for the data processed by Europol (art.38).

The competence of Europol has widened in other ways. An 'on the spot' mobile office providing direct access to all Europol data may be supplied during investigations or operations.[117] Only Europol will have direct access to these, but national units and liaison officers may request the files to be passed on to them, to be applied by national police authorities within their national legal frameworks. This means that, although Europol might have had access to, and registered information originating in, or concerning Norway, Norwegian police would not be allowed to employ this information in their investigation. When MS authorities access Europol data, the national law of the particular MS applies, in addition to the relevant rules of the Regulation. There are additional rules to ensure data protection and legitimate use of the EIS, for example, rules stating that Europol staff must retrieve information only when they are empowered to do so by the Executive Director (art.20 [4]).

Norway has two liaison officers in The Hague HQ of Europol. Within Norway, Kripos, as the Europol National Unit (ENU) has operative dialogue with the Norwegian representatives at Europol. Norwegian police authorities, unlike those of EU member states, may not search for data directly in the Europol Information Database.[118] All information flowing from the Norwegian authorities to Europol, including via the liaison officer, must pass through Europol's operational centre for formal checks of its conformity to Europol rules.[119] Communication takes place through Europol's SIENA information exchange system (Secure Information Exchange Network Application), which is interoperable with national police communication systems, and "tailored to [the national law enforcement officers'] domestic environment and legislation".[120]

Member states may bilaterally exchange information on crimes that fall outside Europol's competences, if this is allowed by national law (ER art.8[4]). One might ask whether Europol should have the task of facilitating such exchanges,[121] and what the point is of limiting Europol's competences, when the limitations may be side-stepped, for example when a tip is received via Europol offices. Europol, acting independently, may not request, information or initiate a Joint Investigation Team, but any MS liaison officer based at the Europol HQ, can do either of these things. Such information exchange does imply the use of Europol technical facilities and possibly the in-put of Europol officials, and therefore to a certain extent involves Europol itself.[122]

Europol does not have autonomous operational police competence, but can exert considerable influence on operational police work. Giving advice and providing material and analysis in ongoing operations, alongside their competence to interlink and analyse the data provided to them, or that they collect independently, gives Europol a strong presence in police investigations across borders. According to Peers, the only limit on the "investigative and operational action" of Europol is that it requires the agreement of the member state concerned, and that member states are responsible for "coercive measures" (which are not precisely defined).[123] Although lacking the competence to order an investigation or coercive measures, it is clear that Europol may act as both initiator and facilitator of investigations, thus becoming increasingly autonomous.

117 Information from the Europol's web site Vaajma IntReg Report 2014.
118 St.prp.nr.98 (2000–2001):15.
119 St.prp.nr.98 (2000–2001):3.3.
120 Europol review 2012:2.3.
121 de Moor and Vermeulen 2010a:1100.
122 Op.cit.:1100.
123 Peers (2007):4. For a critical view of the operational development, see e.g. de Moor 2012.

Norway, as a third state, thus has two problems. One is that EU member states do not have to go through Europol to obtain data, being more able to search themselves. The other is that the group of third-country and -party cooperation partners is growing, both in numbers and diversity. EU MS competent law enforcement authorities may communicate directly with Europol, rather than through their official national units (although always informing these of the communication) (art.7 [5]). Norway, not a member state, cannot do so, which slows down Norwegian access.

Denmark does not take part in this cooperation, in accordance with art.1 and 2 of Protocol no.22, annexed to the TEU and TFEU. This means that the Nordic cooperation has some of the same challenges to access, and also the same incentive to seek information elsewhere.

9.4 Eurojust

Eurojust facilitates cooperation between member states' public prosecutorial authorities, and seeks to coordinate investigation and prosecution in cases involving serious crime, especially organised, crime, concerning two or more member states.[124] This EU body was established in 2002, and its competences were extended in 2008. It sometimes coordinates and directs major police operations between several countries where time may be of the essence. It may assist by directing requests to the right authorities in different countries, or expediting responses to such requests. Although this book does not generally discuss police actions involving the higher law enforcement authorities, a description of the role of Eurojust is required to complete the picture of EU police institutions, and their effects and competences in the MS and Norway.

Eurojust is not a supranational body: it has no competence to overrule member state decisions, or tell them what to do, and this was clearly the intention of the institutions establishing the organisation.[125] Eurojust has, however, some competences that could give it quite a high degree of influence on member states' police investigations and operations. Eurojust can make a "motivated request" to the member states' competent authorities, to initiate an investigation or prosecution of a crime that Eurojust has learned of (EJCD art.10). Such requests may involve transferring responsibility for an investigation to a more appropriate MS; taking over the leadership of joint operations (thus providing supranational guidance, though without 'coercive' authority); initiating joint investigations; passing on to others information required to carry out Eurojust's tasks (within the legal limitations); advising national authorities processing European Arrest Warrants; and recommending legislative changes to promote mutual assistance in criminal matters. Member states are not obliged to comply with Eurojust's requests, but can only refuse if compliance would significantly endanger security interests, a person, or an ongoing investigation (EJCD art.8).

The Eurojust mandate matches that of Europol (EJCD art.4), and may be expanded if member states request assistance to investigate or prosecute other crimes (art.4 no.2). The competences and mandate of Eurojust are quite extensive, which indicates a desire on the part of the EU to secure the Eurojust involvement regardless of changes taking place in the international crime scene.[126] In many situations, it may be difficult to locate the right foreign authority quickly enough. Eurojust solves this problem. According to Henricson,

124 [2002] OJ L 63/1; [2008] OJ L 138/14 art.3(1).
125 Bigo *et al.* 2008:16–17.
126 Henricson 2011:41; Mitsilegas 2009:193–8.

this is particularly valuable when police cooperation takes place between states where prosecutorial functions are not internalised in the police organisation, in the way they are in Norway and Denmark.[127]

Europol and Eurojust have had cooperation agreements since 2004. Cooperation was stepped up as a consequence of the Stockholm Programme, alongside other bilateral cooperation agreements between EU agencies such as OLAF and Frontex.[128] The present Cooperation Agreement, in force since 2010, requires the entities to share information with each other, and gives Eurojust access to the EIS.[129] This amendment meant that Eurojust may initiate an AWF, or establish a target group, which is now presumably equivalent to an operational analysis project (E-E art.9[2]). This extends the scope of Eurojust into an area that was previously the preserve of Europol.[130]

Eurojust is run by a college consisting of members from all 27 member states. Apart from its strategic role, an important function of the college is to settle jurisdictional disputes (art.7). The competences of the national members seconded to the college vary between countries. Some have judicial competence in their home state, others have only an administrative role. This has been criticised for being inefficient. Some representatives cannot initiate investigations in their home state even though they have information justifying such action. The college has no independent operational authority over the liaison officers (LP), but neither does the home state have decisive competence to instruct its representative(s). Decision art.9(1), however, provides that all members should have the same right to access all national police and criminal databases as national judicial authorities.

One minimum requirement is that they have prosecutorial competence, since representatives should be able to initiate urgent prosecutorial decisions without obtaining national authorisation (art.9a[1;2] cf. 9e). National authorities must be informed of such decisions afterwards. In this respect, their powers resemble the cross-border competences foreign police are given in urgent situations under the Schengen cooperation (e.g. arts.41–42 CISA). Sending liaison prosecutors to Eurojust with national competence involves no supranationalism. It may, however, influence which tasks are prioritised or carried out in the national territory, when these are decided in coordination meetings in The Hague. This is like the Europol liaison arrangement: the LP may phone directly to a police district in Norway to initiate an arrest.

Norway has a cooperation agreement with Eurojust.[131] it is not a full member, because of its non-EU status, but this may be of little practical significance.[132] Similarly, Norway is not a member of the College, and the liaison prosecutor does not have national member status (EJCD art.9), which means that Norway cannot formally influence the strategic development of Eurojust. Meetings may be attended on invitation (art.8). Norwegian cooperation consists of activities and competences set out in the Eurojust Decision (art.3 E-N Agreement). This lack of formal influence does not prevent the cooperation being considered very important. Norwegian liaison prosecutors have said that the informal coordination meetings (where Norway does participate) are the most productive of the Eurojust forums.

127 Henricson 2011:42.

128 The Stockholm progamme 2009:8; 36; 41. The book does not cover OLAF, the European Anti-Fraud Office. Norway is not a member of OLAF, which justifies the omission of this important EU police entity.

129 Europol/Eurojust Agreement 2010.

130 Boehm 2012a:155–6.

131 Eurojust Norway 2005.

132 Efjestad 2009:17–19.

In them, the LP may follow investigative leads to foreign countries – something that used to be beset by practical difficulties.[133] Eurojust has insisted that Norway is an important partner, and such events as the 22/7 terrorist attacks made Norway value the partnership too.[134] In its 2012 Annual Report, Eurojust uses the Norwegian case to show what Eurojust, Europol and MS can, could and cannot do when they join forces.[135]

Information exchange between Eurojust and Norway takes place via the liaison prosecutor (E-N art.9 no.2). All information that is "necessary, relevant and not excessive" to enhance "the co-operation between Norway and Eurojust, on combating serious forms of international crime in the areas specified in the Council Decision" shall be exchanged (E-N art.9 no.1 cf. art.2). The Norwegian authorities may, when passing information to Eurojust, make reservations on what use it is put to, access or transfer delimitations, and/or deletion of the information, and must be notified if it is transferred to states or bodies outside the Eurojust member states (art.10). Similarly, Eurojust must signal such limitations when transferring information to Norwegian authorities, and it must not be passed on by Norway (E-N art.11).

Eurojust itself does not perform any investigations involving data gathering independently, but has, its own data system (EJCD arts.14–16), and receives information from member states, third countries, and such organisations/entities, as the SIS; from national registries; and from EAW information. Member states are obliged to provide information necessary for Eurojust to perform its tasks under arts.4–5, cf. 13 no.1. MS must also (art.13 no.6) without "undue delay" inform their national Eurojust member of any case that directly involves at least three MS, and where requests or decisions on judicial cooperation have been passed to at least two MS, and one of three categories of requirements are met. It must be either (a): an offence punishable in the requesting or issuing state (depending on the MS) by a custodial sentence or detention order of at least five or six years, and included on the list in the paragraph on serious crimes;[136] or (b) any offence where there are factual indications that a criminal organisation is involved; or (c) an offence that suggests a serious cross-border dimension or possible repercussions at the European Union level, or that member states might be affected other than those directly involved. Information shall also be provided, although without an expediency requirement, if (a) conflicts of jurisdiction have arisen or are likely to arise; (b) controlled deliveries affect at least three states, at least two of which are member states; (c) requests for judicial cooperation, or decisions on it, have been repeatedly refused, and obstacle put in the way of giving effect to the principle of mutual recognition.

The obligation to share information was substantially extended by the 2009 Eurojust Decision. Information may only be processed by Eurojust when a person is under investigation for criminal matters, or being prosecuted under national law. In some circumstances, information on witnesses may also be processed (art.15[1;2]) (applicable in the E-N relationship, art.9[1] cf. 2[2], though only in cases within the competence of Eurojust (EJCD art.4). A wide range of data that can identify a person may be stored: DNA profiles, finger-

133 Op.cit.:19, referring to interviews with former liaison prosecutors Kallerud and Sundet 2008.

134 Eurojust Annual Report 2007:52.

135 Eurojust Annual Report 2012:25.

136 i) human trafficking; (ii) sexual exploitation of children and child pornography; (iii) drug trafficking; (iv) trafficking firearms, their components, and ammunition; (v) corruption; (vi) fraud affecting the financial interests of the European Communities; (vii) counterfeiting the euro; (viii) money laundering; (ix) attacks on information systems.

prints, photos, investigations in different countries, facts suggesting the case has an international dimension, etc. (EJCD art.15[1] a–n). Sensitive information may only be processed when necessary for the national investigation concerned and Eurojust coordination (art.9[4]). Data processed by Eurojust may be shared with other partners, but this needs approval from the data-supplying state (art.27[1]). This approval is unnecessary when the information is forwarded to EU bodies (such as Frontex or Europol), which fall outside the scope of the agreements of art.26a.

The Norway–Eurojust Agreement refers to the 2002 Council Decision that Eurojust was based on; not the revised version of 2008. Norway is not therefore formally bound by the amended CD (E-N art.2[1] cf. 1[a]). It follows from the Cooperation Agreement art.7, however, that the parties shall meet regularly (at least once a year) to assess how the Agreement is being implemented, and agree upon any amendments (art.20[1]). Given the mutual interest in an ongoing cooperation, this must be interpreted as continuing the cooperation based on the new Decision. The consequences of a Norwegian withdrawal from any cooperation it has entered into in the police and crime control area, are hard to predict. It would be difficult to stay in some, and leave others.[137] The 2008 Council Decision drew a distinction between EU member states and Norway : like Eurojust, Norway cannot make 'reasoned recommendations', only less binding 'requests' (E–N Agreement art.3[3]). This may suggest that requests from, or recommendations to, Norway have less force. Requests may be refused without giving any reason. The E–N agreement does not specify which measures the Norwegian LP may suggest, in contrast to the specifications given in the EJCD art.6.[138] The attitude of Norway to EU or other international forums has, though, rarely been one of negligence or unwillingness. The desire seems rather to be 'top of the class': the Norwegian liaison prosecutor is notably better endowed with competences than many EU MS national members.

9.5 Differences and similarities between the systems

There are important differences, but also many similarities between the various systems of information exchange.

Norway's inclusion in various systems may suggest that it is no mean player in the field of international police cooperation. The key aspects for comparison are: 1) the registration requirements regarding an international dimension; 2) the purposes of the systems, for example, crime or immigration control; 3) the geographic reach of the databases, and what kind of information may be accessed; 4) the potential outcomes of the registrations; 5) the use and accessibility of the various databases; and 6) the threshold for registrations.

All the police cooperation mechanisms may presuppose an international dimension, but this does not have the same meaning for each instrument. The different meanings make potential overlaps interesting because they may or may not be applied in addition to, or instead of, each other, by the same authorities. The international dimension may mean that the registered subject or object involves some kind of cross-border element, as in the case of migrants from another country, a convict escaping into another country or a stolen car being driven into another country. The VIS simply concerns visa applications, and this is the cross-border element. Europol involvement previously required the crime in question to be

137 See Hufnagel 2016.

138 The question was not, according to Efjestad, touched upon in the Norwegian *forarbeid* (2009:18–19).

of a "serious, international, organised" nature, but the requirement for an organised criminal structure was removed in 2002, and "related" crimes are now included. The crime in question must still affect two or more Europol member states.

The SIS covers both national and international crime. The domestic crimes included in the system are those such as murder, theft, and illegal immigration, but they must have an international dimension, as when a perpetrator has fled the country, or an expelled immigrant has absconded. The national aspect also covers the prevention and detection of threats to public order and security, unlike EIS, whose purpose is the investigation of more international serious crime.

Another difference is in whether the systems concern crime control alone, a combination of crime and illegal immigration control, or public order policing. The primary purpose of Europol is crime control. That of Eurodac and VIS is control of illegal immigration. The SIS has both immigration and crime control aims. A major difference between the SIS and VIS is that the latter targets third country nationals, while the SIS holds information on both third country and EU nationals in connection with crime and missing persons.[139] Europol operates worldwide and does not discriminate between nationalities, but only targets criminals or those suspected of crime. Eurodac holds only information on foreign nationals applying for asylum, illegal immigrants and illegal border-crossers.

The targets of immigration databases no doubt vary because of interoperability, and the access available to national and international police. While the SIS is concerned with both crime control and immigration control, statistics show that, in practice, it has been used primarily for immigration control,[140] despite the fact that most of the provisions in the CISA and the SIS Act concern crime control. The databases originally dedicated to immigration control, such as Eurodac and VIS, are becoming ever more accessible to the police. If the effects on the individual's life are *de facto* similar, there are good reasons to feel there has been a purpose-shift in these databases to one with a police or criminal procedure focus. Such a change would strengthen the rights of the individual, and the police activity resulting from information held in these databases would be governed more strictly, according to criminal procedural law.

Some of the databases overlap in geographical scope and in the type of information registered and exchanged. SIS is a search register for many of the same types of crimes as the worldwide Interpol and, like it, registers missing persons and objects. As for passports and travel documents, this overlap is regulated in the legal basis. In the case of the potential duplication of arrest warrants, the SIRENE Manual is the only written guideline, and gives priority to SIS alerts over Interpol alerts. The Interpol system should be used only in exceptional cases, where there is insufficient information available to register an alert in the SIS.[141] The SIRENE Manual also recommends that SIRENE Bureaus cooperate with Europol National Units (ENU) and Eurojust, so that all exchange of 'ordinary' and supplementary information, under the SIS rules or not, pass through the SIRENE office.[142] These practices must take place in accordance with national law, and the SIRENE recommendations are non-binding. Some overlap is thus intended, to fill possible gaps between databases: Where SIS is unavailable, Interpol may be used instead, albeit as a second best. One way of

139 Karanja 2008:300.

140 Op.cit.:304.

141 SIRENE 2013:1.8.3 (relating to SIS II Decision, but identical to the former SIRENE versions).

142 SIRENE 2013:1.6; 1.7.

seeing this is that increasing connectedness and interoperability brings them closer together, and makes them less distinct for users.

Eurodac was the first European police and border control cooperation database that contained biometric data. Such data was also allowed in SIS in 2008, and in the VIS in 2011. Biometric data is also included in Europol's registers. Changes in other databases may suggest a spill-over effect: the SIS seems outdated if it does not have the same functions as other systems. Alternatively, it may just be that technical development is an independent driving force.

These databases are all available, to varying degrees, to the police performing law enforcement tasks, either for crime control, or immigration control purposes. The degree to which the various types of information are accessible to the police differs from database to database, depending on the primary purpose of the system. While Eurodac originally concerns only the prevention of illegal immigration, (and this is still the case for Norway), the SIS always had immigration and crime control purposes, as well as a concern with security in the broader sense, including public security. The VIS has immigration control as its main concern, but since its inception has also allowed access for law enforcement purposes. The interoperability between the systems is viable, as with SIS, in passport information alerts. The aim would be to avoid duplicating the use of resources, and – within legal limits – to make the most of the data held.

A major difference between SIS and Europol registers was their intended outcomes. The former was primarily a search register, for wanted or missing persons or objects, while the latter included an investigative tool.[143] This distinction has become less clear since the advent of more extensive data registration possibilities, and SIS is now more of an investigative resource[144], and thus more like the Europol system. The EIS has centralised searches by authorised personnel in the HQ and national units, but the analysis files are closed, because they contain more information and concern ongoing investigations.

Both Europol and Schengen mechanisms contain substantial measures of information exchange, which differs in use and accessibility, as well as in how it may be applied. SIS is a search register that also prescribes action to be taken after a hit. The Europol systems will also request responses, but action may be initiated on the grounds of data in the systems that supplements or supports the information held by the searching state.[145] This underlines the difference between the centralised capacity of Europol and that of SIS, and the much greater autonomy of the Europol office with its direct and indirect employees (i.e. liaison officers) analysing and producing intelligence that Europol may, to some extent, do themselves.

Perhaps the most notable difference is that the Schengen system is decentralised, and run, fed and analysed by the authorities of the Schengen member states and associated partners (including Europol, Interpol, etc.).[146] In contrast, the Europol databases are tools of the employees of Europol itself, containing working and analysis files that are used, and amended by Europol officials (including liaison officers). Exchange of information with the member states takes place only through the national contact point (Kripos in Norway).[147] This difference is also visible in the liaison officer arrangements; through the Schengen cooperation,

143 E.g. Wold 2004:28.

144 See e.g. Boehm 2012a:279–80; 344–5.

145 On the use of such data as evidence, see e.g. Torgersen 2009.

146 A difference to the other international information systems used to be that searches could only be done in the national databases (N.SIS) (Karanja 2008:305). After the SIS II entered into force, however, all search is also in the SIS carried out in the centralised base (OJ L [2006] 381/4) art.4[4]).

147 [2009] OJ L 121/37 art.8(2).

the liaison officers are based in the member states, while liaison officers seconded to Europol work in The Hague.[148] The differences in access, however, are less important: the Europol Convention decided that the direct access of national units to data related to possible future crime should be restricted. Now, national units may consult theEIS directly (ED art.13; ER art. 20). This was a practical change, initially intended to reduce the burden on liaison officers,[149] but also, perhaps, indirectly facilitating wider access to Europol. The importance of easier access later became apparent in the new access rules of the 2016 Regulation.

For Norway, the various sections of Kripos's international department constitute the contact points with international police forums. The exception is SIS, which is accessible for law enforcement more generally. Kripos is still the national SIRENE bureau (SIS Act sect.2). The fact that the same users will often consult several systems in search of the same data probably creates a degree of synergy between them.[150]

Depending on relevant articles of the CISA, there are different thresholds for data registration determined by the reasons for registration, i.e. the type of crime or immigration law violation involved. The Schengen threshold was that the person had committed or was committing particularly serious crimes, or that a foreigner would in the future commit such crimes. This threshold was later lowered: the requirement for more than one crime was dropped, and the crime in question had only to be serious, rather than particularly grave.[151] The Norwegian Ministry's justification for this was pragmatic: it had turned out to be too difficult to maintain a uniform understanding in the Schengen member states of the "particularly grave" criterion, which hindered the unified practice that is required in the Schengen Area. Another reason was that the threshold for extradition, and the corresponding regulation in the European Arrest Warrant (EAW), was lower. This meant that the lowered CISA/SIS Act rules would not be considered disproportionate.

A basic difference between the information systems is their geographic scope. Apart from Interpol, the other information systems Norway participates in are primarily European. However, while the systems do include players from different areas – the SIS is mainly accessible to the police of Schengen member states – the partial interoperability and cooperation between the systems, at least for users who have access to all systems (e.g. personnel at Kripos or Europol HQ), means that information entered into the systems may reach further than the initial purpose for registration. As a general rule, data processed in the SIS (II) must not be made available to third countries or to international organisations, with the exception of passport data etc. that may be transferred to Interpol.[152] Nevertheless, in accordance with the "data ownership principle" in the SIS II Regulation art.34(2), the MS which registered the information may transmit supplementary information to third countries. Such a transfer may, if allowed in national provisions, take place via Interpol.[153] Issues concerning the proliferation of information then arise, as when there is increased pressure to share information with other parties.

One of the research questions I will address here in part II, is the impact international police cooperation may have on the work of Norwegian police, and whether this is what the

148 Wold 2004:28.
149 de Moor and Vermeulen 2010a:1102.
150 Karanja 2008:308.
151 Ugelvik 2009.
152 [2006] OJ L 381/4 art.39; [2007] OJ L 205/63 art.54–55.
153 SIRENE 2013:1.5.1(b).

population "needs" according to the Police Act sect.1. This account and analysis of the information systems, access rules and possible avenues for cooperation, aim to show the range of resources available to the police for purposes of information exchange, retrieving information giving grounds for further investigation, and establishing the identity of various categories of people. There are differences in the primary purposes of the resources. Some are largely police databases, others have both crime control and illegal immigration control purposes, and others are only relevant to immigration matters, such as visa applications. Because Norway is not an EU member, the access of the Norwegian police to databases, sometimes depends g on whether they are Schengen-relevant or not. In other cases, police access depends on the reason for seeking access: whether it is for (serious) crime control purposes or, say, safeguarding public order. The breadth and the scope of the systems are considerable: of particular note is the Eurodac development whereby the Norwegian Ministry suggests allowing foreign law enforcement authorities access to data that is prohibited for Norwegian law enforcement authorities. These developments challenge the separation of administrative and policiary powers, and the link between the police and the state.

The information retrieved or exchanged through the various instruments may be utilised in operational police activity. The following chapter therefore concerns the practical outcomes of information exchange.

10 Actions following hits in the databases

The traditional notion of international cooperation in criminal matters involves extradition and mutual legal assistance, but even such cooperation presupposes practicalities such as seizure or arrest.[1] Information exchange registers, such as SIS, function as broad search registers for wanted and missing persons and things. But these registers also include requests for foreign police to take action on behalf of the agency that made the registration. Information is, for example, registered to help apprehend a person wanted for a criminal offence or to obtain evidence pertaining to an investigation. This chapter analyses the regulation of arrests and the obtaining of evidence, through hits in databases. The role of the EU bodies Europol and Eurojust is also explored, in relation to arrests, after a brief look at requests for surveillance or specific checks.

10.1 Requests for surveillance or specific checks

Information on persons and vehicles may be registered so that surveillance or specific checks will be performed abroad. The purpose of observation may be to collect evidence or analyse the structure of criminal networks. 'Specific checks' means search in/of a person or object/property. The requirements for this in the original CISA art.99 no.2 refer to "prosecuting criminal offences and the prevention of threats to public security" and "numerous and extremely serious offences" (no.2 a). The wording of the Norwegian SIS Act was changed in 2008, following the SIS II Council Decisions, to remove the requirement that the serious offences should be "numerous and extremely [serious]", thus lowering the threshold for registering such requests quite significantly.[2] The police action requested must be necessary, either because a person is seen as a threat or because there are other threats to internal or external security. Information gathering and transmitting is regulated in CISA art.94. Searches, like any coercive measure, may only be performed according to national rules. Surveillance involves directed, non-coercive watching of and listening to someone or something, and includes the retrieval of information.[3] Surveillance involving coercion, such as wire-tapping or bugging private rooms, is not covered by the Schengen cooperation. This follows from art.40 no.3(e). The CISA does not contain rules on which observation techniques may be applied. The vagueness of the wording opens the way for measures such as

1 Anderson *et al.* 1995:218.

2 [2006] OJ L 381/4; [2007] OJ L 205/63. The lowered threshold, I argue elsewhere, is poorly justified (Ugelvik 2009).

3 Auglend *et al.* 2004; Joubert and Bevers 1996.

DOI: 10.4324/9780429503696-12

police infiltration and controlled deliveries. The latter are specifically mentioned in art.73, which antithetically gives grounds to exclude pure "observation" of the surveillance as applied in arts.40 and 99.

CISA art.99 was transferred into the SIS Act sect.8 (1) and determines when requests for discreet surveillance or specific checks may be registered in the SIS. The purpose must be to fight crime and prevent threats to public security (a) when there is clear evidence ("***konkrete holdepunkter***") that a person is planning to commit, or is committing, a serious criminal offence, or (b) where an overall assessment of a person, especially because of previous criminal acts, makes it likely he/she will also commit serious criminal acts in the future. In the second paragraph, such registration is also permitted when there is clear evidence that information on a person's whereabouts, travel route, destination, passengers, etc., are necessary to prevent a serious threat posed by him/her, or other serious threats to internal or external national security. As shown above, there is a general obligation to cooperate as far as possible within national legislative frameworks (CISA art.39). Norwegian police are not, however, obliged to grant a request from foreign police to put someone under surveillance. If they do so, this must be in accordance with national law. This makes such requests comparable to ordinary international requests for assistance in criminal matters, even though the incentive to comply might seem somewhat stronger.[4] The main difference is how the requests are transmitted, that is, via SIS instead of letters rogatory, for example. Since the action taken must accord with Norwegian national law, art.99 is not analysed further here. This Schengen resource is less of a novelty in the Norwegian policing situation than the one I look at in the next subchapter.

Norway negotiated an agreement with the EU on the European Evidence Warrant (EEW), which facilitates the gathering and transmission of evidence among the member states.[5] The agreement was not ratified in EU MS before the EEW was replaced by the European Investigation Order (EIO), in force May 2017.[6] There has been no agreement (as yet) on a Norwegian association. Since these matters primarily concern court-involved police cooperation in criminal matters, they will not be further discussed here. The Norwegian Europol liaison officers have expressed concern that Norway's efficiency will be seriously reduced by its non-affiliation to the EIO.[7]

10.2 Arrest

10.2.1 Arrest after a SIS hit

Neither the CISA nor any other international treaty provide a legal basis for foreign police or law enforcement authorities to order an arrest in Norway. There are different regulations in Norwegian law, depending which international agreement an arrest request is based on. One could say that the SIS Act regulates the registration of data to facilitate the exchange of arrest requests. Other international police cooperation agreements, such as the Prüm

4 See e.g. Ot.prp.nr.56 (1998–1999) ch.6.2.2. The general obligation to comply with international requests for assistance in criminal matters follows e.g. from ETS 30 (1959), especially arts.1 no.1 and 2 no.1; also and ETS 182 (2001).

5 [2008] OJ L 350/72.

6 [2010]OJ C 165/22.

7 http://www.juristkontakt.no/i/2017/2/juko-2017-02b-19 [08.09.2017]).

cooperation, provide a similar basis for apprehension and arrest, and one might expect such coercive measures to be collected into one act. However, given that the actual legal basis for coercive action is the same in all cases, whether outside or within the SIS Act, this absence of a single act is without legal significance. The Act itself does not give any legal basis for apprehension, arrest or extradition such as follows from the Police Act, the Criminal Procedure Act and the Extradition Act.

A request to arrest a person may be registered in the SIS for extradition purposes (CISA art.94 no.1, SIS Act sect.7 no.1). If a Norwegian police officer gets a SIS hit that requires the arrest and extradition of someone, the officer may apprehend that person. Prior to the arrest, the legality of the alert in the issuing state must be examined (SIS Act sect.5 [3] cf. CISA art.95 no.2). The arrest must be legal in both states (art.95 no.6). The Schengen cooperation does not concern extradition to another member state, only arrest and detention until the necessary procedures can be carried out. Any extradition must be in accordance with existing agreements, typically following an arrest order.

The principle of mutual recognition is a cornerstone of police and judicial cooperation in criminal matters in the EU. The principle does not apply to third states such as Norway, and may thus limit the scope of Norwegian police cooperation. The principle implies a unquestioning acceptance of foreign legal decisions prior to carrying them out in the 'host' state – when, say, extraditing an individual in response to a foreign request. During the negotiations on Norway's agreement with the EU on the European Arrest Warrant (see the following), it became clear that not all EU member states were willing to put as much trust in Norway as the mutual recognition principle takes for granted. Unquestioning acceptance of the decisions of foreign legal systems means mistakes are more likely to happen, which may explain the scepticism of EU states towards including third countries.[8]

To a certain extent, the mutual recognition principle does apply more generally in Norway, and the police cooperation systems are examples of this. A Norwegian Act implementing the Lugano Convention gives a legal basis to the l principle of accepting foreign judicial decisions without further examination.[9] This only concerns civil cases, and customs cases are excepted (art.1 [1]). The principle guiding the Norwegian courts' evidence assessment means that the courts are free to decide whether evidence has weight, and – and if so – how much. The Norwegian Supreme Court has applied this principle so as to allow evidence gathered (legally) abroad that Norwegian police would not have been allowed to gather (Rt. 2002.1744 and Rt.2005.1524).[10] The principle of reciprocity means, however, that if a state's law enforcement authorities request a certain police measure to be taken in another jurisdiction, for example, wire-tapping or surveillance, they must return the favour when the other state asks them to. The Norwegian police should thus not request action in other countries that they would not be able to perform in Norway.[11] Doing so might not be

8 Efjestad 2009:15.

9 Act 08.01.1993 no. 21 art.26, with exceptions in art.27.

10 The Norwegian police may, through SIS, request evidence to be gathered within another state, or to be allowed into that territory to collect such material themselves. Such requests pass through the Ministry, and are not detailed further here (the Extradition Act 1975 sect.24). For the Norwegian courts' use of evidence gathered abroad through investigative measures that are illegal in Norway, see Rundskriv G 19/2001; Torgersen 2009; Bruce 2015.

(The applicable Norwegian processes follow the Forskrift om internasjonalt samarbeid i straffesaker (2012); [2004] OJ L 26/3 and Nordic MLA 1974.

11 Bruce and Haugland 2014:99; 104.

illegal, but it is a clear general rule that Norwegian police must not actively seek to evade national rules.[12]

The 2001 European Arrest Warrant was designed to facilitate extradition between EU member states. Such warrants are automatically legally valid in any member state. An EAW may be issued as an alert in the SIS (EAW Decision art.9 no.2–4; CISA art.95) and be equivalent to an arrest order request until the SIS (II) is capable of holding complete arrest warrants. An affiliation agreement was made in 2006 for Norway's participation in the EAW, replacing traditional extradition with surrendering procedures, and simplifying the process significantly.[13]

The affiliation agreement was finally accepted by the Norwegian and EU parliaments in 2011. Ratification was expected to come in 2013, but the approval required has not been forthcoming, either from the Council or from every EU member state (art.218 TFEU). The Agreement resembles the EAW, but contains some variations allowing, for example, the continued exception of 'political offences' and the ability to refuse to extradite one's own citizens, subject to some limitations. The difficulty of accessing the European Arrest Warrant is one example of a lack of trust between some e EU member states and Norway as a 'third country'.[14]

Norway has alternatives to facilitated arrest orders, such as the 2005 Nordic Arrest Warrant Agreement. Apart from this, extradition following either a Schengen-related arrest or through other cooperation mechanisms must take place in accordance with the regulations in the Extradition Act sect.15 (before the Norwegian Arrest Warrant Act of 2012 becomes fully applicable).[15] The lack of access to EAWs directly in the SIS has no practical consequences as long as the SIS is used as an alert system: CISA art.95 still contains provisions on the transfer of additional information, which usually means a complete arrest warrant.[16]

The requirement to examine the legal validity of arrest requests was criticised for being more laborious than other ordinary international requests. The Norwegian legal solution was simply to give the SIRENE office responsibility to review the arrest regulations in all other member states. SIRENE coordinates the procedure of the public prosecutor in all such cases.[17]

CISA contained restrictions on the arrest of a state's citizens (art.95 no.3). This was changed for the EU member states by the European Arrest Warrant. Norwegian citizens too, may now be extradited from Norway to other countries under the general delimitations within the Extradition Act of 1975 and the European and Nordic Arrest Warrant Act of

12 Riksadvokatens letter of 20.01.2003 about Rt. 2002.1744.

13 [2006] OJ L 292/1, also defined in the Decision defining the Schengen Extradition *Acquis* as regards Norway and Iceland ([2003] OJ L 76/25) (Peers 2011:675 fn.113). The Norwegian extradition rules in relation to the EU rules are detailed in Mathisen 2009; and the relationship between the NAW and the EAW in Mathisen 2010. Mathisen concludes that the NAW is an improvement on the EAW, partly because of the higher level of mutual trust existing between the Nordic countries than between the EU MS. This is contrary to Larsson 2006:462, who argues that the French, Italian and Spanish systems and cultures are, for example, more similar than the Nordic ones. See also Hufnagel 2013 ch.3.

14 E.g. Muth 2006:ch.5.3; Kvam and Suominen 2009.

15 The Extradition Act of 1975 supplied by the Arrest Warrant Act 2012 with its 2012 Circular.

16 On the comparison and implementation of the EAW and the Nordic Arrest Warrant in Sweden, Denmark and Finland, see Suominen 2011:ch.3.3.

17 Ot.prp.nr.56 (1998–1999):60–62.

2012. The latter, however, only applies to Nordic arrest warrants, which means that other arrest warrants from Schengen countries outside the Nordic region must still must follow Schengen or general international extradition procedures.

As regards extradition and surrender procedures, the Norwegian police may thus, for the time being, seem to be excluded from the closer cooperation existing between EU members. Norway is, however, associated with both Europol and Eurojust, and we will now look at the process of requesting arrest through these EU bodies.

10.2.2 Europol and Eurojust arrest

Neither Europol nor Eurojust are autonomous operational police or prosecution bodies. Both entities may, however, have significant roles in police operations involving arrest. Eurojust is a prosecutorial cooperation instrument, and therefore principally outside the scope of this book. To provide an integrated understanding of the measures accounted for in the previous chapter, it is, however, necessary to explore the Eurojust cooperation to a certain extent as well. As seen in Chapter 2.4, the police and public prosecution are partly intertwined in Norway. This combination also explains the following analysis of the EU police and prosecution bodies' role in arrest after information exchange.

Europol does not have power to carry out coercive police activities on its own, but at the request of member states, may assist in such operations. The Norwegian contact point is Kripos,[18] which means it is the only direct hub for information exchange between Europol and the Norwegian police – apart from the contacts the Norwegian liaison officer (LO) makes at the Europol HQ (E-N art.14). In emergencies, communication may take place directly between the LO and the police districts in Norway. Kripos must later be notified of such contact (art.7[2]). This could happen if information from a Europol analysis, for example, revealed a drug courier was driving through Norway. The Norwegian LO could then telephone the Trondheim police district and request immediate arrest. This would be within Norwegian police competence, and carried out by them, but at the instigation of Europol.

The Norwegian Eurojust liaison prosecutor may autonomously initiate coercive measures within Norway that are within his competence as a senior prosecutor. Most of these, (except in emergencies), are limited by a prior court decision (EP CD art.9a). In principle, such action should take place in accordance with the responsible national authority (EPCD art.9c). Following a coordination meeting within Eurojust, or a tip from another Eurojust state or body, the liaison prosecutor may request that Norwegian police carry out a general investigation; arrest a specific person; or set up a joint investigation team to cooperate with, for example, Sweden. The Norwegian Eurojust prosecutor could also, in urgent cases, directly suggest cooperation between police districts within Norway (EPCD art.9d[a]). He/she is entitled to all national information needed to deal with Eurojust cases (EP–N art.5[5]/EPCD art.9b), for example, everything pertaining to a case which may have ramifications in other states.

A supranational European public prosecutors' office (EPPO), suggested on the basis of TEU art.86, will work (initially) only within the field of crime against the Union's financial interests. TFEU art.86 however, opens the way to extending the EPPO's competences to other areas of serious crime with a cross-border element (with similar aims to Europol and

18 N-E Cooperation Agreement arts. 5; 7. For more detail on Eurojust, see e.g. Suominen 2008.

Eurojust), if the Council and Parliament see fit.[19] The declared purpose of the EPPO and the (future) Eurojust is to give bodies at the EU level competence to carry out investigations or prosecutions themselves, since the member states' efforts to prevent fraud are not as "effective, uniform and deterrent as required under the Treaty".[20] Since EPPO representatives would be empowered to carry out investigations, and prosecute in member states' national courts, this body would constitute a new type of legal entity in the international system. The EPPO has met substantial resistance: in 2014, the Council's proposal was sent to the member states for consideration, but did not gain unanimous approval.[21] A so-called enhanced cooperation was initiated instead, and in October 2017, the 20 MS who are part of this (per December 2017), agreed on the Regulation on how EPPO should function.[22] Norway was obviously not included in the approval phase, and will have to adapt to how EPPO will function in practice.

There is no supranational police or public prosecutor in the EU. Nonetheless, national representatives, including from Norway's, adhere to an EU set of rules and procedures. Although these are not binding, there are strong incentives to comply with them, as they are applied more or less uniformly throughout the member states of Schengen, Europol and Eurojust, whatever their member status. The incentives relate both to fighting cross-border crime, and the political advantages of cooperation. Since neither Eurojust nor Europol have operational competences, it is the national authorities that carry out the recommendations – or decisions – of these bodies. Such operations take place within national law of the acting state. For Norway, there is the additional incentive of appearing to be an important partner to the EU and the EU bodies, since its non-EU member status makes it unclear whether it will be included in ongoing and future collaborations.

19 Press release from the Commission, http://ec.europa.eu/justice/newsroom/criminal/news/130717_en.htm [13.09.13].

20 COM/2013/0534 final, Explanatory Memorandum ch.1.

21 http://www.consilium.europa.eu/en/press/press-releases/2017/06/08-eppo/ [15.09.2017].

22 [2017] OJ L 283/1.

11 Liaison officers

Between operational and non-operational cooperation

Norway partakes in the arrangement for seconding liaison officers to several forums. Seconding police officers (*sambandsmenn*) has been a long-standing Nordic tradition. The Nordic Police and Customs Cooperation (PTN) countries exchange liaison officers between themselves and have joint representation in non-Nordic countries. The Schengen cooperation gives an international legal basis for such arrangements between police authorities in the member states. The Europol and Eurojust Agreements with Norway give a basis for seconding Norwegian liaison officers to their offices, and vice versa. Liaison officers may participate in operational meetings, and coordinate such operations as controlled deliveries and cross-border surveillance. The tasks vary between states.[1]

The secondment measures in the CISA (art.47provide for bilateral or multilateral liaison agreements, and are nothing new for Norway.[2] What was new, perhaps, was the encouragement to expand the pool of secondment partners to the rest of the Schengen Area. In the mid-1990s, this was not a very large or diverse group. This changed because of the bilateral and multilateral possibilities for seconding police officers provided for by art.47 and the increase in Schengen member states during the early 2000s

The Nordic model of joint liaison officers, representing more than one country, was unknown in other Schengen member states (art.47 no.4). Liaison officers in the Schengen MS are not authorised to act on behalf of their contracting state with autonomous police authority, but "to provide advice and assistance". They are not permitted to act operationally abroad.[3] Although it excludes coercive measures, this arrangement allows national police to exercise authority on behalf of foreign jurisdictions.

The Europol cooperation also has a system of liaison officers (ER art.8). Every member state's national unit (e.g. Kripos) is obliged to have at least one seconded liaison officer at Europol's HQ. Norway must guarantee that the liaison officer has the necessary technical access to the various databases that his home-based colleagues have access to. Europol is also allowed to station an officer within a particular police body in Norway (E-N art.14 no.4).

Bigo calls the liaison officer "a human interface between various police forces"; according to den Boer, the "personification of the foreign police of nation-states".[4] Norwegian liaison

1 Block 2011:169; Block 2013:105–6.

2 St.prp.nr.42 (1996–1997):ch. 5.5.9.

3 In contrast to the primarily operative liaison officers some countries, such as France, have in Interpol (Block 2013:105).

4 Bigo 2000b:74, den Boer 2010:57. For more general, worldwide details on liaison officers see Nadelmann 1993; Bigo 2000b.

DOI: 10.4324/9780429503696-13

officers do not work as Norwegian police officers when they are posted to other countries or organisations; they are seconded to the particular foreign authority.[5] The police officer seconded to Europol works for Europol, in The Hague; the officer who is seconded to Serbia works in the liaison office for Serbia, Bosnia, Montenegro and Croatia. The liaison officer's main task is to cooperate, in his area of competence, with the authorities of the host state or organisation, on behalf of, but not at the behest of, Norwegian police. They thus give assistance to local police authorities, but in the interests of building relations and solving crime that affects Norway. They do not engage in operational police work, nor do they carry out investigations on their own initiative. Instead, they function as an information link between the police in the host country and the police in the home state. For example, if the Nordic liaison officer in Serbia came across information he though could be important to Norwegian police, he would inform Kripos. Information may sometimes be so precise that it leads directly to an arrest. More vague information is passed on to the relevant police department, which may follow it up in case the information has 'drowned' in an information overflow.[6] Bigo's research shows that Europol liaison officer cooperation goes deeper than other bilateral or multilateral agreements, since all the officers work at the Europol HQ and actually get to know each other through day-to-day contact and cooperation.[7]

Liaison officers may receive information and requests for information from both the home and host state: thus, if customs stop two Bosnian citizens on the border with Norway because they 'suspect something', but the SIS reveals no hits, the customs officers may contact the liaison officer directly. What used to take several days to arrange through Interpol, can now be done by the liaison officer within minutes.[8] However, communications between Norway and the liaison officers must still pass through the Third Countries Office, which assesses the legality of the transfer. Although the new Police Directive sect.1–3 no.1 includes the Norwegian liaison officers in Europol and Eurojust, there is no legal provision authorising them to transfer information, say, during a JIT operation.

Since information from the liaison officer is not necessarily computerised or gathered and analysed in the same way as data in police resources such as the Europol analysis registers, or in the SIS, this information exchange may, in principle, happen outside Norwegian data protection legislation. The limitations in Norwegian law concerning professional secrecy still apply. The Ministry has not considered it necessary to provide a specific Norwegian legal basis for the secondment of Europol liaison officers.[9] The liaison officer thus seems like a closer, somewhat more informal, contact between the countries in question. Since there is ever more police cooperation, both operationally, and as regards information, the role of liaison officers as contact nodes and advisors becomes increasingly important.

5 Council Decision of 27 February 2003 on the use of liaison officers in law enforcement.

6 Interview with Jan Kruszewski in Solberg 2011b.

7 Bigo 2000b.

8 Solberg 2011a:40.

9 St.prp.nr.98 (2000–2001) ch.5. Kvam (2014) argues that there is no proper Norwegian legal basis for the liaison officers.

12 National law enforcement on foreign territory

Operational cooperation

The state's sovereign jurisdiction over its territory is presupposed in Norwegian law, as in the General Civil Penal Code (GCPC) sect.12(1).[1] I argue that cross-border investigative measures challenge these jurisdictional rules. The responsibility for an investigation is supposed to lie with the local chief of police, who may request assistance from Kripos, if their expertise and equipment is needed. Investigative measures must be performed by Norwegian police on Norwegian territory (CPA sect.225; Prosecution Directive (***Påtaleinstrukensen***, PI) 1985 sect.7–5 [1]). The pertinent Norwegian Acts are, however, only applicable with the restrictions imposed by relevant international law or agreements (CPA sect.4; PA sect.3; GCPC sect.2).

The focus has so far been on police cooperation in terms of information exchange, and on actions that may follow such exchange. The following chapters are devoted to more practical police cooperation across borders: cross-border hot pursuit and surveillance, and joint investigations and operations.[2] Either information-related, or operational cooperation may lead to someone being arrested or convicted in another country. Carrying out police operations in a foreign territory is, however, traditionally seen as more problematic. A state's sovereign right to exercise coercive authority within its own territory is normally only challenged in times of war – or, on the basis of international agreements.

I take the Schengen cooperation as my point of departure, since it is the EU cooperation forum into which Norway is most fully integrated. The Schengen Convention is the basic legal agreement for international cross-border police operations, including associated bilateral or multilateral agreements between member states and others.[3] The cooperation obliges

1 There are, however, several issues outside the agreed core of the principle, e.g. suspects based in other countries; crimes partly committed in other countries, or where a partial or full offence took place in different countries. There is no agreed set of international rules on this, at either the UN, Council of Europe or EU level. In contrast to international civil law, where national courts may apply foreign law in their proceedings, courts enforcing national criminal law will generally apply this alone (Peers 2011:823). As a consequence, when the law of one country is applied to a certain criminal offence, the offender will not, as a general rule, be convicted by any other state's court under this law. In addition, many countries will apply jurisdiction on certain offences committed outside their territory, regardless of whether the act was criminalised where it was committed, as follows e.g. from the Norwegian Penal Code sect.5.

2 This corresponds to the contents of the Council's Manual of cross-border operations (CBO Manual 10505/3/09 (REV 3)).

3 Peers 2011:934. Bilateral cross-border police agreements have existed in Europe for a long time, between e.g. France and Switzerland, Austria and Prussia, Austria-Hungary and Germany (Fijnaut 1993:120–1), and later between e.g. the BeNeLux countries. Several such extended bilateral agreements exist in addition to the CISA. On the development of post-1950 police cooperation in Europe, see Hufnagel 2013:36–58.

DOI: 10.4324/9780429503696-14

member states, under certain conditions, to permit the exercise of authority by foreign police, either in the form of hot pursuit or cross-border surveillance, on their territory. The specific measures are not necessarily 'cooperative' in the sense that two or more Schengen member states' police officers work together. Rather, they imply that foreign police officers on their own may, under certain circumstances exercise police authority on the territory of another state. Such action may be understood as 'cooperative', in the sense that the police forces are cooperating on a common police purpose, irrespective of national boundaries.

The Police Act sect.20a was amended in 2001 following Norway's Affiliation Agreement with the Schengen cooperation. The CISA regulations on police cooperation were largely transferred into Norwegian law, permitting foreign police to enforce their home state's jurisdiction on Norwegian territory. Police authority includes issuing commands and prohibitions, and, if necessary, enforcing these by coercive power. This authority was strictly limited: only cross-border continuation of on-going surveillance or hot pursuit was allowed in the Police Act before 2012. Substantial developments have taken place in cross-border police cooperation since the Schengen cooperation of the 1990s. The instruments and measures examined in this chapter, after an initial discussion of cross-border hot pursuit and surveillance, are those concerning controlled deliveries, covert investigation, and joint investigation teams.

12.1 The development and content of the relevant Norwegian legal basis

The Schengen Cooperation was the direct cause of the new Police Act section 20a, but the Government considered it advisable to provide a general legal basis for foreign police activity in Norway.[4] Specific reference to the Schengen Convention was made, however, to limit the access of foreign police, after criticism in the legislative consultation rounds. This reference was seen as limiting the extent of the new international law enforcement on Norwegian territory, and thus also limiting the possible infringement of sovereignty.[5] In 2012, as mentioned above, the reference was removed.

According to the Norwegian Police Act sect.20a(1), foreign police officers may participate in joint investigation teams, or joint police operations, or otherwise perform their policing duties in Norway in so far as this follow agreements with other states. Continued observation or hot pursuit into Norwegian territory are also allowed. These requirements have been changed twice, most recently with a 2012 amendment (which came into force in 2013). The latter removed the distinction made between the various measures. Since 2013, sect.20a has been the legal basis for all foreign officials' activities permitted by mutual agreements. Cross-border hot pursuit, observation, joint investigation teams and joint police operations are specifically mentioned, but the Act does not set out any further regulation of them. Sect.20a is simply the legal basis for any present or future cooperation agreed upon with a foreign state.

Domestically, the general rule on assistance from other national police districts, and the Norwegian police special units, especially Kripos, is that the chief of police in the district remains in charge of the operation in question. The special units do, however, sometimes take over responsibility, or have initial responsibility, in complex or otherwise special cases.

4 Ot.prp.nr.56 (1998–1999):92.
5 Op.cit. The Committee's comments ch.8.

If there are risks involved following ordinary – often more time-consuming – procedures, most decisions may be made outside the ordinary decision-making hierarchy. Requests for assistance from other public bodies or departments, should be directed to the police chief of the district. There are exceptions to this rule in emergencies (PD sects.13–4). Urgent requests for assistance from another police district, can be directly forwarded to lower-level police officers, who should either get permission from their superiors or, alert their superiors after assistance is been given (PD sect.7–4(2)). This accords with the regulations on the procedure that applies when a police officer acts outside his geographical area of service without such a request (to protect persons or goods from imminent danger, or in other pressing police matters) (PD sect.7–2).

Whenever exceptions are sought, assistance must be requested from the proper agency, as soon as possible, and within 24 hours at the latest (PA sect.17d (3)). The strict procedures to be followed in the case of searches are described more fully in the *forarbeid*.[6] According to PA sect.7a, exceptions on searches can only be made by senior officials.

In the case of international cooperation, the Norwegian government did not, in the 1990s, consider the Schengen measures that allowed foreign police officers to enforce their authority in Norway to necessitate any legal amendments. Nordic police cooperation already allowed cross-border hot pursuit and surveillance, because of the vast wilderness areas in the borderlands of Norway, Finland and Sweden. Nor did the possibility of arrest by foreign police officers (CISA arts. 40–41) require new legislation, since anyone could already legally arrest someone caught in the act or fleeing after committing a crime (i.e. 'citizen's arrest', CPA sect.176(1)). The Schengen cooperation police measures were thus not intended either to increase the Norwegian police's power to make arrests, or to provide a legal basis for giving foreign police officers Norwegian police authority.[7] After criticism of the lack of a clear legal basis for (potentially) coercive powers, the Police Act was amended by section 20a. The amended section also required foreign police officers to be subject to Norwegian administrative and penal law *in the same manner as Norwegian police officers* (in accordance with CISA art.42). This, for example, implied that a foreign police officer acting in Norway would be criminally responsible in the same way as domestic police, but also protected under the GCPC sect.155 (threats against police officers). The new legislation thus underlined the difference between ordinary citizen's arrest and the responsibilities and duties of police officers – even ones acting outside their territory.

In the political debates of the 1990s on the Schengen cooperation, concern was also voiced about additional 'soft law' rules. There were doubts about the handbooks on police cooperation, and on maintaining public order and security.[8] The Ministry maintained that the handbooks were mere guidelines. Nevertheless, the cooperation implied that these guidelines should be followed provided they were in accordance with national law. The handbook had to be distributed and followed by the Norwegian police.[9] The question as to

6 Ot.prp.nr.58 (2001–2002):27.

7 Ot.prp.nr.56 (1998–1999):96.

8 The common practices and handbooks of cross-border police cooperation are for example the Schengen Executive Committee's Handbook on cross-border police cooperation [SCH/Com-ex (98)52] ([2000] OJ L 239/407 restricted document); Decision with principles governing the payment of informers ([2000] OJ L 239/417). A similar resolution was adopted by the Council ([1997] OJ C 10/1); Best practice and recommendations regarding Schengen cooperation (Council doc 10842/09, Peers 2011:927).

9 Innst.S.nr.147 (1998–1999):15; St.meld.nr.33 (1998–1999) ch.8.

which guidelines have final authority when those of the Schengen regulatory authorities conflict with those of the Norwegian police, or other authorities, does not yet have a definitive answer.

12.2 Hot pursuit and cross-border surveillance

On 7 August 2012, a brutal bank robbery took place in the small town of Töckfors in Sweden, a few kilometres from Norway. The three robbers then drove across the border. Both Norwegian and Swedish police from neighbouring districts participated in the ensuing search. A helicopter was kept ready on the Swedish side of the border, with permission to enter Norwegian territory if necessary.[10] This is an example of one of the until recently only forms of autonomous police operations allowed on Norwegian territory: hot pursuit and cross-border surveillance.

'Hot pursuit' in CISA is defined as the pursuit of someone caught committing or participating in a serious criminal act, or immediately afterwards, and when there is no doubt that he/she is the offender; or the pursuit of someone escaping a custodial sentence or provisional custody.[11] The general rule is that the home state takes over at the national border (CISA art.41 no.1). If the home state police cannot immediately do so, cross-border pursuit may take place to ensure that the person does not escape. Similarly, if a police officer, is keeping under surveillance someone suspected of committing an extraditable offence, or someone who there is good reason to believe may assist in identifying or tracing such a person, the officer may continue the surveillance in another Schengen country (CISA art.40). In the first scenario, surveillance may continue without notification in particularly urgent situations, and borders may be crossed without prior notice when this is not feasible.[12] At the latest, officers must consult the authorities of the host state as they cross the border. Pursuit shall cease at the first request of the host state. Hot pursuit and cross-border observation are regulated in the Norwegian Police Act sect.20a, which sets the requirements and permissions for both measures. They will therefore be dealt with together in the following, which focuses on the details that arise from the CISA rules.

Exceptions to the general rules can only be made if certain requirements are met. The grounds for border crossing will be described first, including the level of suspicion necessary, the type of crime, and the further consideration of whether or not non-offenders also may be pursued. General rules concerning which types of police may cross borders, whether they can be armed, and whether they may arrest someone in other countries, are dealt with later.

12.2.1 The grounds for crossing borders

Cross-border hot pursuit and surveillance may be applied to those suspected of certain criminal offences. Police may also cross borders in pursuit of someone who could identify the perpetrator of such crimes. Hot pursuit may also take place when someone has escaped from

10 Dagbladet 08.08.12.

11 The definition resembles that of the traditional right of hot pursuit in international law, except as regards flight from custody, see e.g. Poulantzas 2002:11.

12 'Host state' indicates the state upon whose territory the foreign activity takes place, while 'home state' signifies the sending state, or state whose officers are enforcing their powers abroad.

provisional custody, or while serving a sentence involving the deprivation of liberty. These requirements are explained further in the next sub chapters.

12.2.1.1 Suspicion and offences

The original list of offences legitimising cross-border surveillance contained very serious crimes, such as murder, rape, forgery of banknotes, aggravated burglary and robbery, human trafficking, and trafficking in narcotic drugs (CISA art.40 no.7). Two amendments were made after the incorporation into the EU *Acquis*, in 2000 and 2003. The first was technical, the other more substantial: instead of being only someone suspected of an extraditable offence, the subject could now also be a person who there "is serious reason to believe [. . .] can assist in identifying or tracing such a person".[13]

The range of crimes that could justify 'urgent procedures' in art.40 no.2, cf. no.7, was also expanded to include counterfeiting of means of payment, smuggling of aliens, money laundering, participation in criminal organisations,[14] and terrorist offences.[15] The offences listed in art.41 no.4(a) were originally the same as for cross-border surveillance (art.40 no.7), except that they also included the failure to give explanation to the police following a serious accident. Daman shows how varying definitions of the offences may be problematic, particularly in hot pursuits: in Germany, car theft constitutes 'aggravated theft', which is listed in art.41 no.4(a). In France, however, it is merely theft. The many hot pursuits of car thieves in Germany have therefore led to a reclassification of the offence in French law, while German police have reduced the number of such hot pursuits.[16] With the 2003 Council Decision,[17] the list of offences 'justifying' surveillance was significantly extended. MS themselves decide whether the list in no. 4(a) or the 'extraditable offences' alternative should apply. The latter alternative, chosen by Norway, is a wider category.[18]

Requests for legal assistance in criminal matters are regulated by the Norwegian Extradition Act, Chapter V. The refusal grounds are much the same as those in the 1959 Convention with protocols. Sect.23a no.3(c) makes "other weighty reasons" grounds for refusal, such as the fact that the suspect is under the age of criminal responsibility. Other grounds for refusal are certain practical hindrances, and the lack of legal basis in Norwegian law for the requested measure.[19]

The EU Convention of 29 May 2000 regulates mutual recognition and legal assistance in criminal matters between EU member states.[20] Its purpose is to encourage and modernise cooperation between judicial, police and customs authorities by supplementing and facilit-

13 Surveillance of non-suspects was added by the Council Decision 2003/725/JHA; [2000] OJ L 248/1, amended in the PA in 2012.

14 [1998] OJ L 351.

15 As referred to in [2002] OJ L 164/3 on combating terrorism. The wording was also amended for some terms; 'rape' was replaced with 'a serious offence of a sexual nature'. Boucht 2012:208 n.23 shows how art.17 in the second additional protocol has a narrower scope than the CISA.

16 Daman 2008:182.

17 Council Decision 2003/725/JHA.

18 The Extradition Act sect.3 cf. PA sect.20a (before the 2012 amendment).

19 Prop.97 LS (2011–2012):55. If the request does not imply coercive measures, there is no requirement of double criminality in the Extradition Act; the 1959 art.5 no.1(a); nor in the CISA art.51(a).

20 [2000] OJ C 197/01, and the Protocol to the Convention on Mutual Assistance in Criminal Matters between the member states of the European Union established by the Council in accordance with Article 34 of the Treaty on European Union ([2001] OJ C 326/1).

ating the existing instruments; the provisions and application of the 1959 Council of Europe Convention MLA and its 1978 Protocol, the CISA, and the Benelux Treaty of 1962. Some parts of the Convention and its protocol of 2001 were defined as a development of the Schengen cooperation, and thereby applicable to Norway. The others were made applicable through an Association Agreement, which, along with new extradition regulations, was finally negotiated in June 2012, and came into force in early 2013.[21] The rules on mutual recognition and assistance simplify legal assistance and make it more flexible regarding the exchange of legal requests, witness interrogation via video or telephones, phone tapping and surveillance of bank transactions. In terms of operational police cooperation, the agreements provide a legal basis for joint and covert investigation.

Extradition from Norway may generally take place for crimes with a maximum sentence of more than 12 months, or where a foreign court has handed down a sentence of at least four months. The European Arrest Warrant has become the standard extradition instrument in the EU and is decisive and in widespread use.[22] EAWs may be issued for all acts punishable by a maximum sentence of at least 12 months or, where a sentence has been given of at least four months (EAW art.2[1]). Norway, as mentioned above, is not yet party to the EAW cooperation. The practical differences are few, but important: Norwegian citizens will not normally be extradited outside the Nordic countries. And in the Nordic Extradition Act, the requirement for extradition of Norwegian citizens is that s/he has been resident in the requesting state for the past two years, or that the offence in question is punishable by four years or more.[23] Extradition of non-Norwegian citizens to other Nordic countries, however, only requires that the offence may lead to a custodial sentence, or when a verdict deciding such a sentence has been pronounced (Arrest Warrant Act sect.17(1). There is no obligation for officers to check the citizenship of someone they are pursuing, before crossing the border; this would be contrary to the whole idea of urgency in hot pursuit. In the absence of indications to the contrary, officers are only required to judge that the offence and offender objectively fall within the scope of the Nordic Extradition Act.

A clear reference in the PA sect.20a to the requirement for an extraditable offence was removed in 2012. The reference is now general, simply including any applicable international cooperation instruments, under the Norwegian Agreement with the EU MLA Convention (MLA9 and the 2001 Second Additional Protocol to the 1959 European Council (ETS 182).[24] The amendment is not referred to in the *forarbeid*. The threshold for cross-border pursuit or surveillance is presumably the same as before, since nothing different has been stated in the relevant official documents. When hot pursuit takes place under the CISA, the extradition requirement applies (cf. Norway's declaration).

Under the CISA, the offence triggering a hot pursuit is thus required to be serious, such as fleeing from a murder scene, or a robbery, rather than something like speeding. Although an offender cannot be pursued into Norway if the offence is insufficiently serious, a trial may take place in Norway for acts committed by a Norwegian abroad.[25] Only the other Nordic

21 Working programme for EU/EEC matters 2013:62.

22 Daman 2008:181. See Kvam 2008:112–8 for the specifics on the Norwegian relation to EU extradition agreements.

23 Extradition may not take place if the whole offence is committed within Norway (para. 2).

24 [2004] OJ L 26/3; ETS 182 (2001); Prop.97 LS (2011–2012):49–50. There were no objections in parliament to any of the changes (Innst. 331 S (2011–2012):2).

25 GCPC sect.5; Nordisk straffullbyrdingslov 1963; Directive 1963–12–03–1.

authorities are allowed to perform cross-border hot pursuit into Norwegian territory, so in practice, it is the fairly wide Nordic Extradition Agreements that apply. It may be noted that Sweden declared in the *Øresund Agreement* (preamble [5]) with Denmark that hot pursuit into Swedish territory may be carried out by Danish for any offence that is subject to public prosecution.[26] Going beyond CISA, the Agreement allows hot pursuit for traffic offences, and in the interests of public order maintenance in this border region.[27] An agreement, which came into force in 2003, implies there are no restrictions between Norway, Finland and Sweden concerning the application of CISA arts.40–41. There are no material regulations departing from the CISA.[28] The Agreement is not easily accessible. Following my request, the Police Directorate (POD) made inquiries in police districts in the Norwegian border regions. The districts replied that no such agreement exists; they contact the relevant agency on the other side of the border in each specific case.[29] The International Department at Kripos, however, immediately produced the agreement when I requested it. So, the agreement exists, but the Norwegian police in the border regions seem to be unaware of its existence. This might not be a problem in practice, however. Their informal attitude towards the agreement, alongside the absence of restrictions, may signal a very high level of trust between the neighbouring states (or at least the police personnel in question) – so high, in fact, that a formal agreement is not perceived as necessary.

The legality of the PA sect.20a 2012 extradition amendment could possibly be challenged in a Norwegian court.[30] The presiding judge in the receiving state must consider the legal basis of the pursuing state. Assessing this may be difficult, depending on the various definitions of the offences listed either in CISA or in other international instruments. The police in border areas have reported that the requirement for seriousness is problematic, since many of the offences committed by transnational wrongdoers consist of theft, vandalism and shoplifting.[31]

12.2.1.2 Hot pursuit: 'Caught in the act' and the threshold of suspicion

The 'caught in the act' requirement is met, according to the Norwegian *forarbeid*, when a person is seen committing, or immediately after committing an act, and when there is little doubt that this person is the perpetrator.[32] The CISA art.41 does not mention this last aspect of the definition. PA sect.20a formerly stated that observation and hot pursuit could take place if a person was suspected of committing an extraditable offence. Auglend *et al.* emphasise that the deviation from the territoriality principle is so blatant in hot pursuit situations, that the level of suspicion must be high. The *forarbeid* stress that the requirement for qualified suspicion must be part of the threshold of 'reasonable grounds'. The 2003 amend-

26 Declaration to arts. 6 and 8 in The Øresund Agreement 1999. On the Danish supplementary agreements with Sweden and Germany: Henricson 2010:319–21.

27 The Øresund Agreement art.6; also, Henricson 2010:186–7.

28 Rundskriv 2004/004. See e.g. Auglend *et al.* 2004:567; Boucht 2012.

29 Personal communication with POD, 17.06.2014.

30 This could be remedied by the Schengen Border Code for Police Cooperation, but the document is restricted, and this is thus impossible to know. (Not to be confused with the Schengen Catalogue on police cooperation recommendations and best practice, which is unrestricted, but less precise and non-binding. (Council doc 15785/2/10, 25.01.2011).

31 Daman 2008:182.

32 St.prp.nr.42 (1996–1997) ch.5.5.4.

ment of sect.20a extended legitimate cross-border observation and hot pursuit to include persons not suspected of committing the crime, who there was "reasonable grounds" to believe could identify, or contribute to tracking down, the suspect. The amendment certainly emphasised the high threshold required for hot pursuit and the observation of those not themselves suspected of committing a crime.

In 2012, the requirements specific to the Norwegian legislation concerning cross-border hot pursuit and observation were removed from the PA sect.20a. It is not clear whether, or how far, this change was actually intended to alter the material and procedural conditions. Since 2012, foreign officials may perform their national duties, and continue hot pursuit and observation on Norwegian territory, to the extent this is permitted according to international agreements. The headline of the section refers to *police* officers, thus presumably limiting paragraphs 1–3. Unlike sect.20a before the 2012 amendment, this is, however, not specified. Paragraph 2, giving foreign officers (officials) partial police authority cf. sect.20(3), is not limited to police personnel. In other words: foreign officials crossing the border in pursuit or observation are not required to be *police* officers. Any kind of authorised authority within the sending state is permitted. This also seems to have been the intention in the Ministry Consultative Paper.[33] It follows in para.4 that directives may provide more detailed rules and requirements for international cooperation. Such rules do not yet exist (September 2017). The *forarbeid* do not appear to intentionally narrow the requirements governing the measures dealt with in section 3. The lack of precision is regrettable, especially since this legislation is of relevance to non-national officials who may have less-than perfect knowledge of the general Norwegian sources of law.[34]

Hot pursuit must be 'hot': only a relatively short period of time must have passed since the act was committed. A situation where the police are called by someone who has just observed someone setting fire to a building, for example, would be sufficiently 'fresh'. The precise definition of the concept is at the discretion of the national police, thus Norwegian police must accept, say, the Finnish police patrol's assessment of the level of 'heat' and the urgency of the situation.[35]

A 2003 Schengen-relevant Decision extended cross-border surveillance to persons who may identify or help track down a suspected offender.[36] In the Norwegian amendment, this extension was also made applicable to hot pursuit. Auglend *et al.* show how this went unremarked in all the associated *forarbeid*.[37] This extension is not applicable in Denmark,[38] which might suggest that it was more or less unintended. Because of the new general wording post-2012, it is unclear whether the extended legal basis includes subjects of hot pursuit, and thus whether the previous Norwegian wording is applicable, allowing also non-suspects to be pursued across borders. Sect.20a now only refers to agreements with foreign states. Does this mean that the CISA art.41 should be considered outdated, and that the sect.20a reference is to other legal instruments? At present, only CISA gives legal basis for hot pursuit into Norway, so this not, at present at least, a possible alternative.[39] Presuming

33 Consultation paper (høringsbrev) 26.03.2010 to Prop. 97 LS (2011–2012) on international cooperation, ch.14.3.

34 The Handbook of Cross-Border Policing (SCH/Com-ex (98)52) may provide clarification on this – but this is a restricted document whose content are unknown.

35 Auglend *et al.* 2004:575, also Henricson 2010:183–4.

36 Council Decision 2003/725/JHA.

37 Auglend *et al.* 2004:569 n.1360.

38 Gade *et al.* 2005:185–9.

39 Participation in the Naples II Convention on hot pursuit by customs could change this. See e.g. Peers 2011:936.

the extension is still is applicable, the border crossing must be *necessary* to achieve the purposes of the investigation, not merely useful. In addition, there must be an absence of any alternatives that do not infringe sovereignty.[40] Removing this necessity criterion for pursuing a *non*-suspect, implied a lowered threshold for international entry into Norway.[41]

In contrast, cross-border observation of persons not suspected of committing an offence, is not permitted without prior host state consent (art.40. no.2[1]). As we have seen, the distinction between these cross-border activities was not reiterated in the Police Act, and it is somewhat unclear what the situation is. Although surveillance with the intention of solving serious crime, without coercive police measures, was accepted into the CISA in 2003, the threshold for border-crossing is higher in these situations. There must be "serious reason" to believe s/he may identify/locate the suspect, and this knowledge must constitute a "necessary" part of an ongoing criminal investigation. In Norwegian law, the requirement is that the balance of probabilities (*'sannsynlighetsovervekt'*) should suggest this is the case.[42]

The differences between surveillance and hot pursuit regulations vary here in two respects: 1) there are more offences included in the list in art.40 no.7, that allow non-authorised cross-border surveillance, than in art.41 no.4 (a); and 2) cross-border surveillance must also be authorised in the case of those who may assist in identifying a suspected offender (see above). Hot pursuit is, as we have seen, only allowed in the case of offenders. Unauthorised surveillance is, however, not permitted in the case of non-offenders. Furthermore, the wording clearly permits only repressive, not proactive, observation operations.[43] Cross-border cooperation on potential crimes is regulated in art.46, which also seems to be assumed in the Norwegian regulations, where the PA sect.20a previously specified "continuing observation and hot pursuit of [. . .] a person suspected of a criminal offence". Henricson argues that observation such as of football hooligans on their way to a match, may be continued as long as it is part of a criminal investigation, and has started before the border is crossed.[44] "Criminal investigation" may, of course, include investigation of pre-empted crimes. Using the word 'investigation' may not accord with the Norwegian division between investigation and prevention.[45] The results of the observation may of course also be applied to preventing future crimes. The suspicion that a person will commit a murder in Norway is not covered. Host state authorities must in the case of hot pursuit and of observation be notified, at the latest, when the border is crossed (art.40 no.1(3); 41(1)). The pursuit must be stopped immediately if not agreed to by the host state. In such cases, the home state police may demand the arrest of the fugitive, on the basis of the host state's national law, while they await e.g. an order of interrogation (art.40 no.6). The conditions for such emergency measures are listed in no.2 (a) and (b): the authorities of the host state must be notified immediately when the border has been crossed, and a request for assistance, and the justification for the non-authorised border crossing must be submitted at once. Surveillance must also cease instantly if the host state so requests. Technical developments, such as drones, may challenge the practical limitation of such surveillance. The

40 Auglend *et al.* 2004:570.

41 Myhrer 2013 n.119 to sect.20a [04.02.14].

42 Ot.prp.nr.62 (2002–2003) pt.8.4–6; Auglend *et al.* 2004:569.

43 Joubert and Bevers 1996:130–1.

44 Henricson 2011:189.

45 E.g. NOU 2009:15 p.149.

general rule is still that intrusion into a person's private sphere, whether a suspect or not, needs a clear basis in national criminal procedure law.

Art.40 no.6 gives states the option of extending the scope of art.40 bilaterally. For example, Denmark has bilateral border cooperation agreements with Sweden and Germany, cf. art.40 and 41.[46] The agreements somewhat extend the powers of 'foreign' police officers to perform policing activities, although these powers are less than those of national officers. They may not, for example, set up a cross-border police checkpoint for blood alcohol content searches, but they would be allowed to stop a seemingly drunk driver.[47] Traffic policing is more widely permitted, and more direct information exchange and communication between lower-level police officers is allowed, as long as coercive measures are not involved.[48] While Denmark is party to the Schengen Cooperation, it opted out of the JHA following the Maastricht Treaty. Since police cooperation is now fully within the supranational EU area, Denmark has to negotiate special agreements for the parts it wants to participate in. This may explain Denmark's wider range of specialised agreements and negotiations compared with what Norway seemed to need, in its initial outsider position.

12.2.1.3 Persons who have escaped from custody

The pursuit of a person who has escaped from provisional custody, or from serving a sentence involving the deprivation of liberty, is also allowed without prior consent (art.41). There is no requirement as to the reason for, or length of, the incarceration. The proportionality principle laid down in the CPA sect.170a would probably prevent the Norwegian police from starting a hot pursuit after a shoplifter, but escaping police custody may be considered more serious than the offence itself. The lack of further requirements may lead to differences in the grounds for pursuing a fugitive from provisional custody. In a Nordic context, Auglend *et al.* and Gade *et al.* disagree on whether it is a (clear) requirement that the pursuit must take place in direct connection with the escape.[49] The term 'provisional custody' may also be applied differently in MS.[50] Although the custody must be punitive, in other words, not in a child welfare institution, there are different thresholds for the extent and type of custody. Joubert and Bevers show how the wording in two out of three original languages (Dutch and German) of the Schengen Convention excludes escapes from police custody, and that these versions require that the provisional custody must have been decided by a judge.[51] In other words, a pursuit following an escape from police custody could be legal or illegal dependant on the wording in different languages. Such custody is not specified in Finnish law at all,[52] while the Swedish Act uses "*häktad*", which also seems to exclude police custody.[53] The Police Act sect.20a does not specify this. Police custody ("*politiarrest*") seems not to be included; the specification in the *forarbeid* – without further explanation – is "*varetekt*", i.e. remand imprisonment/pre-trial detention.[54] The lack of

46 Gade *et al.* 2005 ch.4.1–4.2.
47 Op.cit.:191.
48 Op.cit.:196.
49 Op.cit.:186; Henricson 2010:184; Auglend *et al.* 2004:575.
50 Joubert and Bevers 1996:245–6; 281.
51 Op.cit.:281.
52 Boucht 2012:216 n. 64.
53 Swedish Act on international police cooperation sect.5. The applicable Swedish Directive (2010:705) does not mention such detention.
54 Ot.prp.nr.56 (1998–1999):pt.8.4.3; also Auglend *et al.* 2004:575.

precision opens the way for challenges in court. Furthermore, including police custody could lower the 'threshold of seriousness'.

12.2.2 General rules for hot pursuit and surveillance

The cross-border 'autonomous' foreign police measures in CISA arts.40 and 41 are emergency exceptions meant for situations when the national police are not available, or not able to take control of an ongoing operation. The articles oblige the host state to allow foreign police officers from Schengen member states to continue their operations in its territory ("shall be authorised": arts.40 no.1 and 41 no.1). Furthermore, they set out the general conditions for crossing the border and give more specific rules for when 'autonomous' and sometimes un-notified operations may take place.

The pursuing authorities must be police officers with due authority in their home state. These officers are listed (by the MS) in CISA arts.40 nos.4–5; 41 no.7. There are, however, also differences between Nordic countries in the types of officers permitted to carry out pursuits: both Swedish and Finnish police and customs officers are permitted to cross borders; in Finland border police officers can too.[55] In Norway, only officers with police authority may perform hot pursuit.[56] Officers must be easily identifiable at all times, with visible identification such as a uniform, brassard or vehicle accessory. Hot pursuit in civilian clothes in an unmarked vehicle is forbidden, and officers must at all times be able to prove that they are acting in an official capacity (art.41 no.5[d]). Except in the case of emergency pursuits, the prior permission to cross the border must also be produced.

Unlike the situation with hot pursuit, those under surveillance are unaware of the police operation: border-crossing officers are not required to have identification marks on cars or uniforms. They must, however, be able to provide proof that they are acting in an official capacity, as well as proof, if obtained, of the host state's permission (no.3 b–c).

Both the CISA rules in arts.40 and 41, and the foreign territory's laws apply to border-crossing officers, including any instructions issued by the competent local authorities art.40 no.2; no.3[a];41 no.1 [3]; no.5 [a]). Although foreign officers do not have ordinary national police competences, they are allowed, in the same way as national officers, to break the national traffic regulations when necessary.[57]

In the context of criminal and civil liability, pursuing officers are considered to be like national police (CISA arts.42–43, cf. PA sect.20a, cf. GCPC sects.155–156, 265, 268). Individuals claiming damages from foreign police officers acting in accordance with arts.40 and 41 may choose whether to put the claim forward in the host state or the sending state. The Ministry emphasised in 2012 that such a responsibility is a natural consequence of subjecting foreign officers to Norwegian law even though they are acting on behalf of their home state.[58] Section 20a was amended to include foreign police officers acting within Norwegian territory, following the affiliation agreement with the EU 2000 MLA[59] and ETS 182 (2001).

The CISA does not limit the number of officers or units that may cross the border. According to Auglend *et al.*, several police units may cross, even though only one unit can

55 Op.cit.:568 n.1356.
56 St.prp.nr.42 (1996–1997):31.
57 See Auglend *et al.* 2004:571.
58 Prop.97 LS (2011–2012):53–54.
59 [2004] OJ L 26/3.

see the individual or vehicle being pursued.[60] The receiving state may, when notified, object, and allow only one entity to cross the border, for example, if the number of pursuing police cars is perceived as disproportionate to the crime in question.

The openness of the PA sect.20a concerning the question of what foreign personnel may legitimately cross the border into Norway, seems to allow any foreign official provided with the necessary authorisation from the home state to cross. And this irrespective of Norwegian demands of police authority for their officers. As shown below in ch.13.1, joint investigation teams may mean that foreign police officers outside the more familiar Nordic police cooperation, operate in Norway.

12.2.2.1 Notification

Pursuing police officers must notify the host state police to obtain authorisation before crossing the border. The notification must be seen as a request to continue the operation, which may or may not be approved. The request must contain the information needed by the host state authorities to assess the grounds for the crossing. In surveillance operations, notification when the border is crossed must contain a request for assistance from the host state (art.40[1]).

The countries involved have listed their contact points in the fact sheet appended to the Manual on Cross-Border Operations. For cross-border pursuit into Norway, chiefs of police in the district in question must be contacted for approval. The border-region districts of Finland and Sweden are listed with contact details.[61]

Notification must always take place, at the latest, when crossing the border.[62] The border may be crossed without preliminary approval when there is particular urgency. Such cases should be rare, given the enhanced communication links established by art.44.[63] MS are obliged to create and sustain communications between police units, particularly in border regions, to secure 'the timely transmission of information for the purposes of cross-border surveillance and hot pursuit' (Art.44). This may be challenging between different languages. Although English is widespread, it is not equally good on all levels in the police. And regardless of language, even between the Scandinavian countries, which use the TETRA network, to secure communication between Norway and her nearest neighbours, there have been serious problems with the implementation and use of this system in Norway. This was for example apparent during the 22 July atrocities, where the victims did not get through to the police because of the high number of callers. In the case of surveillance, emergency continuation is either limited a maximum of five hours, or subject to bilateral agreements.

Authorisation to continue pursuit may also be given when the host state police are unable to reach the scene in time. This means that a form of approval is given to the foreign police to perform host state police tasks simply because they are on the spot. This may well happen

60 Auglend *et al.* 2004:574.

61 CBO Manual fact sheets (10505/4/09):464–5. Boucht suggests that this requirement for such high-level notification contact point may be unnecessarily inflexible, but shows how this may be permitted in the ANPC 2012 sect.4.1 (Boucht 2012:235).

62 Arts.40 no.1(3); 41(1).

63 See e.g. http://www.aftenposten.no/nodnett/Na-kommer-politiradioen-tilbake-7268664.html#.UwxZCXbKwis [25.02.14].

in states such as Norway, that have a long border mainly running through remote wilderness areas.[64]

12.2.2.2 Service weapons

Norwegian police are generally unarmed, unlike most other police forces in the world, including those in the other Nordic countries.[65] During hot pursuit, pursuing officers have an unconditional right to carry their service weapons into foreign territory (CISA art.41 no.5e). The use of the weapons is generally restricted to legitimate (self-)defence. This right does not apply to cross-border observations, where the MS may opt to specifically refuse this (no.5 d). The Norwegian Police Act does not differentiate between the two measures. The nature of urgent border crossing renders it impossible to properly dispose of a weapon before crossing a border; according to the Ministry, this applies to both pursuit and surveillance.[66] The *forarbeid* to PA sect.20a explicitly state, however, that the right to carry arms does not imply the right to be seen to be armed. The prohibition on visible service weapons was meant to ensure that the appearance of foreign police officers does not conflict with the Norwegian tradition of unarmed police.[67] Foreign officers breaching the Norwegian provisions on carrying arms may be punished under the Norwegian Penal Code (CISA art.41 no.5[a] cf. art.42 cf. PA sect.20a[2]). Before the Schengen cooperation, the Norwegian penal code regulations on public officials were not applicable to foreign officers.[68]

12.2.2.3 Geographical limitations

The CISA only allows hot pursuit over land borders. Auglend *et al.* assume that pursuit may also take place in the airspace immediately above land borders.[69] Their statement has no further reference, and is not to be found in other literature on Schengen hot pursuit.[70] On the contrary, several commentators have pointed out the difference between the CISA and Naples II, for example, where hot pursuit is also permitted over the sea and in the air.[71] Hot pursuit on the high seas, however, has long been permissible according to both international and customary law.[72] Danish police in hot pursuit could, for example, follow a suspect across the Kattegat Sea towards Norway. This would, however, be based on other instruments, and the police could not cross into Norwegian territory without special agreement.[73]

64 A similar long-standing and strong cooperation within (and prior to) the EU, is that between the BeNeLux countries, e.g. in the BeNeLux Treaty of 1962. See Spapens 2008; Hufnagel 2013:ch.3.1.1; Spapens and Fijnaut 2005:26.

65 Strype 2005:93, see also Myhrer 2005. UK police are also unarmed, which implied a special agreement on this for the police cooperation with France for the Channel Tunnel (Hufnagel 2013:ch.3.1.3).

66 Ot.prp.nr.56 (1998–1999):97.

67 Op.cit. ch.8.4.6.

68 St.prp.nr.42 (1996–1997).

69 Auglend *et al.* 2004:574. Most of the operational Schengen measures are removed in the book's third edition (2016, ch.26).

70 Joubert and Bevers 1996:246–7; Peers 2011:936.

71 Boucht 2012:214 n.54; Daman 2008:179; 185. Drones may constitute a pertinent example of potential challenges to the airspace limitations, which there seem to be no clear solutions to at present.

72 Poulantzas 2002:11; 347; Fleischer 2000:137.

73 See e.g. UNCLOS 1958 art.23; UNCLOS III 1982 art.111.

Land borders include bridges and frozen lakes or rivers, thus on Norway's southeast border with Sweden there is the Svinesund bridge, and between Sweden and Denmark there are the Øresund bridges.[74] While hot pursuit is simplest when it means entering immediately neighbouring territory, it need not be restricted to this. If Danish police are pursuing someone into Sweden, and no Swedish police are available to take over, the Danish officers may continue across the border into Norway, provided all other requirements are fulfilled. There may, though, be national restrictions on which actions the police from a non-neighbouring state may perform – on arrests, for example.

In the same way, Norwegian police in a hot pursuit in northernmost Norway could pass through Finland, and even want to continue into Murmansk in Russia. The latter is not included in the Schengen cooperation: the pursuit would thus be illegal without a special bilateral agreement or ad hoc approval. There is a police cooperation agreement between Russia and Norway, but this regulates cooperation on information and intelligence exchange, not operational work. Since the Norwegian–Russian border is an external Schengen border, unlike intra-Nordic borders, it is highly controlled by military border garrisons. These though, may have police authority when necessary, which could cover situations where, for example, a person fleeing the Russian police crosses the border (PA sect.20[4]). Illegal border-crossing by people in cars, or those fleeing on foot from the police, is within the remit of the cooperation between the two countries.[75] This must, however, occur on a case by case basis, as it is unfeasible, within the Schengen cooperation framework, to agree routinely to Russian police entering the Schengen Area, despite the fact that the police cooperation mechanisms that exist *de facto* between the two states probably facilitate the Norwegian authorities' consent in individual cases. This appears to apply to cross-border observation between Russia and Norway, but not pursuit, meaning that people cannot be apprehended on Norwegian territory.[76]

According to CISA art.41 no.3, the MS may declare how far into its territory a pursuit may carry on, and for how long. Norway has made no such limitations.[77] According to Daman, no MS has limited the pursuit in time.[78] Distance limits exist in various MS. Neither Sweden nor Finland has such restrictions. Denmark bans Swedish police from going further into the country than 25 km from the end of the Øresund, and the German authorities from going more than 25 km from the German border.[79] For practical geographical reasons, this Danish limit prevents Schengen members south of Denmark continuing a hot pursuit into the other Nordic countries, and thus a Nordic 'closed zone' starts 25 km into Danish territory.

In surveillance operations (art.40), unlike hot pursuit, the host state may not impose time or distance limits, or stipulate that a person can only be followed across land borders. Thus Schengen members who do not have a border with Norway can carry out cross-border surveillance in Norwegian territory by means of ships or aircraft. This means that. Spanish, Polish or Romanian police could be authorised to continue a surveillance operation into

74 Auglend *et al.* 2004:574.

75 Prop.97 LS (2011–2012): 53.

76 Op.cit.:53. A new Norwegian Border Act is currently presumably soon enacted, following the *forarbeid* found among others in Prop.161 L (2016–2017).

77 St.meld.nr.18 (1999–2000) ch.4.3.2.

78 Daman 2008:186 n.88.

79 Gade *et al.* 2005:194; 197–8.

Norway, in emergencies, without prior permission. The operation must have started within the pursuing officers' country, but surveillance can, of course, be carried out through several jurisdictions. The distance between non-neighbouring countries and Norway generally gives pursuing officers plenty of time to request prior authorisation. If, say, a surveillance operation has taken place across the entire Schengen Area, and its object suddenly crosses into Norwegian territory, one could assume Spanish police would have the right to urgent, 'autonomous' border-crossing. In practice, however, in the case of such a major international surveillance operation, the police forces of all relevant jurisdictions would probably be alerted beforehand, and Europol and/or Eurojust would be included.

CISA arts.40 no.3 (e) and 41 no.5 (c) explicitly prohibits pursuing police from entering private homes, and other places not accessible to the public. This means, as Damans emphasises,[80] that they lose a significant share of their coercive competences: national police have wider powers to enter private homes, or other premises, when pursuing a criminal caught 'red-handed'. In hot pursuit, this means that the foreign officers must wait outside. However, following CPA sect.176, risk of escaping justice triggers citizens' arrest, and this would be applicable here.

12.2.2.4 Coercive powers

The only coercive measures allowed are apprehension, together with those available to all citizens defending themselves, or someone or something. The general rule, however, is that foreign police officers are not entitled to apprehend those they pursue.[81] Furthermore, the Convention does not in itself give a legal basis for home state police to hold fugitives and extradite them on the spot: normal extradition procedures must be followed. A cross-border permit does not mean that foreign officers are given the same powers as Norwegian police officers. But there are exceptions to the rules for hot pursuit when the host authorities are unable to reach the scene in time and have not demanded that the pursuit should be stopped (art.41 no.2 [a–b]). The apprehension allowed to foreign officers is only temporary, until the host police can take over, or the person apprehended has been delivered to a host police station (or similar) (art.41 no.2.).[82] Norwegian police may take individuals into custody without there being any suspicion a crime has been committed (PA sect.8). Such apprehension and detention is not a criminal procedural measure, and need not meet the substantial requirements laid down in the CPA sect.171 for there being reasonable cause for suspicion of guilt, and that the crime should be of a certain gravity. Apprehension based on the PA sect.20a will necessarily satisfy requirements similar to those in the CPA, since hot pursuit involves a person caught red handed or escaping punishment over international borders, or

80 Daman 2008:187.

81 CISA left several aspects of hot pursuit to be decided by the MS: whether or not the officer may apprehend the fugitive (Norway allows this)(art.41 [2]); whether there is a restriction in time othere is a restriction in time or distance on the pursuit [3]; and whether the pursuit may take place for any extraditable offence, or only those mentioned in a particular catalogue [4]. The same type of choice exists regarding surveillance (paras.5; 7). Joubert and Bevers 1996:287–8 criticise the CISA for leaving too many options to the MS, since this may lead to a confusing array of regulations for police officers.

82 No. 2(a) states that there is no right to apprehend the fugitive, but (b) he may be "detained". No. 5 f) allows search of the person "apprehended as provided for in paragraph 2(b)", thus showing that the detention mentioned amounts to apprehension – with the purpose of bringing the fugitive before local authorities, and not any other policiary purposes.

lacking permanent residence in the country. This will also lower the threshold for apprehension under CPA, cf. sect.173. The Norwegian legal basis for apprehension by a foreigner is the PA sect.20a, which is the same as the CPA sect.176, i.e. the ability of anyone to apprehend someone under certain conditions.[83] When foreign police officers are entitled to pursue and apprehend, this is dependent on suspicion of an extraditable offence, or fleeing. These requirements accord with the rules in sect.173. The power of home state police officers to apprehend fugitives is based on CPA sect.173, and there is a requirement for proportionality. Supreme Court practice has decided that coercive measures employed under the CPA must also adhere to CPA sect.170a (Rt. 2004.1826).

The person apprehended may be subjected to a security search, and may be handcuffed during transport (Art.41 no. 5(f)).[84] Evidence may be seized. The threshold for necessary or proportional use of force may be different in different countries. The restriction of coercive measures in art.41 may be seen as a precautionary measure to avoid even slightly wrongful coercive activity arising from differences in these thresholds. This limitation has been seen as problematic:[85] the strict embargo on the use of force could mean that a pursuing police vehicle could not block a fleeing car, or that the use of handcuffs was impossible. As long as foreign officers are subject to the law of the host state (in addition to their own), however, there is no legal basis for disciplining them for using 'necessary' force within their national police competences. Foreign officers are subject to and protected by, for example, GCPA regulations. There are no sanctions in the CISA concerning the inappropriate use of force. But MS are free to agree bilaterally upon the delegation of wider competences than those of the CISA. It seems that Finnish legislation goes further than Norwegian and Swedish norms in allowing foreign use of force for apprehension; it allows, for example, a foreign official to use necessary force if a suspect resists or attempts to escape.[86]It may be seen as unfortunate that there are different regulations in these three neighbouring countries: a Finnish official could well be unaware that there was no legal basis for using force when apprehending a fugitive in Sweden. However, since the extension of police cooperation post Prüm, whereby foreign police officers. may gain some police competences in Norway, the necessary use of force in the legitimate apprehension of a fleeing suspect would be unlikely to be deemed illegal in a Norwegian court. It could probably also be accord with the principle of necessity.

If the hot pursuit is ordered to be discontinued, coercive measures may be requested to establish the identity of the fugitive, so also an arrest to be made while awaiting a formal extradition request or interrogation request to be processed (art.41 no.1 (3) cf. no.6).

CISA's division between apprehension and arrest is unclear. Joubert and Bevers' comparison concludes that generally CISA's "apprehension" means "provisory arrest".[87] This accords with the Norwegian regulations, under which foreign police can only apprehend and detain in the way that is available as a public order policing measure.[88] Before the 2012 amendment, the right to apprehend a suspect when necessary was specified in PA sect.20a. It is an open

83 Ot.prp.nr.56 (1998–1999) ch.8.4.4.

84 According to Swedish law, foreign officers engaged in pursuit may carry out a search for reasons of security, or e.g. for the purposes of a specific investigation or trial (Swedish Act on international police cooperation sect.7 no. 2). Similar searches are allowed in Finnish law (Boucht 2012:216).

85 Brammertz 1997:14.

86 Boucht 2012:216.

87 Joubert and Bevers 1996:289–324.

88 Auglend et al. 2004:570–1 cf. 492–3.

question whether arrest to identify someone other than the fugitive, is covered. The Norwegian PA does not provide for the apprehension of a person on such grounds.[89] If the person lacks the status as a witness that is given by the court or the prosecutor, their apprehension is presumably illegal. This, however, could hamper the whole purpose of the hot pursuit; if so, this could lead to emergency subpoenas being issued by the pursuing authorities, to give the fugitive a certain status. (If the national authorities have not been reached in time.)

One could imagine a situation where Finnish police officers pursue someone caught *in flagrante* while breaking into a house (Norwegian GCPC sect.322 cf. 321). Norwegian police are contacted; they stop the getaway car, and take over the pursuit. Neither the Schengen cooperation nor the Police Act permit the Finnish police to immediately take the individual back to Finland; ordinary extradition procedures must be followed. The Finnish police may, though, require that the person be taken into custody for up to six hours, if the person is not a Norwegian citizen. The time limit is extended if an extradition claim arrives before the expiry of the six hours. The time between midnight and 9 a.m. is not counted. Supposing that the Norwegian police then take over the Finnish hot pursuit, and make an arrest based on reasonable grounds for suspicion (CPA sects.171 or 173, possibly cf. 176). Such an arrest may legally result in detention for up to 72 hours (sect. 183), although this *de facto* is limited to 48 hours because of relevant ECtHR court practice. Either way, according to the Police Act sect.8, however, police custody is limited to four hours. This means that if the fugitive is pursued because he/she is escaping from police custody imposed for such non-criminal activity as public disorder, this person could be detained longer than a Norwegian in a similar situation (CISA art.41 no.6[2]), since international agreements take precedence (PA sect.3). The likelihood of such a situation is however, probably slight.

The regulations on apprehension and the use of coercive measures overlap to some extent with those concerning joint operations (i.e. operations where the foreign police authorities do not work autonomously). These are returned to below.

In cross-border surveillance operations, the home police are permitted "neither to challenge nor arrest" the person(s) under observation (art.40 no.3[f]). Situations may then arise where the foreign police, during their surveillance, observe a crime taking place. Since CISA art.41 requires an ongoing hot pursuit by the home state, the surveillance operation could not change character. Police officers would not be allowed to pursue the person who is both under observation, and has been seen in the act of committing a crime which could have legitimised hot pursuit and subsequent detention. If, however, the crime about to take place or taking place is of a certain seriousness, the police officers would be allowed to intervene on the same basis as anyone else, according to the GCPC sects.17–18 (right to self-defence etc.) and/or CPA sect.176 (citizen's arrest'). This is made explicit in Finnish law,[90] but this cannot be assumed to be the case in all the Schengen MS that Norwegian police could continue a surveillance operation into.[91]

12.2.2.5 Duty of reporting and assisting

Following both hot pursuit and surveillance operations, foreign officers must report to, and assist the host authorities. Arts.40 and 41 nos.3(h) and 5(h) are materially identical, obli-

89 PA sect.8(1) no.4 might imply such basis, but this seems not to be the intention. (So also op.cit.:504.)
90 Boucht 2012:210; 213.
91 Joubert and Bevers 1996 ch.4.

ging participating officers, when requested, to give further investigative and judicial assistance following operations. This could mean contributing local knowledge of the location of the crime in question or giving testimony (*litra* h) and appearing as witnesses if a case is taken before a court in the host state. But also for the host state to maintain sovereign control over policing on its territory.

To a greater extent than in the case of surveillance, hot pursuit officers must be available until all the circumstances of the pursuit have been clarified, regardless of whether it leads to apprehension. Both the pursuit itself, and the whole foreign police operation needs to be explained, including. whether further steps are planned, or if the activity was only a part of a larger process.

There is a standard report form in the Schengen Handbook of Cross-Border Police Cooperation, annex 3 to sect.2. There is no specification in the CISA as to how reporting shall take place, which implies that it may be written or oral. According to Daman's research, however, most hot pursuits (at least in central Europe) are not reported at all, perhaps because of the failure of the pursuit (the fugitive managing to escape into unfamiliar foreign terrain) or because of language difficulties.[92] Auglend *et al.* emphasise that the most important thing is to be able to evaluate the operation.[93] (On a more practical level, reporting may be seen as a precautionary measure in case pursuits have unfortunate consequences, such as accidents, or where a report will follow a subsequent trial.)

12.2.2.6 Initial Norwegian reservations towards international police cooperation

Two other international agreements regulate transnational cross-border hot pursuit and surveillance in Europe. Norway signed the CoE 1959 Convention second additional protocol in 2001 (ETS no.182), in other words around the same time as CISA, but it was not ratified until 20.12.2010. The MLA Association Agreement was signed in 2003.[94] The Ministry wanted to legally regulate international police cooperation more formally, making foreign police officials criminally liable under Norwegian law when acting in Norway, whatever the form of police cooperation involved. So, Norway made a reservation (art.33) on cross-border measures, including observation (art.17), and joint investigation teams (MLA art.13/ETS no.182 art.20) upon signing ETS no.182. The reservation was lifted with effect from 2013. Foreign officials crossing into Norwegian territory could not necessarily be expected to be familiar with Norwegian regulations, and the Norwegian Bar Association argued that a broader revision of the Police Act should be made before such a legal expansion.[95] The Ministry underlined that the ETS no.182 art.17 was less expansive and far-reaching than the Schengen arts.40 and 41 current (at the time), even though its contents were materially the same as art.40. It was considered more "practical" that Norway should take advantage of the measures in art.17. The existence of ultimate Norwegian control through the applicability of Norwegian law made the abolition uncontroversial.[96]

92 Daman 2008:198–9. Discussion language challenges in international police cooperation, see Ingleton 1994.
93 2004:573.
94 [2004] OJ L 26/3.
95 Prop.97 LS (2011–2012):52–53.
96 Op.cit. ch.9.4; ch.16.2–16.3.

The need for cross-border observation followed by arrest by a foreign police officer has mostly arisen when Russian police officers cross into Norway, according to the Ministry.[97] The CoE 1959 Convention, however, has been ratified by both Russia and Norway.[98] The other expansions of the PA sect.20a after the 1959 and 2000 protocols, relating to controlled deliveries, are returned to below.[99]

Both the MLA Convention and the ETS no.182 have reservation clauses (art.14 no.4, and arts.33 cf. 19). Denmark, Finland, Sweden and Norway all declared a reservation on cooperation on covert investigation.[100] As with the other reservations on the 1959 Convention, Norway's was lifted on the country's accession to the MLA Convention. The justification given was much the same as in other withdrawals: it was practical for the Norwegian authorities to take advantage of the benefits of cross-border covert investigation cooperation, and that there were no foreseeable risks with such operations, since they would accord with Norwegian law.[101]

Against this background, the Ministry rejected the Norwegian Bar Association's arguments that such covert investigation should be more thoroughly legally regulated before international agreements expanding the measures were entered into. The Association based its argument on the fact that other covert measures, such as communication control, had been regulated without any apparent differences concerning privacy, in much the same way as undercover agent measures. The limits on police provocation and the right of no self-incrimination were, according to the Association, at risk. This argument did not convince the Ministry.[102]

12.3 Controlled deliveries and covert investigation

Cross-border covert investigation occurs when police do not intervene in a criminal activity; controlled deliveries occur when they postpone intervention.[103] These non-coercive measures were previously based only in customary law, but s since the Schengen cooperation and other international instruments, they have been increasingly fixed in law.

12.3.1 Controlled deliveries

Cross-border controlled deliveries mean that the police of one country are aware of illegal activities, such as the importing of drugs or a shipment of stolen cars, and allow them to take place across (and into or out of) another country, in order to get information about a criminal organisation. The international aspect of controlled deliveries takes two forms. One is that foreign authorities notify the Norwegian authorities of, say a shipment of drugs that will soon arrive in Norway. The notification is followed by a request not to intervene before the drugs reach the final destination, so that the broader range of persons involved in the criminal operation can be identified. This implies that the police employ the 'opportunity principle' in not interfering with a criminal activity, or at least not immediately, to uncover

97 Op.cit.:53.

98 http://conventions.coe.int/Treaty/Commun/ChercheSig.asp?NT=030&CM=&DF=&CL=ENG [08.06.2014].

99 The same justifications are applicable for JITs (see Prop.97 LS (2011–2012):49)

100 Boucht 2012:228 n.122; Gade *et al.* 2005:462.

101 Prop.97 LS (2011–2012):51.

102 Op.cit.:51–52.

103 NOU 1997:15 p.84.

other crimes or criminals. A handbook with information on other states' rules of procedure has been produced, to facilitate cooperation in such cases; another handbook concerns general cooperation on fighting drug-related crime, and a third deals with police cooperation across state borders.[104] As an example, Dutch customs authorities stopped a package containing 579 grams of cocaine-chloride on its way from the Dutch Antilles to Norway, and contacted Kripos, before shipping the package to the Norwegian post office. Kripos replaced the narcotics with fake drugs at the post office, before notification of a package awaiting collection was sent to the addressee. Norwegian police kept the post office under surveillance, and arrested the addressee when he showed up to collect the package.[105]

The other form of international cooperation occurs in the same type of operation, but foreign police not only request non-interference, but also ask to carry out and/or participate in surveillance (or arrest, or seizure) on Norwegian territory. Since they include requests for coercive measures, such operations normally, but not invariably, involve the prosecutorial authorities. The Supreme Court (Rt. 1986.779, p.784) states that controlled deliveries without any elements of provocation do not necessitate prosecutorial agreement.[106]

Controlled deliveries are one of the extraordinary or untraditional investigation methods permitted in Norway on a 'soft law' legal basis, when not in breach of GCPC sect. 196.[107] The procedure was legally established in the above-mentioned Supreme Court verdict of 1986 concerning narcotic drugs. Police provocation of the criminal activity observed may, however, challenge the legality of the police operation, and any evidence might be excluded from court proceeding.[108]

Cross-border cooperation on controlled deliveries was first formalised in the CISA art.73, whereby MS permit such deliveries on assumption that territorial MS retained control, responsibility and the right to intervene as they wished.[109] These are, then, quite similar to the requirements for surveillance and hot pursuit described above, with the exception that responsibility for the operation is the host state's. As we have seen, the Norwegian PA sect.20a was previously limited to hot pursuit and surveillance. After the 2012 amendment, under international agreements foreign police are allowed to operate on Norwegian territory. Cross-border controlled deliveries are thus now presumably legally based on this section.

104 St.prp.nr.42 (1996–1997).

105 LG 2013.25651

106 Another case from 2013 involved Lithuanian police using an undercover agent in an amphetamine-smuggling group in Lithuania, who had discovered smuggling to Norway. Lithuanian police requested communication control and continued surveillance in Norway, but did not participate themselves in the Norwegian operation. (LB 2013.112693). In one of the so-called Skrik cases (Rt. 1998.407), foreign agents worked undercover in Norway for the Norwegian police to retrieve a stolen Munch painting. They wanted to testify anonymously in court, which was refused, and their testimonies were not accepted as evidence. There were, according to the Court, several other weaknesses in the covert investigation. The accused was acquitted of the theft.

107 Prop.97 LS (2011–2012):47; NOU 1997:15 p.81–2.

108 NOU 1993:3 and Ot.prp.nr.64 (1998–1999) ch.16.2. The regulation of controlled deliveries and investigative methods of a provocative nature was considered by the Norwegian Methods Committee in 1993, and in a subsequent *forarbeid* (1999). After considering the reported 'failure' of the legal regulation of such methods in Denmark (in practice, the methods were hardly ever used by Danish police), the Committee and Ministry concluded that such regulations would endanger police efforts to uncover serious crime. The methods were considered sufficiently limited and regulated in soft law, i.e. by several Supreme Court verdicts (Rt. 1992.1088; Rt. 1993.473; Rt. 1998.407; later Rt. 2008.1659).

109 Art 73. Art.74 decided that searches for drugs should take place, as far as possible, inside member state territory, not on the borders between the MS. The MLA Convention does not contain such a preference.

As shown above, there are no rules in the CISA on which observation techniques may be used in cross-border surveillance. Controlled deliveries may therefore be interpreted as allowed under CISA art.40, although they are more specifically regulated in art.73. Art.73 was repealed in 2000 and replaced with articles 12, 15 and 16 of the 2000 MLA Convention.[110] These were Schengen-relevant and thus binding for Norway. The MLA rules permitting controlled deliveries are practically identical to those in art.18 of the CoE ETS no.182. The controlled delivery must take place during investigation of extraditable offences according to national law. In Norway, this is regulated by the extradition act sect.3, which has as a general requirement for a minimum one-year sentence for the crime in question.[111]

Norway originally made a reservation on art.18 cf. 33 no. 2, which meant that controlled deliveries were not automatically accepted from non-CoE members. The reservation was lifted in 2012.[112] The only difference from CISA art.73, is that art.73 regulated only controlled deliveries of narcotics and psychotropic substances, while no such limitation exists in the MLA or ETS no.182.

The Ministry's justification for the change in PA sect.20a was that such operations did not entail any transfer of authority or control, since they would take place in accordance with national law and under the direction of national authorities. There were thus no discussions in the consultative papers of these changes.[113]

The international instruments contain no clear definition of 'controlled deliveries'.[114] The Danish Circular on them states that the deliveries or transports may contain: a) objects it is illegal to possess, e.g. weapons or drugs; b) objects involving tax or toll evasion; and c) human beings who have no right to enter the country. This corresponds with the description set out in the UN Convention of 1988.[115] Art.12 and ETS no.182 and MLA art.18 also require that each situation is individually considered and decided upon by the competent authorities of the state where the crime is to be temporarily 'allowed'. The operation must accord with the procedures and national law of the host state. Finally, the right to "act and to direct and control" operations lies with the host state. Thus, even though a truck containing stolen goods might be kept under close, continuous surveillance through Europe and into Norway, and be on its way out of Norway into another jurisdiction, Norwegian authorities could abort the operation if it did not comply with Norwegian rules.[116]

Several issues arise in connection with controlled deliveries. One is whether the police should strike at an earlier stage, in another country. Another is how free the police are to choose which country should be the dominant one in the final police action; which state's police should make this decision; and whether all offenders should be transported to the final state to be prosecuted together.

There may be various reasons for deciding that a controlled delivery should pass through many countries before ending up in the state chosen for the arrest and prosecution. This could in fact amount to jurisdiction shopping, and questions about how the 'final destination' is chosen should at least always be asked.

110 [2000] OJ C 197/3 art.2(2).

111 Utleveringsloven 1975.

112 Consultation paper 2010 on int.coop.:70–1.

113 Prop.97 LS (2011–2012):47–48.

114 Gade et al. 2005:456.

115 Art.1(g) UN Convention against illicit traffic in narcotic drugs and psychotropic substances (1988).

116 [2000] OJ C 197/1 art.12. This is also reiterated in the Directive on a European Investigation Order ([2010] OJ C 165/22 art.26, see fn.595).

It would hardly be allowed to emphasise the general sentencing frameworks for crimes, so that – contrary to the popular fear that Norway may become a 'safe haven' for criminals – the higher frameworks for sentencing drug crimes in Norway could make it a 'haven' for police who want criminals to be punished 'as severely as possible'. The police and prosecution authorities, however, can to some extent choose whether to investigate and prosecute. While serious crimes generally will be investigated, this opportunity principle also allows police to choose the appropriate approach, and timing.[117] From the nation-state point of view, an issue arises if foreign authorities are able to decide whether the national police should investigate or stop a crime. In the Danish DPP's Circular, the purpose of controlled deliveries should be to learn the identity of the receiver of the illegal goods or persons.[118] Such a purpose is not stated either in CISA, the MLA Convention, or the ETS no.182 protocol. No binding regulations exist for the Norwegian police: they are free to choose the purpose of a controlled delivery. The controlled delivery should, however, be within the general legitimate purposes of the police.

Europol and Eurojust can be influential through giving advice on where and how investigations should be carried out. Although they are not supranational entities, the overview and contact mechanisms they possess, make them well-equipped to assist member states on controlled deliveries. The emergency powers of the national public prosecutors, who are always present in the Eurojust HQ in The Hague, make possible the prosecutorial decisions needed to make an arrest the moment a pursued car stops, or to search the hotel room where the passengers of an observed car have spent the night. Since the decision on allowing illegal goods to cross borders must be made by judicial authorities – 'low level' police cannot decide this – the coordinating function of Eurojust, through the seconded national members present in The Hague, makes a significant contribution to the success of such cooperation.[119]

12.3.2 Covert investigation

Cross-border covert investigation refers to operations going beyond the surveillance described above. It means that foreign police officers investigate a crime under cover, outside their jurisdiction.[120] Covert police work is by nature more or less invisible; it is supposed to be secret from those policed. This enables police to act without being as easily controlled, and is or may therefore be legally challenging. And this is not less challenging when non-national police are permitted covert policing.

National covert investigation using secret or false identity, known as 'infiltration' or 'undercover operations', is unregulated by current Norwegian law. It is, however, considered a valid police method.[121] It is one of various so-called extraordinary or untraditional investigation methods, which are generally subject to two basic requirements: 1) they must not be used if conventional methods, such as surveillance, may suffice to accomplish the investigatory purpose, and; 2) the targeted person(s) must be suspected of committing serious crime.[122]

117 Auglend et al. 2004:851.

118 Circular of 31.07.2002:3, quoted in Gade *et al.* 2005:456.

119 Prop. 97 LS (2011–2012) ch.9.1.

120 Peers 2011; Prop.97 LS (2011–2012):51. For a detailed account of covert investigation using coercive measures in Norway, see Bruce and Haugland 2014.

121 NOU 1997:15 p. 119.

122 Myhrer 2007b:420; 434; RG.2013.615.

(I return to the level of seriousness in the following.) The measures must be decided by the competent authorities. In contrast, a decision by the police to infiltrate does not have to be made by a Public Prosecutor. Police infiltration and controlled deliveries are not subject to as strict a proportionality requirement as other covert measures.[123]

The core of infiltration is that the person under surveillance is unaware of the identity of the undercover officer. Undercover agents are passive in their interaction with suspects – unlike agents involved in provocation. Provocation may, however, result from both infiltration operations and controlled deliveries. In principle, police provocation is prohibited in Norway, but is to some extent allowed in other states (see, however, some Norwegian exceptions in the following).

Cross-border covert investigation involve intelligence gathering before a criminal case has been initiated, and during the early stages of an investigation. It can include surveillance; communication control; bugging of private or public rooms or buildings; hidden photographing or filming; or the use of informants.[124] If the measure is coercive, infringing, for example, privacy rights (phone-tapping, etc.), it must be in accordance with host state law. If not coercive, or where there is no contact with the suspect(s), it may be classed as surveillance. There can be different understandings of what under-cover operations are, which may be why the details of such operations must be agreed specifically upon, particularly in the international instruments.

Methods going beyond surveillance were not part of the Schengen cooperation.[125] They are, however, regulated in the MLA Convention art.14 and the ETS no.182 art.19. These are identical, and regulate cross-border covert investigation, understood as "officers acting under covert or false identity". The action is now formally regulated in the Police Act sect.20a, under the general provision permitting foreign duties performed on Norwegian territory. What is involved in such cooperative assistance, as described by the Ministry, is assisting foreign police to gain access to criminal environments as 'undercover agents', to gather information and identify and map members of a criminal network.[126]

Three types of covert investigation are covered by the the applicable conventions: 1) foreign authorities – the Polish police, say – ask Norway to allow a Polish official to perform covert investigation in Norway (or the other way round); 2) the Norwegian authorities ask the Polish authorities to send an official to Norway to assist in a covert investigation; and 3) the Norwegian authorities request a Polish official to assist Norwegian officials carrying out a covert investigation in Poland.

The requirements for mutual assistance in covert investigations are:

- Each request must be considered individually by the competent authorities in the member state receiving the request, paying due regard to that country's national law, cf. arts.14 and 19 no.2 (in both articles).

123 Hopsnes 2003:77.

124 Prop.97 LS (2011–2012):50. There is no clear definition of 'covert operations' in the [2000] OJ C 197/1 art.14, but also Boucht 2012:228 identifies infiltration as part of such operations. See e.g. Brodeur 1995 on differentiating between passive and active undercover policing.

125 The Naples II Convention ([1998] OJ C 24/1) art. 23, however, provides for such cooperation for customs officers.

126 Prop.97 LS (2011–2012):50–51.

- The duration of the covert investigation, detailed conditions and legal status of the officers involved shall be agreed between the member states with due regard to both/all parties' national law and procedures, cf. no.2.
- The covert investigation shall take place in accordance with the law and procedures of the territory concerned, cf. no.3.
- All member states involved shall cooperate to ensure the security of the officers acting under false identity, and that all operations are "prepared and supervised".

It is thus not permitted to go undercover in another country without the knowledge and approval of the host state.

There are no requirements as to which types of offences may warrant a cross-border undercover operation. Boucht argues that such operations are mostly connected with serious crimes, such as organised crime, abduction, forgery and weapons theft.[127] In national law, infiltration is one of the extraordinary police methods which are only considered lawful when used to combat very serious crimes. Such extraordinary methods as communication control and concealed search, that are legal under the Criminal Procedure Act, require the crime in question to be punishable by 10 years or more – which, in the Norwegian legal system, means that it is very serious. This could imply a *de facto* requirement that crimes be 'serious' – which, of course, is also practical as regards police resources. Nevertheless, according to Myhrer, the methods mentioned above mostly involve provocation, which raises various issues concerning due process rights, that are less significant when it comes to infiltration.[128]

Another covert investigation technique is the use of a police officer as a 'stool pigeon' (*lokkedue*) to lure someone into committing an offence. Norwegian Appeals Court practice has allowed this even for offences with a low sentencing frame. In the absence of a clear legal regulatory requirement, the court stated, the criterion should be whether the police method is proportionate to the crime. In one such case, an undercover officer used a cell phone and "showed" a suspect that it was kept in an easily accessible pocket.[129] Phone theft is not in itself considered a serious crime, but the court emphasised that the sentencing frame alone does not determine whether certain methods of investigation are acceptable. The centre of Oslo has seen a huge growth of pickpocketing, with a 122 per cent increase in reported offences in the period from 2006 to 2012. It has turned into a major social problem. The social impact of less serious crimes should therefore also justify untraditional investigation, when ordinary methods fail (Rt.1993.473). A conclusion following this is that the offence in question needs either to be serious in terms of its penal code classification or the sentence it attracts, or have a high social impact. Even the suspicion of relatively petty crimes may thus justify covert investigations such as infiltration. The case just mentioned involved the use of a stool pigeon, not infiltration. The same considerations apply, regarding the offences that may 'legitimise' infiltration, at least until the operation turns into provocation.

Cross-border operations must conform to the national law and procedures of the host state. The above-mentioned instruments contain no general requirement regarding the purpose of covert investigations. The Norwegian Director of Public Prosecution (DPP) emphasises in the circular concerning police provocation that it should be used to "improve

127 Boucht 2012:228.
128 Myhrer 2007b:420.
129 RG.2013.615.

[the police's] knowledge of or control over a course of action".[130] Although this purpose is wide-ranging, it presupposes that the undercover agent is actively seeking to gain information in a specific case or environment, thus excluding, say, knowledge randomly acquired by a police officer privately attending a football match.[131] Presumably this also applies to other similar measures.

Police agents in infiltration operations may be civilian, according to several Norwegian Supreme Court verdicts.[132] Peers shows that the officers involved in such operations within the Naples II Convention may be both customs officers and "officers acting on behalf" of a member state's administration.[133] He says the latter may include private detectives authorised by a state. While the Naples II Convention is not an applicable legal instrument in this context (and Norway is not a member of this cooperation), the Police Act and consultative works contain no regulations on who the officers performing covert investigation in Norway may be. The Norwegian Police Act sect.20a refers to an "officer" (*tjenestemann*). An undercover agent who is not a police officer in his home state may also have temporary Norwegian police competences delegated to him (sect.20[3]). Thus, if a private investigator in Spain is tasked with going undercover in a mission in Norway, Norway must be notified of the legal status of the undercover agent, and the details of the operation must be agreed upon between Spanish and Norwegian authorities, in accordance with both states' laws and procedures – but in Norwegian law, there are no regulations limiting the types of personnel taking part in such operations. If agreed by the two states, a private detective could also be given temporary police powers, and thus perform coercive measures. Though most such operations would be subject to prosecutorial authorisation, some will follow directly from ordinary police powers. Covert operations must be agreed upon, but, of course, unforeseen situations may occur. As Brown points out, it is often advisable to keep as few people as possible informed of major undercover police operations, since the stakes are high, and the crimes and criminal networks involved are formidable.[134] It may therefore easily happen that an undercover agent is 'too undercover' to be trusted by ordinary police officers, who then apprehend him because he is in possession of drugs received from the group he is infiltrating.

As a general rule, legitimate police provocation cannot be carried out by civilians under Norwegian law, but if a civilian – a private detective, say – is given temporary police competences in the country he is engaged in the undercover operation, this prohibition is of no consequence.[135] The Norwegian guidelines for undercover officers are given in a directive that is classified for security reasons.[136] This is understandable, but implies that foreign undercover agents are in contact with the levels of Norwegian authorities who can reveal its contents. In infiltration cases, the decision to go undercover does not have to be made by a public prosecutor.[137]

130 Rundskriv nr. 2/2000:3 (my translation).
131 Hopsnes 2003:78.
132 E.g. Rt. 1994.319; NOU 2004:6 p.92.
133 Peers 2011:938.
134 Brown 2008.
135 Hopsnes 2003:69–70; Rt. 1994.319. The human rights limitations following ECtHR case law concerning civilians acting as police agents would apply.
136 NOU 1997:15 p.121.
137 Hopsnes 2003:77.

The legal issues arising from covert operations were debated in connection with the legal amendments in the Norwegian CPA concerning, for example, the police's right not to testify on certain aspects of their operation.[138] Sect.292 regulates the right to make exceptions to the duty to bear witness, if information is not significant for the specific case, or a point has already been sufficiently proven.[139] As mentioned above, police provocation is generally prohibited in Norwa. However, if covert operations include an element of provocation, the Circular of the DPP no.2/2000 contains the legal guidelines applicable to the police.[140] There may be an element of provocation when, for example, the police purchase drugs or stolen objects to prove the criminal offence (smuggling or theft) has taken place. The provocation of crime, on the other hand, is when, say, the police ask for a large quantity of cocaine, which *because of the request* is smuggled from Colombia to Norway – and then, when it arrives, the police arrest all the parties involved. In such a case, the crime would not have taken place if not provoked by the police. There seems to be a relatively clear scale of legality for such investigative measures. Infiltration is the first step; the next is provocation, which, if it constitutes provocation of crime, is generally a reason for acquittal in Norwegian law.[141] The added requirement of legality developed in Norwegian law, which demands that the police investigation should have no other serious flaws, might create further uncertainties.[142] Police provocation may lead to evidence which could be used in a criminal case. Such evidence may, under certain conditions be admissible in Norwegian courts (Circular G 19/2001 on international cooperation in criminal cases).

Cooperation also raises potential issues concerning the question of reactive versus proactive crime control. Police methods should be as non-intrusive and non-coercive as possible, which makes infiltration a good option. The sanctity of private spaces and intimate relations of course, points in the opposite direction. There are also issues to do with the control of covert investigation.[143] If the basic requirement of no provocation of crime is met, abuse may be prevented. And there is no particular advantage in having offenders, whether domestic or foreign, policed only by national police officers. This also accords with the ECtHR, in the Lüdi case[144], in which it was established that, although police infiltration may infringe a person's private life, as protected by the ECHR art.8, this right may not be invoked while engaging in serious criminal activity. In this case, after a tip-off from the German police that Lüdi – a Swiss national – was dealing in cocaine, the Swiss authorities brought an undercover agent into the investigation. What he discovered, in addition to phone taps, created sufficient evidence to arrest Lüdi. The Court said that although both the infiltration and the telephone tapping infringed his privacy, he inevitably risked encountering undercover agents by engaging in cocaine dealing. Such police measures were thus seen as "in accordance with law" and "necessary in a democratic society" for the

138 Ot.prp.nr.64 (1998–1999) ch.16.1. There must be due regard for the prosecutorial and private life rights of the person under observation; ECHR arts.6; 8; the CPA sect.226 on covert coercive measures does to some extent imply fewer rights for those being observed.

139 The right to access was reduced in broader covert investigative measures, in a CPA amendment in 2013, because "certain types of crimes have developed in the past few years that in themselves may threaten societal stability" (auth. translation, Prop. 147 L (2012–2013) ch.3.4).

140 Rundskriv nr. 2/2000. On police provocation as an investigative measure in Norway, see Hopsnes 2003; and NOU 1997:15.

141 E.g. Rt. 1993.319; Rt. 2000.1223; op.cit.; and Teixeira de Castro v. Portugal 44/1997/828/1034, 9.6.

142 Rt. 1998.407.

143 See e.g. Bruce and Haugland 2014; Marx 1995b.

144 Lüdi v. Switzerland 12433/86 15.06.1992, Series A 238.

"prevention of crime".[145] Nevertheless, although such police methods may be accepted in the courts, both nationally and internationally, infiltration that is not coercive may, as Halvorsen argues, still be morally questionable because the manipulative element of infiltration challenges the value of individual autonomy.[146]

Peers points out the accountability issues arising from extensive undercover police operations across borders.[147] The question of whether it is possible to know if an undercover agent is acting on behalf of the police of host state (which may or may not have been informed), or on behalf of police officers from abroad, is potentially problematic. Conspiracy theorists might think that police officers from member states of the MLA Convention or the ETS no.182 could agree to be undercover agents in each other's states, away from the environments where they were previously known. If the police could be suspected of deliberate circumvention of various legal restrictions legal restraints would have little effect. This may be more likely in some MS than others, given different histories of policing. Fijnaut and Marx, for example, point out the undercover characteristics of the original French police model, in contrast to the British tradition.[148]

It is possible that the intentions and actions of persons within infiltrated networks may be manipulated.[149] Also of concern is the lack of control on how evidence or general data obtained by a foreign undercover agent is applied abroad. There have been several occasions on which Norwegian courts ruled evidence inadmissible, because it came from an infiltrator secretly taping conversations.[150] Norwegian authorities, once they have permitted foreign undercover activity, have little control on how such evidence is used in foreign courts, where other rules may apply. The case law from the ECtHR, which is applicable in all courts in question (within the EU and/or CoE members), does however set up strict limitations designed to safeguard due process in these matters. ECHR art.6 no.1 and 3(d) prohibits the presentation of evidence when the privilege against self-incrimination and to contradiction in court has been broken.

The international instruments also state, as mentioned above, that all member states involved shall cooperate to ensure the security of the officers acting under false identity, and that all operations shall be "prepared and supervised". The first point follows the Schengen cooperation model. Since operations must follow national laws and procedures, undercover agents are, under the PA sect.20a, considered criminally and civilly liable in the same way as Norwegian officers. This also follows from the MLA Convention arts.15 and 16; ETS no.182 arts.21–22.[151] The sufficient 'preparation and supervision' by a high-level authority could perhaps be argued to constitute another requirement. It is notable that the MLA Convention arts.21 and 22 on the officer's criminal and civil liability do not apply to art.14 situations.

145 Op.cit. para. 2. Joubert and Bevers 1996:193–5 criticise the case for giving too little attention to (suspected) criminals' privacy rights, arguing that the interpretation of ECHR art.8 must be wider since e.g. the presumption of innocence is challenged in these operations. Marx 1995a also points out similar challenges, though he considers these as ethical considerations in a democratic society.

146 Halvorsen 2003.

147 Peers 2011:538.

148 Fijnaut and Marx 1995.

149 Joubert and Bevers 1996:194.

150 E.g. Rt. 2009.567; Rt. 1999.1269.

151 Prop.97 LS (2011–2012):50–1; 53.

12.4 Considering the operational cooperation

Through the Schengen cooperation, which has been duly incorporated into the Norwegian Police Act sect.20a, foreign police officers may continue hot pursuit or surveillance operations started in their own country, into Norwegian territory. In situations of particular urgency, in pursuit of persons who have committed serious crimes, or who are suspected of committing them, such border crossing may take place without prior authorisation from Norwegian authorities. Norwegian regulations and laws apply, and foreign police may only apprehend the persons in certain circumstances.

The more detailed Schengen regulations are implemented in various ways in the member states, as regards, for example how far foreign police are allowed to come into the country or whether they may be armed and use force. There are also some differences in national definitions of crimes and police measures. The states Norway mainly cooperates with are Sweden and Finland, whose regulations are similar to Norway's. The major difference between Norway and Schengen *and* EU members concerns extradition regulations. For EU members, the European Arrest Warrant (EAW) sets out the applicable rules, which lower the threshold for the extradition of citizens. This threshold may determine which crimes may legitimise hot pursuit.

Apart from extradition of Norwegian citizens, the relevant Norwegian and Nordic regulations are similar in practice to those within the EU regime. The possibility of autonomous foreign police authority being enforced on Norwegian soil was controversial in Norwegian public debate. Such enforcement however, as we have seen, is subject to detailed regulations, and must always comply with the national law of the territory where the pursuit is carried out. Despite the obvious infringement of the territorial sovereignty of national police, the actual encroachment on national control appears to have been less than critics feared. Daman points out that the array of conventions and treaties in central Europe makes hot pursuit uncommon.[152] Hufnagel's research, on the other hand, shows that the police like having a range of alternatives, which enables them to choose the appropriate tool for a situation.[153] It is undoubtedly important that the police are able to carry on the pursuit of an offender fleeing the crime scene, in view of the open borders between the Schengen members. Interestingly, in recent legislative amendments, the focus has moved away from the hot pursuit measures.

The less visible forms of police work are increasingly emphasised as important in targeting the most serious border-crossing crimes, as well as 'ordinary' crime. The situation in Norway regarding cross-border policing has changed in recent years: there used to be restrictions on foreign police operating covertly, but these have been removed. Alongside this wider acceptance, came a lowered threshold for initiating such measures, and thus making far more offences possible grounds for covert policing.

A key concern in this book is possible infringement of sovereignty following from foreign police in national territories. What emerges from this chapter is that there have been significant changes in the foreign or international police measures that are allowed on Norwegian territory. Hot pursuit is a long-standing tradition on the high seas, and has also happened informally over land borders. The Schengen regulations formalised these practices. The same is largely true of cross-border surveillance operations, though the possibilities for

152 Daman 2008:203–5.
153 Hufnagel 2013.

foreign police to engage in this have been extended since the original Schengen rules. Hot pursuit allows more foreign action on a host territory, while various surveillance or covert operations simply *appear* less intrusive to public, and even perhaps to the state. 'Less visible' then equals less infringing on the monopoly of violence – because people do not get to see foreign police enforcing foreign power. Another, more practical interpretation, is that the technological possibilities of covert policing and communication between police, e.g. during controlled deliveries, have improved. Such an improvement may be related to practical needs: international, serious crime is steadily growing and becoming more complex. New police methods and instruments are necessary to counter this.

One the one hand, the developments may be traced to changes and even international and EU pressure. New cooperation instruments, such as the MLA Convention have been established, and Norway fears becoming a safe haven for criminals. On the other, when it comes to perceptions of which police methods are necessary, it may be hard to separate national from international currents, that arise from changes in perceptions of crime and risk in the general population, and fluctuations in crime rates.

13 JOINT OPERATIONS AND INVESTIGATIONS

In 2010, Operation Golf, led by the UK Metropolitan Police (MET) and Europol, involved a Joint Investigation Team (JIT) consisting of officers from the Romanian National Police and the MET. The aim of the JIT was to stop a Romanian organised crime network that was trafficking and exploiting children from the Roma community in the UK. The operation led to the rescue of 28 children and the arrest of 126 individuals suspected of offences such as human trafficking (including internal trafficking within the UK), money laundering, benefit fraud, child neglect, perverting the course of justice, theft and handling of stolen goods. Europol had an active role in assisting the national police authorities by giving analytical support on all levels and at all times – providing mobile offices both in Romania and in the UK (with on-the-spot intelligence to support search and arrest); identifying links to other EU countries' criminal networks, especially Belgium and Spain; and giving expert advice on setting up the JIT and planning strategic and operational activities.[1]

The above is an example of foreign police officers actively doing police work in the continuation of their home state jurisdiction. This is different from the more exceptional Schengen regulations and information exchange independent of state borders. If one thinks of the Weberian monopoly of legitimate force, and the idea that police work within state borders, and the military outside them, such joint operations and investigations certainly seem to constitute a challenge for sovereignty and for Weber's concept of the state.

The controlled deliveries and covert operations described above are also joint operations, to some extent. The Police Act sect.20a regulates the crossing of foreign police officers into Norwegian jurisdiction to continue hot pursuit or observation, and sometimes to enforce coercive powers on behalf of their national authority. Such actions are not so much cooperation, as the continuation of national police powers enforced, with limitations, in other jurisdictions. JITs involve detailed exchange of plans, and foreign police operating on national territories, alongside the domestic authorities. A specific Nordic alternative is also discussed.

While joint investigation operations seek to uncover criminal offences, joint patrols and cross-border assistance are concerned with public order policing. Joint cooperation in public order policing, at least the kind formally based in law, is a relatively new invention.[2] The term is not new: it is widely used with various meanings throughout the world.[3] The main idea

1 Solberg 2011a; Solberg 2011b.
2 Verhage *et al.* 2010:7–8. Similar cooperation exists in South-East Asia, but there too is mostly unregulated in law (Hufnagel 2014).
3 Block 2008:78.

DOI: 10.4324/9780429503696-15

behind joint investigation teams is that a police operation will be more successful when officers from several jurisdictions cooperate. Joint operations involve the influence and action of officers from two or more jurisdictions, and often the coordination of simultaneous operations in multiple places. There can be many benefits. Suppose that, as in the example above, individuals from Romania are suspected of engaging in criminal activity in England; the Romanian police could assist in matching corresponding facts and situations in their home state, providing information on, for instance, local patterns of child exploitation. If action is taken simultaneously in the suspects' home state and the 'end destination' of the offence this may prevent suspects elsewhere being alerted to the discovery of the criminal network.

This chapter examines first joint investigation teams and then joint operations in the forms of patrolling and assistance in mass gatherings. The relevant international instruments are primarily the MLA Convention and the ETS no.182 Additional Protocol (AP), the Nordic Police Cooperation Agreement, and – to some extent – the Schengen Agreement.

13.1 Joint investigation teams

A joint investigation team (JIT) may be described as a team of law enforcement officials and/or other authorities from several states working together on the investigation of a case of international or cross-border crime.[4] The main purpose of JITs is to facilitate mutual assistance in criminal matters by avoiding time-consuming formal requests between states for investigative steps to be taken in other states. Avoiding possible parallel investigations may also be in the interest of suspects, since it lessens the risk of multiple convictions.[5] Joint teams were introduced in the 1997 Amsterdam Treaty, but were not regulated before the ETS 182 art.20 and the MLA Convention art.13[6] with the related Framework Decision on Joint Investigation Teams.[7] Both the EU MLA Convention art.13 and the CoE ETS no.182 art.20 regulate JITs. The material requirements are the same: member states may, for specific purposes and for a limited period of time, agree to set up a joint investigation team to cooperate on investigating criminal cases in one or more of the parties' jurisdictions (MLA art.13 [1]). The investigation must always adhere to the national laws of the host state. For the sake of brevity, the articles of the MLA Convention appear as references in the following, unless specified otherwise. There are also regulations in the Nordic Police Cooperation Agreement on joint investigations.[8] The following describes the possibilities and pitfalls of joint investigation teams, examining the national and international requirements for such operations, and comparing them with Schengen measures when relevant.

JIT mechanisms involve cross-border police and prosecution activities, which has led, and maybe still leads, to some disagreements or confusion on what kind of legal animal this

4 E.g. de Moor 2009.

5 Cameron *et al.* 2011:138.

6 [2000] OJ C 197/01, with [2001] OJ C 326/1.

7 [2002] OJ L 162/1. A speedy implementation attempt failed in March 2000. A new successful attempt followed, and the Decision was established after the 9/11 events. Art.13 was taken out of the MLA Convention, providing a Framework Decision for more rapid implementation provision than the Convention in general (Block 2008:78; Block 2012:91). The Decision ceases to apply when the Convention has come into force in all member states (FD art.5). The FD does not diverge from the Convention, but until this comes into force, there is an additional need for the EU member states to implement a national legal basis, since an FD cannot be an autonomous legal basis for the establishment of JITs (Rijken and Vermeulen 2006a:21).

8 2012 ANPC.

is. Some have argued that JITs should not be regulated in the MLA Convention, since they primarily concern police, not prosecutorial cooperation measures. Others hold that much of the cooperation takes place between prosecutorial authorities in charge of investigations, depending partly on the structure of the police and prosecution system in the various states.[9] Prior to the Lisbon Treaty, the basis was (initially) art.31 of the 1992 TEU. Arts.82 and 85 TEU (judicial cooperation) are included in art.85 (within police cooperation), giving a legal basis for the Council's conditions and limitations on which judicial authorities can operate in other MS' territory.[10] In Norwegian legal literature, at least in the standard works,[11] this could explain why the international elements of prosecutorial and police regulations are treated somewhat briefly, it simply seems of little concern to Norway as a non-EU member.

Joint patrolling (i.e. various kinds of assistance) across national police district borders is based in the Norwegian Police Directive sect.7–4, and in principle, is compulsory. The legal basis for joint investigation teams across national district borders is the Prosecution Directive (*Påtaleinstruks*) sect.37–5, which requires the offence(s) in question to be organised, or otherwise serious. In such cases, Kripos and the relevant local police or DA may set up joint investigation teams. There are no further guidelines or requirements. The National Authority for Prosecution of Organised and Other Serious Crime (NAST) has the higher public prosecution responsibility for such cases, where Kripos do not themselves have competence (sect.38–1).[12] Until 2012, there were no specific regulations on international cross-border joint investigation teams, apart from those between the Nordic countries. The regulation now following from PA sect. 20a is intertwined with the international legal basis described below.

13.1.1 Requirements for JITs

The conventions do not specify which types of offences or situations can justify a JIT. The JIT must, though, have a specific purpose set out in advance, and there must be a temporal limitation, which can be extended. JITs may be set up "particularly" when there are "difficult and demanding" investigations that have links with other MS, or when several MS are conducting investigations that need to be coordinated (art.13 [1] a–b).[13] The requirement for a specific purpose and a clear time limitation means there must be a particular crime in question. The demand that the crime be linked to more than one state suggests that only serious and complex crimes are relevant.[14] There is a requirement for a proper legal basis. At the EU level, this is the Convention, but a JIT must also have a national legal basis. This follows from several paragraphs in art.13, requiring the activities of the JIT to be either within both states' rules, or that of the host state of the team's investigation, and the activity of the seconded members within *their* respective jurisdiction's rules. This only indicates

9 Gade *et al.* 2005:457–8; Plachta 2005:285–6. De Busser argues that JITs are judicial in the cooperation form, with reference to the treaty basis being the MLA Convention.

10 De Busser 2006:140–1.

11 Andenæs and Myhrer 2009; Fredriksen 2013; Kjelby 2013. More interest is shown in the most recent edition of Auglend and Mæland's *Politirett* (2016).

12 Note that the Norwegian system has police entities including a prosecutorial department, and others that are solely prosecutorial authorities. The chief and assisting chief of Kripos have prosecutorial competences at the chief of police level (CPA sect.55[1], Ot.prp.nr.77 (2004–2005)).

13 Peers 2011:939.

14 Rijken and Vermeulen 2006b:15.

some criminalised activity, or the suspicion of it; in contrast to, for example, the hot pursuit rules, there is no requirement for it to be an extraditable offense, or to have a cross-border element.[15] In MLA's Explanatory Memorandum, organised crime is mentioned as a particular concern, while the Framework Decision's preamble focuses on trafficking in drugs and human beings, and on terrorism and terrorism-related crimes.[16]

The JIT's formal purpose must be clearly specified in the agreement setting up the operation. De Busser's fieldwork shows that JITs also often have *in*formal purposes.[17] Formally, the JIT studied by de Busser was established "in relation to investigating the drug trafficking activities of a criminal organisation operating in the Netherlands and England & Wales". The main purpose was to dismantle the organisation in the Netherlands, using evidence and intelligence provided by the two other parties. There were also undeclared aims, however: to seize property and assets, and gather information on other, related cases. Strengthening the police cooperation between the UK and the Netherlands was another informal purpose. The regulations do not prohibit additional purposes, as long as there is also a formal requirement.

National regulations on when to use JITs vary. De Busser shows member states have different guidelines on what cases warrant a JIT.[18] Dutch guidelines apply a proportionality criterion, whereby a JIT should only be used as a last resort, when traditional forms of mutual (legal) assistance cannot achieve the same results. Swedish and Finnish legislation follow art.13 regulations as described above.[19] The British legislation show no requirements for the use such methods, it must just be advantageous. There is no mention of requirements in the Norwegian policy documents, at least not in unclassified ones, which may imply a similar situation to the British one. Many of the specifics have, then, been left to the member states to regulate. Nevertheless, Europol and Eurojust have suggested a set of uniform rules for individual agreements.[20] The suggestions take the form of a Council Resolution, which is not binding. Participants and establishment. In addition, a JITs Practical Guide has been developed by a Network of National Experts on Joint Investigation Teams[21], in cooperation with Europol, Eurojust and OLAF. The objective of the Guide is to provide practical information, guidance and advice to practitioners on the formation of JITs.[22]

A request to set up a JIT may be made by any of the member states concerned (MLA Convention art.13 [1] a). Thus, if Norwegian police suspect that a major pickpocket gang operating in Norway is based in a Lithuanian city, they may suggest to the Lithuanian police that a JIT should be set up there. The initiative need not come from the state where the investigations will be carried out.

The MLA Convention (art.13 [2]) refers to the 1959 Convention art.14, which lays down that the request to set up a joint investigation team shall contain information similar to that in an ordinary request for mutual legal assistance, together with a proposal on the

15 De Buck 2007:255.
16 [2000] OJ C 379/7 p.17; [2002] OJ L 162/1 preamble 6–7 (2002/465/JHA).
17 De Busser 2006:138–9.
18 Op.cit.:138–9. See her text for the specific member state references.
19 Boucht 2012; Cameron *et al.* 2011:140. There is no mention of it in the Danish literature (Gade *et al.* 2005; Henricson 2010).
20 [2017] OJ C 18/1.
21 Council Document establishing the JITs network, doc. 11037/05.
22 Joint Investigation Teams Practical Guide, doc. 6128/1/17 (https://www.europol.europa.eu/publications-documents/jits-practical-guide)

composition of the team. Europol and Eurojust have produced a request form containing the elements specified in art.13, to facilitate the setting up of teams. A Model Agreement for a team to be set up is appended to the resolution.[23] The Model Agreement asks for example for information on the member state, which body the officer is seconded from, his/her name, rank and affiliation (judicial, police or other competent authority) – in the case of the leaders – and the "role" of other participants.

While this is just a suggestion from Europol/Eurojust, the document is (supposedly) based on practitioners' needs, and may indicate details that should be kept in mind. JITs carry out investigations, and will therefore generally consist of police officers of various kinds, as well as investigative judges from states, such as France, that have them.[24] Members from other organisations, such as EU bodies like Europol, may be part of the teams, subject to national law and international regulations (art.13 no.12).

JITs can be established either 1) top-down, when it is decided either at a high level of the police/prosecutorial hierarchy, or even by a government agency, that a certain area of crime needs international cooperation; 2) bottom-up, where investigating officers realise that transnational joint investigation is necessary for further success; or 3) outside-in, when the authorities of other states have an on-going JIT, and ask another state to join it.[25] The higher national level – the contact point – will in all cases be involved, before (potentially) delegating participation to a local agency.

Kripos is the Norwegian international contact point. It is not specified in the Norwegian consultative works precisely who in the Norwegian police may suggest such operations.[26] The Swedish Act requires that a national preliminary investigation should already be on-going, if seconded members of a JIT operating in Sweden are to be allowed to take investigative measures under the simplified procedure of art.13.[27] Norwegian legislation is silent on this matter.

Art.13 (1) of the Convention concerns investigations within the territory of the member states. Thus, a joint investigation within a third state cannot have a legal basis in the Convention. As shown immediately below, officers of third states, or personnel from EU bodies may participate as members (art.13 [12]). A drug JIT could for example be investigating in Norway, with members from other transit and destination countries in Western Europe, and even cooperating with a country of origin such as Colombia. While such agreements with third states can be made, research suggests that police are sceptical as to the efficiency of such operations.[28] Competent authorities of the host state (state of operation) may request assistance from a state that is not party to the JIT, or from a third state, following applicable instruments or regulations (8). The conventions do not therefore give

23 [2017] OJ C 18/1. The recommendation for such model agreements comes from the Stockholm Programme, point 4.3.1.

24 Gade *et al.* 2005:458.

25 Mayer 2006:204–8. Both Mayer and Block 2012 argue that top-down initiatives, for various reasons, are far less likely to succeed. It is likely that the participants' internal enthusiasm for the cooperation influences the success.

26 In Sweden, it is the Prosecution Authority (or a particular authority leading an on-going investigation); the National Police Board or the police authority designated by the National Police Board; the Swedish Customs Service; or the Swedish Coast Guard that can set up a JIT, after consulting other affected Swedish authorities (Sect.3 paras. 1–2, referred to in Cameron *et al.* 2011:140 and n.553; 141). It follows that, if not specifically agreed/allowed by another state, such requests from Sweden shall be communicated via the Swedish Ministry of Justice.

27 Op.cit.:141–2.

28 De Busser 2006:136–7. See in depth on the cooperation in pre-operational phases of JITs in de Wree 2006.

extra justification for such requests. It follows also from art.13 (11) that the conventions should not be prejudiced in favour of other arrangements, or regulations regarding joint investigation teams or cooperation.

There is no obligation in the Convention to comply with a request to set up a JIT. As with all international (police) cooperation instruments, it may be assumed that there is always, a strong incentive to comply with requests from state parties that one wishes to maintain a good relationship with. If, however, a JIT is suggested without the involvement of higher-level officials, in other words, without 'political weight' behind the request, budgetary considerations may obstruct its realisation: the desire to 'achieve good stats' may count against complying with a JIT request.

13.1.2 Members, leadership and competences of seconded members

A JIT agreement is required to set out the details of the operation, specifying it the participants, which may include non-police officials and officials from non-state bodies such as Europol. The team should be organised and based in the MS where the (majority of the) investigation is expected to be carried out (art.13[1]2). Deciding which state will be the main location is important, since the competences and rights of the host and the non-host (seconded) members are different (art.13[4]). Investigation may be carried out in all participating states, following the initial agreement.

The team leader shall be a representative of the host member state (art.13[3]a). This is normally also a requirement for obtaining the necessary police authority. The leadership may change, several times even, if the investigation moves to another member state.[29] Block shows that leadership is one of several unclear aspects of JIT operations, which may lead to variations in how orders are executed. The wording of the regulation may be interpreted as meaning the JIT stays in a single location, under one leadership (which how the Dutch authorities perceive it), while the French, for instance, allow teams to be set up in different participating states – and these teams coordinated their efforts. Special agreements may be made: the French authorities have standing agreements on designated team leaders with Spain and Germany, and the French police may cross borders to assist neighbouring police, without further notification.[30]

All participating states' requirements, as set out in the specific JIT agreement, must be duly considered (no.3[b]). The host state is responsible for making the necessary organisational arrangements for the team to operate (no.3[c]). Team members are subject both to their national law and that of the host state (art.13[3]b). The investigation regulations for Norway are found in the Criminal Procedure Act (CPA) on the use of coercive measures – in Part Four – and on investigation more generally in Part Five, Chapter 18. As mentioned above, police competences outside investigative measures are regulated in the Police Act with adjoining directives and circulars, on, for example, when to investigate, police conduct when investigating, etc.[31] The team does not have operational powers outside the host state, but may request assistance from authorities in other MS (art.13 no.7).

The Norwegian regulation on the police and public prosecution hierarchy is found in the applicable Directive, which, however, has not been updated to include JITs. Sect.2 simply

29 Gade *et al.* 2005:459.
30 Block 2008:79–80, also showing how mundane issues such as working languages are unregulated.
31 Påtaleinstruksen (PI) 1985; Riksadvokatens rundskriv 1/2014.

states that it also applies to foreign police officers in Norway, following an agreement within the Schengen cooperation.[32] The applicability of the Directive gives a direct legal basis for foreign police officers being subject to the Norwegian obligations to obey – and in some situations, give – orders.

Foreign police may enforce home state police powers on host territory within JITs. JIT members seconded from foreign jurisdictions may be given certain police competences, and may even be allowed to take some coercive measures during operations. This was an innovation of the MLA Convention.[33] Thus, Latvian, Spanish or German police officers participating in a JIT in Norway, that was investigating a human trafficking case, could, under certain conditions, arrest someone and seize their belongings. Seconded members are entitled to be "present" during investigative measures taken by the JIT, unless the leader, "for particular reasons", and in accordance with the state's law, decides otherwise. The competent authorities in both host and seconding state must approve. A "particular reason" could be the questioning of a child victim of sexual abuse, where the presence of multiple police officers would be inappropriate. Operational considerations may also be relevant justifications, according to the Council's Explanatory Report.[34] Barring someone from participation simply because the seconded member is not a host state national is prohibited.

The seconded member may, accordingly, be entrusted by the team leader to perform "certain investigative measures" (art.13[5–6]). This is a change from the traditional legal order, that also applies in Norway. De Busser shows how different member states have implemented the Convention differently, as regards autonomous investigative competence. One assumes these issues are dealt with in the JIT agreement. The type of investigative measures is not specified. It might be that the leader of the team delegates to the seconded officers the same powers as domestic officers have. These must not, however, exceed the powers the seconded member has in his home state, and must, of course, follow host state law.[35] The guidelines state that such use of authority must be approved both in the initial agreement and at later stages.[36] The Model Agreement[37] suggests conferring these powers on third state participants too. But this is not, it seems, suggested for MS participants.

In contrast to the police measures based in the Schengen cooperation, JITs make it possible to delegate coercive competences to foreign officers. In JITs, foreign police officers are under host-state leadership; these competences are not, as with Schengen, enforced autonomously.[38] In both situations, however, enforcement may be carried out on behalf of the sending state.

Much as in the Schengen regulations, seconded members shall be regarded, according to art.15 of the MLA Convention, as host state officials during a JIT operation if offences are committed by or against them. This matches the Norwegian regulation in PA sect.20a (3).[39] In contrast to the Schengen regulations, however, there is nothing in JIT regulations that obliges seconded officers to be available as witnesses, or to aid the host

32 RPOD–2010–5.

33 Block 2012:89.

34 [2000] OJ C 379/7.

35 Mayer 2006:2010–11; Boucht 2012:221.

36 Guide to EU MS JIT legislation p.6.

37 Appendix II no. 3 ("Specific arrangements").

38 Henricson 2010:191. Denmark had (in 2010) trained ten police officers to participate in a force targeting international ventures in which crimes relate to Denmark (ibid n.164).

39 Like covert investigations and controlled deliveries (see ch. 12.3).

state in subsequent trials etc.[40] This accords with some jurisdictions' law (e.g. Dutch law), but not Norway's. Cameron *et al.* show how the Swedish International Police Cooperation Act was made deliberately vague on joint investigation teams, in the interests of flexibility.[41] They maintain there are sufficient restrictions in the due process regulations of Swedish procedural law to prevent abuse, despite the vagueness of the legal text. This is probably the attitude taken by the Norwegian Ministry in these matters, since nothing is said on the subject, other than "no legal amendment required". In contrast, the Swedish Act limits JITs in the same way as the Nordic Police Agreement of 2012, to those within the MLA Convention and the corresponding Framework Decision, and the connected Agreement between Norway/Iceland and the EU of 2003.[42] It is noteworthy, though, that seconded members in Swedish JITs are not allowed to carry out "exercises of public authority", such as performing searches.[43] No such restriction exists in the Norwegian Police Act sects.20 or 20a.[44]

If seconded members want an investigative measure to be taken in their home state, they can make a request to the competent authorities there, just as they could if they were at home (art.13[7]). For example, if, during a JIT operation in Norway, a seconded Dutch member learned of evidence held at a location in Amsterdam, s/he could request search and seizure by the Dutch authorities, following standard Dutch procedures. This is proper facilitation of cooperation with other states, comparable to what can be done through Eurojust or Europol. The wrong way to go about it would be for a police officer who learned of such evidence while investigating in Norway, to use SIS, Interpol or Europol channels to request or suggest a search or seizure in Amsterdam, by which time it might be too late.

13.1.3 Finance and funding

Article 13 of the MLA is silent on financial questions. The Explanatory Memo suggest, however, that the financial issues should be dealt with in the specific JIT Agreement.[45] This was also included in the Model Agreement of 2010, which suggested for example (4.4.1) that the cost of technical equipment (office space, telecommunications etc.) and other expenses should be borne by the member state in which investigative measures are taking place. These costs are presumably implied in "the necessary organisational arrangements", referred to in art.13(3b). Since 2010, costs incurred by Europol staff participation are also included (4.4.2). As Mayer suggests, travel and accommodation are the main expenses when police officers work abroad. Other expenses may be divided equally between the participating states, or otherwise, as agreed.[46] This seems fair, but might create problems, because of the high cost of living of countries such as Norway, where foreign police forces with limited budgets would find lengthy participations in a Nordic JIT financially burdensome. A feasible solution would be that Norway should cover more of the expenses when acting as host-state. Cost considerations could thus influence where JITs are set up. It is note-

40 Plachta 2005:302; Schalken and Pronk 2002:75.
41 Cameron *et al.* 2011:139.
42 Op.cit.
43 Op.cit.:141 with further references.
44 The Finnish legislation appears similar to the Norwegian (Boucht 2012).
45 [2000] OJ C 379/7 e.g. p. 18; 26.
46 Mayer 2006:2010–11.

worthy that Eurojust may fund JIT operations, thus ensuring that financial problems do not hinder the establishment and success of JITs.[47] Norway received funding from Eurojust in two cases in 2016.[48]

In the most recent model agreement of 2017, the direct suggestions related to financing are taken out. Under pt.18, facilities and costs etc. are mentioned under "Organisational arrangements", but there are no preliminary suggestions from Europol/Eurojust.

13.1.4 The role of Europol and Eurojust

While Europol is clearly not an operational police force, Europol officers are through JIT participation part of operational groups that may do police work in cooperation with MS.

JITs normally consist of prosecution and police members with varying competences, depending on the member states. When international coordination and/or participation are required or desired, JITs will therefore consist of members both from Europol and Eurojust. Involving these bodies in a JIT may have several benefits. They have knowledge of investigations and crime situations in several countries, and can convene meetings of authorities from different member states. Europol experts may also carry out investigations and analysis. Europol may ask member states to set up JITs, and its staff may participate in these (ER art.4 and 5 [5]). Eurojust has, as mentioned, significant competences in, and knowledge of the prosecutorial systems of all its member states. Both the MS's national members and the Norwegian liaison members may take part in joint investigation teams and in authorising controlled deliveries (Eurojust CD arts. 9–9f), and through coordination work, Eurojust can help identify operational cases suitable for JITs. According to Groenleer, Eurojust has been less reluctant than Europol to exert informal pressure on member states, to initiate investigations. Member states must provide formal justification for refusing to involve Eurojust in investigations and prosecutions – this encourages cooperation. As a result, cases are sometimes referred to Eurojust for coordination purposes alone, without a formal request from the Agency.[49]

Following the MLA (art.13[12]), JIT members from EU bodies such as Europol may have rights similar to those conferred upon seconded members, when this is specifically stated in the JIT agreement. This means that Europol officers may assist in all activities performed by JIT members and seconded members, and exchange information with them. They may not, however, "apply coercive measures, in carrying out their tasks" (ER art.4 [5]). The lack of clear guidelines on which actions may be legally performed, and the 'barring' of Europol officers from taking part in any operational task, have been criticised.[50] The wording of the Europol Regulation is contradictory, particularly in the unclear relationship between "assist in all activities" and the prohibition against coercive action.[51] It was unclear whether assisting in (not applying) coercive measures is legitimate – could a Europol officer be present during the interrogation of a suspect in an assisting capacity? It was suggested that the 2003 version opened the way for Europol members to be given wider operational rights by the leader of the team.[52] But also the 2017 JIT Practical Guide makes clear that

47 Eurojust Grant Programme for 2014. See art.3 of [2002] OJ L 63/1, amended by [2008] OJ L 138/14.
48 Eurojust Annual Report 2016 p.20.
49 Groenleer 2009:319–320.
50 Mitsilegas 2009:171.
51 De Buck 2007:260–1.
52 Op.cit.:261.

Europol "shall not take part in any coercive measures" (pt. 2.2). The 2010 and 2017 Model Agreement on what Europol staff could and could not do, seemed to remove this possibility. The Model Agreement states that staff could, under the guidance of the leader(s) of the team, be present during JIT operational activities (Appendix pt. 3). The presence is purpose-limited: it shall be "in order to render on-the-spot advice and assistance to the members of the team who execute coercive measures", and must conform to host state regulations.[53] No further clarification on this matter followed in the new Europol Regulation.

Europol participation requires that the JIT, unlike the general requirements for JITs, deals with offence(s) within Europol's mandate (ER art.5 [1]). The threshold of crime is in principle not high: Europol may act in cases of crime such as racism, fraud, grievous bodily harm and motor vehicle crime (ER Annex 1). The information Europol officers obtain during the JIT operations may be included in the Europol database, as long as the MS providing the information consents, and that MS is in charge of the JIT (ER art.5 [4]). Legal responsibility for information remains with the state that has provided it. Several authors have argued that, although Europol does not have operational competences, their presence and advice have significant operational impact.[54] Both Europol and Eurojust may be assumed to have a much better understanding of legal differences than any single member state, drawn from wide experience of cases from all its member states. Europol knowledge can help resolve problems involved in deciding which country to set up a JIT in.[55] Europol may have a coordinating role in JITs, and even satellite tracking via Europol is allowed by MS to secure admissible evidence that will ensure prosecution in various member states.[56]

The participation of Europol and Eurojust in JITs naturally affects communication between them and their (seconded) members. While communication between Norway and Europol mainly passes through Europol's third country office, this will obviously be different when the members of a JIT are working together. Given Norway's general keenness to participate in EU police cooperation instruments and mechanisms, this is presumably seen as beneficial. It may, however, be questionable in terms of notoriety and control over information exchange. A practical consequence may be that, since almost all information going from Norwegian police to foreign authorities must pass through Kripos, there is a more or less formal requirement for the (police) officers taking part in JITs to be employed or 'authorised' by this office. Mitsilegas expresses concern about the degree of informality in JITs, in particular as regards Europol participation.[57] Formal cooperation has had a tendency to be time consuming and inefficient, and this may have motivated the creation of JITs.[58] The extension of the informality traditionally existing between MS police officers to JITs (and other multinational units), will now also include Europol officers, and, thus – as we have seen – have consequences for the information that will be entered into Europol databases. Information gathered in this way, according to Mitsilegas, lacks regulation that ensures transparency and control.

53 [2017] OJ C 18/1.
54 Plachta 2005:291; Schalken and Pronk 2002:74–5.
55 Plachta 2005. On the structure of Eurojust and competence towards the member states see e.g. Suominen 2008, particularly pp.222–4.
56 Gerspacher 2005:429.
57 Mitsilegas 2009:171.
58 E.g. op.cit.:117.

13.1.5 Use of information from JITs

The information and evidence obtained during a JIT investigation may be fully shared between its members.[59] JIT members may supply colleagues with information available to them in their seconding states, for use in the investigation they are conducting (MLA art.13 no.9). A seconded member may 'be present' when certain investigative measures are carried out in a JIT host state, regardless of whether they would be legal in the seconding state. Information resulting from such measures may be used in a member state, even though it would be illegal to get it in that way. Art.13 nos.9–10 set out the regulations. Information gathered through investigation or intelligence requested outside the territorial state that would not normally be accessible to a member state's authorities can be used, provided that: a) the information is used only for the purposes for which the JIT was set up; b) the information sharing MS had, prior to the information gathering, given its consent (which could be withheld only under very special circumstances[60]); c) this is to prevent an immediate and serious threat to public security, and without prejudice to subparagraph (b) if subsequently a criminal investigation is opened; and d) the information is used for a purpose agreed upon by the MS when the team was set up. As Rijken and Vermeulen argue, third states are probably also bound by the consent of the JIT member state where information became available, under no. 10(b).[61]

Thus, if a JIT operating in Norway realises that wire-tapping a suspect in Spain could greatly assist their investigation, the Spanish seconded member may ask colleagues in Spain to do this– under Spanish law – and then pass on the results to him (art.13[7]). Such information should be considered as resulting from a national investigation (in Spain), and thus available to the Spanish seconded member of the Norwegian JIT, as if he were at home. Rijken and Vermeulen argue that, although there is an (informal) agreement on mutual trust between the members of a JIT, there are no regulations in the Convention restricting the information gathered in such an 'indirect' manner from being used in other situations.[62] This is less likely when the information or police measures required are from third states, or states outside the original JIT members. This request must be made by the host state's competent authorities to the other state, in other words, not directly by the 'ordinary' members (art.13[8]). Although not explicitly stated, the request will have to state the purpose for which it is required. They should also be informed if the information is re-used, or further disseminated, for example, because new members have joined the JIT.[63]

Cameron *et al.* argue that the limitations in art.13 (10) on using information could threaten the rights of individuals, since they would mean that the Norwegian police could not give an accused person access to data or information that has been gained through another JIT member state or a cooperating third state.[64] Although it is not mentioned specifically in the *forarbeid*, the purposes referred to in art.13 (10a; d) that the Norwegian members can agree upon, must accord with Norwegian law to be regarded as legal: Norwegian police officials cannot agree with the other members of the JIT to share information for

59 Block 2012:89.

60 Where use would endanger criminal investigations into the Party concerned or into a serious threat to public security, and without prejudice to *litra* b.

61 Rijken and Vermeulen 2006a:17.

62 Rijken and Vermeulen 2006b:16.

63 Op.cit.:17.

64 Cameron *et al.* 2011:142; also Jonsson 2010:122.

purposes that are illegal in Norway. The national law still limits their activities, regardless of their cooperation partners. In theory, it is unlikely that this restriction would be an obstacle, since the purposes of JITs are generally consonant with the general aims of the Norwegian police.

Essentially, investigative measures are meant to be used the same way as they would be if the investigation team consisted entirely of Norwegian police officials. National regulations apply to actions performed in Norway, while ‘foreign’ rules govern those taken abroad. Among the practical benefits of JITs is access to the general know-how and experience states’ officials have of certain forms of crime or criminals; another, regulated in the conventions, is the ability to exchange more detailed knowledge.

One key question is whether practitioners differentiate between information that may and may not legally be put to use across borders under Norwegian law when they exchange information and best practice with police officers or other people from foreign countries. The police have a duty of confidentiality, but this duty is lifted in many situations, for example, when information is revealed to prevent or avert crime (Police Act [PA] sect.24 (4) no.2)). This is, of course, the overall purpose of police work (PA sect.1). The exchange of information with foreign police is limited: preventive and deterrent (*avvergende*) measures are included, but the maintenance of order (*ro og orden*) is excluded. Furthermore, information regarding the investigation or solving of specific criminal cases is regulated by the confidentiality regulations of the General Procedure Act. However, in the *forarbeid* of 1995, the maintenance of order was not considered a sufficiently serious purpose for information exchange. The *forarbeid* said that to avert was appropriate in a situation where criminal activity seemed imminent, whereas ‘prevention’ applied if there were no clear indications, but the available information helped hinder future acts of crime.[65]

13.1.6 The Nordic joint investigation teams

The Nordic Police Cooperation Agreement also regulates joint investigation teams. The 2002 Agreement, ch.8, stated briefly that “the Nordic countries’ police authorities may establish joint investigation teams for purposes of criminal investigation”. The 2012 Agreement ch.8 (sect.21) expands this: Nordic JITs should be established in accordance with the MLA Convention art.13 and the relevant Norwegian/Icelandic Association Agreement. The JIT chapter thus has little added value to the MLA. Until Norway and Iceland had an agreement with the MLA the 2002 Nordic Agreement could, however, serve as an intermediate JIT basis. Since the Ministry in the 2012 consultative works states that the Police Act sect.20 (3) has not been applied to give police competences to foreign police, there was presumably no basis in Norwegian law for such foreign competences before the 2012 Police Act amendment.[66]

65 Ot.prp.nr.22 (1994–1995): ch.V, comment on sect.24. One of the purposes of the legal amendments in sect.24 was precisely to bring together the regulations on police confidentiality and the references to the applicable rules, in one legal section. The section refers to the general procedure act for the regulations applicable when a criminal investigation is started, and the general administrative act with the additions of the police act, for all other police activity (ibid ch.6.10.1). The administrative act sect.13 (b) no.5 was not considered to permit information exchange with foreign authorities, and since this was considered imperative, the police act needed specific regulation of these situations (ch.6.10.2).

66 Prop.97 LS (2011–2012):49.

The Agreement does not regulate police powers in such operations; the focus is on the national contact points and information on these levels if a JIT is established. This is also emphasised in the section concerning participation in evaluating major events etc. in the Nordic countries. The general suggestion is that all such recommendations should pass through the national contact points. At present, unlike most other police cooperation measures, such recommendations must pass through the Police Directorate (POD) (ch.13 sect.26).

13.1.7 Discussing the legal changes of foreign police powers

The 2001 amendment of PA sect.20a was pared down, during the consultative rounds, so that it gave a legal basis only for Schengen-related measures, despite the then government's assessment that it was most practical to give a general legal basis for foreign police authority enforcement in Norway.[67] The enforcement of authority was limited both regarding the measures that could be taken, and by the Norwegian police's control over coercive measures. Section 20a was amended – not to give foreign police officers any wider powers – but to give a clearer legal basis for the existing right for anyone to arrest someone *in flagrante* provided in the Criminal Procedure Act sect.176. While this still applies, the argument based on a formalisation of foreign police officers' access to arrest cf. sect.176 has been abolished.[68] In 2010, the Schengen limitation was considered outdated; it was more important to regulate the present situation and the future potential of foreign police officers acting in Norway.

Only in exceptional cases can Norwegian police authority or powers be extended to non-police, according to the Police Act sect.20(3). The original *forarbeid* to this section explained the need to do so when "the public good requires that somebody be given police authority within a limited field", which mainly means surveillance tasks in e wilderness areas and at sea, where the police lack resources to operate.[69] The Ministry has the power to bestow such police authority. In 2012, the Ministry included the conferral of Norwegian police authority on foreign police officers in sect.20(3).

The initial agreements establishing JITs create a common judicial space for members from various countries, in which communication problems can be avoided. As seen above, the implementation of the regulations that are the basis for making JIT agreements, however, differs widely from state to state. The Netherlands has introduced quite detailed provisions, while Sweden has introduced the same general idea as Norway into its law.[70] The perceived need for a detailed Act may be greater in Central Europe, because cross-border investigation is more common. Norwegian law, it seems, has still not fully accepted that Norway is concerned about transnational crime, and taking part in the fight against it. Some clarification is suggested in the proposed new Criminal Procedure Act (NOU 2016:24), but this is still far from having been politically approved.

Stortinget has, as we saw above, agreed almost unanimously to every amendment suggested since the Norwegian Schengen Agreement. Similarly, only one objection was

67 Innst.O.nr.89 (1998–1999):23–24.

68 The Swedish Government put forward a similar argument when introducing the new Swedish Act on International Police Cooperation (Jonsson 2010:321–2).

69 Ot.prp.nr.22 (1994–1995):pt.6.4.1.

70 Block 2012:97.

raised before the amendment of the Police Act in 2012: the Norwegian Bar Association argued that the suggested changes that would give foreign police officials wider competences in Norway should be subject to far more thorough analysis.[71] The Ministry claimed that foreign officials would rarely exercise police power, and that it was important for Norwegian officers to participate in joint investigation teams to fight crime with cross-border elements. Local knowledge was considered vital for operations to succeed. The availability of coercive measures was also important: foreign police officials could be given the powers necessary when JIT members lived in different places, and a seconded member might suddenly have to follow a suspect moving into another state's territory.[72] Take the case of a Dutch official participating in a JIT based in Norway, and stationed in a city close to the Swedish border. At short notice he needs to pursue a suspect across the border into Sweden. In principle, such an action would be legal on the basis of the Schengen cooperation, regardless of the amendment of sect.20a. This would not be so if the seconded official was part of a Norway-based JIT established under the ETS no.182, and from a country outside the Schengen Area, such as the UK or the Ukraine.[73]

To some extent, the Ministry replaced the Schengen restriction with the time and purpose limitations that follow from the Police Act sect.20(3). It is interesting that Norway has never imposed temporal or geographic limits on the cross-border police activity set out in sect.20a following the Schengen cooperation. Sect.20(3) was originally understood as providing for wilderness supervision tasks, as mentioned above. In 2012, the Ministry argued that, in view of the international crime situation, the PA sect.20a was too narrowly limited.[74] It has been replaced by the general restriction in sect.20(3) giving ordinary police exceptional competence. The opportunity to delegate limited police powers to foreign police has thus always been present in sect.20a. What is new is the equating of foreign police with other Norwegian authorities. The former sharp distinction between the international police work described in sect.20a, and other provisions is removed. It seems it is of less importance to the Norwegian government to uphold the strict internal sovereignty aspect of absolute monopoly of national police.

With reference to the various requirements noted above, there seems to be little regulation of joint investigation teams in Norwegian law and practice (in publicly available sources, anyway). The Ministry simply said that general and covert investigations by foreign officers in Norway should be conducted to the same standard as those performed by national police officers. Because there is now a possibility to specify the details of each operation and impose general regulations, such operations are considered sufficiently subject to the rule of law.[75]

The Ministry thus leaves responsibility for the activities of JITs (and for resolving any disagreements) to the police or prosecutorial authority in question. The Police Act contributes little to the guidelines for police cooperation – and even less since the legislative amendment in 2012, when the Schengen limitation applied.

The Ministry does not, then, consider that the new police cooperation instruments have much impact on the Norwegian policing situation, at least not one necessitating legal regulation. The only effect of the sect.20a amendment is that foreign police officers, for a limited

71 Prop.97 LS (2011–2012):50.
72 Op.cit.:50.
73 Both have ratified the protocol; with no reservations on art.20.
74 Prop.97 LS (2011–2012).
75 Prop.97 LS (2011–2012):51.

time and probably for a limited purpose, have full Norwegian police competences while acting on behalf of their national authority. It is indisputable that Norwegian law applies to seconded members, the measures open to them, and the operation in general. As regards such measures, there are quite substantial differences between member states. This may not accord with one of the founding principle of the Norwegian police: that there should be a close link between police and place. This objection, of course, may be trumped by the argument that fighting serious, cross-border crime must be prioritised. We return to this issue in Chapter 15.

There are several issues that the Ministry does not discuss. JITs may consist of members from countries other than the Nordic neighbours, and Block points out how legal differences in, for example, how investigative roles and powers are allocated, may result in misunderstandings and identification issues.[76] Regardless of whether Norwegian law is followed, this implies that the content of important concepts and terms may vary. Different rules on applicability and the gathering of evidence may also challenge national frameworks: covert phone interception, for example, may be legal in Norway and the Netherlands, but illegal in the UK and Sweden.[77] As regards procedural rights, there are also different disclosure rules to consider: for example, defence lawyers are authorised to meet their clients at very different stages of investigations in cooperating countries.[78]

13.1.8 The parallel investigations alternative

Before the JITs were formally invented, mutual legal cross-border cooperation could take place through parallel investigations. Parallel investigations in different countries into similar or corresponding criminal cases is, naturally, still used. According to the JITs Practical Guide (pt.3.1.2), such investigations already exist in the vast majority of cases where JITs are established.[79] There are still situations in which parallel investigations are superior to JITs.[80] Simplified information exchange between law enforcement authorities, which bypasses slower Interpol and Europol channels, was already covered by CISA art.39, and information exchange was further eased in 2006 ('the Swedish Initiative'). In some situations, a JIT would simply take too long to set up, as would sending letters rogatory. Parallel investigations need no written arrangements under the FD.[81] The FD was Schengen-relevant, so Norway is also party to this cooperation. The exchange of information under Norwegian law is regulated in detail in the Police Register Directive (PRD) sects.65-1–65-19.[82] Both Block and Spapens argue that some JITs' failures may be due to the cumbersome structure of the project, top-down prioritisation, and differences in how MS implement JIT rules.[83] Rijken points to some projects where the parties could not even

76 Block 2012:93 ff.
77 Tak 2000:348–53, Block 2012:94.
78 Kvam challenges the legality of Norwegian exchange of information with foreign authorities through JIT, and liaison officers' competence to share data in Norwegian police registers (Kvam 2014:249–50). The applicable regulation is the *politiregisterforskrift* (PRD) for Norwegian police registry information, while non-registry information exchange, e.g. of investigative case information (observations, etc.) may be shared within the team.
79 JIT Practical Guide Doc. 6128/1/17.
80 Spapens 2011:255–6; Hufnagel 2013:216.
81 [2006] OJ L 386/89.
82 For a detailed account of the Norwegian rules on information exchange under these regulations see Kvam 2014.
83 Block 2008:100.

arrive at a common understanding of the case to be investigated.[84] Many consider JITs to have fewer advantages than was hoped for when invented. It was hoped that the JIT would be the "desired instrument to facilitate mutual assistance", but most evaluations suggest that this hope has been disappointed.[85]

On point of interest is that different rights are triggered, depending on which investigatory approach is chosen. When a measure is used against an individual through JIT cooperation, that person will most likely be investigated in the country where the JIT is based, which gives him/her procedural rights vis-à-vis that state. In the case of traditional mutual legal cooperation, a measure carried out in Spain at the request of Norwegian police does not give the individual any rights vis-à-vis Norway; carrying the measure out in Spain may rather give it the status of an administrative 'operation' that does not imply any rights under the ECHR art.6[86]

13.2 Joint operations

The 'Prüm measures' were established to meet a perceived need for even closer cooperation. Data exchange facilitated between police in the member states, and direct searches in member states' fingerprint, DNA and vehicle databases, are much trumpeted benefits of the Prüm cooperation. The Prüm Decision[87] is, however, also the international legal basis for operational cooperation such as joint patrols and operations, and assistance in connection with mass gatherings, disasters, and serious accidents. This includes notification of such situations, coordination of joint responses and sending personnel and equipment onto the territory of another MS. The measures are related to the Schengen rules that have already been implemented. To combat illegal migration, and assist in repatriation, document advisers were seconded to source or transit countries. Joint patrols and mutual assistance in the context of major events[88] imply a tendency towards low-level police cooperation on low-level policing issues. It seems as though once 'emergency measures' were in place to deal with serious border-crossing offences, ordinary policing measures followed.

13.2.1 Overview

Joint operations and joint investigations have different purposes: the latter concern criminal offences, the former belong to the field of public order and security, and crime prevention.[89] The issue to be explored here is how far police can cooperate internationally on matters that do not exclusively concern crime, focusing on public order and security policing in the form of joint patrols and cross-border mutual assistance, in other words, chapter V of the Prüm Decision of 2008.[90] What is particularly interesting about these police cooperation measures

84 Rijken 2006:22–23.

85 Op.cit.:99; Spapens 2011:259.

86 Jonsson 2010:214–5, also Hufnagel 2013:216; Block 2008.

87 [2008] OJ L 210/12.

88 The information cooperation measures are widely covered and raise an array of data protection questions that fall outside the ambit in this book. See references in ch.1.4.2.

89 As used in CBO Manual 10505/3/09 (REV 3):25.

90 The Prüm Convention of 2005 was a 'test lab' for some EU states in the way the Schengen cooperation was initially. The cooperation was incorporated into the EU *Acquis* with the Prüm Council Decision ([2008] OJ L 210/1), with an implementing Decision ([2008] OJ L 210/12).

is that they consist of 'ordinary' policing in other jurisdictions. Public order policing – patrolling the streets – is central to low-level policing, which is a vital part of internal sovereignty in the form of maintaining the public's perception of security. The types of offences or situations that trigger such operations, what their requirements are, who may be seconded, and what powers they may enforce abroad, will be explored.

Public order and security are not easily defined, and are understood differently in different countries. Some measures related to public order and security have been agreed on at the EU level, but remain subject to national discretion. In the Residence Directive (art.27[2]),[91] an EU citizen may have his/her fundamental right to freedom of movement restricted if s/he is considered a sufficient, genuine and present serious threat to one of the fundamental interests of society, which include "public policy, public security and public health". The threat must be based on an assessment of the "personal conduct of the individual concerned". Although it has been difficult to agree on further definitions, the situations where police cooperation measures, for example, are allowed have been interpreted by the EU Court as satisfying this requirement.[92] Public order and security may be the legitimate aim of police cooperation, for example, in the prevention of illegal immigration, in the form of joint patrols or specific police operations in border regions, in cases of mutual assistance in catastrophes or serious accidents, and in the control of large events such as concerts or football matches and major political meetings such as the G8 political summits. Control of illegal immigration is part of maintaining public order and security: illegal migration is thus considered part of the field of public disorder and insecurity. Border controls were abolished after the Schengen cooperation entered into force and, though customs officers can search for illegal goods on borders, the police must control illegal immigration elsewhere. Police may close borders, however, and carry out targeted checks, in situations such as the 22/7 bombing of the Government headquarters in Oslo. There have been many cases of temporary border control because of the need to protect public order and security, to the extent that this is a current state of exception due to the terror attacks in Europe the past few years. In Norway, the temporary control has been renewed for three months at a time for around two years at the time of writing (December 2017).

The Amsterdam Treaty introduced the area of freedom, security and justice that was to be created, safeguarded and upheld by the Union and its member states, partly through police cooperation measures. The aim was reiterated in the Europol cooperation and in the Lisbon Treaty, emphasising "peace, its values and the well-being of its peoples" (art.3 TEU), which necessitated the balancing of free movement and "the prevention and combating of crime". While international police cooperation has largely dealt with serious cross-border crimes, there are other events and activities that may threaten the peace, freedom and security of individuals. The Norwegian Police Act sect.1, thus lays down that the police shall ensure security under the law, i.e. safety and welfare in general. Police work will often aim to prevent crimes, rather than stopping them or reactively searching for the perpetrator. Not all disturbances of safety and security, though, are of a criminal nature, and not all disturbances end in crime. Preventive work on crime control has also been done in the EU, relating both to international crime control at EU or other levels, and to how member states target crime in their individual countries. Efforts intensified with the Lisbon Treaty art.84, whereby the EU was enabled to take measures to support states' attempts to

91 [2004] OJ L 158/77.
92 Henricson 2010:308.

prevent crime that were previously considered the sole responsibility of member states. There was a wide-ranging Resolution on Crime Prevention in 1998, and a crime prevention network (EUCPN) whose latest legal basis is found in.[93]

The Prüm Decision art.18 makes it possible to assist other member states in major events and disasters. Additional rules on assistance in major crises, involve other types of officials than the ordinary police. The Council Decision on Cross-Border Intervention Teams[94] provides for foreign special intervention units to enter other member states, in the case of "a criminal offence presenting a serious direct physical threat to persons, property, infrastructure or institutions in that Member State" (art.2[b]). The regulations on such operations on the host state's territory are similar to the Prüm Decision arts.17 and 18.[95] This form of assistance does not apply to Norway,[96] so the additional rules on assistance are important.

A common framework for joint operations and investigations has been developed, to which the Prüm measures are central. As noted above, the parallel agreement for Norway's accession to the Prüm cooperation was accepted by the EU in 2011. The Association Agreement came into force when a technical update of the police databases for DNA and fingerprints had taken place, and the Police Register Directive was fully in force, which happened 1 July 2014. *Stortinget* unanimously agreed both on Prüm and the deepening measures[97] in May 2016.

The Police Act amendments of 2012 related to joint investigation teams, and were intended to encompass the Prüm cooperation, so the legal framework seems complete.[98] The agreement has been struck. Finally, in May 2016, following summary debates in *Stortinget,* this was presented and approved.[99] Some technical improvements and evaluation of data security measures are required before it comes into force.[100]

The measures on joint patrolling and assistance in more ordinary situations are interesting because they indicate the extension of EU action from cooperation on serious crime, to cooperation on low-level public order matters.

As with joint investigation teams, foreign police may exercise police powers on the host state territory. Art.17(1–3) of the Prüm Decision allows "designated officers or other officials (officers)" to participate in operations in other member states' territory, for example, police patrols. The seconded officers are obliged to follow the instructions of the host state authorities, and are subject to host state national law.

There are many types of cross-border joint operations. Europol's Manual of Cross-Border Operations (CBO) lists examples of operations that may be initiated in Norway under the Prüm Decision art.17. The CBO is not sufficient legal basis alone; such work is dependent on additional provisions or implementation in the national law in question (in Norway PA sect. 20a and 20[3]).[101] The list includes joint patrols, tourist assistance and the security of tourist sites, traffic controls, accompanying supporters, personal and document checks,

93 [1998] OJ C 408/1 and [2009] OJ L 321/44, respectively.

94 [2008] OJ L 210/73.

95 See e.g. Schumacher 2011; Balzacq *et al.* 2006; Bigo 2000b; for relevant discussions.

96 CBO Manual 10505/3/09 (REV 3):466.

97 CD 2008/615/JIS and CD 2008/616/JIS, see Prop. 54 S (2015–2016) and Innst. 225 S (2015–2016).

98 Meld.St.7 (2010–2011):74–6.

99 An agreement of 08.05.2012 with the USA on intensified police cooperation, the PCSC Agreement, was accepted simultaneously. See Prop. 54 S (2015–2016).

100 Prop. 54 S (2015–2016):7.

101 CBO Manual 10505/3/09 (REV 3):26.

(mutual) support during major events (the G8 summit, the football world cup), sending equipment and operators (e.g. water cannons), and joint exercises for the kind of operations covered by art.17. The Manual recommends that member states "provide to allow" foreign police officers autonomous police competence (the use of such powers is returned to below), and that such joint operations should be as practical and pragmatic as possible.

13.2.2 Regulations common in Articles 17 and 18

Both for joint operations (Prüm Decision art.17[1]), and assistance connected with mass gatherings and serious accidents (art.18[1]), the purpose of seconded police assistance shall be to maintain public order and security, and to prevent criminal offences. While the offences need not be serious for assistance under art.18, situations should have a cross-border impact.

Joint patrols and assistance in mass gatherings are treated similarly in the CBO Manual, and are largely subject to the same regulations in the Prüm Decision. Before some of the specifics of the two types of operations are explained, the regulations common to both can be noted: these concern the purposes of the operations, employer responsibility for the officers, and reimbursement rules for damages. The powers foreign police may exercise, and the rules on arms and uniforms, are covered later.

There are no restrictions as to time or space for the operations, which may take place in the air, at sea or on land, and for as long as member states see fit.[102] However, operational powers delegated to foreign police (in Norwegian law) must be time and purpose limited.

Host states have a responsibility to provide "the same protection and assistance to (foreign) officers performing their duties" as they do to national officers (art.20). Arts.21–22 contain general rules on seconded officers' civil and criminal liability, which are much like those in the Schengen and JIT agreements. The rules on responsibility for joint patrols and mutual assistance are somewhat different, however. For the former, the sending state has civil liability for damage caused during operations by the seconded officers, whilst the host state is responsible for this in mutual assistance operations (art.21 nos.1; 4). Art.21 sets out reimbursement rules for the host and seconding states. The main rule is that victims of officer misconduct should direct their claims to the state where the activity took place. Nevertheless, there will be no reimbursement in art.18 cases, where only "gross negligence or wilful misconduct" *may* lead to the host state's reimbursement (art.21[4]). This difference may suggest a distinction between the assistance given under art.18, which may be considered as beneficial to one state – the host state – whilst joint operations under art.17, as the term suggests, concern activities that are mutually beneficial. The criminal liability regulations are the same in both cases, unless specifically agreed differently (art.22).

Although seconded officers operate in foreign jurisdictions, art.23 underscores that they are subject to their home state's employment law. Regardless of whether the host state takes a leadership role, the seconded officers are still regarded as employees of their own jurisdiction's authority. Employer responsibility includes. the leadership and decision competence for the entire operation, and thus what kind of risks personnel may be exposed to, and secondary matters such as questions of rehabilitation and the discipline and education of officers.[103] Disciplinary rules are particularly emphasised in the Manual.[104] While employer

102 CBO Manual:25.
103 Nordisk samtjänstgöringsrapport 2009:16–7.
104 CBO Manual 10505/3/09 (REV 3):28.

relations concern very practical issues, these are important for officers' sense of belonging and identity. The laws of the host state must be respected, but the seconded officers work for their home state, as in JITs – unlike liaison officers.

13.2.3 Joint patrolling

In the Dutch border town of Venlo, where many Germans go shopping every weekend, German and Dutch police patrol together so regularly that some patrol cars have dual liveries: they have the colours of the Dutch police on one side, and the German colours on the other.[105] While Prüm Decision art.17 gives little guidance on what joint patrolling is, border areas show what it may become in practice. According to the CBO Manual, joint patrols may have various aims.[106] One is to facilitate "access to law enforcement for citizens from the different member states" – a citizen focus. Another is to improve cooperation between authorities and officers, by giving practical and linguistic assistance. Two typical forms of joint patrols are envisaged: one is patrolling border areas. While border control is prohibited within the Schengen Area, Prüm art.17 allows control in border *areas*, rather than *at* the border.[107] Local authorities should have power to set up such patrols in "a very quick, pragmatic and efficient way", whenever necessary. They thus resemble the parallel investigations described above (ch.13.1.8). While member state authorities must agree on the patrols, there is no requirement for patrols to consist of representatives of both (or all) parties. With agreement, such patrols may act within one MS alone, or cross repeatedly between jurisdictions.[108]

The other type of joint patrol targets specific events. The CBO Manual mentions football matches or other major events, as well as assistance to tourists, traffic controls, or patrols on international trains. For several years, Norwegian police have been present in the Swedish border town Strømstad when Norwegians go shopping there in the Easter holidays.[109] They have mainly operated as observers and liaison officers, but the Prüm Decision allows them to have delegated police competences. Tourist police forces operate on the French Riviera. In future there could be Norwegian police patrols in areas on the Spanish coast where there is a large Norwegian retirement population.

There are two particularly interesting aspects of joint patrols. One is the impact the presence of foreign police may have on ordinary or regular policing situations, in other words, on Norwegians' view of the Norwegian police, or on the police themselves. This is discussed below (ch.14.1). Another more practical issue is the competences police officers have abroad when participating in joint patrols. These powers will be assessed, after a résum of the rules on assistance in connection with mass gatherings.

105 Spapens 2011:174.

106 CBO op.cit:29.

107 Joint external border patrolling has long been taking place, especially on the Southern and Eastern external borders of the Schengen – and outside (Baldaccini 2010, e.g. pp.254–5). See e.g. Hungarian and Ukrainian joint patrolling (http://media.bordermonitoring-ukraine.eu/2014/02/04/during-the-joint-patrolling-border-guards-of-ukraine-and-hungary-detained-6-illegal-migrants/ [01.07.2014].

108 CBO op.cit.

109 http://www.nettavisen.no/nyheter/3597406.html [02.04.14]. Twenty to thirty Norwegian police officers observe and assist in Strømstad every Maundy Thursday, while seven (in 2013) Swedish officers accompanied the Norwegian police across the border to the Norwegian town of Halden, where a large gathering of Swedes and Norwegians party in the evening.

13.2.4 Public order assistance

To deal with disasters or serious accidents, and large political gatherings and demonstrations, the member states' competent authorities must have in place practical arrangements for cooperation with their neighbouring states (Prüm Decision art.18). By the Police Act sect.2 and the Police Directive ch.2 the police are obliged to maintain public order and security, and protect the community against any general threat towards its security; this obligation goes further than taking action against criminal activity – it is a general responsibility for safety and security, and includes preventing crime or threats to security.[110] Several provisions concern mass gatherings. The Norwegian Penal Code (GCPC) ch.35 deals with the disturbance of public order, and sect.350 criminalises breach of the peace by fighting, making a loud noise or other improper conduct. Sects.136–7 criminalise causing or participating in a riot. The Police Act also has several provisions for police intervention in mass gatherings. It may be difficult to draw a line between the coercive measures of the criminal procedure regulations, and interventions that are almost the same, but *de jure* part of the administrative – not procedural – powers of the police. Provisions in the Police Directive (sect.8–2[1–2]) oblige the police to take action in major fights, riots, gatherings, etc. when traffic or public order are disrupted. The intervention must be necessary and appropriate to the circumstances. Such arrangements for assistance between national police districts exist in the Police Instructions sect.7–4, which obliges police from all districts to assist each other if necessary. There is, however, no such legal basis for international assistance.

It is natural there should be mutual assistance across land borders, given the arbitrariness of borders, which should not prevent police officers from assisting foreign colleagues if an incident is taking place close to them.[111] Under art.18, MS must assist each other in three ways: a) by notifying other states of situations with a cross-border impact, and exchanging relevant information; b) by taking and coordinating necessary policing measures within their own territory; and c) sending officers, specialists, and equipment if this is requested by a member state where such a situation has arisen. The CBO Manual (p.30) lists the following obligations in such cases: exchange of contact points and contact procedures, notification procedures in situations that may have a cross-border impact, definition of security or disaster plans, and arrangements for supplying equipment. If necessary, all or any of these should by coordinated by the authorities concerned.

A similar provision exists in art.25 of the original Prüm Convention (the predecessor of the Decision), which provides for a form of *negotiorium gestio*. Art.25 allows police observing an urgent situation outside their national territory to intervene to avert imminent danger to the physical integrity of individuals. Unrequested assistance must comply with the host state's national law. This seems in line with Norwegian law: Norwegian customary emergency law allows such interference on behalf of an individual, and arguably, in aid of the home state's police, if they are not immediately able to intervene.

110 Andenæs and Myhrer 2009:847.

111 O'Neill 2011:131; Spapens 2010:164. Other cooperation instruments preceded the Prüm cooperation, relating to international football matches ([2002] OJ L 121/1 and the connected resolution with requirements [2006] OJ C 322/1), and the protection of public figures [amended last in [2009] OJ L 283/62]. Both these police cooperation instruments set out recommendations for manuals to facilitate cooperation in such matters.

13.2.4.1 Foreign police powers

Both the efficiency of a police operation and the security of the participating officers may be improved if seconded officers are given police powers, either ordinary, e.g. to direct traffic or instruct someone to move away from an area, or coercive, e.g. to pin down and handcuff a trouble-maker. Art.17(2) of the Prüm Decision regulates foreign police powers, but art.18 also concerns a form of joint operations, where powers must be specifically agreed upon. Art.17 regulations are also applicable to assistance in mass gatherings, setting out two alternatives for foreign officers enforcing power in host territories: certain executive powers may be conferred by the host state, or they may be allowed to enforce those of their own jurisdiction. The seconding state must also agree to the delegation of powers, and the enforcement must comply with officers' own national law. This means that if, say, Spanish police officers are called to Norway because of a public order problem involving Spanish immigrants, this must be legal under both Norwegian and Spanish law. There are no strict regulations on who the officers should be, as regards rank, for example, but they must have a state approved capacity. A private person acting on behalf of a security company could not be given powers under Art.17.

The Norwegian Police Act sects.20(3) and 20a, allow foreign police to participate in joint operations and perform general police activities (*tjenestehandlinger*) under international agreements, such as the Prüm. In exceptional cases, Norwegian police powers may be conferred. 'Exceptional' has the meaning defined in PA sect.20(3). The *forarbeid* do not make this a strict limitation. While the original suggestion was that foreign police officers may be given police powers, the word "exceptional" seems only to signify that such a need would not often arise.[112] This is similar to the empowerment of non-police officials under certain circumstances in Norway (sects.20a[2]; 20 [3]) The reference in 20a to 20(3) underlines that the restrictions on national temporary police competence also apply to foreign police: the competence is 'total', i.e. the same as that of a Norwegian police officer, but functionally and temporally limited.[113]

Enforcement of police powers on foreign soil should, as a rule, be exercised under the guidance of host state officers, and in their presence (PD Art.17 [2]). The Norwegian Ministry emphasised this in their remarks on the sect.20a amendment, though primarily in the context of the joint investigation teams dealing with criminal offence*s*, not public order. According to the Ministry, the key to success is often familiarity with national legislation on coercive measures, practice, language, and local conditions.[114] Nevertheless, the rationale for joint patrols and similar operations is that foreign officers have knowledge that the local authorities do not possess. It is only implicit in the Police Act, but Art.17(2) clearly states that seconded officers given Norwegian police competence under these rules are also subject to Norwegian law. Although the seconding state continues to have employer responsibilities, the host state is responsible for foreign officers' actions. Situations where foreign officers enforce authority on their own, without national police officers present, are expected be very rare.[115]

The foreign police use of force is subject to Norwegian regulations. After a foreign officer has apprehended someone, his/her legal status may be unclear for a time. As seen above,

112 Prop.97 LS (2011–2012):50.
113 Op.cit. ch.9.2.
114 Op.cit. pt.9.2.
115 Op.cit. pt.9.2.

Norwegian police may take individuals into police custody without officially arresting them (CPA sects.176 cf. 175). The 176 provision also allows private persons or foreign police to apprehend someone caught *in flagrante;* this person must be handed over to the police as soon as possible (176 [2]). When the police, without a court or prosecutorial order, apprehend such a person, or when seizure has been made under sect.206, the person acquires the status as criminally charged (CPA sect.82).[116] This, however, seems not to be the case if people lacking police competence, under the Police Act sect.20, take such emergency coercive measures. This creates an interesting difference. People may be apprehended in hot pursuit and surveillance situations, as previously laid down in PA sect.20a, but it is unclear whether this is so in emergency surveillance situations, under the 2012 amendment. Such apprehension follows the same principle as that of citizen's arrest in CPA sect.176[117] and thus does not give the subject the status possessed by someone who has been charged. In joint patrol situations, however, the temporary police powers delegated under PA sect.20a are the same as those of any Norwegian police officer without prosecutorial competence (CPA sect.176 cf. PA sect.20[3]). It does not seem from the *forarbeid* that delegating police competences to foreign police officers in joint operations and investigation teams was intended to enhance the procedural rights of those affected by them. This may be seen as an added benefit that should, perhaps, be added to the regulations on the Schengen measures. Note that, while there is an absolute prohibition in the CISA measures on entering homes or areas restricted from public access, JITs and joint operations with delegated police powers have no such restriction, given that officers simply become Norwegian officers temporarily.

In practice, when officers patrol together, the host state officers usually enforce any coercive measures. Joint Hit Teams (JHT) have been established by Belgian, French, German and Dutch police to patrol border regions, particularly known drug courier routes from the Netherlands into the other three countries. According to Spapens, JHTs have successfully retrieved and exchanged information very rapidly and informally (they may, for instance, have their local offices checking national classified data systems in real time). The international composition of the teams also means that they can question people in their native language.[118] They are like joint investigation teams (JITs), except that hit teams are less strictly regulated. Interestingly, cross-border crime need not be involved: JHTs may simply convene to maintain "public order and security and prevent criminal offences" (Prüm Decision art.17).

Given the limited Norwegian legal regulation, it is useful to look at how neighbouring countries have implemented the cooperation. Both Swedish and Finnish law authorise giving foreign officers police powers. Finland enacted legislation implementing these Prüm measures, with regulations similar to the Convention.[119] Finnish police officers may assign foreign officers the same powers as they have themselves (sect.3). These powers may only be used under supervision, unless there is imminent danger to life or health, and no Finnish officer is available (sect.4). The Norwegian regulations are thus less strict, or at least vaguer, with no such limitation on enforcing police powers. Further regulations may be given in a directive when the Prüm Association Agreement is in force, as anticipated in the

116 Skaflem (2014) n.458.
117 Ot.prp.nr.56 (1998–1999) pt.8.4.4.
118 Spapens 2010:175.
119 Boucht 2012:226–7; Act 277/2007 sect.3 (http://www.finlex.fi/sv/laki/alkup/2007/20070277 [28.03.14].

PA sect.20a (4). Foreign police officers, especially leaders, must be familiar with the model agreements and cross-border cooperation manuals before entering into such joint operations. These rules largely govern foreign police operations, where police powers are entrusted to non-Norwegian police officers. These situations raise serious questions of competence-sharing, and it seems that the regulations should be quite clear, and set out in the Police Act itself, rather than hidden away in a circular or directive.

The Swedish Act on International Police Cooperation, and the related Directive,[120] differ slightly from the Finnish and Norwegian rules. Section 4(2) of the Directive explicitly prohibits Swedish officers engaged in a joint operation with a Prüm basis from enforcing police powers abroad. There is no mention of foreign powers enforced in Swedish territory. To judge by the Swedish Act sect.12, such enforcement seems unwanted. Sect.12 regulates the use of police powers (*myndighetsutövning*) by foreign police on Swedish territory under the regulations in the Act, which clearly deal with operational powers enforced in Sweden. Sect.12, however, has the heading 'common regulations for the Schengen and Øresund cooperation measures', and this would appear to exclude the Prüm cooperation, which is dealt with elsewhere (sects.16–23). Further details on the Prüm Decision can be found in the requirements for assistance in joint operations, the request for which must come from the state where the event is taking place. Although the Decision sets out an obligation to cooperate in art.18 events, sect.4 of the Swedish Directive states that such assistance may only be given if the authority in question has the necessary resources, and competence. This obligation clearly has no supranational force, and states retain sovereign power to consider resource prioritisation and capacities. Similarly, there is no obligation *per se* for member states to take part in joint patrols. The fact that a state enters into the Prüm cooperation implies, however, a willingness to provide such assistance upon request.[121] And as with all international agreements, it might seem a political *faux pas* to refuse a reasonable request.

13.2.4.2 Arms and uniforms

Uniforms and arms are central to how foreign police are perceived on host state territory. Whether they are armed, and under what rules, are also important issues in joint operations. Officers abroad may wear their national uniforms (Prüm Decision art.19). They may also carry arms and ammunition, as allowed in their home state, unless the host state has prohibited this (art.19[1]), for example, if they are more heavily armed than host state officers. While Norwegian police are generally unarmed, emergency situations in art.19 cases could justify both seconded and Norwegian police officers being armed; generally, though, it is unlikely that foreign police officers would be allowed to carry firearms in Norway. This differs from the urgency in hot pursuits provision under Schengen rules, when weapons cannot be safely stored. Annexed to the manual on cross-border operations are fact sheets on the cross-border instruments of various EU member states, and of Iceland, Norway, Switzerland and Liechtenstein, which are published and regularly updated by member states.[122] Norway's states that Norwegian police officers generally do not carry firearms, but that

120 Law 2000:343, with Directive on international police cooperation.

121 Henricson 2010:321.

122 CBO Manual fact sheets (10505/4/09); op.cit. The information is not, however, fully updated. The Norwegian Police Act sect.20A dates from before the significant 2012 amendment. There might be more up-to-date versions circulated among the police.

> short or long batons may be included in the standard equipment. The individual chief of police may permit officers to carry a handgun on ordinary car patrols. In that event, the handgun would be a revolver or pistol, with ammunition, and would be required to be kept in a locked compartment in a sealed bag or gun case.

Conditions and regulations are detailed in the Ministry's circular of 1989; however, the fact sheet also gives an overview of the specifics of the Norwegian police's weapons regulations.[123] For purposes other than legitimate self-defence or defence of others, the *use* of arms and other equipment must accord with host state law, and be allowed by the leader of the operation (art.19[2]).

Only in urban areas are Norwegian police allowed firearms, which are locked in a safe in the police vehicle. In more rural areas, officers have to get firearms from police stations.[124] In the Nordic border regions cities and towns are small. Foreign officers participating in a joint operation would normally carry firearms and so have them more readily available than their Norwegian colleagues in an emergency.

Icelandic and Norwegian police are generally unarmed, unlike their Danish, Finnish and Swedish counterparts. Regulations on how and when firearms should be used are also different,[125] which raises the issue whether Norwegian police participating in a joint operation in another Nordic country should carry firearms. The Norwegian police were indeed temporarily armed from November 2014 until February 2016, following a lengthy 'state of exception' because of the 2014 terror attacks in Paris, etc., and risk assessments from the Norwegian Secret Service. The exception did not lead to permanent changes in the arming of police. The debate still continues, and the PST has recently (November 2017) recommended police armament – in contrast to the conclusion from the Governmental Committee (NOU 2017:9 *Politi og bevæpning*).

Police may be more heavily armed in the case of mass gatherings (Weapons Instruction sects.17–18). This is appropriate in particularly dangerous situations. The decision must, as far as possible, be taken by the chief of police. The weapons referred to in sects.17–18 are batons and gas. Only in exceptionally dangerous situations may firearms be considered (sect.19). According to the Ministry, such situations may arise when mass gatherings become uncontrollable and constitute a threat to vital societal interests.[126] In such cases, firearms must only be used to disperse crowds. Arms may also be necessary when arresting persons suspected of serious offences, or who are considered to endanger state security (sect.19b). Terrorist attacks fall within this category. A major consideration is whether an offender could give foreign authorities information of vital importance to Norway's security. When a situation primarily concerns state internal security, this could be seen as inherently excluding foreign police from being involved in the operation.

13.2.5 A Nordic version

The Prüm measures are largely described innovations. For Norway, it is important to explore alternatives to the EU cooperation measures, especially if some aspects of EU regulations

123 Op.cit. p. 466–8; Politiets våpeninstruks.

124 Nordisk samtjänstgöringsrapport 2009:13.

125 Op.cit. In Finland, firearms are limited to self-defence, or, under certain circumstances, use by an officer with the necessary competences (sect.4[2]). See e.g. Strype 2005; Knutsson 2005.

126 Politiets våpeninstruks pt.19.3 (to § 19).

exclude Norway as a non-EU member (such as EAWs). Interestingly, there was a Swedish initiative on Nordic joint patrols back in 1999, though it was abandoned, without any reason being mentioned, when the Schengen cooperation came into force,[127] despite the absence of any regulations in the Schengen cooperation that would have prohibited it.

According to the consultation paper in 2010, such an agreement on Nordic joint operations (*samtjenestegjøring*) will be agreed upon,[128] but there is no sign of it yet. Such joint operations are not mentioned in the Nordic Police Cooperation Agreement of 2012. The Nordic Committee's 2009 suggestions have not been implemented.[129] Still, the suggestions shed light on the Prüm regulations.

Joint patrols were defined in the Nordic report as joint police work designed to maintain public order and security, or uncover or prevent crimes or criminal activity.[130] Such cooperation could prevent too many national police officers getting tied up in one place or operation, if other Nordic police could assist. In sports events, concerts and the like, seconded officers are valuable in targeting persons from their home state that might create trouble. The report emphasises that the mere presence of police officers from a person's home state, in addition to an increased number of police officers in general, may have a preventive effect.[131] Members of the public could, of course, perceive the presence of foreign police as a provocation, particularly if they are in uniform. Although police uniforms are less symbolically loaded than military uniforms, the presence of foreign state paraphernalia, even if it does not suggest a warlike situation, can certainly signify a form of intrusion or general state of unrest. Nevertheless, if the intention is to make citizens of the seconding state aware of the presence of their national police, uniforms are essential.

Rapid assistance in more urgent police operations was also envisaged. In border regions, foreign police might get to crime scenes quicker than national police. Such joint operations could even be considered as a more long-term solution, although of course, not a permanent one.[132] In the event, the agreement suggested by the working group of the Nordic Committee of Senior Officials for Legislative Issues (EK-LOV) did not go further than the Prüm Decision art.17.

Such cooperation raises interesting questions at the levels of immediate response, and more ordinary public order policing, which seem to open the way to coordinating police work beyond the area of cross-border crime. In December 2013, the Norwegian Minister of Justice contacted Sweden about the possibility of renting cells in Swedish prisons. The Norwegian correctional services had a substantial waiting list of convicted people waiting to serve their sentence, while the prison population in Sweden is declining. The request was declined on the grounds that it would breach Swedish legislation.[133] Arguably, however, joint operations for largely practical purposes seem somewhat akin to renting prison cells. Legal systems, however, have barriers against employing or 'renting' other – even neighbouring – states' system of coercive powers, i.e. police officers and prisons cells. Further,

127 Nordisk samtjänstgöringsrapport 2009:6.

128 Consultation paper 2010 on international cooperation p. 75; Politiet (2012):50.

129 Boucht 2012:227; Nordisk samtjänstgöringsrapport 2009.

130 Nordisk samtjänstgöringsrapport 2009:2.

131 Op.cit.:8.

132 Op.cit.:8.

133 http://www.svd.se/nyheter/inrikes/inga-norska-fangar-till-sverige_8955336.svd [30.04.14]. Both parties were ready, however, to consider creating such Nordic cooperation in the future (http://www.nrk.no/norge/ma-endre-loven-for-a-ta-imot-fanger-1.11538718 [30.04.14]).

these barriers may just represent system inertia, and it may be merely a matter of time before we see the necessary changes in legislative frameworks. On the other hand, we may be talking about quite sturdy mechanisms that are central to state capacities. It is notable that Norway since 2015 have rented prison cells in the Netherlands (the Norgerhaven prison). The legal status from Norway's point of view, is that this is a department of the Norway-based Ullersmo prison.

The opportunity principle also applies in situations of rapid assistance, regarding the police's right and obligation to make an independent assessment of a situation and of the best way of resolving it.[134] This principle must be seen as inherent in the police role; foreign police too (in the absence of specific orders), must judge for themselves what is the best way to react. The principles of the least infringing measure, and proportionality, follow from PA sect.6(2). The principles of non-discrimination and objectivity must also be respected. Auglend *et al.* also emphasise the rule that the police must never take sides in a conflict, for example, a strike. These are all provisions that are challenged in public order policing operations involving foreign police, though perhaps less so in the case of Nordic cooperation.

The report was delivered before the Prüm was implemented in the EU, and, as Boucht argues, states may consider it less worthwhile to pursue a special Nordic agreement now that these measures exist in the Prüm cooperation.[135] It might be 'unpopular' if the Nordic countries had special local agreements. Although more far-reaching bilateral agreements are common in central and Southern Europe, it might be frowned upon if, say, Sweden, which has limited its Prüm implementation slightly, allowed more competences through the Nordic agreements.

The governmental perception of the Nordic importance in police cooperation issues, is also seen in the delegation of Norwegian police powers. In a 2004 amendment, people without Norwegian citizenship could have limited police authority, when, for example, working as guards at detention centres or as reindeer police. The Ministry argued that cross-border cooperation with Sweden and Finland meant removing the absolute citizenship requirement. There was never a requirement for citizenship for positions in the police not conferring police powers.[136] While it was considered most practical to give legal provision for foreign police activity in Norway, the Government explicitly stated that the Schengen convention was the immediate motivation for the new police act sect.20a.[137] Initially, it was intended to provide for cross-border hot pursuit and surveillance. After criticism from several consultative bodies, however, the power of foreign police to enforce their jurisdiction in Norway was limited to the use of police authority under the Schengen Convention. The committee preparing the 1999 proposal emphasised the importance of this limitation, without any specific explanation of its significance.[138] This reference was removed in January 2013. This is a change explicitly related to the state's perception of the policing restrictions. The previous hesitation about giving Norwegian police competence to foreign police authorities, was removed, without any real justification: it was just more practical.[139]

134 Auglend *et al.* 2004:851–2.
135 Boucht 2012:227.
136 Ot.prp.nr.61 (2003–2004) ch.5.4.
137 Ot.prp.nr.56 (1998–1999):92.
138 Op.cit. The Committee's comments ch.8.
139 There is, for example, no provision in Swedish law to allow Norwegian police Swedish police competence when they are cooperating in Sweden (SOU 2011:25).

Exercising foreign police authority in Norway has clearly been an exception to the normal rules. The Schengen measures permitting border crossing even without prior notification, are limited to emergency situations, and to the (presumably) brief period before Norwegian police can arrive and take over control of the situation. An interesting development is the growth of more routine policing abroad. Perhaps inspired by the central EU regions such as Maas-Rijn, a Swedish-Norwegian region, Vaajma, was established as a Scandinavian InterRegion Project. It is an EU initiative designed to coordinate Swedish and Norwegian police in efforts not only to stop cross-border crime, but to co-localise the police forces of both countries, and thus ensure a greater presence of visible police (independent of nationality) throughout the region.[140] The 2014 Report also suggests that the Norwegian police should introduce the neighbourhood watch networks (*grannsamvärkan*) run by Swedish police, where ordinary citizens are trained to aid the police by, for example, sending text messages if they observe suspicious cars, persons or incidents in their neighbourhoods. The Report suggests coordinating such a Norwegian network with the Swedish networks in border regions, so that the Norwegian and Swedish police may "have ears and eyes paying attention everywhere throughout the entire region".[141] Making ordinary citizens part of low-level, or voluntary policing may be seen as a return to the traditional, local police functions.[142] It seems, then, not to be one of the official tasks of Norwegian police, which must still be strictly within state competence and the police authority of the Police Act, at least when organised as a police service and not private security. This sort of thing might be precisely what communities need: greater focus on proximity policing, and the involvement of citizens to increase the perception of local security. Possible negative effects will be discussed below.

Police cooperation in the form of joint patrolling is a good example of the multi-layered new reality, which involves a network of bilateral, regional and EU developments. Swedish and Norwegian culture and history are closely connected, thus joint patrolling and co-localisation of the police forces of the two countries are not perhaps a radical departure in the relationship between the state, police and the citizens of Norway. However, since these cooperation measures also reflect developments at the EU level, the next step may be police officers from more diverse countries being co-situated, performing joint patrols, and having citizens from all over Europe texting them when they see or hear something suspicious. This may be fine from a crime control and security production perspective, and there is no intention here to discourage such a development, but it is one the Police Act and the existing Norwegian regulations are not designed to fit.

13.3 Managing investigation in Norway

None of the EU police mechanisms imply supranational operational police powers *per se*. As a clear general rule it is the national (member) states that have ultimate control over and say in police matters; the police are *national* forces (albeit with some national variations). Although there is a general obligation in the Schengen Cooperation to cooperate (art.39 CISA), the state, for example, receiving a request through SIS is not obliged to comply

140 Vaajma IntReg Report 2014. The challenge of police cooperation between Norway and the Swedish neighbour was also discussed in SOU 2011:25, particularly ch.3.4 on joint patrolling.

141 Vaajma IntReg Report 2014:41–42 (my translation).

142 So also Garland on the public-private partnership in crime control (Garland 2001).

with requests and petitions from other countries *because* these are directed through the SIS. Such obligations may, however, follow from other agreements such as the European and Nordic Arrest Warrants (see, for example, Chapter 10.2.1), and may even be hard to consider independent of each other.

Surveillance and non-coercive police measures are permitted on foreign territories, but foreign police may not make decisions of investigation outside of their home state. Even for EU member states, there are no regulations that give basis for, for example, a German prosecutor's decision to start a police investigation in Sweden. The principle of mutual recognition could become such a basis, but it is currently not. The German prosecutor may send such a request, and this request should then be considered as a home-state request, but it must then follow home-state procedures. Nor can a Swedish police officer call his German colleague and ask him to request of him, in Sweden, something that Swedish officers would not normally be allowed to do. This could imply a certain circumvention of original national procedures.

The rules giving legal basis to requesting initiation of an investigation could challenge the hierarchical structure of the police and prosecution (Chapter 2.4), as well as general principles of prioritisation. A relevant aspect concerns the choice of which officer or body at which level that should make decisions on investigation or e.g. the use of coercive measures. This concern is, however, in a sovereignty perspective, less pertinent since there basically is no *obligation* for the MS to comply with Europol or Eurojust requests. If the request implies use of coercive measures, these must be performed (in Norway) according to the regulations in the Police Act (PA) or Criminal Procedure Act (CPA). They could of course in principle still be limited or altered by binding international agreements, etc.[143]

It is, however, a possible challenge to the principle of opportunity: The public prosecution has no absolute duty to prosecute criminal acts (e.g. the CPA sects.69 and 70), the police are not absolute obligation to investigate any crime (CPA sect.224 and the Police Directive (PD) sects.7–4 and 7–5). The decision not to investigate may also be legitimated based on the prioritisation between police tasks according to PA sect.6 and generally according to available resources.[144]

International bodies may to some degree *influence* the initiation of investigation within other states. Europol may request that the competent authorities of the member states (MS) initiate, conduct or coordinate investigations (Art.6 ER). The MS are not obliged to comply with the requests, only to give them 'due consideration'. The competent authorities must inform Europol of the reasons in case of refusal, unless legitimised as harming national security interests (art.6 no.3a) jeopardising on-going investigations or the safety of individuals (no.3b). Some procedural rules apply: Europol must inform Eurojust prior to initiating measures (no.4). In cases where the MS supply Europol with various results of their investigations, such information must as a main rule be passed through the competent MS authorities (art.7 no.5). This would mean that a police officer who, for example, disagrees with his superiors' decision to not share information with Europol may not report this to the Europol office outside the official channels.[145] The regulation largely mirrors the

143 PA sect.3.

144 See more on this in Auglend and Mæland 2016:657ff; Kjelby 2013; Fredriksen 2013 esp. ch.4.1–2.

145 Nonetheless, the regulations on liaison officers may hollow out this regulation, as the liaison officers may have less strict procedures to adhere to.

Eurojust Decision on the initiation of investigations,[146] and the connection is implicitly acknowledged in the report requirement from Europol.[147]

In the Eurojust case, such concerns may arise, for example, when several countries have issued an arrest warrant on the same person. The sending state then determines which state will receive the wanted person, but Eurojust may act in an advisory capacity (EJ Decision art.16 no.2). This gives Eurojust the role both of coordinator of arrest warrants and of an expert body, possibly with a significant impact on the MS procedures in a particular case.[148] The Eurojust assistance related to the 'choosing' of jurisdictions to carry out investigation and/or various measures in, may even entail a supranational 'puppeteer' function, especially when Eurojust may know that they may evade troublesome hindrances to investigation a specific national jurisdiction.

The fact that both Eurojust and Europol may request investigation by the MS may imply an increased pressure to initiate investigation. Such pressure may be seen as a symbol of the blurring between police and prosecutorial/judicial functions at the EU level.[149] This hints at the differences between MS's criminal justice and legal systems, where, in contrast to many other countries, the Norwegian police and prosecution are partly intertwined.

The Norwegian Europol Agreement does not base an obligation for Norway to provide information to Europol in the same way as the Convention did (arts.3,4,10) the Decision and Regulation, since Norway is not a full-fledged member.[150] The 'ordinary' MS must provide reasons for their possible refusal to comply with Europol requests, unless this would harm essential national interests or jeopardise ongoing investigations or the safety of individuals. (art.7[3]). Apart from the reasons given, this does not necessarily imply much of a difference; there are no formal consequences are involved if refusing to comply with the request. The incentives to follow up on requests would thus presumably be the same for Norway as for the proper members: the common goal of crime prevention and crime stopping and the political will to be seen as a 'compliant' MS.

Through the harmonisation of criminal law in the EU, there is a degree of supranational obligation for the member states to criminalise certain acts.[151] While this does not concern the practical leadership of investigations, the harmonisation process may imply a managing of national penal law contents. And this may also imply a duty for the national police to investigate new kinds of crime. On one hand, this might interfere with the priorities of the national police locally, but also political budget priorities, if the EU were to *de facto* decide how the national resources should be distributed. This could be seen as unreasonable infringement on government's sovereign budget authority. On another side, the harmonisation of regulations must be 'taken seriously', and be dutifully implemented within national legislation. This may imply e.g. the right of victims of certain such crimes to have their cases investigated by the police of the country in question. Since the criminalisation of the crimes in question is rather uncontroversial, the *practical* challenge may not be that serious.[152] As

146 [2009] OJ L 138/14 art.6 no.1a.
147 Mitislegas 2009:169.
148 Efjestad 2009:26.
149 Mitsilgas 2009:169.
150 E/N Agreement 2001; Wold 2004:56.
151 E.g. Perron 2005:19–20. See also Bruce and Haugland 2014:34–35.
152 Fijnaut has shown, however, that the common shaping of investigation priorities in the Meuse-Rhine Euroregion has led to conflicts, for example, when the Belgian police initiate a large-scale investigation, and it turns out they need a substantial Dutch contribution, which the latter are unable or unwilling to provide (Fijnaut 2010:117ff.).

discussed above, the Schengen concerns raised by the minority fraction were assured by the argument concerning the *impracticability* of infringing activities. If the harmonisation influence issue would be challenged politically in Norway, the impracticality of unreasonable outcomes could probably settle the matter. EU harmonisation does not follow *de jure* for Norway from the Schengen cooperation, nor from the applicable EU regulations, apart from the EEA. In streamlining the cooperation with the EU countries, the harmonisation expectation may still be considered to be an important development in shaping also the Norwegian situation.[153]

From a Norwegian point of view, then, the autonomy of the national police and public prosecutor to decide whether an investigation or prosecution should be initiated or not, is not truly challenged. The political management may of course be significant in terms of, for example, which results are expected in which fields, and these may be more or less influenced either by signals from political cooperation partners, or by a political desire to appear 'Europe friendly', or generally 'tough on crime'.[154] This type of influence is discussed further in Chapter 15.4.2 *inter alia* on threat assessments along with the possible *reasons* for political steering.

13.4 Discussing the development of operational cooperation, joint operations and investigations

In the consultative works for the 1995 Police Act, the Ministry underlined the right to extraterritorial police enforcement,[155] particularly in the case of national ships and aircraft operating in international seas or airspace, as well as in Norwegian Waters. Extraterritorial police jurisdiction in other states' territory was not covered. As we have seen in this Part II, extraterritorial police enforcement in the sense of various cross-border transnational measures and instruments, is far more extensive than seemingly presupposed then.

The aim has been to show that the plethora of international police cooperation measures and instruments has resulted in a new policing situation. From the Norwegian point of view, the Norwegian Schengen negotiations, which took place around the time of the introduction of the 1995 Police Act, may arguably mark the change from 'old' to 'new'. The relevant regulations have been explored in detail and presented in (approximately) chronological order, as they multiplied, and extended cooperation on more ordinary policing levels, and increased access to a wider range of information on people in more countries.

Practical issues arising from the new situation have been analysed, such as foreign police officers' right to bear firearms in Norway when working with unarmed Norwegian police, and different understandings of terms and concepts, and different interpretations of common cooperation agreements. Rules governing the leadership of JITs may alter the traditional Norwegian hierarchy. Norwegian police officers may find themselves, when participating in a JIT abroad, subject to host state leadership (art.13[3a]). The rules of both the host state and the home state must be followed, but officers can take part in investigative measures that may be, if not illegal, at least "culturally different". Since the seconded officers also act

153 It is interesting to note that also the *Danish* situation is criticised for having too little influence in the development of EU criminal law (Baumbach 2012). Albeit EU member, Denmark has opted out of several certain criminal law and policing measures, which, as with Norway, entails lessened influence on a steady development throughout Europe.

154 Specific steering of *individual* cases is not acceptable.

155 Ot.prp.nr.22 (1994–1995) note to sect.3.

within national competences and national hierarchical structures, conflict may arise if their national superior and the JIT leader require different things of them.[156]

A new section, 20a, was added to the Police Act in 1999 (in force from 2001), empowering foreign police, under certain conditions, to enforce their jurisdictional competences in Norway. In principle this would breach the Police Act's presupposition that Norwegian police perform policing in Norway, apart from the limitations in sect.3 on applicable international law and agreement (in line with an internal sovereignty point of departure). Until the amendment, the only exception was the delegation of temporary police competences in sect.20(3). The consultative notes made clear that non-police personnel may be given temporary police powers when performing tasks that, to a significant extent, involve the prevention or investigation of crimes.[157] Such extraordinary police competence is described as limited, but this is only in time and purpose.[158]

The first amendments of sect.20a extended the competences of foreign police to hot pursuit and surveillance of a non-suspect in certain situations (2003). The year 2012 saw the removal of requirements that had followed in sect.20a, and, foreign police officers could now be given Norwegian police competence, such as that described in sect.20(3).

Chapter 12 dealt with national police forces' cross-border activities for home state purposes, including hot pursuit of someone fleeing a murder scene, continued surveillance from one country to the next, and undercover policing in foreign territories. The present chapter also described a new form of police cooperation: joint operations and investigations, which imply more operational cooperation, rather than police work that crosses a border into the next jurisdiction. It is also new in involving countries which do not share a common border: as well as Finnish police crossing the unguarded border into Northern Norway, Romanian police patrol Norwegian streets.

Both Interpol and Europol have been accused of having an inflated bureaucracy that prevents efficient police cooperation.[159] Supranational police bodies may be involved in JITs and joint operations, but these may mainly be seen as instruments facilitating more direct cross-border cooperation between national police, for example, in avoiding letters rogatory, and increasing the presence of neighbouring police officers in each other's jurisdictions. JITs, however, initially suffered from the challenges that inevitably arise when real transnational cooperation between member states is being carried out. Despite the obligation to apply the JIT Framework Decision before 1 January 2003, only 14 member states had adopted it by August 2004.[160] By 2005, only one JIT had been formed, increasing to 21 in 2006, and 38 in 2009.[161] There is, however, a significant increase in the recent years: according to Eurojust, 69 new JITs were established in 2016 alone, including with third states. Three were involving Norway.[162]

156 Mayer 2006:212–3.
157 Ot.prp.nr.64 (1998–1999) note to sect.20.
158 Myhrer 2007a:3
159 den Boer 2010:43.
160 COM (2004) 858, 07.01.2005; [2002] OJ L 162/1 art.4(1).
161 As far as is known. See Peers 2011:940 and Block 2012:98–99. The JITs set up concerned Basque and Islamic terrorism (between France and Spain); left-wing terrorism (France and Germany); and drug trafficking (between the UK and the Netherlands). Finland is reported (based on an interview) to have had seven JITs, mostly with Sweden and Estonia.
162 Eurojust Annual Report 2016, p. 18.

As Mitsilegas points out, having police officers from foreign states operating on state territory clearly challenges traditional ideas of state sovereignty, especially when their operational powers go beyond the limited Schengen provisions on hot pursuit and surveillance.[163] Other obstacles to employing JITs in practical police work are the general uncertainty regarding the national implementation of the EU regulations, and lack of funding, since JITs may be expensive to negotiate and operate.[164] Hufnagel's research shows that the processes facilitated in the MLA Convention, were not always perceived as quicker and more effective by practitioners.[165] Tak argues that lack of knowledge is a major obstacle, because transnational cooperation is perceived as too complicated.[166] Sheptycki shows that skilled police officers may use the fragmented situation for forum shopping.[167]

It may be that there is an unwillingness to cooperate on this level, perhaps because the primary focus is on EU cooperation solely between member states, and the complications of including non-full-fledged members to cumbersome. If there is nothing to gain by international cooperation, there is no point carrying out such complex processes. It may also be that this is perceived as too far from MS national interest, in other words (to some extent, at least), not in line with internal sovereignty, understood as prioritising full control over the internal territory. However, the rather radical increase in numbers may indicate that the processes appear less complex, due to for example the facilitated Europol and Eurojust guidelines, better possibilities for financing, and the options for support from the JITs network secretariat. The lowered threshold for involvement from Europol may also play a role, simply because they may more easily be of assistance – and encouraging police work in more areas.

For Norway, the amendment of PA sect. 20a, cf. 20 (3) clearly opens the way to the use of non-police officers in national investigation operations (in JITs). This may challenge the national structures and hierarchies of the police organisation. It does not, though, necessarily raise the issue of differences between police forces in different countries, since operations have to be carried out under host state law. There are still some legal gaps concerning evidence and information obtained while taking part in JITs. A common set of suspect and defence rights has not yet been agreed upon at EU level. In the meantime, it seems possible that police officers who know jurisdictions well will go 'forum shopping', and that such shopping may jeopardise individual rights.

The legal regulation of JITs at the EU level, in combination with the other multinational units mentioned, implies that much is left to the discretion of police officers, and to ad hoc arrangements made between the authorities concerned.[168] Where joint operations target mass gatherings, it may be a problem that host and seconded officers have prevention as a common goal, but lack a common understanding of what constitutes a 'danger'. It is problematic that seconded officers may be operating alone in situations that are inevitably stressful and require urgent action. Norwegian police officers' presumed close link to the Norwegian state and culture is the rationale for the requirement for Norwegian citizenship in PA sect.20(1).[169] Regardless of whether Norwegian law is applicable, or whether the

163 Mitsilegas 2009:170.

164 https://www.europol.europa.eu/activities-services/joint-investigation-teams [08.12.2017].

165 Hufnagel 2013:216–18.

166 Tak 2000; also Block 2012:94.

167 Sheptycki 2002:89.

168 Mitsilegas 2009:171 and Rijken 2006:102.

169 NOU 1981:35 p.85 ff; St.meld.nr.42 (2004–2005):10.

leader of an operation is Norwegian, it seems that the temporary (yet possibly lengthy) delegation of full police competences to foreign police officers may challenge the value set on cultural proximity when it comes to perceiving risks and threats.[170] One possible problem is where foreign police apprehend and detain someone, and the witnessing before Norwegian courts, as to the Norwegian judge's consideration of risk-assessments, for example, how specific and concrete the risk to be prevented, must be for the police to intervene with various level of force. The police have wide discretion, and police are not required to have grounds for suspicion to apply the measures provided in the Police Act; the decision rests on their judgement.

Previously, a restriction that seems likely to be based on sovereignty considerations relating to providing supranational bodies' competence to start and take part in operational investigation teams would perhaps be considered to challenge national sovereignty. Europol could not request access to participate in JITs. Actual practice could, though, be different, given that those working in the EU police and prosecution bodies are mainly liaison officers who are not subject to the same restrictions. With the new Regulation, this prohibition is removed.

And on an other hand, there seems to have been little supranational impact on the structure of EU states' police systems. There is a distinct 'openness' underlying the diversity of the police system. Thus, there is the open-ended and flexible word "officers" in the JIT Decision, instead of "police officers", "constables", or "persons with police authority". We clearly do not yet see an EU police force: these bodies are all still basically governed by their own national law, insofar as other police forces may not enforce their national law on foreign territory if it conflicts with this territory's law. 'Soft' and 'hard' cooperation instruments, training sessions, and role models, undoubtedly have effects that cross borders, however. What these chapters have shown is that, on several levels, there has been a 'communitarisation' of the police forces of the different countries through the development of EU instruments, and there is no reason to believe that the Norwegian police remains unaffected.

170 On the different risk perceptions of citizens and police, Balvig 1987; Finstad 2000.

14 Impact on the Norwegian police

In Part I, Chapters 7 and 8, the way Norway entered into the EU police cooperation was considered from two sovereignty perspectives. One perspective focused on internal sovereignty, where I argued that the Norwegian government failed to justify the actual consequences of the cooperation to its citizens, and thus made the informed enforcement of popular sovereignty impossible. The other perspective emphasised elements of external sovereignty, where I argued that Norway's place in the EU institutional and political hierarchy makes the agreements (as a whole, at least) infringing on the Norwegian government's possibility to *de facto* act internationally in a fully uninhibited way.

The police were first night watchmen, then suppliers of most welfare services, then a detective force tasked with preventing, stopping and solving crime. They are now still some of this, but also involved in a wide range of international police cooperation mechanisms. This development may suggest that there has been a shift in the notion of what sort of phenomenon 'the police' is, who they work for and where they are organised. The wealth of detail given so far in Part II will serve as a basis for a discussion of this development based on two other perspectives on internal sovereignty. This chapter and the next concern the ways the Norwegian police may be influenced by the rapidly expanding police cooperation.

Following one logic, the constitution of the modern state is intimately connected to the police, because a state that cannot get anything done, because of an unorderly internal situation, is not a state. Policing, Bayley argues, is an intensely political matter, sensitive to the prevailing pattern of state-making and the prevailing character of resistance to it.[1] And the point of departure of this book is the Weberian notion of the police as the state's tool of coercion within its territory, where only the police can legitimately enforce violence in peacetime. This legitimate force is made operational by and through the police. For Weber, this is a defining feature of the state.

It is easy to contest the idea of this monopoly in contemporary European states. There are, for example, far more private security guards than police. Private security forces, however, are regulated by the state, which thus, I argue, retains its monopoly. Furthermore, public police, unlike private security staff have *autonomy* to carry out coercion or threaten it. Except for citizen's arrest and the right to defend oneself and others, this autonomy is an exclusive prerogative of the police within the state's territory.

Part II above described international agreements and regulations on what the police may and may not legally do. The focus now will be on what the more general impact of the

1 Bayley 1975.

DOI: 10.4324/9780429503696-16

international cooperation regulations and operations may be – and more specifically – on the possible effects of international police cooperation instruments, measures and operations on the Norwegian police (the present chapter), and the Norwegian society (chapter 16).

In this chapter, I will address my third research question:

> *In what ways does the development of operational police cooperation regulations and measures impact on the Norwegian police?*

More specifically I will discuss issues such as how these developments fit with the Norwegian policing tradition, what sort of influence foreign police officers working in Norway may have on their Norwegian peers, and how the work of foreign agencies, like, for example, Europol threat assessments, may affect Norwegian policing practices.

14.1 The wider effects of the Norwegian Schengen cooperation

The Schengen cooperation and later instruments, such as the 2000 MLA Convention,[2] were intended to permit foreign police to enforce their national police authority on Norwegian territory, and vice versa. This was not supposed to imply a surrender of ultimate Norwegian police authority rooted in a 'state organ' – the national police, but the police cooperation measures described above, may cast doubt on this.

The question here is whether these measures develop in line with the predictions made in the Norwegian policy documents of the mid- and late 1990s. It was assumed that hot pursuit and cross-border surveillance, and to some extent information exchange in the SIS, would mean foreign states' police competence being enforced on Norwegian territory, but these measures were not expected to be used frequently. Other consequences were not considered, not to mention the breadth and depth of how the development would expand through the years to come. The most striking feature of the various forms of police cooperation channels and instruments available to the Norwegian police today, is their topical breadth and geographical extent. The mandates of the various organisations and forums vary, especially as to the expected outcomes. This is in no way reflected in the political debates and processes, at the time of agreement or through later amendments.

Sheptycki argues that historically entrenched differences in police and justice systems in different countries, along with local influences on police work, means that "the changes to the architecture of policing is understood differently in different places".[3] He maintains, however, that homogenisation can, for example, result from technological innovation, which has similar effects across jurisdictions on how the police are organised. The very notion of policing has changed with the development of technological intelligence, which Haggerty and Ericson call the 'surveillance assemblage'.[4] This book does not deal with the differences between police forces in the European states with which Norwegian police may cooperate. The following reflections are therefore based on the differences set out in documents relating to the negotiations and agreements, as shown above.

2 [2004] OJ L 26/3.

3 Sheptycki 2002:138, also Marenin 1982.

4 Ericson and Haggerty 1997, see also Lomell 2007.

14.1.1 Changes in the policing situation and crime focus

The Norwegian police have generally had a positive attitude to innovations and amendments to do with police cooperation. This is hardly surprising since any professional will want to have as many useful tools available as possible. A constant worry of the police (and some politicians) has been that, as a non-EU member, Norway could be left outside if non-EU international instruments were abolished by the EU states, and thus liable to become a safe haven for criminals.[5] This may be a valid concern, but no empirical data has shown that this situation is imminent. Reported crime in Norway is the lowest for 20 years, according to Statistics Norway.[6] This may, of course, be because of improved police cooperation. Police success is hard to measure, since optimal police work has no positive, countable results: no crimes committed, no disorder reported. In other European states, the new initiatives on cross-border cooperation agreements and measures have been criticised for not being based sufficiently on police officials' own perception of what is necessary. The fact that the police have little influence on policing policy, makes them less efficient, according to Block, who argues that professional rationality is indispensable for success, and for the correct assessment of success.[7] Bigo takes a similar line, pointing to a progressive marginalisation of police practitioners in debates. Their replacement by European specialists is justified by the advanced technical aspects of international policing.[8] This is not the impression given by the consultative works relating to Norwegian police cooperation.[9] There might, however, be a discrepancy between the state of affairs suggested by the various legal proposals, and the reality of the instruments in use.

While, then, the police response to new cooperation agreements and measures has been generally positive, are these novelties put into practice? The Office of the Auditor General's assessed the police's efforts against organised crime in 2010.[10] Severe criticism was voiced:

- The cooperation between national police districts was inadequate; it was difficult to make police districts take charge of investigations that went across district borders (a complaint made by almost all police districts).
- Several measures had been instated, and police budgets have increased, without there being any proportional effects.
- Police districts reported a greater need to make use of 'extraordinary' measures such as covert search, surveillance and communication control. Reports showed, however, a decline in the use of these measures in the period 2005–2008.
- There was no strategy to fight organised crime.[11] Action plans and documents that had been developed, were not followed up in the districts, and their work in the area of organised crime could not be measured because of a lack of control parameters.

5 Kvam 2008:167; Juritzen 2009:10.

6 https://www.ssb.no/sosiale-forhold-og-kriminalitet/artikler-og-publikasjoner/faerre-tyverier-og-narkotikalovbrudd [30.11.2017]

7 Block 2012:90.

8 Bigo 2000a.

9 Such variables may of course depend on differences between the police sources who are interviewed in research, and those giving feedback in consultative documents, which may be a division between 'low level' and higher-ranking police employees, but these differences have not been researched here.

10 Dok. 3:10 (2009–2010). There has also been a report on the fight against crime for gain (2012), but nothing else related to this area of police and prosecutorial efforts.

11 This was remedied soon after in Meld.St. 7 (2011–2012).

There may be several reasons why cooperation agreements and measures are suggested, but then not used as much as intended. One might be that such instruments are implemented hastily, without sufficient analysis of their necessity, to demonstrate a quick political reaction, to concerns voiced in the media, for instance, what kind of concerns become prioritised and how.

Organised, transnational crime has become a 'great concern' of our time. According to Bowling and Sheptycki, the notion of transnational organised crime first emerged in the 1970s, and was subsequently developed in official UN discourse.[12] Their point is that there has been a trend whereby 'international crime' which used only to cover political crimes and terrorism, now includes ordinary crime.[13] This corresponds with the development of EU international police cooperation instruments.

How crime is explained and defined naturally has a major impact on everyday police work. Human trafficking and illegal immigration received more attention after police were made aware that organised crime groups were often behind such crimes.[14] It seems a fair deduction that many types of crime have increased as a result of the abolition of border controls between the Schengen/EU member states and, perhaps also, of the more thorough control of the borders surrounding the Schengen Area. Trafficking becomes ever more profitable as the risks of punishment and the difficulty of 'getting in' increase. Tax rates in western countries, and especially in Norway, make smuggling and forgery of heavily taxed products very profitable. Recently, the maximum sentence for breaching an Immigration Act prohibition on entry into Norway – in other words, returning to the country after being expelled – was increased from six months in prison to two years, with a government direction that, in ordinary cases, sentences of not less than one year's imprisonment should be given for a first-time breach.[15] The usual sentence given before the amendment was 35 days. In cases of repeated breaches, the maximum increases to four years' imprisonment (CPA sect.61). The reason for this radical increase, according to the Ministry, is that illegal entry and residence undermines the goal of regulated immigration. Control of foreigners' identity and residence in Norway was argued to be very important for security reasons, given the Norwegian authorities' diminished control post-Schengen. The growth in 'entry crime', expected to result from globalisation and increased general mobility, makes the general and individual deterrence effects of harsher punishment seem necessary.[16]

According to the Oslo police district, most cases of people smuggling were discovered through border control of persons. Concern was expressed about moving border controls to public spheres such as urban areas (see the 1988 Immigration Act sect.44), which could be seen by foreigners as a more offensive kind of control. However, 'covert border control' is not a legitimate purpose for checking IDs in urban areas.[17] The Ministry considered it necessary to include deportation by the police from Norwegian territory if it was necessary because the person was a "threat to public policy, national security or the international relations". The Ministry claims that this was no different to the assessments the police already carried out under §27e, only the wording was different (Ot.prp.nr.56 (1998–1999): 28–29).

12 Bowling and Sheptycki 2012:34.
13 Op.cit.:36, see also Larsson 2004.
14 St.prp.nr.50 (1998–99):16.
15 Innst. 48 L (2013–2014), amending the Immigration Act sect.108.
16 Op.cit. ch.1.2.1; 3. The argument is also put forward in America, see such as Stumpf 2006.
17 op.cit.:19, Ugelvik 2013. See art.5 pt.1, leading to the 1988 Immigration Act new sect.27j

The Oslo Police District argued that there should be a distinction between people expelled for breaching the Immigration Act (such as those overstaying a temporary residence permit) and those expelled following a criminal conviction. The Ministry emphasised that any expulsion would be based on the foreigner's lack of respect for Norwegian law, and underlined the correlation between foreigners committing crimes and foreigners breaching the Immigration Act. The Ministry thus defined an area combining administrative law and criminal law as a serious crime problem. This is, then, another example of the increased weight put on the international aspects of social problems. The general justification is that, as more and more police resources are devoted to foreign criminals with no permanent connections to Norway, harsher sentences for the Immigration Act breaches often committed by them in addition to other crimes will assist the fight against organised crime.[18] Discussion has shifted from the benefits of a Europe with free travel and trade to the issue of people without the desired status or purpose taking advantages of open borders. Increased intertwining of immigration policing and other forms of policing may also be seen in the interlinking of administrative and police databases that were previously kept strictly apart. This, I argue, can be seen as imposing a shift in police attention to areas that were intended differently; as a positive, free-travel concept of a borderless Europe. When it instead – or at least seemingly excessively – becomes police and policing concerns, this requires a more thorough public and political consideration to maintain internal sovereignty.

The 2011 bombing of Government Headquarters, and the mass-murders at Utøya, shook Norwegian society to its foundations, but the reactions of the public were far less punitive than one might have expected: there were few demands for more severe punishment, the introduction of the death penalty, or a tougher, more militarised, police. The police, however, came under severe criticism from the political authorities, and several reports followed.[19] In its evaluation of police performance during and following the atrocities in 2011, the Evaluation Committee concluded that the police failures did not primarily result from insufficient resources or legislation, a deficient organisation, or changes in values.[20] Like the Office Auditor General, they argued that the failure was more to do with leadership, lack of cooperation, and the general culture and attitudes of the police.

The subsequent analysis in NOU 2013:9 resulted in a call for police reform. One hundred years after the 1912 Committee issued its thorough report, a new wide-ranging report – the Police Analysis (*Politianalysen*) – was published. It suggested major reforms, including further centralisation of the police by reducing the number of police districts from 27 to 6, as well as a general improvement of management and efficiency. The report said that the police of the future must be able to "tackle complex, serious and cross-border crime, and at the same time deliver a good service where the population lives".[21] Like the 1912 Committee, it considered that the Norwegian police force was not sufficiently centralised,[22] and that

18 Op.cit. ch.1.2.1; 3. The Police Act (sect.14 1)) was recently amended, allowing municipalities to prohibit begging under local bylaws. Aggressive begging could already be dealt with by the police under PA sect.7 (1) nos.1 and 3 if considered to breach public order (Fredriksen 2014:398–403). The 2013 restriction also serves as an example of poor people being hindered from taking advantage of mobility within the Schengen area (Prop. 152 L (2012–2013)).

19 E.g. NOU 2012:14; Meld.St.21 (2012–2013).

20 NOU 2012:14.

21 NOU 2013:9 p.9, my translation.

22 Op.cit.:18. Mathiesen (1979) even argues that the state seems to have an ever-growing desire to have overarching, centralised control of the police, since this is considered to increase the Ministry's efficiency.

recent social developments challenged the Norwegian police model, and brought new requirements, and different views on what a 'good police service' is.[23] The analysis concluded that, although the crime rate throughout Europe is declining, the crime that does take place is ever more complex, cross-border and organised.[24]

Organised crime has always been a key EU target area. Particular emphasis has been put on counterfeiting and other crimes affecting the financial interests of the Union.[25] A general strategy for fighting organised crime was formulated in 2005,[26] and a contemporary Joint Action established an inventory of competences to deal with it.[27] A resolution has been adopted on the policing of international crime routes[28] and another has established a model protocol on public/private partnership against organised crime.[29] There have also been Council decisions on targeting organised crime by 'mobile groups'.[30]

In such a reality as this, the local management of police work was considered to be inadequate; most northern European countries had reached the same conclusion.[31] This view was criticised because of its overemphasis on the value of efficiency as against other principles of the Norwegian police, and because the report in no way took into account national or international academic research on good policing.[32] Is it valid to conclude that, despite a falling crime rate, crime is becoming so serious that successful local police models must be abandoned? May one anticipate further centralisation moving decision-making away from not only local and regional levels, but also from national level?[33] The special nature of the Norwegian police arguably results from the ten principles described in Chapter 2.1):[34] such principles as that the police force should reflect the ideals of society, should be united, civilian and prevention-oriented, should interact with the public, should have officers that are generalists, and be decentralised and integrated into local communities. Provided the Norwegian police follow these principles, the "needs of the community" requirement stated in the Police Act sect.1 should be met.[35] Of course, the meaning of the ten principles depends on how the concepts they mention are defined.[36] The way these concepts have constantly acquired new meanings will now be examined.

There has, I argue, been a change from more and more focus on organised crime, on the expense of more ordinary crime, and so also more extraordinary police measures and forms of cooperation. It is continuously reiterated that there is increasingly more crime, and that the crime is more serious. The question here is whether these changes in focus come also

23 From researchers: Ellefsen, B 2013., Johannesen, S in DN 02.07.13; *Høringssvar fra Riksadvokaten 2013.*
24 NOU 2013:9 p.18.
25 E.g. [2001] OJ L 329/1 (criminal investigations).
26 COM (2005) 232 2 June 2005.
27 [1996] OJ L 342/2.
28 [1999] OJ C 162/1.
29 [2004] OJ C 116/20.
30 E.g. Council conclusions on setting the EU's priorities for the fight against organised and serious international crime between 2018 and 2021 – Council conclusions (18 May 2017), doc. 9450/17.
31 NOU 2013:9.
32 Halvorsen 2013.
33 den Boer and Doelle 2002 note that, while there are considerable variations in European countries, there is a general trend towards centralising police systems (p.9). All systems may be seen as changing because of the perceived advantages of new technologies, although some core differences are maintained (Sheptycki 2002:139).
34 NOU 1981:35; NOU 1987:27, Ot.prp.nr.22 (1994–1995):13; Innst.S.nr.192 (1991–1992), etc.
35 According to NOU 1981:35 ch.5.
36 E.g. Charbonneau 2008:11.

from the police, or more from the external (EU) level, and whether they may have unwanted or unforeseen consequences on the police.

It was emphasised above that the police force works on behalf of a state, and that this is a core feature of the modern police function. The police, however, is arguably also made up of individual officers, who may be motivated by their own interests or those of their organisation. According to Walker, when policing is perceived as a matter of technical skill, its practitioners – especially those working internationally – are more likely to be treated as respected professionals and less likely to be subjected to close scrutiny, because they are experts.[37] This may, in turn, influence how the police officers perceive their role in or obligation towards the community. The issue here is whether internationalisation and increased autonomy weaken the link between the citizens and the state.

The police may become more autonomous through the processes of internationalisation and of the development of police cooperation. Deflem believes that various police institutions gained a degree of formal separation from their governments by the establishment of the International Criminal Police Commission in 1923.[38] This embodied a structural condition of institutional autonomy, supported by the fact that the organisation was established independently of Governments, by police officials alone. The same thing may of course happen through other forms of international police cooperation, such as those of the EU, which had a more detached role vis-à-vis nation-states' governments.

Interpol has long been criticised for being an old boys' network which lacks transparency.[39] Thus, one of the benefits of police cooperation being formalised and expanded within the EU and Schengen was closer regulation and increased transparency. But do Europol and other international police organisations extend their autonomy simply by enhancing the importance of their function? Den Boer and Doelle answer this by arguing that some EU initiatives may even indirectly create competition between MS police, because evaluation mechanisms make them strive to achieve better results.[40]

According to Auglend *et al.*,[41] the growth of international police cooperation measures and agreements has been driven by the police themselves. If this is true, it might go a long way towards explaining the gap between the plethora of cooperation agreements, conventions and treaties, and the actual need for or use of them. Many have thought that international police cooperation should be allowed to develop freely, unrestrained by legal regulation.[42] Auglend *et al.* argued that legislators, both politicians and ministries, basically were uninterested in the matter, and left it to the police to make the most of the tools available to them, and to develop informal or lower-level cooperation agreements.[43] The challenges now arising from a greater involvement of politics and the law in policing are similar to the general challenge of the so-called juridification of areas of society that traditionally belonged to the political sphere.[44] The body of treaties, conventions and agreements is increasing, and the formalisation of police measures (within and across national boundaries)

37 Walker 1993:42

38 Deflem 2002:174.

39 Anderson *et al.* 1995:74. On police culture within Europol, see e.g. Groenleer 2009:293 ff.

40 den Boer and Doelle 2002:33; den Boer 1998.

41 Auglend *et al.* 2004:1036 ff.; also, Henricson 2010:16; Bowling and Sheptycki 2012.

42 Joubert and Bevers 1996:36, referring to the Memorandum of the European Treaty on Mutual Legal Assistance in Criminal Matters.

43 Auglend *et al.* 2004:1037. Note that this is not repeated in the second edition (2016).

44 E.g. Sand 2010.

may make them less accessible, both to those who might make use of them and to those who might be subjected to them. The further development of the regulations may also be entrusted to bureaucrats rather than practitioners such as police officers and detectives.

Contrary to what Auglend *et al.* found, political attention now seems to have turned to the international and transnational field of police and crime control. Fighting an 'ever-growing' amount of international, organised and serious crime, associated with expanding sections of society, has become a vital target for any political party or government in Europe. The political structure of the EU, especially post-Schengen, is also more oriented towards governing cooperation on policing and justice. Regardless of whether the development of the police is politically driven or police driven, it seems inevitable that cross-border measures will be introduced, and that there will be a move towards more centralised control. I would also suggest, however, that the police are at the same time becoming more powerful actors in their own development, in the context of resource allocation, and of the development of a 'bigger and better tool box'.

14.1.2 Examining a changed Norwegian police culture

This chapter explores whether Norwegian police culture has become, or is becoming, different because of international police cooperation agreements, and the increasing focus on 'international' challenges to Norwegian society represented by cross-border crime and increased immigration. The term 'police culture' refers here to a shared mind-set within the police force: the way police employees make sense of their social world, use their time, and interact with people in different settings.[45] Police culture may influence the law and policy of a particular state or local community.[46] The chapter considers the overarching question of possible changes in the relationship between the state, the community and its police when the police force is influenced by new and more international developments. As such, this clearly affects the tightness of whether the police increasingly work on behalf of themselves, rather than the state – composed by its citizens. But also on who the police, among themselves, perceive as part of the community they serve. This, I argue, is at core of sovereignty, as it relates to defining both who is part of the citizens and the state, in the concepts of the PA sect.1. The impact on police culture will be explored, including questions relating to the arming of police officers, and the possible conflict between efficiency and other values in everyday police work.

14.1.2.1 Impact from joint patrols and training

The Norwegian Police Academy was the first state police body, and was set up before the 1927 and 1936 Police Acts. It was considered imperative to have a state institution that would ensure a national operational standard. The Academy was a vital part of the first wave of efforts of centralising the police function towards state control. From this point, one may argue, the education of police officers was central to the management of the state monopoly on legitimate violent force. The fact that police officers can be now sent abroad to train, may itself be said to begin the erosion of the 'unity' purpose of Norwegian police officer training.

45 Loftus 2009:15. The term 'police culture' is loaded with meanings, and has given rise to a whole body of research which I do not seek to add to. Some classic studies show that police culture may vary between rural and urban police (e.g. Cain 1973) and be dependent on hierarchical ranks (Manning 2007).

46 Cockcroft 2012.

In addition to the idea that citizenship is a safeguard, because Norwegian citizens are assumed to share 'Norwegian values', the citizenship requirement is also meant to satisfy the Norwegian principle of proximity policing.[47] The Schengen cooperation and other international police cooperation instruments depart from the principle that only Norwegian state-employed police should enforce powers on the national territory. Even if the exceptions made to this are strictly limited, f international influence may challenge the proximity policing model. When the reason for emphasising proximity is that it leads to an increased perception of security and safety, opening the way for foreign police and foreign policing models, may be seen as a deviation.

In Chapter 13, it was noted that, alongside the legal aspects of giving foreign police officers Norwegian police powers in Norwegian territory joint patrols also had other sociologically interesting aspects. The presence of foreign police may have a cultural impact on the police. The mere presence of foreign officers may affect how the Norwegian police are perceived by citizens, or even by the police themselves. In addition to being members of Norwegian society, and thus impacted like other citizens by, for example, political statements on, and media coverage of, international crime, police officers may also be influenced in work-specific ways. This may be as a result of policy documents or regulations that will have impact on resource allocation and the priorities assigned by the Police Directorate, say, or the Director of Public Prosecutions. But it may also come about through changes in the police personnel's perception of what they are supposed to do, what their role should be, whether they should expect their work to be dangerous, and if so, in what ways, and finally which people represent a risk, and how they can be recognised. All these issues are conveyed by the term 'police culture'.

Police practice can change more or less spontaneously and by chance, because new people are made to work together, or indeed, simply because they are shown a television series. However, there seems to be an increasing tendency for police in various countries to be subjected intentionally to international, centralising influences. International training is not a new development. Interpol has, for example, police training and development as a core activity.[48] The extent and intensity of such efforts, however, increase when they are encouraged by, and take place through, the EU, as part of general policies of the Area of Freedom, Security and Justice. A police force controls the society and community in which it works, and thereby has great effect on how it is shaped and acts, what the population perceives as safe and unsafe. One point in this matter is the question of the police carrying weapons.

The possibility that foreign police officers might bring their service weapons into Norway when in hot pursuit of a criminal was a particular concern in the Norwegian Schengen negotiations.[49] Because of the generally high level of trust, and informal regulations, between the Nordic countries, Boucht argues that, while there are not currently any measures agreed between the Nordic countries that are 'deeper' than those in EU instruments, such measures could more easily be developed, due to cultural similarities. One of his suggestions is that it should be made mandatory for police officers in training to spend some time in another Nordic country.[50] The Nordic joint cooperation report emphasises that it is

47 The model is characterised by small police units, close cooperation with the public, integration in the local community, representativeness and little division of tasks (NOU 1981:85, St.meld.nr.42 (2004–2005):10).

48 See e.g. Martha 2010:123–4.

49 Innst.S.nr.229 (1996–1997):14. On differences in police use of arms in the Nordic countries, see Strype 2005; Knutsson 2005; Hendy 2014.

50 Boucht 2012:235.

essential that officers who are going to cooperate abroad should be trained, and that language skills, for example, will be important for the success of an operation.[51] And the growth of international police cooperation measures may necessitate an increased focus on joint training schemes. The Schengen cooperation can be taken as a point of departure since, as mentioned previously, this led to the first formalised operational regulations. Even though the rules on hot pursuit in CISA art.41 have always been considered to be quite complex, the Schengen instruments did not include provisions on joint training.[52] The European Police College (CEPOL) has relatively recently gained the status of an EU body; its purpose is to serve the citizens of Europe.[53] This appears similar to the purpose of the Norwegian police as expressed in the Police Act sect.1, except for the fact that the citizens involved are European, not just those of a nation-state. An increased focus on the training of Norwegian police officers with the 'care' of European citizens in mind may be a fine goal. To play devil's advocate, however, one may ask whether joint training within the ambit of an international EU body such as CEPOL does not stretch the purpose set out in the Police Act. How the police are trained is important and may even be decisive for ensuring they act according to the national police culture and national traditions. As shown in Chapter 2.4, Norwegian police officers must be Norwegian citizens, and this citizenship is assumed to ensure that they are sufficiently trustworthy to be granted the wide range of discretionary powers that Norwegian police officers enjoy.

14.2 Extraterritorial proximity policing

Current cultural and financial challenges are impacting European countries very differently. Many of the agreements concerning police and judicial cooperation within Schengen/the EU are initiated by certain EU member states. Germany and Austria, for example, have a long tradition of active police cooperation. The reason is, of course, their geographically central position in Europe, and shared cultural traditions resulting from their historical connection with Prussia, the strong (police) state.[54] This tradition may be said to be carried forward in important European police cooperation measures.

This might lead one to think that the Norwegian police are, to an extent, enforcing crime control policies that are based on other states' traditions and historical developments, rather than Norwegian ones. This in turn may have a significant impact on the way the Norwegian police develops, in style, tasks, and priorities. As with the harmonisation of criminal law, this is not 'hard' influence: there are no legal regulations on how the police should and should not think and work. Given the traditionally strong relationship between citizens, police and state, these 'foreign' and/or international influences may still raise questions as to whether certain changes to the police are in fact needed or wanted by Norwegian citizens. On the other hand, with more open borders and a far more diverse Norwegian community, the international impact may be precisely what is needed, when citizens are less homogeneous

51 Nordisk samtjänstgöringsrapport 2009:17–8.

52 Daman 2008:179.

53 https://www.cepol.europa.eu/who-we-are/european-police-college/mission-vision-and-values [21.05.14].

54 See e.g. Anners 1997, Liang 1992. Germany, for example, made the first proposal for police joint investigation teams in 1994 (Block 2012:89). Ulrich Beck argues that Germany, through its financial power, has come to dominate the EU (http://www.social-europe.eu/2013/03/germany-has-created-an-accidental-empire/ [04.07.14]). As Germany is one of the main proponents of enhanced police cooperation, it is likely that this power may help support more far-reaching EU initiatives.

than in the past, and the sense of community assumed in the Police Act is more difficult – perhaps impossible – to achieve. The effects of changes in the Norwegian police on the people being policed is the topic of the next subchapter.

One of the core principles of the Norwegian police is proximity.[55] In the 2012 DPP circular concerning the focus of the Norwegian prosecution authorities' investigations, theft and burglary are judged to be the main crimes that people are victims of. The DPP stressed that it is important for people's general feelings of safety, and for their trust in the police, that these everyday crimes should be solved. The police solved for example around 13 per cent of burglary cases in Norway in the period between 2006 and 2012.[56] Are the consequences of legislation what citizens of the member states expect? Is legislation based on a view of security that is shared by citizens? Does the law meet their needs? In other words, is the social contract transferable from the level of the nation-state to that of EU cooperation, and is whoever who is now responsible for this contract, aware of the results that citizens expect to get for their trade-off? The EU legislative frameworks are necessarily common to all member states, and national exceptions are rarely made.[57] It might be hard, even impossible, to anticipate all consequences of legislation. Thus, when intending to enforce their popular sovereignty, it is necessary for citizens to be presented the alternatives, for the government to show them what the consequences may be and what the citizens should be aware of. These are things that signalise that this does not unfold in the same manner when it takes place in or from the EU or transnational police cooperation level; locally and/or more nationally.

14.2.1 A skewed police focus?

Norwegian police districts have complained that the increased requirements for contingency planning take away resources from ordinary police work, so that serious backlogs build up.[58] It is now a requirement that the police should be able to prevent major crime events or disasters such as the terrorist attacks in Oslo and at Utøya in 2011. International police cooperation may be well suited to prevent and stop cross-border crime. It might, though, lead to a skewed perception of security and safety, if the threat and risk assessments the allocation of police resources is based on, focus unduly on serious, cross-border crimes committed by foreigners. International cooperation instruments now also apply to parts of what remains of national order policing. The development international police cooperation

55 '*Nærpoliti*' may also be translated as 'community police', but this has other connotations. I choose therefore to use the term proximity policing, since this suggests the aspect of geographical distance that is pertinent when considering the international versus the national levels. Both terms have been used in translations before, see Holmberg 2005 and Larsson 2010.

56 Prop.1 S (2011–2012):100–101, DPP Circular 1/2014:3–4.

57 This is the main rule. Supranationally, however, the picture is not black and white. In the case of policing, practical implementation will consider national differences, e.g. that officers enforcing EU competences such as arrest after a mutual recognition order, must also be competent to perform the action under national law.

58 http://www.aftenposten.no/nyheter/iriks/--Beredskap-har-apenbart-gatt-ut-over-etterforskningen-7572205.html#.U4MztXY4VaQ [26.05.14].

59 Proximity and local police work is, of course, not unique to Norway. See e.g. Sheptycki 1995; Bayley 1985, Anderson *et al.* 1995:168. See Fredriksen 2014:373–5 on the different characteristics of 'public order' versus 'security' as grounds for the Norwegian police's coercive (but non-CPA) interference in the individual's personal life, and on the contents of the 'legal standard' of 'order'. He discusses, for example, how intervention must be based on a disturbance of public order, not merely a breach of general moral societal standards (pp.380–385). This is, of course, harder to assess for police officers who are not members of the community they police.

that is more oriented towards order policing can be said to amount to what could be called a rise of 'extraterritorial proximity policing', based on the proximity principle of the Norwegian police (this is returned to below).[59]

The modern welfare state may appear an updated version of historical conceptions of the well-ordered police state: it is an advanced bureaucracy with a complex state administration that has numerous directive and regulatory functions.[60] Such a view is in line with Neocleous's 'good police', to mean the reaffirming of general good order.[61] Changes in the purpose, methods and function of the police may be necessary to meet fast moving technical and social developments. The question is whether the changes made are ones that are wanted or expected by a particular society. There are signs that more repressive forms of control have taken place since the Norwegian Schengen cooperation came into force.

A securitisation trend started in the early 1990s. Securitisation entails an expansion of the security focus to include the security of the nation-state.[62] According to Buzan, security at the state level implies the absence of threats against the survival of the state itself – a fundamental need for communities as well as individuals.[63] Huysmans noted that security is often defined merely by its opposites: threats are described, but not the ideal secure situation.[64] The concept of 'societal security' also developed in this period, amid 'the new threats' assumed to be arising both internally, from society itself, and externally, from migrants.[65] Securitisation processes hinge on certain (professional) actors' construction of (statistical) 'truths', according to Bigo.[66] In the early 1990s too, international police cooperation measures and agreements really started to gain momentum. It is notable that it was only in the later stage of the negotiations on the drafting of the Schengen regulations that the security challenges of open borders were emphasised.[67]

The point argued here is that the development has been somewhat skewed, over-emphasising really serious, cross-border crime, at the expense of local crime which may also be very detrimental to people's lives. Arguably, this is part of a general trend towards contingency, 'hard', high-level policing, with less attention to, and perhaps less allocated resources for, proximity policing and run-of-the-mill policing tasks. Simultaneously, however, there has been a move to cross-border assistance in more low-level policing tasks, in the form of joint patrols. The development may also be seen as flawed because it disadvantages foreigners of various statuses, which seems contrary to how the cooperation agreements were initially presented.

The term 'security' has been defined and operationalised in a broader sense in later EU policy development,[68] erasing the traditional borders between foreign and security policy,

60 Raeff 1983:254.
61 Neocleous 2000.
62 Bigo 2000a:343.
63 Buzan 1991.
64 Huysmans 2006.
65 Buzan and Wæver 2003; Bigo 2000a:345.
66 Bigo 2000a. For the further security state theory, see Neocleous 2000; Walker 1993, Charbonneau 2008 ch.1, also Loader 2002a, and Anderson *et al.* 1995: especially p.175; 179.
67 A German representative of the Ministry of Interior inserted a reference to the security-deficit the reduction of border controls would lead to. The security deficit arguments gained momentum up to and during the negotiation of the second version, the CISA. When this was drafted, instead of transport and trade ministers, interior and justice ministers did the negotiating, assisted by working groups of mostly police experts (Parkin 2011:3; also e.g. Chapter 6.2).
68 NOU 2012:2 p.689. European Security Strategy 2003; 2008. See also Anderson *et al.* 1995 ch.5.

and justice and home affairs. Security measures include targeting crime; civil and military crisis management strategies; anti-terror politics; and general foreign and security policies. Despite the fact that only parts of the Union's work may be applied supranationally (as discussed previously), its influence is significant because of a growing body of mechanisms that may have a great impact on member states – on the lives of citizens as well as on the development of policies and regulations. Formerly, cross-border police cooperation, whether international, transnational, or including international bodies such as Europol, concerned only the most serious, organised crimes. I have argued that cross-border police cooperation measures and instruments now seem to cross over into public order policing.[69] The main purpose of the establishment of Europol was to target cross-border crime, that is, crime thought to have a European dimension.

The level of trust in the police is very high in Norway today.[70] Næshagen argues that one of the reasons for the long-standing tradition of democratic and 'proximate' policing has been the absence of internal conflicts and violence. Næshagen notes that, since the 14th century, there have been extremely few violent clashes between citizens and the authorities, and the few examples there are (three between the early 19th century and the early 20th century) resulted in hardly any physical damage.[71] One explanation of the general absence of conflict is the fact there were no major insider/outsider divisions.[72] Norway's relatively subordinate position in political unions for most of its history since 1300, created a very strong sense of in-group community within the country. There have always been Danes or Swedes to be the outsiders. A strong sense of solidarity has resulted from this. The pressing question is whether this traditionally strong mutual trust, and relatively peaceful community may be disrupted by external forces focusing on security threats that require a change to a different style of policing.

14.2.2 Threat assessments and the Norwegian perception of reality

A specific way of considering the where the police gaze should be directed, is through threat assessments. Such threat assessments are produced at national, regional and 'universal' levels, by national and international institutions (such as Kripos and Europol). They are designed to give practitioners and policymakers the best foundations for resource allocation and prioritisation in the crime control field.[73] These assessments can be seen as pure information, but also as a as a way of influencing the risk perceptions of readers. This is an important consideration, because how threats are defined is a central factor in what the community perceives as police tasks and obligations.[74]

69 De Moor and Vermeulen 2010a:1103. Loader also discusses this securitisation through the enhanced transnational policing capacity (Loader 2002a).

70 For example, Runhovde 2010; Thomassen *et al.* 2014.

71 Næshagen 2000; Johansen 1977. Somewhat different, though, in Dørum and Sandvik 2012, but this may be definition-dependent.

72 Barth 1996.

73 The importance of threat assessments when considering which police methods to apply was emphasised, for example, in NOU 1997:15 p.23.

74 In the Police Directorate's Crime Tendencies (*Kriminalitetsanalyse*) of 2014, the assessments of international organisations are mentioned as one of the report's sources. In the previous report, they were not mentioned. A more general reference to "analyses from our own and other departments, and information concerning international trends" may, however, mean the same. (PODs kriminalitetsanalyse 2010–2012; 2014.

In recent years there has been increasing emphasis on future risk assessments. Thus, instead of European Organised Crime *Reports,* there are Crime *Assessments* (emphasis added).[75] These are based on Europol's analysis work files, and on data from external partners, member states, third countries, Frontex and Eurojust, alongside various academic contributors.[76] According to Europol, these threat assessments are the basis for the development of an intelligence model of European policing.[77] One of Europol's obligations is to provide these annual threat assessments for the member states and EU bodies. They include recommendations on what to target in, for example, national crime prevention work.[78] Eurojust also contributes to the assessments. These Serious and Organised Crime Threat Assessments (SOCTA) are intended as strategic documents to aid and influence national and supranational decision-makers when identifying priorities. These then shape the operational work of law-enforcers nationally, regionally and locally. Until 2013, the reports focused on organised crime alone. Serious crime was included after the new multiannual policy cycle was established in 2013 to ensure effective cooperation between the "Member States' law enforcement agencies, EU Institutions, EU Agencies and relevant third parties in the fight against serious international and organised crime".[79]

The feeling of fear and insecurity is not necessarily directly related to actual dangers, and risks of crime; this is a classic criminological finding. Individuals' perception of their safety and welfare is dependent on many factors – both personal, such as sex and age, and cultural, that is how the world (including the local crime problem) is being presented.[80] Many different suppliers of information influence the perceived level of safety or crime. Media coverage is one important factor.[81] The national crime statistics are another, but these may be less easily understood and thus less accessible to the public.

In 2013, a new contributor to the assessments appeared: the COSI (the Standing Committee on Operational Cooperation on Internal Security). COSI is an EU Council body with a mandate to facilitate, promote and strengthen the coordination of EU states' operational work in the field of internal security. On the basis of threat assessments, the Council agrees on priorities for their work; since the 2011 assessment, eight priorities have been set for the period. These are then translated into strategic goals, and explicit projects are launched to coordinate the member states' and EU bodies' action in these policy areas.[82] Only MS' justice departments are admitted to the COSI meetings, only in the COSI Mix Committee, and thus allowed to influence the policy cycles. While the policy priorities established here are not binding for Europol MS, they are decisive for which areas Europol prioritises for funding. While this might be less important for Norway, funding may be an important factor in deciding which crime types and areas to tackle in less well-off countries in Europe. This may mean that motorcycle gang crime, for example, which is seen as a

75 Mitsilegas 2009:172.

76 SOCTA 2013:2.

77 EU Organised Crime Threat Assessment 2011 (File.no. 2530–274 28/4–11).

78 ED art.5 (1)f.

79 SOCTA 2013:9. The present policy cycle covers 2013–2017 and has four key steps: 1: SOCTA; 2: Policy-setting and decision-making (strategic and operational action plans overall and within the MS); 3: Implementation and monitoring of the action/plans in (2); and 4: Review and assessment – before the cycle starts over again.

80 Hindelang *et al.* 1978.

81 E.g. Cohen 1987; Jewkes *et al.* 2014.

82 SOCTA 2013:9. The eight projects for the period 2011–2013 were West Africa, the Western Balkans, Facilitated illegal immigration, Synthetic drugs, Smuggling in shipping containers, Human trafficking, Mobile (Itinerant) Organised Crime Groups and Cybercrime. See also den Boer and Monar 2002.

problem in Norway, but not prioritised in the EU, may not be tackled in Hungary or Portugal – although the issue could be dealt with more effectively by a cross-border approach.

A similar national coordination body (the *Samordningsorgan*) was established in Norway in 2010 to strengthen the national effort against serious and organised crime, especially organised cross-border crime.[83] The *Samordningsorgan* say their decisions are based primarily on national strategic analyses and steering documents.[84] This may mean they are less affected by international entities, but since the body is composed of the assistant chiefs of the Police Directorate, the Director General of Public Prosecution's office, and the heads of Kripos and the Oslo Police District, it may also be that the steering documents (instructions, etc.) have already been influenced by international assessments.

The reason for focusing on the actors creating threat assessments is that any assessment of the future is speculation. Arguably, the perception, experience and anticipation of threats and risk are dependent on the hegemonic group most able to enforce its views.[85] The threats believed most important by the EU may not correspond to those thought significant by individuals in a local area. Perceptions will undoubtedly vary in such a diverse area as Europe, Europol threat assessments have been criticised for being unreliable and irrelevant.[86] Another consideration is that organisations such as Europol and Interpol depend on their members believing that international policing is necessary to fight transnational crime. Thus awareness may need to be raised in the member states to ensure they participate at both policy and operational levels in the effort against trans- and international crime.[87] Without sufficient awareness, and/or too much confidence in their sovereign national ability to deal with crimes on their own, the member states may reduce the efficiency of the international police organisations. Thus, threat assessment is an important tool for raising awareness.

Fifteen years on, the European states are more closely connected, at many new levels, than at the time of the Committee's report of 1999. The international threat assessment reports assessing broader cross-border trends are arguably necessary to understand the Norwegian policing situation. It may, however, also be the case that these international reports on crime and disorder emphasise these issues disproportionately, at the expense of 'national characteristics' or trends that have gained less attention.[88]

An important thing to understand about threat assessments is that they employ an 'optic of fear', thereby creating a 'state gaze' that focuses on threats through a lens made elsewhere.[89] The state focus may then affect how reality is perceived by its citizens. Crime policies increasingly pass through transnational and global institutional channels.[90] The meaning of central terms, such as crime, security and police, are informed by the existing

83 Instruction of 12.05.2010, replaced by Instruction of 01.05.2013 (Samordningsorganets årsrapport 2014).

84 2014 report p.8.

85 Schumacher 2011:1.

86 van Duyne and Vander Beken 2009.

87 Gerspacher 2005:422–5; 433. Based on her interviews, Gerspacher also emphasises the importance of training and education from international police when it comes to raising concerns. See her article, which applies an organisation perspective, to the roles international police organisations take to maximise their utility and effectiveness, in contrast to or in cooperation with nation states.

88 Ot.prp.nr.56 (1998–1999):150. One of the changes suggested by the committee was the centralisation of border control resources. Such coordination was held to increase the efficiency and rationality of the control system. This change was eventually made, ten years later (NOU 2009:20).

89 Scott 1998.

90 Karstedt 2004.

legal and wider social culture. This should, of course, not be taken to imply that the information and perceptions in these assessments are wrong. Threat assessments from abroad should obviously be taken into consideration. They do, however, require active interpretation. They may help alter the relationship between citizens, state and police. This is not necessarily either good or bad, but its effects should, be studied and explicitly discussed. And this is not visible in Norwegian public or political debates over the past 20 years or so.

14.2.3 Security and order

When the 1912 Committee, working on the first Norwegian Police Act of 1927, discussed police responsibility for providing public order, they meant order in the broadest sense: whatever was necessary for social prosperity and safety. The police should protect society against all internal disruptive forces. The 1981 Aulie Committee's report, towards the 1995 Police Act, argued that this was far too wide an ambit. According to the Committee, it was 'unnatural' to give the police a task that would mean the surveillance of all law-abiding citizens.[91] It was further emphasised that the police's task of creating order was twofold. On the one hand, the police are expected to deliver a real situation of social safety and security; on the other, they should provide a *feeling* of security in the population.

It is generally agreed that the understanding of 'order' is specific to a particular time and place. Despite the contextual specificity of the term, it may nonetheless be useful to attempt to arrive at a more general understanding of its contents, to judge whether there are characteristics that constitute a Norwegian 'model', and whether a Norway-specific policing model is a necessary condition for, say, the emphasis on proximity policing. On the one hand, expression must be given to society's condemnation of certain *acts* (not individuals), and they must be punished in a way that society deems to be fair. Policing-wise, this is a challenging idea, because it emphasises the investigation, not the prevention of crime, and is blind to the impact of a crime, as long as 'society' perceives an act as offensive. On the other hand, prevention still had to be considered as part of the legislative mix. While police preventive efforts could stop crimes from happening, they could also extend state control into areas traditionally seen as outside the police ambit (such as schools and health care), and make the distinction between care, and control by a coercive police force harder to see.[92] Though the Norwegian police are still governed by national regulations, there may arguably be a tendency to move away from the traditional, locally oriented, civilian police force.

The majority fraction of the 1997 hearings underlined 'normality' in the CISA art.46.1: its wording is so similar to the 1995 Police Act sect.2 no.2 that it should only be seen as complementing, not changing, the ordinary tasks of the police.

Public order police cooperation is central to the Schengen cooperation, and the SIS regulations do indeed also focus on the prevention of threats to public order and security (CISA art.93). In contrast to the SIS cooperation, the investigation of transnational, more serious crime is the main purpose of other agreements and measures. Research has suggested that gathering and sharing information relevant to the policing of events like major sporting events, or important political meetings, was precisely what the Schengen regime was

91 NOU 1981:35 p.92–3.
92 Lorentzen 1981:232.

intended for.[93] Europol has also been involved in what may be termed 'transnational public order policing', as in the policing of protests and street demonstrations related to the G8 meetings in Gothenburg in 2001 and in Genoa in 2010.[94] Norway is not a full-fledged member of Europol, but we have just seen that this is not necessarily a significant hindrance. Norway still makes use of Europol information, also that which mainly is available through participation in Europol investigation groups. Operational international police cooperation often builds on information exchange, including the SIS: the various systems work alongside one another.

Even less serious crimes, such as burglaries and car thefts, are often seen as local manifestations of cross-border, international criminal networks that may necessitate "concerted European action".[95] Kvam argues that Europol cooperation was of less consequence for Norway than for the EU member states, since the threshold for Europol involvement is a serious criminal activity that affects two or more member states.[96] This wording excludes situations where the criminal activity in question concerns only Norway and one other EU state. One could, however, also argue that the EU would interpret most of the crimes within Europol's mandate as threats to the 'internal security' of the Schengen area. The EU Internal Security Strategy regards various forms of organised crime as the first of the "most urgent challenges to EU [internal] security". In this context, it is difficult to imagine cases where the Norwegian authorities would have an interest in cooperation with international police on crime that did not in some respect concern more than two states. It seems, rather, that international policing may extend into the local sphere in more cases than originally intended.

One area where the focus of international police cooperation has obviously shifted, is in the development of Europol competences: formerly, they concerned only serious, organised crime, but now even Europol may be involved in order policing. Different procedures and rules may be applicable, depending on whether the cooperative work with Europol, or 'through' Europol, has an investigative or preventive purpose (e.g. public order policing), but, either way, Kripos remains the national contact point. No matter if the police work is formally subject to the Director of Public Prosecutions, the Police Directorate, or the Ministry of Justice, Kripos is still the responsible party.[97] The purpose involved may generally be said to determine whether a police activity should be seen as investigative or not. This question is important because there are different rights and regulations associated with different kinds of police work, and the kind of measures involved. Among the issues that arise is the question whether specific criminal procedure legislation is applicable both to the rights of the subject and the procedures of the acting law enforcement authorities, or whether administrative law and procedures, especially the Police Act and the Police Register Act, should be applied instead.[98]

It may be difficult to draw a line between investigation and preventive police work when the police are dealing, for instance, with crimes such as those associated with major political meetings or football matches.[99] It is noteworthy that complaints cannot be made about a

93 De Moor and Vermeulen 2010b.
94 Op.cit.
95 COM(2010) 673 final:4, see also den Boer and Bruggeman 2011:144–9.
96 Kvam 2008:136.
97 E.g. Rieber-Mohn 1996; Torgersen 2011.
98 RA 99–238.
99 Myhrer 2001; Wold 2004:60.

police decision on the execution of measures with a general peace and order purpose, nor does a police officer need to justify his decision to the subject in such cases.[100] There are few possibilities for control and legal oversight in this type of policing, which t may have quite a significant impact on the public life of many individuals. A Latvian police officer might well arrest a Latvian citizen in downtown Oslo, without that person, or any bystanders being given the right to demand an explanation, or lodge a complaint about the decision (unless there is police brutality, which may, of course, still be reported to the Norwegian Bureau for the Investigation of Police Affairs [SEFO]).

The maintenance of public order is a different objective than that of preventing and combating crime, even though they overlap in practice.[101] De Moor and Vermeulen point out that the principle of speciality, according to which powers are assigned for a particular purpose, is threatened when international police are used to (or themselves decide to) act outside their proper framework or competence.[102] Actions may breach rules and regulations concerning, for example, data protection specific to the entity. Before the Europol Decision, assistance with public order policing was considered incompatible with Europol's objective, i.e. in breach of the purpose specification principle.[103] Europol has now, however, a legal basis for providing intelligence and analytical support in connection with major international events with a public order policing impact.[104]

Several analyses of Europol and other forms of international police cooperation criticise the shift in policing emphasis.[105] Most international police work or cooperation focuses on 'high policing functions'. The problem, as Anderson notes, is that the growth of proactive methods – in other words, clandestine and undercover methods – at the European level may inspire increased use of them on the national level. Areas of policing previously seen as 'ordinary' may now warrant 'extraordinary measures'.[106] These observations by Anderson *et al.* were made as early as 1995, before international police cooperation had really gained momentum. They may be said to have had a certain prophetic quality.

International or supranational extraterritorial proximity policing may not be particularly successful. Sheptycki suggests three reasons for why changes in policing may contribute to growing levels of social anxiety and fear of crime and insecurity.[107] A change 'from above' takes place because police are used to dealing with certain transnational crimes. By contrast, the rise of 'intelligence-led' policing, which uses a wide range of technological developments, is a change 'from within'. The marketisation of security, with a growing middle-class able to pay for private security provision, changes the police 'from below'. Seen in combination, these changes may distract attention from wider social, economic and political factors which may underlie. transnational organised crime.

What all this *does not* mean is that if Norway had more sovereign authority in policing matters, and was less influenced by the outside world, the police regulations described

100 Forvaltningsloven sects.24 and 28 cf. its directive (Forvaltningslovforskriften) sects.21(b) and 30(b).

101 Sheptycki has even argued that there has been a quiet revolution in favour of transnational rather than local policing (Sheptycki 2002; Sheptycki 1995).

102 De Moor and Vermeulen 2010a:1103.

103 Op.cit.:1103.

104 [2016] OJ L 135/53 art.4(1) e.

105 E.g. Bowling and Sheptycki 2012:65–66.

106 Anderson *et al.* 1995:175; 179.

107 Sheptycki 2002:145.

above would be completely different. It does not mean that the Norwegian police would be strictly 'proximity based', and based mainly on forms of social control other than coercion. Societies, technologies and mobility are changing, and require the mechanisms and measures of policing to change too. On the other hand, a better understanding of which interests are actually being promoted, and of which should be regarded as important for Norway as a community, may shed light on the policing situation. This may be likened to Christie's idea of the benefits of informal, primary social control, in contrast to the more formal secondary control exercised by the police, the courts, etc.[108] Christie criticises the development of the modern social order because it tends to lessen the effect of primary control, which is less intrusive and more accurate than secondary control. In his view, a low level of primary control creates an assumption that some problems can only be solved by the police.[109] This, in turn may engender impotence when it comes to dealing with one's own problems in a constructive manner, and an increase in the fear of crime, and other problems, that one needs experts to deal with. This may also be relevant to the discussion of the relationship between the fear of crime and actual crime rates.[110] In the early 19th century, it was seen as vital for the cultivation of a strong sense of trust in the police that the most local police, the *lensmen* were always seen to be the highest authorities in their communities. It would, it was thought, break down trust between the community and the *lensman* service if this were challenged by non-local ('outsider') police officials.[111] Does this line of reasoning – old-fashioned though it may seem – apply to situations where foreign police officers take part in, or autonomously carry out, local policing tasks?

We may start from the assumption that proximity policing is the Norwegian way, and vital to the success of Norwegian policing. A clear criticism of Christie's arguments is that he overlooks the fact that certain problems are impossible to solve by means of informal primary control.[112] The question is whether international cross-border crime simply cannot be dealt with within the framework of traditional national police structures and policies, however desirable this might be. In societies where they are quick to exercise social control, people are also more inclined to want and use formal control instruments such as the police. While the fact that states cannot act 'autonomously' implies increased police cooperation, one could argue that, in the case of. more repressive joint police cooperation measures, or increased harmonisation leading to harsher sentences, Olaussen's assertion that more primary control also implies a high level of secondary control, means that there will be less cooperation and influence from below.

This chapter has addressed the issue of what how the development of operational police cooperation regulations and measures may be said to impact the Norwegian police. To summarise, there may be several effects of international cooperation regulations and operations for the Norwegian police. Europol is a key example of a move towards an increased impact from cooperation on national policing. It has been argued that police cooperation, and measures and instruments generally introduced from elsewhere may lead to more punitive solutions and greater repression, even when these are not necessarily what

108 Christie 1995:28–30.

109 Christie 2006:65.

110 Sheptycki 2002:142.

111 Ot.prp.nr.59 (1920):52.

112 Olaussen 2007. He also underscores the collective legitimacy of secondary control mechanisms inherent in police and courts, in contrast to the far more subjective primary control (mechanisms) (Durkheim 1933:64; 96).

Norwegian society requires for the best possible balance between security and freedom. The 'soft' impact of international or foreign threat assessments that are increasingly applied in the development of national security and policing may have a significant impact not only on perceptions of risk and crime control needs within society, but also on the way the state understands its citizens' needs. And this, in total, I argue, can be seen as a possible challenge to Norwegian sovereignty, in the sense that it changes the state's ability to define the police situation within its territory.

15 Impact on Norwegian society

The etymological meaning of *polizei* or *police* implies binding rules given for the benefit of the community (*gute polizey*). What was beneficial was not based on democratic decision-making rationality, but on the expectations one might reasonably have of a good prince.[1] Today, the citizens' acceptance of the democratically negotiated powers of the state in criminal matters grants legitimacy to state power. This in turn reinforces sovereignty translated into the capacity of the state to impose power.[2] Thus there is a demarcated territory, an ultimate sovereign, and a people constituting the sovereign. The people, a nation, comes into being in various ways: one might be a common perception of what constitutes risks and dangers that bind people together through the creation of insider/outsider categories[3]. A common perception that significant risks and dangers are beyond the capacity of the nation-state to handle, may lead citizens to lose trust in the national sovereign as a supplier of security. Sovereign power may have less to do with territory than with authority.[4] Hence it is not impossible that the EU could be a sovereign, a good prince, if it is competent to carry out the citizens' will and create security. Assuming there are some security threats, such as cross-border crimes, for which the EU is a better criminal justice actor than nation-states might be, does the notion of the EU as a sovereign criminal justice actor present any problems?

There has been a substantial increase in the number of EU and Schengen police cooperation measures. The previous chapter discussed the effects this development has had or may have on the Norwegian police, and their role in the future. There is a close connection between effects on the police, and consequences for citizens. In this final chapter I will addresses my fourth and final research question:

> *In what ways may the development of operational police cooperation regulations and measures impact on Norwegian society and the Norwegian public?*

More specifically, I will discuss issues such as whether citizens' (i.e. understood as the population legitimizing the sovereign) capacity to make informed decisions about policing policies and practices is diminished when the EU, an entity further removed from the general Norwegian public, becomes an important decision-making arena. To what extent

1 Nuotio 2004:178.; Stolleis 1988:369 ff.
2 Mitsilegas 2009:321.
3 In line with Beck 1992; Durkheim 1933.
4 Agnew 2009 ch.2.

DOI: 10.4324/9780429503696-17

are current developments in the international police cooperation field based on citizens' experience of increased cross-border crime? In what ways may this affect the composition of relevant insider/outsider categories from the point of view of the Norwegian public? And do the developments described in this book influence the legal standing of Norwegian citizens vis-à-vis domestic and foreign police forces? My hypothesis is that when the function and organisation of the police changes, the service offered to the population will change as a result.

15.1 The public

EU regulations and cooperation instruments allow police and justice authorities in several countries to investigate individuals or groups suspected of cross-border crime, or crimes that may have connections to other countries. The international police cooperation this facilitates makes it harder for suspects to know where they may claim their fundamental procedural human rights. Practical issues may arise: if investigatory steps are being taken in several countries, when and where are they entitled to a defence lawyer? Instruments protecting citizens' rights in criminal proceedings have been extremely hard to produce – far harder than the repressive measures states can take. EU measures, for instance, include subjecting citizens via EAWs to foreign jurisdictions for freedom of expressing opinions which are criminalised abroad. This was the case with Holocaust denial in Denmark.[5] In transnational trials, the balance between the prosecution and the individual's resources is upset. Europol and Eurojust may even fund Joint Investigation Teams, which requires resources that an individual can rarely match when preparing for a court trial.[6] This is not an infringement of sovereignty, but could be said to challenge the fundamental values of a state's constitution.

On the other hand, if an Area of EU criminal justice has been established, it is beneficial to citizens that a supranational court and regulations ensure that procedural and other human rights are attended to, even if people are arrested and promptly extradited to another EU member state, or if their personal data is exchanged between national police authorities.

The EU area of criminal justice is primarily concerned with serious cross-border crime, and the notion of seriousness has always raised serious problems of definition, since it is interpreted differently in the various states. This may be problematic in that EU criminal justice has different effects in different countries, and this might result in legal uncertainty – for police, individuals and states.

15.1.1 Repressive effects

Since the 1980s, internal security has increasingly been interpreted as including the fight against organised crime. This change of focus has made the protection of citizens from external threats a core concern.[7] Organised crime, then, is, seen as an important outside threat.

It has been argued that the new, collective experience of crime and general insecurity is related to factors other than the actual crime level. Garland describes how late modern

5 E.g. CF Decision amending 2002/475/JHA; Wade 2013:64, also Sassen 2008.

6 Wade 2013.

7 Ahnfelt and From 1996:30; 285, Anderson 1994.

communities have developed a culture of crime control where an ever-increasing crime rate is perceived to be a 'fact of life'. It is seen as so obvious that this state of affairs will continue that the threshold for intervention in public and private space is significantly lowered.[8] Garland's analysis draws on Beck's notion of late modern societies as 'risk societies', characterised by citizens' sense of omnipresent risks and dangers that they and their states are largely powerless to ward off.[9] One way of interpreting the proliferation of police cooperation instruments is that states are attempting to respond to risk perceptions by promoting a tougher and more active attitude towards crime. This, in turn, may signal the beginning of a shift from Norway's traditional welfare society, to a social order more in line with the ideas promoted in the international cooperation project of market liberalism. From that perspective, crime control is more efficient and more valued than other ways of dealing with problems in society.

It has also been argued that no particularly new types of crime arose in the period when the police cooperation project started making real headway, and that there must have been other reasons for the increased emphasis on certain types of crime. Anderson pointed out that organised crime was seen as a 'novelty' in the internal security debate in the EU, and that four factors contributed to this: 1) The realisation that the 'war on drugs' had been lost meant that new methods should be attempted, e.g. more international police cooperation. 2) The changes post-1989 in the relationship between eastern and western Europe, and the increasing focus on the rising threat from the east posed by mafia-like organisations and organised crime. Ahnfelt and From argue that such changes can generally be understood as linked to major social changes.[10] The military threat from the east, then, has been replaced by a crime threat, along with an increasing flow of immigrants that the Iron Curtain used to keep out of Europe. 3) The general increase in reported crime – and in the fear of crime – within the EU. Open borders and increased interaction may in themselves lead to increased insecurity, and such insecurity could challenge the whole Union project. 4) Finally, Europol as a European police force, with or without supranational powers and jurisdiction has itself had an impact.[11] Ahnfelt and From's study concludes that police cooperation has been driven by various public and political projects, not a general increase in risk and crime.[12]

The term 'harmonisation' is often used in relation to the goal of creating coherence between EU member states' regulations. 'Harmonisation' and 'approximation' are used interchangeably[13] either way, the intention is to bring national legal systems closer together and make them more similar.[14]

Harmonisation of crime control and police practices may also be seen as bringing the citizens of Europe closer together; it may even contribute to the development of a common European identity. The desire to make a given area more harmonious may make external boundaries more important. The closer the residents of the Schengen/EU Area are, the more they feel like members of a community, the more they will exclude 'outsiders', who

8 Garland 2001.
9 Beck 1992.
10 Ahnfelt and From 1996:31, also Knepper 2011 arguing that this is nothing new.
11 Anderson 1994.
12 Ahnfelt and From 1996:33.
13 Both terms are used in e.g. TFEU art.67.
14 Mitsilegas 2009:59.

do not belong to it. It is a basic sociological insight that community and similarity within a group is constituted and strengthened by differentiating and excluding an outsider group.[15]

From this perspective, an increased focus on transnational crimes and the risks connected to mobility, strangers and open borders, may diminish the safety, security and welfare of those who are not insiders, and not part of the harmonisation project.[16] Whether it is right or not to differentiate between insiders and outsiders in this way, may be contested, but history shows that such a divide is inevitable when limited resources (in the widest sense of the term) are being allocated. The issue of the 'final goal' of the Schengen project arises: How do you strike a balance between efficiency regarding security and control, and the ideal of a calmer and more orderly society? It has been argued that security provision is not a zero-sum game. This is not true when security or order measures include human or material resources; in such cases, welfare as well as security goals may well run up against resource restrictions. And it is a convincing argument that Høigård makes; the Nordic policing model is linked to the strong and generous Nordic welfare states.[17] The question is then whether the harmonisation with the EU community's understanding of necessary or appropriate police and repression, constitutes an unwanted impact on the Norwegian community's understanding of this. Not least when the influence – as shown in *forarbeid* and the political framing of Schengen, and the EEA for that matter, was clearly mainly economic.

On the question of whether harmonisation may lead to increased repression, it is argued here that differences in criminalisation, and in imprisonment rates may be seen as gauges of general differences between countries. The original purpose of the EU was economic cooperation, albeit with peacekeeping mixed in. The EEC member states committed themselves to creating equal legislation on national areas that affected international trade. Today, there are extensive regulations on forms of cooperation that go a lot further than economic matters. These developments, and the general EU spirit of harmonisation, also influence Norway and the Norwegian police.

TFEU art.67(1) proclaims that the European Union constitutes an Area of Freedom, Security and Justice, where the fundamental rights of citizens, and the member states' legal traditions and systems are respected. To achieve a high level of security in the Union Area, measures should be taken to prevent and fight crime, via coordination and cooperation between police and other law enforcement authorities, and mutual recognition of law enforcement decisions, and – if necessary – by approximation of national penal law (art.67[3]).

Harmonisation and cooperation require a measure of common understanding of the issues and concepts involved. The core characteristics of many types of crime are generally agreed upon. For others, such as terrorism, there is consensus on the gravity of the crime. Nevertheless, it has proved difficult to agree on a general definition of the *mens* and *actus reus*, and on the kinds of related activity that should be criminalised, and the level of punishment.[18] Terrorism may have hideous outcomes, and the necessary law enforcement tools

15 Barth 1996.

16 'Globalisation' refers here to closer interaction throughout the world, both in terms of economic trade, easier communication and migration between countries, and generally increased international and transnational cooperation (e.g. Aas 2007, Bauman 1998; Sassen 2008).

17 Høigård 2011.

18 Elholm shows for example that where Sweden and Finland set a maximum penalty of six years based on a framework decision, Denmark set eight years (Elholm 2009:221). Such minor differences are seen within the Nordic countries. One may expect variations throughout the EU to be greater.

should be available to prevent it. However, the criminalisation of acts related to a terrorist offence, such as purchasing large quantities of fertiliser that could be used to make bombs, raises various issues. Deciding which actions to criminalise, what stage in a presumed preparation cycle should be the threshold for criminalisation, and which preventive measures the police may apply in pre-emptive investigation (i.e. before there has been any criminal activity as normally understood), are difficult elements in the general balancing of civil rights and security. The core question is what level of repressive control a given society considers acceptable, to protect the security and safety of the state, the community and individual citizens.

Den Boer and Doelle compared the convergence between national police forces in Europe in the late 1990s and early 2000s to examine the degree of 'communitarisation' resulting from the intensification of EU police cooperation in the late 1990s.[19] On the basis of reports from 14 EU member states, they found that, although the different states retained significant and persistent characteristics, a process of approximation was taking place. This would, they argued, follow a pattern of variable geometry and incremental logic, that is, it would vary in much the same way as the states themselves vary.[20] Since then, the pace of harmonisation and approximation through police cooperation instruments has quickened. The level of crime control can be said to signify the level of general state repression. And differences in crime control levels may be an important part of the variations between states that cooperate on policing and crime control.

A common way of measuring the level of crime control in a country is to compare its prison population with those of other countries.[21] The number of police officers per capita could also be used as a gauge, but since police organisations are so diverse, these are more difficult to compare than prison rates.

Between 1950 and 2006, the prison population in Norway and Sweden rose from about 50 to about 75 per 100,000 inhabitants.[22] The Dutch, and English and Welsh prison populations increased from around 50 to 150 per 100,000 inhabitants in the same period, while the German population has been quite stable, at around 100 per 100,000. Newer EU members have higher rates: Latvia, the Czech Republic and Poland have, respectively, prison populations of 314, 220, and 218 per 100,000.[23] There are many reasons for the differences, some historical, and to do with national cultures, but some, as Lacey argues, to do with government structures.[24] While all the European states are democratic, the economic management objectives in governance are different. Arguably the intensified focus on EU cooperation based on economic principles (both at Schengen and EEA levels) may help move management objectives in this direction. According to Lacey, the variation between states in economic, political and governance structures is so great that they are impervious to significant outside influence. Her discussion compares the US and Western Europe. The

19 den Boer and Doelle 2002.

20 See also Walker 2000.

21 Not an uncontroversial gauge (see e.g. Nelken 2010 for criticism). The prison population may, of course, be a measure of many other issues, for example, something as basic as the level of inequality within the society.

22 The numbers are based on statistics from the International Centre for Prison Studies' World Prison Brief, available at http://www.prisonstudies.org/ [01.07.2014]. See also Cavadino and Dignan 2006, Christie 1993 and Wacquant 2009.

23 The figure for the US is 750 per 100,000, and Rwanda and Russia are in 2nd and 3rd place, with 595 and 568 respectively. See also Ugelvik 2014.

24 Lacey 2008:55 ff. The same conclusions on non-convergence between US and UK crime control policies are drawn by Jones and Newburn 2004.

resemblances between EU member states are arguably greater than those between the EU and the US, and these resemblances may facilitate harmonisation. Whatever may be intended, globalisation and systems for cooperation themselves lead to a certain degree of similarity. The question is which state or international entity will represent the ideal that others seek to emulate, and in which context.

Imprisonment rates suggest that Europe in general is becoming more repressive. One reason may be financial: the resources of the welfare system are being spent on an influx of black market workers – many of them migrants. This may lead to a decrease in the general level of welfare provisions. Lacey argues the change from welfare to workfare in the US implied a greater use of control and registration practices.[25] We will now examine whether more repressive European societies may be seen as inimical to the original ideas behind Norwegian participation in the EEA and Schengen cooperation, because selective security is promoted at the expense of free travel and circulation.

15.1.2 Policing, security and immigration control

Imprisonment rates and the general purposes of punishment may impact how threats and risks are perceived in a society, and thus influence the demands made of the police force. While the ten principles of the Norwegian police are part of what is deemed to be the police service 'needed' by the community (Police Act sect.1), the current concerns of the population must also be taken into account. So far, the focus has been on harmonisation and general repression as possible consequence of increased police cooperation. Are there, though, particular individuals or groups that are being targeted as a consequence of the cooperation instruments? Most European states have, to varying extents, seen an increase in their prison populations in recent years. The increase has (in Western Europe) disproportionately affected non-citizens and non-ethnic citizens of the states.

15.1.2.1 Circulation and mobility

The oft-reiterated traditional (Norwegian) welfare-oriented goals of reintegration and rehabilitation are now ignored. Questions of inclusion and exclusion are of course highly significant for understanding the concepts in the Police Act sect.1; 'citizens' are emphasised before others, and the 'community' seems to be reserved for those who 'initially' belonged there.

The proportion of foreign nationals in the Norwegian prison population has increased significantly in recent years.[26] Even allowing for a certain police bias, one must assume that a substantial amount of crime is being committed by people who were not born in the Norwegian community mentioned in the Police Act sect.1.[27] There may also be a perception of foreigners as *risky*, a perception that may lead to calls for more action by the state and police.[28] Globalisation processes are linked to risk perception in the risk society.[29]

25 Wacquant 2009; Lacey 2008:131.

26 Ugelvik 2014.

27 Repression levels do not seem to decrease under the influence of other countries or cultures (as I have discussed elsewhere: Ugelvik 2012). 'Looking to Scandinavia' seems to be a trend in international penal policies, but the trend seems not (yet) to be leading to substantial outcomes.

28 Garland 2001.

29 Beck 1992; Beck 2009, see also Mitsilegas 2012.

As shown above, the EEA, the EU and (to an extent) the Schengen cooperation had as their main purpose the improvement of economic relations between the member states, albeit with variations, and by means of different instruments. Arguably the fact that these international organisations and cooperation mechanisms have become as significant as they undoubtedly have, is because of their overarching focus is on trade, markets and capital. More neo-liberal societies may adopt less inclusive social structures:[30] those who cannot take part in economic life (by paying taxes) may be not be valued. While increased circulation was intended to further free travel and trade (i.e. capitalist purposes), its consequences have neo-liberal aspects, and thus an increased level of mobility control. The change in what is in focus may be seen as also problematic for policing, since the increased focus on organised and international crime seems to put more people from certain groups in prison. Making the reintegration of the offender into society the main penal purpose is called into question if large groups of offenders are not seen as belonging in the first place.[31] How is reintegration work to be carried out if society does not want to welcome the offender back into its midst? This challenges the liberal democratic principle that punishment should have a purpose other than simple incapacitation.[32] Non-citizens can more easily be imprisoned to prevent them from committing crime while they are incarcerated. This is also the purpose explicitly given by the Ministry for the recent increase in sentences for immigration crimes.[33] From a wider perspective, the justification and purpose of punishment are perhaps becoming increasingly instrumental.

The modern police developed to deal with increased circulation and urbanisation in the cities of Europe in the 18th and 19th centuries.[34] In modern times, the four freedoms of the EU – particularly the free movement of people – seem to resemble this circulation. The open European market is designed to facilitate circulation between member states in a delimited market. Increased circulation means that the social control mechanisms that exist in smaller, more enclosed and stable communities, are weakened. Increased circulation brings both economic benefits and challenges to security.

The four freedoms, especially since Schengen, establish new forms of circulation that could be seen as a new type of 'city structure'.[35] Thus the Schengen area is a kind of city, where goods and people freely circulate, and where Norway is one borough among many. The circulation in the city, between boroughs, and from the suburbs and rural areas into the centre, is more extensive than before. This parallel is drawn here to question the meaning of the term 'community' in the Police Act. There is a growing tension between the local and national community (the intended meaning of the term in the Police Act), and the internationalised community that exists because of open borders, common policies and international agreements. In terms of the city metaphor, the 'new' European migration to more prosperous countries like Norway is hardly surprising. However understandable it is, though, such mobility is not always welcome: The Norwegian Vagrancy Act of 1900, abolished in the 1990s, is now being reconsidered for reinstatement, because foreigners 'are taking advantage' of the EEA and Schengen rules on free movement, without being qualified for proper (tax-paying) employment. According to many politicians, the high number

30 Lacey 2008.
31 Young 1999, Garland 2001.
32 E.g. St.meld.nr.37 (2007–2008).
33 Innst. 48 L (2013–2014).
34 As shown above (in particular 1.2.3), see e.g. Dubber 2005:3; ch.3; Anners 1997:25 ff.
35 See also Marx 1997.

of beggars and buskers of foreign origin is problematic.[36] The 'migrant issue' and the pressing need to control them and deal with the (potential or actual) social problems they represent, is nothing new, as is clear from police reports in the early 20th century.

There are clear parallels to be drawn between these earlier times of industrialisation and urbanisation and today's Schengen development. The migration from countryside to cities that happened then is paralleled today by migration across territorial borders. Improved communication and more open structures give more people opportunities, while social differences between individuals and groups are more visible. Mobility and early city planning led to the invention of the modern police forces. Will increased circulation in the Schengen area lead to a similar watershed in control mechanisms?[37] People and goods are *supposed* to circulate; circulation may be understood as a common good, and mobility and circulation seen as a general social resource "advancing all humanity", as Levi put it.[38] Nevertheless, when circulation is an important part of the structure of the city (state, or area), obstructions to circulation may be experienced as diminishing welfare, and even as reducing security. The police purpose in Norway is, as described, to prevent and stop threats to the community as a whole.[39] As Foucault said: "The object of police is everything from being to well-being . . . the well-being of individuals is the state's strength."[40] It may, however, be difficult to establish which individuals who are part of the state's responsibility – but also, in the sovereignty perspective, which individuals constitute the strong state.

One might expect those being controlled by the police, and having their freedom of movement restricted, to have a perception of 'outsiderness' – more or less deliberate exclusion from the core community.[41] This might be seen in relation to the experience of the legitimacy of crime control: the legitimacy of legislation (and the state's power in general) is dependent on its being based on an autonomous decision by citizens in a proper election.[42] Police control exercised on the basis of the legislation is heteronomous, but legitimate to the extent that it takes place in accordance with previously accepted regulations. Citizens do not need to accept arrest by the police for an action that is not illegal. But as a citizen, according to social contract theory, one more or less automatically accepts the regulations, including the criminal law, set by the state.[43] According to contract theory, one must also accept the contract following voluntary entry into other states. This does not, though, require that the state's legislation is recognised as just or reasonable. And this is one of the reasons why the impact of police work is so important.[44]

What about cases when the link between state and citizens seems less clear? International conventions and agreements extend the scope for police action, and the police's duty to act, both nationally and internationally. This being so, should the group referred to in the Norwegian Police Act, the group that national or international police forces must protect

36 For example, http://www.agderposten.no/nyheter/vil-gjeninnfore-losgjengerloven-1.7786764 [23.04.13]; http://www.aftenposten.no/nyheter/iriks/Hoyre-vil-forby-tigging-6821935.html [23.04.13].

37 Scott 1998.

38 Levi 2008:178–82. Following Foucault, the police's early core responsibility was linked to controlling the active circulation of individuals, because this increases the state's resources, capacities and the general control of the territory: what he calls "splendour" (Foucault 2007 ch.12).

39 PA sects.1 cf. 7,10–12 (Auglend *et al.* 2004:401).

40 Foucault 2007:328.

41 Turner 2007.

42 Beetham 1991.

43 Dubber 2005.

44 See also Zedner 2006.

and control, be enlarged or narrowed? The community in question, one may argue, is no longer delimited to include or even prefer only the Norwegian citizens.[45] It seems, from the perspective of international obligations, difficult to argue that the Norwegian police have a greater commitment to the welfare of Norwegian citizens than to that of foreigners on Norwegian territory.

According to Garland, the new 'culture of control' associated with crime control in the risk society also diminishes trust between citizens, and between citizens and the state. Prison rates may also be seen as indications of the sorts of crime and other social problems the police prioritise, and are able to 'see'.[46] Thus, there may be distortions embedded in police control that, together with other significant structural factors, mean there is systematic differentiation between insiders and outsiders that favours insiders.[47] Lacey suggests that issues concerning citizens are redefined as welfare issues, while criminal sanctions are more often imposed on immigrants and foreigners.[48] Foreign residents are disproportionately represented in crime statistics,[49] but this does not necessarily say anything about the level of crime among Norwegian citizens. There are wide variations between different groups of migrants in terms of being imprisoned: obviously the number of people in prison for immigration-related crime will vary according to the numbers migrating from different countries.

The police are increasingly used in the control of mobility, and many of the offences foreigners are charged with relate to exploitation of open borders.[50] States now control crime to do with illegal mobility to a greater degree than before. This development was certainly not an important justification for the opening of borders post-Schengen membership. Even though the EU project was first and foremost an economic project, it has had important social and peacekeeping side purposes, but may it also lead to increased social differences? Mobility-related crime is a foreseeable consequence of the EU and Schengen; and it makes it challenging for the various nation states to consider the responsibilities to non-citizens. If one recalls the purposes of punishment mentioned above, it could be argued that, if foreseeable crime and disorder result from the abolition of border control,[51] nation states have an extra obligation to non-citizens. Perhaps there should be ways of dealing with these challenges that include positive differentiation? Instead, there are ever louder popular demands for stricter controls on immigration and on crime associated with this particular group. The unintended consequence of the EU and Schengen projects seems to be the creation of an insider versus outsider split as regards the right to freedom, security and justice.

Cultural schemas in the media involve 'dangerous foreigners' rather than national criminals.[52] There are other tendencies, however: a recent directive from the Romerike Police District resulted from the fact that too many unresolved cases concerned family violence and rape; the directive ordered the police in the district to halt all other investigations, and shelve all action on a long list of crimes, such as theft (also aggravated), car theft, fraud,

45 These issues have been discussed in a similar vein by, for example, Bowling and Sheptycki 2012 and Duff 2007.
46 Statistics Norway on the police's role in who are imprisoned: Stene 2002.
47 Lacey 2008:123 ff.; Wacquant 2009; Sollund 2007.
48 Lacey 2008:129.
49 Skarðhamar *et al.* 2011.
50 According, at least, to Wacquant 2009 (French numbers).
51 E.g. Innst. 48 L (2013–2014).
52 See also Cere, Jewkes and Ugelvik 2013.
53 Rundskriv 2014/03683-3502.

simple drug offences and order disturbances.[53] This may strengthen the worry that prioritising cross-border policing and more serious transnational crimes takes away the resources from what actually concerns Norwegian citizens and police.

15.1.2.2 Immigration control and police work: Legitimate differentiation?

The abolition of internal border control in the Schengen Area changed the role of the police: while they have always had responsibilities for controlling strangers and foreigners, this responsibility became more important when borders could no longer be controlled.[54] The Police Act says the state must provide the police *needed* by the community. The needs seem altered by the changed border control regime. Arguably it is increasingly hard to determine what sort of policing effort is 'needed' as the population becomes more heterogeneous. The outcomes of policing may not be answering the needs of an increasingly diverse Norwegian society.

The concepts of the nation-state and of citizenship are inherently discriminatory.[55] And while immigration control is discriminatory, this is generally considered a legitimate form of discrimination, relating to states' responsibility to care for and control citizens. This does not necessarily mean it is legitimate seen in relation to the purposes set out in the Police Act.

A central police task that is not clearly described in the Police Act is participation in immigration control, which is part of the wider task of external Schengen border control. The Schengen cooperation prohibits, with a few exceptions, controls by the Norwegian state on travellers going to and from other Schengen countries. Control may take place, however, at a sufficient distance from the borders.[56] For example 'regular immigration control' permits the police to "stop a person and request proof of identity when there is reason to assume that the person in question is a foreign national and the time, place and situation give grounds for such a check".[57] This provision, then, gives the police the opportunity to stop and check anyone that looks 'different' or 'non-Norwegian' in the city streets, although there should be some other grounds for checking, such as time, place or situation.[58]

The territorial borders are thus drawn inside Norwegian territory, or even everywhere, as Lyon[59] and others have stated. Immigration control happens within the territory, to protect the Norwegian state, Norwegian citizens and – one must assume – others with legal residence permits. The Circular on foreign control stresses that such control should be incorporated into the general crime-fighting activities of the police.[60]

The police's role today, then, involves crime control, immigration control, and being the friendly face of the welfare state. This role is not just paradoxical; it could be considered

54 Another interesting discussion that is not in focus here, would be the similar implications for the customs authorities, who have taken over some of the former responsibilities of the border police.

55 Bosniak 2006.

56 [2004] OJ L 158/77 art.21.

57 Immigration Act 2008 sect.21. It follows from sect.22 that the police are responsible for border control in general, and that any foreigner that arrives from a third country must report to the police or border office (sect.14[2]). The latter will normally be the National Police Immigration Service (PU).

58 Ot.prp. nr. 75 (2006–2007):410–11. The provisions are meant to clarify the requirements on when the police should perform immigration control. It does not regulate when a police officer may perform 'policiary control' outside of immigration control.

59 Lyon 2005.

60 Circular 2001/021 pt.2.

impossible, when the purposes are so diverse and the target group unclear. The purpose of the Immigration Act is to regulate immigration: to control entry and exit, residence and expulsion, and foreigners' security under the law (sect.1). The official translation of the Immigration Act sect.1 uses the words "ensure legal protection", in contrast to "security under the law", the phrase used to translate sect.1 of the Police Act. Both phrases express the Norwegian word *rettssikkerhet*. There is no indication in the policy documents that that they have different legal meanings.[61]

The target group (including citizens of EU, and third country nationals?) of the Police Act may be said to have changed since the Schengen dissolution of border controls. This has a bearing on the implications of the word 'needed' in the Police Act sect.1, I argue, because members of Norwegian society have different perceptions of, say, the value of security or the ability to circulate. Should some needs be only those of citizens? An often reiterated argument is that welfare state benefits are something citizens have paid for through taxation. Even the wealthy Norwegian state has to set priorities, and 'as much security as possible' is an impossible goal. The issue at stake, then, is how far it is reasonable to balance security, seen by many as a 'universal' good against resource considerations. And again, the internal sovereignty of ability to maintain order and security in the territory: in whose interest is this?

If one reads the Norwegian Police Act from this point of view, one may identify a certain hierarchy in the candidates for the protection of the Norwegian state. In the context of policing there is no division between citizens, but there is a division between the citizens of Norway, citizens of EEA countries, and citizens of third countries. It is unclear whether these groups equally part of the responsibilities of the Norwegian police, as set out in the PA purpose statement. Given that immigration control takes place on the streets of Oslo, and that this immigration control is seen as part of international police cooperation to fight, for example, drug crime, and given the further complication that foreign police officers may participate in these control activities, more or less reasonable differentiation may be expected to occur.

Concerns about discrimination in immigration control were also voiced in relation to the use of the Schengen Information System (SIS).[62] One issue debated in the mid-1990s *forarbeid* was whether the wording of CISA art.96, giving legal basis for registering a person in the SIS if he or she is "a threat to public policy or public security or to national security", should be understood in the same way as the Police Act sect.2 nos.1 and 2. These terms, the Government stated, needed to be understood in a discretionary, practical manner, the same way as in national and Schengen rules. The legal texts state clearly which persons may be registered in the SIS, and under what conditions. While presented as a police investigation tool, the provision was largely used in various control efforts directed at foreigners. In the late 1990s, Mathiesen found that the great majority of hits in the SIS were third country nationals who were refused re-entry, and that an immense body of data resulted in a limited number of hits retrieved by the authorities. Mathiesen therefore did not consider the SIS a suitable tool to fight ordinary (serious) crime: it worked more as an immigration control

61 The consideration of security under the law is stated in the 2008 Immigration Act, and the *forarbeid* of the 1988 Act have a clear focus directed on 'legal administration' when security under the law is discussed. (e.g. Ot.prp. nr.46 (1986–1987)]:258). Note that only the Norwegian version has legal status and is continuously updated by the Ministry of Labour and Social Inclusion (https://www.regjeringen.no/en/dokumenter/immigration-act/id585772/ [11.12.2017].

62 This concern had already been voiced regarding the 1988 Norwegian Immigration Act (see, e.g., Sollund 2007; Finstad 2000).

tool, which was not the purpose the Norwegian government had in mind when they argued the necessity for Norwegian Schengen cooperation accession.[63] The government response was that the SIS worked both as an essential tool after internal border control was dissolved, and as a necessary tool for the police. Its primary benefit as a police tool was perceived to be its search system mechanism, hence its value could not be measured in numbers.[64]

Schengen member states have different registration practices. Some register anyone denied asylum status, while Norway, for example, only registers expelled foreigners. Since the reason for an alert will be noted in the system, this should not in theory have any unreasonable consequences.[65] According to art.96, one reason for registering an alien so that s/he may be refused entry to the Schengen area is that s/he constitutes a threat to public order or security, or the internal security of the state. The police may decide to give someone the status of 'threat' on the basis of. criminal convictions, for assault, say, or clear evidence that s/he will commit serious criminal offences. But it may also be based on the fact that s/he is unwanted in the Schengen territory (if a third country national) or in one of the states because s/he has not complied with national immigration regulations on entry, residence or deportation.

The regulations do, then, leave room for differentiation. The *forarbeid* to neither the Immigration nor the Police Acts promote such differentiation, which was doubtless unintended. But the fact that there is a textual difference in the Police Act, may make it different to interpret the Act's purpose.

Another possible effect could be a form of displacement. If Norwegian police successfully target crime problems before they reach Nordic soil, might this not just move crime to other jurisdictions where other, maybe less well-equipped, police forces have to deal with them? In the *Samordningsorgan's* 2014 report, there is an account of a Kripos project on Lithuanian gangs. Seven Norwegian police districts, in addition to Kripos, received financial support to achieve three goals: 1) to make Lithuanian criminals see Norway as a less attractive destination, 2) to make them feel there was an increased risk of being caught, 3) to ensure their criminal activities are more severely punished.[66] While it is mentioned that the local Lithuanian authorities should, as part of the project, be given assistance to improve their efforts to stop domestic crime, the Norwegian police focus is – naturally – primarily on removing the problem from Norwegian territory. This section has shown there has been a shift in how crime is viewed, including the definition of crime, and in what is seen as the most important security concerns. The shift may result in an increased differentiation between policing service for citizens and non-citizens, and even between 'ethnic' and 'non-ethnic' citizens. This may also be seen as a result of a situation where the diverging logics of the benefits of open borders, the risks these open borders entail, and the importance of international markets are mixed in unpredictable ways.

Present-day globalised Norwegian society is undoubtedly less limited, both regarding its state borders and the composition of its community. This may not result from the Schengen cooperation or the police cooperation instruments in themselves. The police are, however, linked to the community in a way that may make it hard to provide security, safety and welfare to those perceived as outsiders.

63 Innst.S.nr.229 (1996–1997):40; Mathiesen 1997:50–51.
64 Innst.S.nr.229 (1996–1997):40.
65 See more on irregular migration e.g. in Peers 2011 ch.7.
66 Samordningsorganets årsrapport 2014:19.

It seems clear that 1) it is the Norwegian sovereign that has ultimate control over the police as a legitimate enforcer of state violence, and 2) it is the Norwegian people that constitute the sovereign. We have seen that the sufficient justifications are necessary from the sovereign, for the citizens to make informed choices when they enforce their sovereignty through popular elections. I have criticised the Norwegian government's lack of honesty or of necessary knowledge in this process. The question is, then, whether the link between the police and the community, as described in the purpose section of PA sect.1 needs to be reconsidered in light of this development. because a limitation in the internal sovereignty perspective, I argue, makes this purpose incompatible with a sufficiently acceptable policed territory.

15.2 The concepts of the Police Act section 1: what do 'state' and 'community' mean?

The nation-state monopoly on legitimate violence may be seen to be challenged by the fact that other states, and state and non-state entities have entered the Norwegian policing scene. The first section of the Police Act, quoted above, is apparently self-explanatory. Under the title "Responsibility and purpose", it sets out clear guidelines on how the Police Act's provisions should be understood, by police officers, the courts, people in general, and those who think they have suffered unfair treatment by the police. If one wants to understand what sort of phenomenon a police service is, and what its purpose is, one important source of information is the Police Act. It is a general principle that the 'natural' linguistic understanding of legal terms should be the basis of interpretation, since anyone must be able to know their legal position before deciding to commit a crime. In this section, I discuss some of the concepts in the PA sect.1 that are central to notions of sovereignty.

The wording of an act may be unclear, ambiguous or old-fashioned. if so, it must be interpreted using legal sources, such as the act's purpose provision. This book explores whether this seemingly straightforward provision has become more complicated because of the development of more advanced and more efficient police cooperation agreements and measures, especially those of the Schengen cooperation.

Does the notion of a monopoly on legitimate violence have any contemporary relevance? The state is not unbiased: it represents the polity as a whole, at least in principle.[67] A central goal of the welfare state is to provide safety and security to all citizens. However, the police may also be seen as a societal institution constitutive for the existence of a modern society.[68] The police are such an indispensable part of the state that, while most other occupational roles of society may be dismissed, the whole societal order would change if the police did not perform its normal functions. The police are (meant to be) blind to political, economic and private differences between citizens; the responsibility to protect and secure welfare and security is *public*, which is designed to ensure the principle of equality before the law. This accords with Bayley's notion of public and professional police. In contemporary Norway, a state committed to international cooperation through, for example, the Schengen and EEA agreements, the question is whether the social form has already changed, without the police function having been able to keep up.

67 Thorburn 2010; Loader and Walker 2007.
68 Birkeland 2007:39.

Harmonisation and standardisation may lead to the dissolution of the link between citizens' needs and the work of policy makers and resource allocators, I argue above. Also Loader sees transnational police cooperation as implying a standardisation process, which significantly disempowers those subjected to the particular police, and its democratic legitimacy is therefore questionable.[69]

Still, the 'state' mentioned in the purpose statement does not have to be the nation-state. Historically, there is no inextricable link between the state and the provider of policing functions. The definition now relevant is linked to territorial delimitation. 'The state' is a geographical area with a sovereign ruler. This is a firm international principle. The clear assumption is that no entity other than the Norwegian state may legitimately enforce coercive power on Norwegian territory; nor may Norwegian authorities enforce state power outside its borders. The state has the monopoly of legitimate power, a monopoly that is connected to the responsibility to ensure general order, security, and so on, in this area, and for the resident community.[70]

Walker emphasises these two characteristics (monopoly on violence and the provision of security) as the traditional instrumental links between the state and the police service, what I describe as aspects of internal sovereignty. He also points to two symbolic couplings: the political and constitutional integrity connected to control of the police service, and to the collective identity marker the national police service can be said to be. These links underscore the connection between the development of the nation-state, and its ongoing construction. If the monopoly on violence seems challenged, the state may appear unable to ensure safety and freedom independently. It is open to question, of course, whether the creation of a monopoly was necessary; what may be more important is whether the state is actually able to provide the police service needed to protect its citizens and community, monopoly or not. And this emphasises even further the value of what sovereign respect and control outside the more formalistic arrangements.

Understanding the concept of 'community' referred to in the Police Act, includes seeing how the Act sect.1 distinguishes between 'citizens' and 'community'. Section 2, regulating police tasks, speaks of 'citizens' as well as 'persons' when referring to individuals: the Norwegian police must "protect persons, private and public property [. . .] maintain public order and security and [. . .] provide protection against any threat to general security in the community".[71] The police also shall "provide citizens with assistance and services in situations of danger [. . .] and otherwise when the circumstances are such that assistance is required and natural". Are these groups distinct, or do 'citizens', 'community' and 'persons' mean the same thing? The question is important on several levels apropos the 'purpose and objectives' in the Police Act sect.1: What is the police service 'needed', and how is that need determined? The perception of what "security under the law, safety and welfare in general" may depend on the group, community or society in question. The role of the police is paradoxical: they must simultaneously protect the state as a whole, and each individual, both from other individuals, and from the state if it abuses its powers.

There is no proper definition of 'society' or 'community' in the Police Act. One of the *forarbeid* implies the state simply represents society's interests.[72] Such a simplistic reading is

69 Loader 2004.
70 Walker 2000:227–9.
71 Sect.2 nos.1 and 4.
72 NOU 1981:35 p.68.

in line with classic societal contract theory. We may understand 'the state' as consisting of those who elect the government – a government that, by being elected, commits to protecting its constituent citizens, who thus become members of the nation.[73] The Police Act sect.1 is, in at least one reading, built on such a contract theory, and read such, the community referred to must consist of the group that constitutes (or could constitute) the Norwegian state through elections – Norwegian citizens.[74] In democratic states, legislation binding individuals is dependent on their autonomous consent, through constituting, via elections every four years, of a legitimate government (the legislative powers). Policing is thus a result of such an autonomous acceptance of national legislation. Although police activity itself is heteronomous, prior acceptance makes it legitimate. Precisely for this reason, the delimited impact area of legislation is important: it is decided by citizens, and binds citizens on the territory where they live.

In earlier times, the police had responsibility for all the modern welfare state's tasks.[75] Police tasks were thus more diverse than today, even though the police do many things that are outside what most people associate with 'police work'.[76] There are different ways, as we have seen, to understand the police and their core tasks. Dubber suggests conceptualising the state in two different ways, depending on its ways of controlling and governing.[77] Looked at through juridical glasses, the state is an institutionalisation of a political community consisting of free, equal individuals. The role of the law is to manifest and protect the autonomy of these citizens. Looked at through police glasses, the state looks more like a household or large family, and the police role is that of a *pater familias* whose responsibility is to ensure the household's welfare.[78] By classifying everything and everyone either as a contribution, or a threat to the family's welfare, the police make sure that the family or household functions as well as possible.

According to the Ministry, the provision of citizens' security and welfare is the over-arching purpose of the police.[79] As regards the Police Act sect.1's safeguarding of 'security under the law', the purpose is somewhat more obvious: the police must prevent and stop crime, because crime damages and/or disturbs individuals and/or general interests.[80] On many occasions, the Norwegian police have made good use of cooperation with foreign police. Crime control and investigation are, however, not the only things involved in the provision of security. The role of the police is also to supply a subjective perception of these values, targeting crime, and also the fear of crime. This perception will naturally vary.[81] In

73 E.g. Hobbes 1998 [1651].

74 This is an understanding of citizenship in line with, for example Sassen 2008:ch.6, presented as the traditional point of departure: several rights bound to the political membership of a nation state, and the rights primarily being recognised as hereditary. By 'constitute', I refer to those who are legally entitled to vote in elections and form the basis of the Government (sovereign), similar to the procedural legitimacy mentioned above (ch. 7).

75 E.g. Silver 1967; Foucault 2009:334; Anners 1997.

76 Finstad 2000.

77 Dubber 2005:3.

78 As in Rousseau 1958 [1762].

79 Ot.prp.nr.22 (1994–1995):13.

80 This is also in accordance with the UN police ethics codex (which is non-binding), where police personnel at any time must fulfil the duties placed on them in law, by serving society and by protecting all persons against illegal actions in accordance with the important responsibility imposed by their profession. (From Ot.prp.nr.22 (1994–1995):13.)

81 NOU 1981:35 pt.5.1. Also in more recent police reform works, e.g. St.meld.nr.42 (2004–2005):60 ff. and in the general police theory (e.g. Auglend *et al.* 2004:195, Walker 2002:310).

the *forarbeid*, two main challenges are mentioned to the peace and safety: traffic and the fact that many, particularly senior citizens, have their freedom of movement inhibited by fear of assault in public spaces – hardly cross-border police cooperation issues.

15.3 An EU sovereign?

The EU differs from other international organisations in many ways – in simple terms, the EU has gained so much power in so many areas that in many ways it looks – and acts – like a state. Constitutional sovereignty most often refers to the nation-state. When assessing whether the EU is sovereign, meaning that it is entitled to give rights, the assumption is that the EU is not a state: it is a new kind of political and legal entity. It is, however, claimed by many, including, as mentioned above, the ECJ, that the Union has become a legal entity of a special nature. Through case law from the CJEU, and more or less tacit unquestioning with the case law and legislation of EU organs, the Union may be said to have achieved constitutional status[82] and to have given the citizens of the member states positive rights, despite what the governments of the member state might think (EU rights have 'direct effect' in the member states). The Union, then, has 'its own' citizens – all citizens of the member states.[83] When the Union acts at a supranational level, the member states could also be considered to resemble 'citizens' in a traditional nation state: Union bodies have power to legislate on behalf of the majority of states, while the minority have to live with whatever the majority decides, if they want to remain within the state (of the EU).

Throughout many paradigm changing moments in history, after lengthy wars resulting in great loss of life and resources, acute needs for greater stability and new forms of power and control arose.[84] Similarly, at the turn of the 19th century, anarchists and terrorists were perceived as having cross-border connections with each other, and drug trafficking and money laundering were seen as crimes with international consequences that warranted a concerted international cooperation if they were to be successfully defeated. The nation-state, as ultimate sovereign, is, it seems, inadequate to deal with the contemporary globalised world, and coordinated efforts must be orchestrated at a higher level.

We have seen that part of the social contract is the citizens' trade-off of freedom for security'. Freedom' is multi-faceted concept that may have many different kinds of content matter. A positive definition views freedom as the ability to actively influence the development of security and justice. It may be questioned whether the strengthening of the rights catalogue at the EU level, both through the Lisbon Treaty and the establishment of the CFREU, create a more difficult balancing act. Who determines how rights are balanced? The EU, the member states or their citizens? Do we, post-Lisbon, need a new definition of the legitimate use of force? Or a new concept of state sovereignty?

The EU is not a state. The EU, so far, has no army, no common police force, and no taxation authority. In many ways, the latest treaty amendment, the Lisbon Treaty, infringed state sovereignty less than did the Single European Act and the Maastricht (Union) Treaty.[85] On the basis of this analysis, the question arises whether the time has come for a European Police Force, given that a European Public Prosecutor's office recently has been agreed

82 With reference to e.g. Op.cit., see also more generally on constitutionalisation in Weiler 1991.
83 Art.20(1) TFEU.
84 See e.g. Kirchner and Sperling 2007.
85 [1987] OJ L 169/1 and [1992] OJ C 191/1 (see details in ch.4.1 above).

upon between 20 of 28 MS (per December 2017).[86] Member states still assert their monopoly of legitimate violence, as is seen in their restrictions of CJEU's jurisdiction regarding the acts of member states' police or law enforcement authorities. If there was a supranational European Police Force, it might increase security by preventing borderless crime more efficiently. It would also be a big step towards the constitution of a European State. Whether or not it did actually promote security and justice more successfully than individual nation-states, such a development would undoubtedly challenge the idea of state sovereignty as we know it, and thus also the concept of freedom.

The founding treaties of the EEC contained no reference to the protection of human rights or the principles of the rule of law. The fundamental rights of the EU were those connected to the four freedoms: the free movement of goods, persons, services and capital. Of these, freedom to do with trade has little to do with human rights as we traditionally know them.[87]

Which entity is competent to provide which rights? The monopoly on legitimate violence belongs to the state. At the same time, only the state or sovereign may give citizens and inhabitants rights that can be claimed on its territory. The EU is generally considered to have developed into a new form of sovereign entity, *sui generis*, through CJEU jurisprudence in the 1960s.[88] If one accepts this view, the EU is an entity that gives fundamental rights connected to the four freedoms. The boundaries between 'fundamental' and 'human' rights are blurred. EU and other international or supranational bodies, such as the UN, may call for states to give people rights. There is, however, a difference between more or less universal human rights and the fundamental rights given to citizens within a state. Palombella sees human rights as fundamental too, but while human rights such as the right to life are abstract, fundamental rights are tied to and formative of a specific society, constituting "a basic pillar within it, and an objective which orientates institutions and policies".[89] Yet another difference is that fundamental rights concern the self-determination of the individual, whilst fundamental boundaries concern the autonomy and self-determination of communitie*s*.[90]

Giving rights and policing individuals (constraining their freedom) are at opposite ends of the spectrum. The reinforcement of borders and exclusion of third country nationals, altogether denying their rights, is an increasingly important part of present-day policing. One might even say, following Agamben,[91] that the EU is creating a form of centralised sovereignty through the common project of excluding non-EU citizens. The area of freedom, security and justice, and free movement is defined by its external borders, protected by police cooperation organs such as Frontex, and the member states' own police. The external borders are being fortified, to compensate for the not entirely positive internal freedom. Protecting the freedom and security of the citizens of the EU means also protecting them from the world outside the borders. And this is traditionally a core facet of sovereignty.

86 EPPO has established through the so-called enhanced cooperation mechanism in TFEU art.87, because of no consensus for the original EC proposal. In line with the development e.g. of the Prüm cooperation, this is probably only a matter of time.

87 This safeguarding may be seen as a prerequisite for the legitimacy of the European Union and the member states' loyalty. See also Brouwer 2007.

88 The first one being the Van Gend en Loos v Nederlandse Administratie der Belastingen 26/62, 5 February 1963. Weiler is one of the influential *sui generis* theorists (Weiler 1998; 1999).

89 Palombella 2006.

90 Weiler 1999.

91 Agamben 1998.

The EU may, then, be said to have become an entity that has a measure of sovereignty, meaning that, at least in some areas, it has the ultimate decision-making competence over its citizens. Any sovereign will attempt to legitimate its power, as this will help stabilise and increase it.[92] The strengthening of the citizens' fundamental rights can be understood as a legitimation of power. Part of establishing the EU as an entity *sui generis* is that EU citizens are given specific rights under EU legislation. Eriksen identifies a distinct, new type of legitimacy, unconnected to the member states, based on this conveyance of rights.[93] However, these rights given by the EU sovereign, are economic rights, related to the expansion of the free, market in Europe. As we have seen, these rights have been considered legitimate. Does this remain the case as the legal and political scope of the expands far beyond the purely economic sphere, to include, for example, a pan-European public prosecutor, prosecuting crimes formerly dealt with by national organs, on the basis of the work of Europol, before member states' national courts? This question is particularly relevant when the rights rub up against the reality of Norwegian policing.

15.4 Concept change in a post-Westphalian system

Like the nation-states, the EU may have two legitimate reasons for subjecting individuals to EU criminal justice. One regards offences harming the EU itself: it seems reasonable that these should be handled at EU level.[94] The harm in question may be to the Union as an institution, as in the case of euro fraud, or to all EU citizens, as in cases of environmental crime. The second regards the obligation the EU, as a supranational entity, has to citizens as individuals, namely to ensure their freedom and security – a form of social contract promise made in the treaties. The problem though, as with the notion of serious crime, is that there may be different perceptions of what freedom and security mean, how this translates in practice, and which measures and instruments are best calculated to achieve these values. A contrary perception is that EU criminal justice – or similar expressions of EU sovereignty, such as border control, may have the opposite effects. The increase of right-wing nationalism, it is suggested, may indicate a sense of insecurity resulting from states' increased participation in integrative or globalised sovereignty exercise in an expanding and more financially challenged Union. I want to consider whether it makes sense to say that we have a situation with competing sovereigns.

It is essential for the legitimacy of EU criminal justice that EU activity does not enable member states to circumvent constitutional rights granted to their citizens.[95] This may be challenging: member states may take the credit when EU criminal justice measures work, and blame the EU when they do not. This may challenge the perceived legitimacy of the CJEU.[96] Then again – if the EU did not also constitute an area of criminal justice – would it become an area facilitating crime and creating insecurity, while also providing free movement of workers, capital, etc.? If citizens do not perceive their interests as being better served by EU criminal justice, the whole arrangement may be viewed as illegitimate in an outcome perspective.[97]

92 Beetham 1991.
93 Eriksen 2009.
94 See op.cit.:26.
95 Wade 2013.
96 Op.cit.:63
97 Op.cit.:54.

Chayes and Chayes argue that sovereignty in the contemporary international system is no longer exercised unilaterally, but through participation in regional and global regulatory regimes.[98] They argue that the 'new' sovereignty consists of an alternative managerial model which relies primarily on a cooperative, problem-solving approach rather than a coercive one. Thus, states avoid going to war against each other because the international agreements they enter into and entities they form together give them more power and success than wars. As regards (external) sovereignty, it is important that the exit option is always open, if the agreement or entity fails to produce the desired results. While many point to the diminished importance or content of state sovereignty, it is not claimed that states have lost the sovereign capacity to withdraw consent to international agreements they have entered into.[99] The exit option is rarely exercised, however, because staying in improves the chances of negotiating a better position than being excluded from multilateral fora.[100] It seems possible, then, that sovereignties can overlap.

At least one understanding of internal sovereignty in any representative democracy, makes the citizens' right to be able to participate in public discussions of developments in the criminal justice area, fundamental. There is a marked lack of such debate in Norway, both inside and outside politics. The right of citizens of EU member states to participate in elections directly influencing EU policy development provides procedural legitimacy. Deliberative legitimacy is not perfect for citizens of either EU or non-EU states such as Norway. This makes the influence of EU criminal justice problematic from the point of view of sovereignty, if sovereignty is defined as a form of self-government by a people that can deliberate and participate in decision-making processes on current developments.

My aim has been to discuss the relationship between the state and other states, and between the state and its citizens, and vice versa. Under the current Norwegian Constitution, Norwegian citizens may not take part in the constitution of the EU.[101] Transfer of sovereignty does not necessarily mean that another state or institution 'takes over' this sovereignty, thus constituting a new super-sovereign, but there might, be a limit to how many national sovereignty functions may be transferred to other levels.

In Europe's area of criminal justice, the internal aspects of sovereignty are weakened, because there is less national debate on, and involvement in, the international development of the criminal justice and police regulations that impact on the nation-state. Does this mean that criminal justice within the nation-states is of a poorer quality than would be the case, were the country completely outside the EU criminal justice system? International and transnational crime related to terrorism, or internet fraud must probably be dealt with by some kind of multilevel governance system. Regardless of the development of the Schengen or EU area border, many crimes and risks are truly borderless in the contemporary world, in which the strength of the EU as a criminal justice actor is that it is a union constituted of many countries. While EU institutions are growing more autonomous, the union model is built on the idea that no one member state is powerful enough, either economically speaking

98 Chayes and Chayes 1995.

99 International criminal law, among others the ICC, may be an exception. Since the Nüremberg trials, there has been a general consensus that some types of crimes are universal, and that states may not 'opt out of' them. The fact that modern western states such as the USA do not adhere to the ICC, signals that the power of these so-called universal crimes with universal jurisdiction, is hardly very potent.

100 Cananea 2010:996–7, so also Slaughter 2004.

101 This is a common interpretation of the Constitution sect. 1, which states that the Kingdom is "free, indivisible and inalienable", with a monarchical form of government.

or by any other measure, to dictate EU actions. Although it has its weaknesses, this idea implies a certain level of joint engagement in this criminal policy.[102] Hence the cooperating nation-states may individually stand stronger inside rather than outside f the cooperation.

The nation-state concept is challenged in many ways in contemporary Europe – through trade agreements and environmental regulations, for instance.

In my view, however, the monopoly of violence is central to national sovereignty, and the definition of the nation-state. And the relationship between state, territory and citizen has changed, considered in the light of the international police cooperation measures described in part II, and their effects and consequences described in part III. How should these changes in the relationship between state borders and territory, between non-citizens, citizens and society, be understood? The Norwegian government has voluntarily entered into various international agreements that entail partial transfer of Norwegian sovereignty. Such transfer is within the sovereign's competence. The Norwegian government can agree to empower other entities to regulate the market and competition regulations for factories; give international bodies such as the European Court of Human Rights the 'final word' in the Norwegian legal system; and through Schengen, delegate to other political institutions the right to decide who shall be able to move freely within Norwegian territory, under the Schengen cooperation. But even if agreements entailing transfer of sovereignty are entered into legitimately because 1) the agreement is carried out by properly empowered persons, and 2) these are democratically elected by the people, can all the functions of a state be delegated to outside entities, and the state still remain a state? If the (nation-)state cannot, on its own, provide the police service that is needed by the community, does the state remain a state in the same sense as before?

It is hard to say the Norwegian state has a strict 'monopoly' on violence, once foreign police officers have acquired the competence to enforce other states' police authority on Norwegian territory. One could also question the legitimacy of foreign police forces' use of their powers, if legitimacy is related to voters demonstrating approval of the powers of their local police through general elections. If the monopoly no longer exists, it may seem that the (nation-)state has been unable to provide the 'needed' police service to those who are members (either by citizenship or residence permit) of the community in question.

It seems that current Norwegian police legislation does not fully embrace the changes described in this book.[103] If police responsibility now includes the entire Schengen Area, it may no longer be legitimate to limit the purpose of the police service to Norwegian society. On the other hand, the Norwegian state may simply lack the competence to determine what kind of police service is needed in the context of the Schengen area. 'Circulation' is a central goal of the Schengen area: the absence of borders clearly improves circulation, but also has other consequences. On the one hand the police operating in a given territory may now be foreign, and may, to some extent be removed from the society that constitutes the state they are employed by. On the other hand, the majority of police personnel that remain on their own territory may look at – and must look at – foreigners and migrants, in new ways and work harder at limiting their circulation.

102 Nuotio 2004:220–1.

103 Reform work on the Criminal Procedure Act started Fall 2014, because of the increased internationalisation of crime (http://www.regjeringen.no/upload/JD/Vedlegg/mandat_utvalg_straffeprosesslov.pdf [10.07.2014]). The Comittee's report was finalised November 2016, and is currently sent to applicable parties for comments. This reform is also argued by Backer 2013.

Understood thus, the purpose of the police includes control of foreigners to ensure peace and order on the territory, while, in the case of citizens, it is more often to provide subjective security under the law. There is a further divide between different types of foreigners: those who may circulate within the Schengen Area and those who absolutely should not.

Bowling and Sheptycki argue that the idea of a monopoly on violence is outdated in a globalised world where the Westphalian nation-state system has turned into a transnational state system.[104] The global neo-liberal market – and the 'regionally global' market within the Schengen area – is more complex than in Weber's day, as concerns both crime, and governance and crime control structures.

Does all this have a bearing on the Norwegian Police Act? This book presents just a fragment of the total *forarbeid* concerning Norwegian police reform, which may seem perpetually ongoing. This might be inevitable in a dynamic era. The previous public law reforms began about the same time as the 1995 Act came into force. The social developments singled out as particularly challenging for the police of the future are seen to relate to the "international dimension": "globalisation, migration, cultural and religious differences, technological developments and the use of drugs".[105] A two-front war is envisioned, where the police are torn between demands relating to Norwegians' perception of security, and the increasingly international and more brutal crime that must be dealt with in other ways, without these necessarily having much to do with the subjective perceptions of security and safety 'at home'.[106] Officially, there are clear expectations that the 'proximity policing' model, the focus on prevention, and the strong police presence in communities will be maintained. At the same time, the police organisation is undergoing a rapid process of centralisation and specialisation, with a concomitant growth in repressive and 'extraordinary' policing methods. One suggestion is that this introduces a distinction between the police service for internal 'household' affairs, and the other designed to police strangers.[107]

15.5 Outlook: A return to proximity policing

This concluding chapter has addressed the question of in what ways the development of operational police cooperation regulations and measures may impact on Norwegian society and the Norwegian public. In a more complex modern reality, I suggest a return to an emphasis on proximity policing, together with a focus on informal social control mechanisms. One of the most serious crimes committed in Norway since the Second World War, the 22/7 terrorist attacks, could perhaps have been avoided or dealt with more efficiently if there had been more local police, with better resources. Someone could have noticed that a person owning a farm was buying large amounts of fertiliser, but not using it and was not doing any farming at all.[108] The increased fear of crime, combined with the weakening of

104 Bowling and Sheptycki 2012:35 ff.

105 St.meld.nr.42 (2004–2005):23, my translation. The early 2000's police role report mainly upholds the principles of the 1980s (St.meld.nr.22 (2000–2001)).

106 Ibid.:60. On the perception of safety in Norway, see the field study of Aas *et al.* 2010b; Aas *et al.* 2010a. One of their findings is that several of the measures identified by people as improving their perception of safety, were not related to crime-prevention, but to well-being, such as "well-maintained outdoor spaces, meeting places and removal of graffiti and tagging" (2010a:65).

107 Stumpf 2006; Aas 2007; Ugelvik 2013.

108 As in fact neighbours were said to have noticed (http://www.nrk.no/ho/nabo-vurderte-a-ringe-politiet-1.7726020 [13.07.2014]. I owe this point to Kai Ekanger, the leader of the Police Role I Committee (NOU 1981:35) at *Polithistorisk møte* 07.05.14.

informal social control and increasing international cross-border crime, all call for a greater local police presence: officers dealing with local crime, and showing that the state is carrying out its responsibilities and protecting its citizens. This would point to a state that is less biased than the security providers normally seen in public spaces, who are private security guards, acting at the behest of various market actors. A signal sent by the recent Police Analysis, although it still underscores traditional Norwegian police values, is that the trend of drastic centralisation and specialisation will continue. One may even interpret the wording of the title as implying this: it calls for the police to be better '*rustet*', which means 'equipped', but also 'armed' or 'prepared for war'.

The purpose section of the Norwegian Police Act was introduced at the beginning of this book. While its wording, and the purpose declared, are obviously just parts of the whole picture of police work and responsibilities, it is crucial for an Act to represent reality, not least because legal interpretation of the Act happens in light of its purpose. Legal texts inevitably become outdated, and social changes are often rapid, while legislation processes are slow. If the purpose section is outdated, the entire Police Act becomes vulnerable and its contents less predictable for both subjects and users. If the purpose section is outdated, one might even say that the entire act is outdated.

The 2005 report to *Stortinget* shows an awareness of developments that were changing the challenges facing the police: In the future, the Government stated, one should emphasise particularly the police's "cooperation with other public and private actors in contributing to enhanced security in society. The citizens' safety must be increased through reduced crime, greater accessibility, and targeted information."[109] Sweden published a major government report on international police cooperation in 2011. A report was given in 2016 on Norwegian police in Schengen 1996–2016.[110] This gives a contribution to an overview of the police cooperation, but it does not address sufficiently, as I see it the scope of, and possibilities and pitfalls inherent in, Norwegian police cooperation with EU. The question needs to be asked again: Who are the citizens? It has been argued that security should be one of the fundamental, universal human rights,[111] in other words a right independent of where in the world a person is. Risks in the globalised world, whether risks of international or national terrorist actions, environmental catastrophes or property theft, do not respect territorial borders. On this ground, there could be good reasons to argue that security and safety should be globally available common goods.[112] The wording of a legal provision is important because rights mean little if there is nowhere to claim them. There must be an entity that recognises the right, and is willing to protect the person entitled to protection, or control the person threatening others' security. It seems doubtful that the Norwegian Police Act sufficiently reflects the current distribution of responsibilities.

Law is a part of society. Major changes in society, and changes of the perception of what 'society' is, necessarily have consequences for law. We now see a discrepancy between the purpose and the area of impact of the Norwegian Police Act, and the regulations in the Schengen cooperation and other international agreements building on these measures that Norway is bound by. Over the twenty years or so that have passed since the Police Act was enacted, there have been changes in the meaning of 'state', 'police' and 'society'. The

109 St.meld.nr.42 (2004–2005):6 (my translation).
110 POD 2016
111 E.g. Goold and Lazarus 2007.
112 Loader and Walker 2007:ch.9.

current weakening of national police responsibility may lead to the idea that supranational actors are needed for successful policing of borderless territories.

Norway is situated geographically on the outskirts of Europe, and the Norwegian attitude towards EU police cooperation is affected by this: Norway appears to seek to compensate for its remoteness and small population by being the most eager participant. This is a long Norwegian tradition, and one that is still important, for example, in Norwegian relations with the UN, the Council of Europe, and recently NATO. A problem for the EU project has been resistance by member states to agreeing on measures and implementing them; change has been slow. This has not been the case with Norway. Norway seems to want to manoeuvre towards a more central position in international cooperation mechanisms than its geographical position and population size would lead one to expect. While this may be interpreted as a small state striving for better status, it may also signify a feeling of dependence. After all, Norway was part of Nordic unions from 1397 up until 1905. This book shows that major influence is exerted by the EU on the development of policy and regulations in Norway. EU police and prosecutorial bodies, as well as other states' police forces, also influence the Norwegian policing situation. During the Swedish-Norwegian Union from 1814 to 1905, Norway had a great degree of independence, practically and politically, but was still not a fully sovereign country. The Norwegian situation related to the EU is quite similar.

In this book, I have raised four specific research questions in order to discuss the impact of EU international police cooperation on Norwegian sovereignty. According to the influential Norwegian legal theorist Aschehoug in 1866, Norway's social order is in its nature a dependent one, due to the various unions it had been part of over the centuries.[113] These meant that changes to the Norwegian constitutional situation had happened because of events or decisions made *outside* of Norwegian authority and territory, without the necessary close contact between decision-makers and society. This distance still challenges the perceived legitimacy of 'European' decisions that are made relevant for Norway. This history of dependency could imply both that Norway presently has an added ambition of sovereignty. But it could also imply that she more easily is comfortable with various forms of foreign influence. This book has attempted to shine some light on important challenges that may be argued to affect Norwegian sovereignty, when seen in the context of the Norwegian place inside and outside the EU.

113 Aschehoug 1866:D §1.

16 Bibliography

Aas, G, S Runhovde, J Strype and T Bjørgo (2010a): *Trygghet i det offentlige rom: I åtte norske kommuner og bydeler.* Oslo: Politihøgskolen.

Aas, G, S Runhovde, J Strype and T Bjørgo (2010b): "Perceived safety in the public space: A survey study of eight Norwegian municipalities and boroughs". M Cools et al. (eds): *Police, Policing, Policy and the City in Europe.* The Hague: Eleven International Publishing.

Aas, KF (2007): *Globalization and Crime.* London: SAGE.

Agamben, G (1998): *Homo Sacer.* Stanford, CA: Stanford University Press.

Agnew, JA (2009): *Globalization and Sovereignty.* Lanham, MD: Rowman & Littlefield Publishers, Inc.

Ahnfelt, E and J From (1996): *Politisamarbeid og europeisk integrasjon.* Oslo: Ad notam Gyldendal.

Andenæs, J (1998): *Statsforfatningen i Norge.* Oslo: Tano Aschehoug.

Andenæs, J and TG Myhrer (2009): *Norsk straffeprosess.* Oslo: Universitetsforlaget.

Anderson, B (2006): *Imagined Communities: Reflections on the Origin and Spread of Nationalism.* London: Verso.

Anderson, M (1994): "The agenda for police cooperation". M Anderson and M den Boer (eds): *Policing across National Boundaries.* London: Pinter Publishers.

Anderson, M, P Cullen, WC Gilmore, CD Raab and N Walker (1995): *Policing the European Union.* Oxford: Clarendon.

Andreas, P and EA Nadelmann (2006): *Policing the Globe: Criminalization and Crime Control in International Relations.* New York: Oxford University Press.

Anners, E (1997): *Brottet, straffet och polisen i den europeiska rättsutvecklingen.* Stockholm: Norstedts juridik.

Apap, J and M Anderson (2002): *Police and Justice Co-Operation and the New European Borders.* The Hague: Kluwer Law International.

Arai, Y (2006): "The system of restrictions". Pv Dijk, Y Arai and GJH van Hoof (eds): *Theory and Practice of the European Convention on Human Rights.* Antwerpen: Intersentia.

Archer, C (2005): *Norway Outside the European Union: Norway and European Integration from 1994 to 2004.* London: Routledge.

Aschehoug, TH (1866): *Norges offentlige ret.* Christiania: Feilberg & Landmark.

Auglend, RL and HJ Mæland (2016): *Politirett.* Oslo: Gyldendal akademisk. (3rd edition of Auglend, Røsandhaug and Mæland's *Politirett*).

Auglend, RL, K Røsandhaug and HJ Mæland (2004): *Politirett.* Oslo: Gyldendal akademisk.

Axtmann, R (1992): "'Police' and the formation of the modern State: Legal and ideological assumptions on State capacity in the Austrian lands of the Habsburg Empire, 1500–1800." *German History.* 10 (1), 39–61.

Backer, IL (2013): "I lovgivningsperspektiv: Er straffeprosessloven moden for revisjon?" *Tidsskrift for strafferett.* 13 (4), 447–456.

DOI: 10.4324/9780429503696-18

Baldaccini, A (2010): "Extraterritorial border control in the EU: The role of Frontex operations at sea". B Ryan and V Mitsilegas (eds): *Extraterritorial Immigration Control: Legal Challenges.* Leiden: Martinus Nijhoff.

Balvig, F (1987): *Hvid som sne: Kriminalitet og kontrol i Danmark og Schweiz.* Holte: Socpol.

Balzacq, T, D Bigo, S Carrera and E Guild (2006): "Security and the two-level game: The treaty of Prüm, the EU and the management of threats". Brussels: Centre for European Policy Studies.

Banton, M (2005): "The policeman in the community". T Newburn (ed.): *Policing: Key Readings.* Collumpton: Willan.

Barker, R (2001): *Legitimating Identities: The Self-Presentations of Rulers and Subjects.* Cambridge: Cambridge University Press.

Bartelson, J (1995): *A Genealogy of Sovereignty.* Cambridge: Cambridge University Press.

Barth, F (1996): "Ethnic groups and boundaries". J Hutchinson and AD Smith (eds): *Ethnicity.* New York and Oxford: Oxford University Press.

Bauman, Z (1998): *Globalization: The Human Consequences.* Cambridge: Polity.

Baumbach, T (2012): "Strafferetten og EU". T Baumbach and P Blume (eds): *Retskildernes kamp: Forholdet mellem national offentlig ret og udefra kommende ret.* København: DJØF.

Bayley, DH (1975): "The police and political development in Europe". C Tilly (ed.): *The Formation of National States in Western Europe.* Princeton, NJ: Princeton University Press.

Bayley, DH (1985): *Patterns of Policing: A Comparative International Analysis.* New Brunswick, NJ: Rutgers University Press.

Bayley, DH and CD Shearing (2001): *The New Structure of Policing: Description, Conceptualization, and Research Agenda.* Washington, DC: National Instutute of Justice.

Beck, U (1992): *Risk Society.* London: SAGE.

Beck, U (2009): *World at Risk.* Cambridge: Polity.

Becker, HK (1973): *Police Systems of Europe: A Survey of Selected Police Organizations.* Springfield, IL: Charles C. Thomas.

Beetham, D (1991): *The Legitimation of Power.* Atlantic Highlands, NJ: Humanities Press International.

Beetham, D and C Lord (1998): *Legitimacy and the* EU. London: Longman.

Bellanova, R (2008): "The 'Prüm Process': The way forward for EU police cooperation and data exchange?" F Geyer and E Guild (eds): *Security Versus Justice? Police and Judicial Cooperation in the European Union.* Aldershot: Ashgate.

Benyon, J (1994a): *Police Forces in the European Union: A Summary.* Leicester: Centre for the Study of Public Order.

Benyon, J (1994b): "Policing the European Union: The changing basis of cooperation on law enforcement". *International Affairs.* 70 (3), 497–517.

Benyon, J (1996): "The politics of police co-operation in the European Union". *International Journal of the Sociology of Law.* 24 (4), 353–379.

Benyon, J, L Turnbull, A Willis, R Woodward and A Beck (1993): *Police Co-Operation in Europe: An Investigation.* Leicester: University of Leicester.

Berg, JP (2011): Kommentar til Lov om Schengen Informasionssystem (SIS). (Available at: http://abo.rettsdata.no/browse.aspx?grid=51728&terms_and=sis [14.07.2014]).

Bergo, K (2000): *Høyesteretts forarbeidsbruk.* Oslo: Cappelen akademisk.

Bergström, M and AJ Cornell (2014): *European Police and Criminal Law Co-Operation.* Oxford: Hart.

Berlin, I (1969): *Four Essays on Liberty.* Oxford: Oxford University Press.

Berlin, I, I Harris and H Hardy (2002): *Liberty: Incorporating Four Essays on Liberty.* Oxford: Oxford University Press.

Bigo, D (2000a): "When two become one: International and external securitisations in Europe". M Kelstrup and M Williams (eds): *International Relations Theory and the Politics of European Integration: Power, Security and Community.* London: Routledge.

Bigo, D (2000b): "Liaison officers in Europe". JWE Sheptycki (ed.): *Issues in Transnational Policing*. London: Routledge.

Bigo, D, W Bruggeman, P Burgess and V Mitsilegas (2007): *The Principle of Information Availability*. Paris: CHALLENGE.

Bigo, D, L Bonelli, D Chi and C Olsson (2008): "Mapping the field of the EU internal security agencies". D Bigo (ed.): *The Field of the* EU *Internal Security Agencies*. Paris: L'Harmattan.

Birkeland, Å (2007): "Politigeneralisten, den moderne staten og politiets legitimitet". HI Gundhus, P Larsson and TG Myhrer (eds): *Polisiær virksombet: Hva er det – hvem gjør det? Forskningskonferansen 2007*. Oslo: Politihøgskolen.

Bittner, E (1970): *The Functions of the Police in Modern Society: A Review of Background Factors, Current Practices, and Possible Role Models*. Chevy Chase, MD: National Institute of Mental Health, Center for Studies of Crime and Delinquency.

Bittner, E (1990): *Aspects of Police Work*. Boston, MA: Northeastern University Press.

Block, L (2008): "Combating organized crime in Europe: Practicalities of police cooperation". *Policing*. 2 (1), 74–81.

Block, L (2011): *From Politics to Policing: The Rationality Gap in the* EU *Council Policy-Making*. The Hague: Eleven.

Block, L (2012): "EU joint investigation teams". S Bronitt, C Harfield and S Hufnagel (eds): *Cross-Border Law Enforcement: Regional Law Enforcement Cooperation: European, Australian and Asia-Pacific Perspectives*. London: Routledge.

Block, L (2013): "EU policy-making on liaison officers". M den Boer and L Block (eds): *Liaison Officers: Essential Actors in Transnational Policing*. The Hague: Eleven International Publishing.

Boe, E and F Sejersted (1999): *Schengen og grunnloven*. Oslo: Universitetsforlaget.

Boehm, F (2012a): *Information Sharing and Data Protection in the Area of Freedom, Security and Justice: Towards Harmonised Data Protection Principles for Information Exchange at EU-Level*. Berlin, Heidelberg: Springer.

Boehm, F (2012b): "Information sharing and data protection in the Area of Freedom, Security and Justice". S Gutwirth et al. (eds): *European Data Protection: In Good Health?* Dordrecht: Springer.

Bonde, A (1994): *For lov og rett i 250 år: Oslo politikammer 1744–1994 med spesiell vekt på de siste 50 år*. Oslo: Oslo Politikammer.

Bosniak, L (2006): *The Citizen and the Alien: Dilemmas of Contemporary Membership*. Princeton, NJ: Princeton University Press.

Boucht, J (2012): "Cross-border use of police powers within the EU: A Finnish, Norwegian and Swedish perspective". *European Criminal Law Review*. 2 (3), 203–235.

Bowling, B and J Sheptycki (2012): *Global policing*. Los Angeles, CA: SAGE.

Brammertz, S (1997): "Schengen et la poursuite transfrontaliere". *Vigiles: Revue du droit de police*. (1), 8–20.

Brett, AS (2011): *Changes of State: Nature and the Limits of the City in Early Modern Natural Law*. Princeton, NJ & Oxford: Princeton University Press.

Brodeur, J-P (1983): "High policing and low policing: Remarks about the policing of political activities". *Social Problems*. 30 (5), 507–520.

Brodeur, J-P (1995): "Undercover policing in Canada: A study of its consequences". C Fijnaut and GT Marx (eds): *Undercover-Police Surveillance in Comparative Perspective*. The Hague: Kluwer.

Brodeur, J-P. (2007): "High and Low Policing in Post–9/11 Times". *Policing: A Journal of Policy and Practice*. 1 (1), 25–37.

Brodeur, J-P (2010): *The Policing Web*. Oxford: Oxford University Press.

Brogden, M (1982): *The Police: Autonomy and Consent*. London & New York: Academic Press.

Brogden, M (1989): "The origins of the South African police: Institutional versus structural approaches". *Acta Juridica*. 1 (1989), 1–19.

Brouwer, E (2007): "Effective remedies in EU migration law". A Baldaccini, E Guild and H Toner (eds): *Whose Freedom, Security and Justice?* EU *Immigration and Asylum Law and Policy.* Oxford: Hart.
Brown, SD (2008): "Controlled deliveries". SD Brown (ed.): *Combating International Crime: The Longer Arm of the Law.* London: Routledge-Cavendish.
Bruce, I (2015): "Praktisk politi- og påtalesamarbeid i EU". *Tidsskrift for strafferett.* 15 (4), 447–468.
Bruce, I and GS Haugland (2014): *Skjulte tvangsmidler.* Oslo: Universitetsforlaget.
Bruggeman, W (2002): "Policing and accountability in a dynamic European context". *Policing and Society.* 12 (4), 259–273.
Bull, H (1997): "The Schengen cooperation and Norway". P-C Müller-Graff and E Selvig (eds): *The European Economic Area: Norway's Basic Status in the Legal Construction of Europe.* Berlin: Berlin Verlag A. Spitz.
Buzan, B (1991): *People, States and Fear: An Agenda for International Security Studies in the Post-Cold War Era.* New York: Harvester Wheatsheaf.
Buzan, B and O Wæver (2003): *Regions and Powers: The Structure of International Security.* Cambridge: Cambridge Uuniversity Press.
Cain, ME (1973): *Society and the Policeman's Role.* London: Routledge.
Cameron, I (2000): *National Security and the European Convention on Human Rights.* The Hague: Kluwer Law International.
Cameron, I (2014): "Council of Europe: Standards on police data storage and sharing". M Bergström and AJ Cornell (eds): *European Police and Criminal Law Co-Operation.* Oxford: Hart.
Cameron, I, M Thunberg Schunke, K Påle-Bartes, C Wong and P Asp (2011): *International Criminal Law from a Swedish Perspective.* Cambridge: Intersentia.
Cananea, G della (2010): "Procedural due process of law beyond the state". A von Bogandy et al. (ed.): *The Exercise of Public Authority by International Institutions.* Berlin Heidelberg: Springer Verlag.
Castberg, F (1955): *Innledning til forvaltningsretten.* Oslo: Akademisk forlag.
Castberg, F (1961): *Juridiske stridsspørsmål i Norges politiske historie.* Oslo: Universitetsforlaget.
Cavadino, M and J Dignan (2006): *Penal Systems.* London: SAGE.
Cere, R, Y Jewkes and T Ugelvik (2013): "Media and crime: A Comparative analysis of crime news in the UK, Norway and Italy". S Body-Gendrot m. fl. (ed.): *The Routledge Handbook of European Criminology.* Abingdon: Routledge.
Chaims, G (2003): *The Limits of Nationalism.* Cambridge: Cambridge University Press.
Charbonneau, B (2008): *France and the New Imperialism: Security Policy in Sub-Saharan Africa.* Aldershot: Ashgate.
Chayes, A and AH Chayes (1995): *The New Sovereignty: Compliance with International Regulatory Agreements.* Cambridge, MA: Harvard Univerity Press.
Christie, N (1993): *Kriminalitetskontroll som industri: Mot Gulag, vestlig type?* Oslo: Universitetsforlaget.
Christie, N (1995): *Hvor tett et samfunn?* Oslo: Universitetsforlaget.
Christie, N (2006): "Criminal justice policies: Trends and their impact on prison health". *International Journal of Prisoner Health.* 2 (1), 63–68.
Cockcroft, T (2012): *Police Culture: Themes and Concepts.* Abingdon: Routledge.
Cohen, S (1985): *Visions of Social Control: Crime, Punishment and Classification.* Cambridge: Polity Press.
Cohen, S (1987): *Folk Devils and Moral Panics: The Creation of the Mods and Rockers.* Oxford: Basil Blackwell.
Connolly, WE (2002): *Identity\Difference: Democratic Negotiations of Political Paradox.* Minneapolis: University of Minnesota Press.
Cornell, AJ (2014): "EU police cooperation post-Lisbon". M Bergström and AJ Cornell (eds): *European Police and Criminal Law Co-Operation.* Oxford: Hart.

Coudert, F (2017): "The Europol Regulation and purpose limitation [. . .]". Blog post 18.04.2017 (09.09.2017).

Cryer, R, T Hervey and B Sokhi-Bulley (2011): *Research Methodologies in* EU *and International Law*. Oxford: Hart.

Daman, M (2008): "Cross-border hot pursuit in the EU". *European Journal of Crime, Criminal Law and Criminal Justice*. 16 (2008), 171–207.

Davis, J (1991): "Urban policing and its objects: Comparative themes in England and France in the second half of the nineteenth century". C Emsley and B Weinberger (eds): *Policing Western Europe: Politics, Professionalism, and Public Order, 1850–1940*. New York: Greenwood.

de Buck, B (2007): "Joint investigation teams: The participation of Europol officials". ERA *Forum*. 8 (2), 253–264.

de Busser, Ed (2006): "Judicial cooperation in criminal matters: Mutual legal assistance". C Rijken and G Vermeulen (eds): *Joint Investigation Teams in the European Union: From Theory to Practice*. The Hague: Asser.

de Moor, Ad (2009): "The role of Europol in joint investigation teams. A foretaste of an executive European police office". *Gofs Research Paper Series*. 2 (2009), 329–358.

de Moor, Ad (2012): *Europol, Quo Vadis? Critical Analysis and Evaluation of the Development of the European Police Office*. Antwerp: Maklu.

de Moor, Ad and G Vermeulen (2010a): "The Europol council decision: Transforming Europol into an agency of the European Union". *Common Market Law Review*. 47 (4), 1089–1121.

de Moor, Ad and G Vermeulen (2010b): "The 'new' principal task for Europol to support member states in connection with major international events: The blurring of boundaries between law enforcement and public order?". *Journal of Police Studies*. 3 (16), 121–138.

de Wree, E (2006): "Law enforcement information exchange in the pre-operational phase of a JIT". C Rijken and G Vermeulen (eds): *Joint Investigation Teams in the European Union: From Theory to Practice*. The Hague: Asser.

Deflem, M (2002): *Policing World Society: Historical Foundations of International Police Cooperation*. Oxford: Oxford University Press.

Deflem, M and S Sutphin (2006): "Policing post-war Iraq: Insurgency, civilian police, and the reconstitution of society". *Sociological Focus*. 39 (4), 265–283.

den Boer, M (1994): "The quest for European policing: Rhetoric and justification in a disorderly debate". M Anderson and Md Boer (eds): *Policing across National Boundaries*. London: Pinter.

den Boer, M (1998): "Internationalization: A challenge to police organizations in Europe". R Mawby (ed.): *Policing across the World: Issues for the Twenty-First Century*. London: University College London Press.

den Boer, M (2002a): *Organised Crime: A Catalyst in the Europeanisation of National Police and Prosecution Agencies?* Maastricht: European Institute of Public Administration.

den Boer, M (2002b): "Towards an accountability regime for an emerging European policing governance". *Policing and Society*. 12 (4), 275–289

den Boer, M (2010): "Towards a governance model of police cooperation in Europe: The twist between networks and bureaucracies". F Lemieux (ed.): *International Police Cooperation: Emerging Issues, Theory and Practice*. Cullompton: Willan.

den Boer, M and W Bruggeman (2011): "Policing and internal security in the post-Lisbon era: New challenges ahead". S Wolff, FANJ Goudappel and Jd Zwaan (eds): *Freedom, Security and Justice after Lisbon and Stockholm*. Den Haag: T.M.C. Asser.

den Boer, M and P Doelle (2002): "Converge or not to converge. . . that's the question: A comparative analysis of Europeanisation trends in criminal justice organisations". M den Boer (ed.): *Organised Crime: A Catalyst in the Europeanisation of National Police and Prosecution Agencies?* Maastricht: European Institute of Public Administration.

den Boer, M and J Monar (2002): "11 September and the challenge of global terrorism". G Edwards and G Wiessala (eds): *The European Union: The Annual Review 2001/2002*. Chichester: Wiley-Blackwell.

den Boer, M and N Walker (1993): "European policing after 1992". *Journal of Common Market Studies.* 31 (1), 3–28.
den Boer, M and W Wallace (2000): "Justice and Home Affairs: Integration through incrementalism?". H Wallace and W Wallace (eds): *Policy-Making in the European Union.* Oxford: Oxford University Press.
den Boer, M, C Hillebrand and A Nölke (2008): "Legitimacy under pressure: The European web of counter-terrorism networks". *Journal of Common Market Studies.* 46 (1), 101–124.
Dubber, MD (2005): *The Police Power: Patriarchy and the Foundations of American Government.* New York: Columbia University Press.
Duff, RA (2007): *Answering for Crime: Responsibility and Liability in the Criminal Law.* Oxford: Hart.
Durkheim, É (1933): *The Division of Labor in Society.* New York: The Free Press.
Dørum, K and H Sandvik (2012): *Opptøyer i Norge 1750–1850.* Oslo: Scandinavian Academic Press.
Eckhoff, T and JE Helgesen (2001): *Rettskildelære.* Oslo: Universitetsforlaget.
Eckhoff, T and E Smith (2006): *Forvaltningsrett.* Oslo: Universitetsforlaget.
Efjestad, JS (2009): "Eurojust: EUs påtalesamarbeid og norsk deltakelse". Oslo: Stortingets Utredningsseksjon (Perspektiv).
Elden, S (2013): *The Birth of Territory.* Chicago, IL: University of Chicago Press.
Elholm, T (2009): "Does EU criminal cooperation necessarily mean increased repression?" *European Journal of Crime, Criminal Law and Criminal Justice.* (3), 191–226.
Ellefsen, B (2013): "Det politianalysen ikke sier noe om". *Dagsavisen.* 23.09.13.
Emsley, C (1996): *The English Police: A Political and Social History.* London: Longman.
Emsley, C (1999a): *Gendarmes and the State in Nineteenth-Century Europe.* Oxford: Oxford University Press.
Emsley, C (1999b): "A typology of nineteenth-century police". *Crime, History & Societies.* 3 (1), 29–44.
Emsley, C (2001): "The origins and development of the police". E McLaughlin and J Muncie (eds): *Controlling Crime.* London: SAGE.
Emsley, C (2011): *The History of Policing.* Farnham: Ashgate.
Ericson, RV and KD Haggerty (1997): *Policing the Risk Society.* Oxford: Clarendon.
Eriksen, CC (2009): *The European Constitution, Welfare States and Democracy: A Study of Conflicts between the Four Freedoms and National Administrative Discretion.* Oslo: Det juridiske fakultet, Universitetet i Oslo.
Eriksen, EO (2008): "Norges demokratiske underskudd". *Nytt norsk tidsskrift.* 25 (4), 368–379.
Eriksen, EO and JE Fossum (2001): *The* EU *and Post-National Legitimacy.* Oslo: ARENA.
Ewald, F (1986): *L'Etat providence.* Paris: Grasset.
Fichera, M (2009): "The European arrest warrant and the sovereign state: A marriage of convenience?". *European Law Journal.* 15 (1), 70–97.
Fijnaut, C (1993): *The Internationalization of Police Cooperation in Western Europe.* Deventer: Kluwer Law and Taxation Publishers.
Fijnaut, C (1995): "International policing in Europe: Its present situation and future". J-P Brodeur (ed.): *Comparisons in Policing: An International Perspective.* Avebury: Aldershot.
Fijnaut, C (2010): "The Meuse-Rhine euroregion: A laboratory for police and judicial cooperation in the European Union". F Lemieux (ed.): *International Police Cooperation: Emerging Issues, Theory and Practice.* Cullompton: Willan.
Fijnaut, C and GT Marx (1995): "Introduction: The normalization of undercover policing in the west: Historical and contemporary perspectives". C Fijnaut and GT Marx (eds): *Undercover-Police Surveillance in Comparative Perspective.* The Hague: Kluwer.
Finstad, L (2000): *Politiblikket.* Oslo: Pax.
Fleischer, CA (1981): *Juridisk betenkning til Justisdepartementet. Bruk av militær makt, militært utstyr mv.i indre konflikter: Spørsmål om rekkevidden av Grunnlovens § 99 annet ledd.* Oslo: Justisdepartementet.

Fleischer, CA (2000): *Folkerett*. Oslo: Universitetsforlaget.

Fosdick, RB (1915): *European Police Systems*. New York: Century.

Fossum, JE and EO Eriksen (2014): *Det norske paradoks: om Norges forhold til Den Europeiske Union*. Oslo: Universitetsforlaget.

Foucault, M (2007): *Security, Territory, Population: Lectures at the Collège de France, 1977–78*. Basingstoke: Palgrave Macmillan.

Fredriksen, HH and G Mathisen (2012): *EØS-rett*. Bergen: Fagbokforlaget.

Fredriksen, S (2013): *Innføring i straffeprosess*. Oslo: Gyldendal juridisk.

Fredriksen, S (2014): *Ro, orden og frihet: En fremstilling av politiets adgang til å gripe inn i den personlige frihet ved utførelse av ordenstjeneste*. Bergen: Universitetet i Bergen.

Frostad, M (2008): "Militær politimyndighet". *Tidsskrift for Strafferett*. 8 (2), 257–289.

Frostad, M (2009): "Regjeringens bruk av militær makt mot borgerne: Grunnloven § 99 annet ledd". JP Rui (ed.): *Rettshjelp fra kyst til vidde: Festskrift til jusshjelpa i Nord-Norge 20 år*. Oslo: Gyldendal Akademisk.

Furuhagen, B (2009): *Från fjärdingsman till närpolis: En kortfattad svensk polishistoria*. Växjö: Växjö universitet, Polisutbildningen.

Føllesdal, A and S Hix (2006): "Why there is a democratic deficit in the EU: A response to Majone and Moravcsik". *Journal of Common Market Studies*. 44 (3), pp 533–62.

Gade, I, et al. (2005): *Det politimæssige og strafferetlige samarbejde i Den Europæiske Union*. København: DJØF.

Gammelgard, P (2001): "International police cooperation from a Norwegian perspective". DJ Koenig and DK Das (eds): *International Police Cooperation: A World Perspective*. Lanham, MD: Lexington Books.

Garland, D (2001): *The Culture of Control*. Chicago, IL: University of Chicago Press.

Gerspacher, N (2005): "The roles of international police cooperation organizations: Beyond mandates, toward unintended roles". *European Journal of Crime, Criminal Law and Criminal Justice*. 13 (3), 413–434.

Gerspacher, N (2008): "The history of international police cooperation: A 150-year evolution in trends and approaches". *Global Crime*. 9 (1–2), 169–184.

Giddens, Anthony (1987): *Social Theory and Modern Sociology*. Cambridge: Polity Press.

Glasser, L (2006): *Schengen: En bibliografi: Et utvalg*. Bergen: European Documentation Centre.

Goldsmith, AJ and J Sheptycki (2007): *Crafting Transnational Policing: Police Capacity-Building and Global Policing Reform*. Oxford: Hart.

Goold, BJ and L Lazarus (2007): *Security and Human Rights*. Oxford: Hart.

Grimm, D (2015): *Sovereignty: The Origin and Future of a Political and Legal Concept*. New York: Columbia University Press.

Groenleer, M (2009): *The Autonomy of European Union Agencies: A Comparative Study of Institutional Development*. Delft: Eburon.

Gundersen, FF (2010): *EU etter Lisboa-traktaten: Institusjoner, rettssystem og rettsregler*. Oslo: Gyldendal akademisk.

Habermas, J (1987): *Knowledge and Human Interests*. Cambridge: Polity.

Habermas, J (1996): *Between Facts and Norms: Contributions to a Discourse Theory of Law and Democracy*. Cambridge, MA: MIT Press.

Hagen, R (2010): "Hva betyr kollektiv binding? Niklas Luhmanns bidrag til en teori om det politiske systemets funksjon.". L Hilt, K Venneslan and B Mortensen Vik (eds): *Luhmann og magt: En antologi*. København: Unge Pædagoger.

Halvorsen, V (2003): "Utradisjonelle etterforskningsmetoder i et samfunnsvitenskapelig og etisk perspektiv". Trond Myklebust and Gunnar Thomassen (eds): *Det utfordrende politiarbeidet: Om krisehåndtering og utradisjonelle etterforskningsmetoder*. Oslo: Politihøgskolen.

Halvorsen, V (2013): "Gjørv-kommisjonen i et komparativt og historisk perspektiv". *Materialisten*. 41 (1–2), 85–97.

Harding, R (2012): "State monopoly of 'permitted violation of human rights': The decision of the Supreme Court of Israel prohibiting the private operation and management of prisons ". *Punishment & Society.* 14 (2), 131–146.
Heivoll, G (2017): *Lovens lange arm?: En studie av politibetjenters rolle som rettshåndhevere i den norske demokratiske rettsstaten.* University of Agder. PhD thesis.
Helle, K, S Dyrvik, T Grønlie and E Hovland (2013): *Grunnbok i Norges historie: Fra vikingtid til våre dager.* Oslo: Universitetsforlaget.
Hendy, R (2014): "Routinely armed and unarmed police: What can the Scandinavian experience teach us?". *Policing.* 8 (2), 183–192.
Henricson, I (2010): *International politiret.* København: DJØF.
Heringa, AW and L Zwaak (2006): "Right to respect for privacy (Article 8)". Pv Dijk, Y Arai and GJHv Hoof (eds): *Theory and Practice of the European Convention on Human Rights.* Antwerpen: Intersentia.
Hindelang, MJ, MR Gottfredson and J Garofalo (1978): *Victims of Personal Crime: An Empirical Foundation for a Theory of Personal Victimization.* Cambridge: Ballinger.
Hobbes, T (1998) [1651]: *Leviathan.* Oxford: Oxfor University Press.
Holmberg, L (2005): "Policing and the feeling of safety: The rise (and fall?) of community policing in the Nordic countries". *Journal of Scandinavian Studies in Criminology and Crime Prevention.* 5 (2), 205–219.
Holmøyvik, E (2013): " 'Sikker konstitusjonell praksis'? Grunnlova og Noregs avtaler om suverenitetsoverføring". *Nytt norsk tidsskrift.* 30 (2), 117–125.
Hopsnes, R (2003): *Provokasjon som politimetode.* Oslo: Universitetsforlaget.
Hov, J (2007): *Straffeprosess.* Oslo: Papinian.
Hufnagel, S (2013): *Policing Cooperation across Borders: Comparative Perspectives on Law Enforcement within the EU and Australia.* Farnham: Ashgate.
Hufnagel, S (2014): "Strategies of police cooperation along the southern Chinese seaboard: A comparison with the EU". *Crime, Law and Social Change.* 61 (4), 377–399.
Hufnagel, S (2016): " 'Third Party' status in EU policing and security – Comparing the position of Norway with the UK before and after the 'Brexit' ". *Nordisk tidsskrift for politiforskning.* 3 (2), 165–180.
Huysmans, EF (2006): *The Politics of Insecurity: Fear, Migration, and Asylum in the* EU. London: Routledge.
Høigård, C (2005): *Nytt politi? En kommentert bibliografi over nyere nordisk politiforskning.* Oslo: IKRS.
Høigård, C (2011): "Policing the North". *Crime and Justice: A Review of Research.* 40, 265–348.
Imsen, S (1997): "Communalism and state-building in Norway, 1537–1648". *Scandinavian Journal of History.* 22 (1), 21–29.
Ingleton, R (1994): *Mission Incomprehensible: The Linguistic Barrier to Effective Police Co-Operation in Europe.* Avon: Multilingual Matters.
Jessop, B (1990): *State Theory: Putting the State in its Place.* Cambridge: Polity Press.
Jessop, B (2009): "State Theory". R Kitchin and N Thrift (eds): *International Encyclopedia of Human Geography vol. 2.* Oxford: Elsevier.
Jewkes, Y, R Cere and T Ugelvik (2014): "Media and crime: A comparative analysis of crime news in the UK, Norway and Italy". S Body-Gendrot et al. (eds): *The Routledge Handbook of European Criminology.* London: Routledge.
Johansen, NB (2008): *Sosial kontroll i byer: To tradisjoner etter Durkheim og Tönnies.* Oslo: IKRS.
Johansen, NB, Thomas Ugelvik and KF Aas (2013): *Krimmigrasjon? Den nye kontrollen av de fremmede.* Oslo: Universitetsforlaget.
Johansen, PO (1977): *Menstadkonflikten 1931.* Oslo: Tiden.
Johansen, PO (1989): *"Samfunnets pansrede neve": Statspoliti og ekstraordinær overvåkning 1918–1941.* Oslo: Gyldendal.

Johansen, PO (2006): *På siden av rettsoppgjøret.* Oslo: Unipub.
Jones, T and T Newburn (2004): "The convergence of US and UK crime control policy: Exploring substance and process". T Newburn and R Sparks (eds): *Criminal Justice and Political Cultures: National and International Dimensions of Crime Control.* Cullompton: Willan.
Jonsson, A (2010): "Gemensamma utredningsgrupper i gränsöverskridande brottsutredningar". *Europarättslig tidsskrift.* 2, 312–334.
Joubert, C and H Bevers (1996): *Schengen Investigated: A Comparative Interpretation of the Schengen Provision on International Police Cooperation in the Light of the European Convention on Human Rights.* The Hague: Kluwer.
Juris, HA (1971): "The implications of police unionism". *Law & Society Review.* 6 (2), 231–245.
Karanja, SK (2001): *Norwegian Border Control in a Europe without Internal Frontiers.* Oslo: Institutt for Rettsinformatikk.
Karanja, SK (2008): *Transparency and Proportionality in the Schengen Information System and Border Control Co-Operation.* Leiden: Nijhoff.
Karstedt, S (2004): "Durkhem, Tarde and beyond: The global travel of crime policies". T Newburn and R Sparks (eds): *Criminal Justice and Political Cultures: National and International Dimensions of Crime Control.* Cullompton: Willan.
Kirchner, E and J Sperling (2007): *EU Security Governance.* Manchester: Manchester University Press.
Kjelby, GJ (2013): *Mellom rett og plikt til straffeforfølgning: Den relative etterforsknings- og påtalepliktens rettslige rammer og rettslige utvikling i norsk straffeprosess.* Bergen: Cappelen.
Kleiven, ME (2012): "Nordic police cooperation". S Bronitt, C Harfield and S Hufnagel (eds): *Cross-Border Law Enforcement: Regional Law Enforcement Cooperation: European, Australian and Asia-Pacific Perspectives.* London: Routledge.
Kleiven, ME (2013): "Seamless law enforcement cooperation: The Nordic police liaison officers". M den Boer and L Block (eds): *Liaison Officers: Essential Actors in Transnational Policing.* The Hague: Eleven International Publishing.
Knepper, P (2011): *International Crime in the 20th Century.* Basingstoke: Palgrave Macmillan.
Knutsson, J (2005): *Politiets bruk av skytevåpen i Norden.* Oslo: Politihøgskolen.
Krasner, SD (1999): *Sovereignty: Organized Hypocrisy.* Princeton, NJ: Princeton University Press.
Krasner, SD (2001): "Sovereignty". *Foreign Policy.* (122), 20–29.
Kvam, B (2008): *Norge og Schengen: Et svekket samarbeid mot kriminalitet.* Oslo: Cappelen akademisk.
Kvam, B (2014): *Politiets persondatarett: En studie av hjemmels- og formålskrav ved politiets utlevering av personopplysninger til utlandet.* Oslo: Gyldendal juridisk.
Kvam, B and A Suominen (2009): "Skjær i sjøen for Norges strafferettslige samarbeid med EU". *Lov og rett.* 48 (8), 478–492.
Lacey, N (2008): *The Prisoner's Dilemma.* Cambridge: Cambridge University Press.
Larsson, P (2004): "Organisert kriminalitet: Myter og realiteter". P Larson and T Myklebust (ed): *Organisert og økonomisk kriminalitet: Myter og realiteter.* Oslo: Politihøgskolen.
Larsson, P (2006): "International police co-operation: A Norwegian perspective". *Journal of Financial Crime.* 13 (4), 456–466.
Larsson, P (2010): "Ideology as a cover up: Community policing in Norway". A Verhage et al. (eds): *Policing in Europe.* Antwerpen: Maklu.
Lavenex, S (2010): "Justice and home affairs: Communitarization with hesitation". H Wallace, AR Young and MA Pollack (eds): *Policy-Making in the European Union.* Oxford: Oxford University Press.
Levi, R (2008): "Loitering in the city that works: On circulation, activity, and police in governing urban space". MD Dubber and M Valverde (eds): *Police and the Liberal State.* Stanford: Stanford General.

Liang, H-H (1992): *The Rise of Modern Police and the European State System from Metternich to the Second World War.* Cambridge: Cambridge University Press.

Lipset, SM (1963): *The First New Nation: The United States in Historical and Comparative Perspective.* New York: Basic Books.

Loader, I (2002a): "Policing, securitization and democratization in Europe". *Criminology and Criminal Justice.* 2 (2), 125–153.

Loader, I (2002b): "Governing European policing: Some problems, and prospects". *Policing and Society.* 12 (4), 291–305.

Loader, I (2004): "Policing, securitisation and democratisation in Europe". T Newburn and R Sparks (eds): *Criminal Justice and Political Cultures: National and International Dimensions of Crime Control.* Cullompton: Willan.

Loader, I and A Mulcahy (2003): *Policing and the Condition of England: Memory, Politics and Culture.* Oxford: Oxford University Press.

Loader, I and N Walker (2007): *Civilizing Security.* Cambridge: Cambridge University Press.

Locke, J (1824) [1689]: *The Works of John Locke, vol. 2 (An Essay concerning Human Understanding Part 2 and Other Writings).* London.

Loftus, B (2009): *Police Culture in a Changing World.* Oxford: Oxford University Press.

Lomell, HM (2007): *Selektive overblikk.* Oslo: Universitetsforlaget.

Lomell, HM, HO Gundhus and KF Aas (2009): *Technologies of InSecurity.* Abingdon: Routledge-Cavendish.

Lorentzen, H (1981): "Politiet i 70-årene". AM Støkken et al. (eds): *Politiet i det norske samfunn.* Oslo: Universitetsforlaget.

Lund, K (1996): *Rapport til Stortinget fra kommisjonen som ble nedsatt av Stortinget for å granske påstander om ulovlig overvåking av norske borgere (Lund-rapporten).* Oslo: Stortinget.

Lyon, D (2005): "The border is everywhere: ID cards, surveillance and the other". E Zureik and M Salter (eds): *Global Surveillance and Policing: Borders, Security, Identity.* Cullompton: Willan.

Maguire, M (2012): "Criminal statistics and the construction of crime". M Maguire, R Morgan and R Reiner (eds): *The Oxford Handbook of Criminology.* Oxford: Oxford University Press.

Manning, PK (1977): *Police Work: The Social Organization of Policing.* Cambridge, MA: MIT Press.

Manning, PK (2007): "A dialectic of organisational and occupational culture". M O'Neill, M Marks and A-M Singh (eds): *Police Occupational Culture: New Debates and Directions.* Oxford: Elsevier.

Manning, PK (2010): *Democratic Policing in a Changing World.* Boulder, CO: Paradigm Publishers.

Marenin, O (1982): "Parking tickets and class repression: The concept of policing in critical theories of criminal justice". *Contemporary Crises.* 6 (1982), 241–266.

Marshall, LS (1993): "The English and American industrial city of the nineteenth century". C Emsley (ed.): *Essays in Comparative History: Economy, Politics and Society in Britain and America 1850–1920.* Buckingham & Bristol: Open University Press.

Martha, RSJ (2010): *The Legal Foundations of INTERPOL.* Oxford: Hart.

Marx, GT (1995a): "Undercover: Some implications for police". C Fijnaut and GT Marx (eds): *Undercover-Police Surveillance in Comparative Perspective.* The Hague: Kluwer.

Marx, GT (1995b): "When the guards guard themselves: Undercover tactics turned inward". C Fijnaut and GT Marx (ed.): *Undercover-Police Surveillance in Comparative Perspective.* The Hague: Kluwer.

Marx, GT (1997): "Social control across borders". WF McDonald (ed.): *Crime and Law Enforcement in the Global Village.* Cincinnati, OH: Anderson.

Mathiesen, T (1979): *Politikrigen.* Oslo: Pax.

Mathiesen, T (1997): *Schengen: Politisamarbeid, overvåking og rettssikkerhet i Europa.* Oslo: Spartacus.

Mathisen, G (2009): *Utlevering for straffbare forhold.* Oslo: Gyldendal akademisk.

Mathisen, G (2010): "Nordic cooperation and the European arrest warrant: Intra-Nordic extradition, the Nordic arrest warrant and beyond". *Nordic Journal of International Law*. 79 (1), 1–4.

Mawby, RI (ed.) (1999): *Policing across the World: Issues for the Twenty-First Century*. London: University College London Press.

Mayer, M (2006): "Sociological aspects regarding the set up and management of a joint investigation team". C Rijken and G Vermeulen (eds): *Joint Investigation Teams in the European Union: From Theory to Practice*. The Hague: Asser.

McLoughlin, E (1992): "The democratic deficit: European Union and the accountability of the British police". *British Journal of Criminology*. 32 (4), 473–487.

Miller, D (1995): *On Nationality*. Oxford: Oxford University Press.

Mitsilegas, V (2009): *EU Criminal Law*. Oxford: Hart.

Mitsilegas, V (2012): "Immigration control in an era of globalization: Deflecting foreigners, weakening citizens, and strengthening the state". *Indiana Journal of Global Legal Studies*. 19 (1), 3–60.

Mitsilegas, V, S Carrera and K Eisele (2014): "The End of the Transitional Period for Police and Criminal Justice Measures Adopted Before the Lisbon Treaty: Who Monitors Trust in the European Criminal Justice Area?" *Liberty and Security in Europe Papers* No. 74 (December 8, 2014). Available at: https://ssrn.com/abstract=2537321

Moravcsik, A (2002): "Reassessing legitimacy in the European Union". *Journal of Common Market Studies*. 40 (4), 603–624.

Mosse, GI (1975): *Police Forces in History*. London: SAGE.

Myhrer, T-G (2001): "Etterforskningsbegrepet". *Tidsskrift for Strafferett*. 1 (1), 6–30.

Myhrer, T-G (2004a): "Taushetsplikt". R Bunæs, KO Kvigne and B Vandvik (eds): *Utlendingsrett*. Oslo: Universitetsforlaget.

Myhrer, T-G (2004b): "Tvangsmidler". R Bunæs, KO Kvigne and B Vandvik (eds): *Utlendingsrett*. Oslo: Universitetsforl.

Myhrer, T-G (2005): "Politiets bruk av skytevåpen: Rettslige problemstillinger". J Knutsson (ed.): *Politiets bruk av skytevåpen i Norden*. Oslo: Politihøgskolen.

Myhrer, T-G (2007a): "Begrenset politimyndighet". HI Gundhus, P Larsson and T-G Myhrer (eds): *Polisiær virksomhet: Hva er det – hvem gjør det? Forskningskonferansen 2007*. Oslo: Politihøgskolen.

Myhrer, T-G (2007b): "So-called extraordinary of untraditional investigative methods a contribution towards a common understanding of terminology". *Scandinavian Studies in Law*. 51, 419–436.

Myhrer, T-G (2013): Kommentar til Lov om politiet (Politiloven). (Available at: http://abo.rettsdata.no/browse.aspx?bid=autoComp&sDest=gL19950804z2D53 [accessed 13.07.2014]).

Nadelmann, EA (1993): *Cops across Borders: The Internationalization of U.S. Criminal Law Enforcement*. University Park: Pennsylvania State University Press.

Napoli, P (2003): *Naissance de la police moderne: Pouvoir, normes, société*. Paris: Découverte.

Nelken, D (2010): *Comparative Criminal Justice: Making Sense of Difference*. Los Angeles: SAGE.

Neocleous, M (2000): *The Fabrication of Social Order: A Critical Theory of Police Power*. London: Pluto Press.

Neocleous, M (2003): *Imagining the State*. Maidenhead: Open University Press.

Neumann, IB (2001): *Norge – en kritikk: Begrepsmakt i Europa-debatten*. Oslo: Pax.

Nouwt, S (2009): "Towards a common European approach to data protection: A critical analysis of data protection perspectives of the Council of Europe and the European Union". S Gutwirth et al. (eds): *Reinventing Data Protection?* London: Springer.

Nuotio, K (2004): "On the significance of criminal justice for a Europe 'united in diversity'". K Nuotio (ed.): *Europe in Search of "Meaning and Purpose"*. Helsinki: Publications of the Faculty of Law, University of Helsinki.

Nuotio, K (2005): "Harmonization of criminal sanctions in the European Union: Criminal law science fiction". EJ Husabø and AStrandbakken (eds): *Harmonization of Criminal Law in Europe*. Antwerpen: Intersentia.

Næshagen, FL (2000): "Norway's democratic and conservative tradition in policing". *Scandinavian Journal of History*. 25 (3), 177–196.

O'Neill, M (2011): "A Europe that protects: Moving to the next statge of cross-border law enforcement cooperation". *The Police Journal*. 84 125–150.

Occhipinti, JD (2003): *The Politics of EU Police Cooperation: Toward a European FBI?* Boulder, CO: Lynne Rienner.

Olaussen, LP (2007): "Kontrolltyper, kriminalitet og samfunn". *Tidsskrift for samfunnsforskning*. 48 (1), 91–124.

Palombella, G (2006): *From Human Rights to Fundamental Rights: Consequences of a Conceptual Distinction*. Florence: European University Institute.

Palombella, G and N Walker (2009): *Relocating the Rule of Law*. Oxford: Hart.

Parkin, J (2011): *The Difficult Road to the Schengen Information System* II*: The Legacy of "Laboratories" and the Cost for Fundamental Rights and the Rule of Law*. Brussels: CEPS.

Pedersen, RB. (2004): "Behandlingen av asylsøknader etter Dublin-forordningen". R Bunæs, KO Kvigne and B Vandvik (eds): *Utlendingsrett*. Oslo: Universitetsforlaget.

Peers, S (2007): *Europol: The Final Step in the Creation of an "Investigative and Operational" European Police Force*. London: Statewatch.

Peers, S (2009): *EU Decision-Making after the Treaty of Lisbon: A Quick Guide*. London: Statewatch.

Peers, S (2011): *EU Justice and Home Affairs Law*. Oxford: Oxford University Press.

Pelinka, A (2011): "The European Union as an alternative to the nation-state". *International Journal of Politics, Culture, and Society*. 24 (1–2), 21–30.

Perron, W (2005): "Perspectives of the harmonization of criminal law and criminal procedure in the European Union". EJ Husabø and A Strandbakken (eds): *Harmonization of Criminal Law in Europe*. Antwerpen: Intersentia.

Plachta, M (2005): "Joint investigation teams: A new form of international cooperation in criminal matters". *European Journal of Crime, Criminal Law and Criminal Justice*. 13 (2), 61–86.

Police Directorate/*Politidirektoratet* (POD) (2010): *Tendenser i kriminaliteten: Utfordringer i Norge i 2010–2012*. Oslo: POD (Crime Tendencies)

Police Directorate/*Politidirektoratet* (POD) (2010): *The Police in Norway*. Oslo: POD.

Police Directorate/*Politidirektoratet* (POD) (2012): *Politiets Omverdensanalyse*. Oslo: POD.

Police Directorate/*Politidirektoratet* (POD) (2014): *Tendenser i kriminaliteten: Utfordringer i Norge 2014*. Oslo: POD. (Crime Tendencies)

Police Directorate/*Politidirektoratet* (POD) (2016): *Norsk politi i Schengen 1996–2016*. Oslo: POD.

Politiets samordningsorgan (2014): *Samordningsorganet: Årsrapport 2014*. Oslo: Samordningsorganet.

Poulantzas, NM (2002): *The Right of Hot Pursuit in International Law*. The Hague: Martinus Nijfhoff.

Prainsack, B and V Toom (2013): "Performing the union: The Prüm decision and the European dream". *Studies in History and Philosophy of Biological and Biomedical Sciences*. 44 (1), 71–79.

Raab, CD (1994): "Where are we now: Reflections on the sociology of education policy". D Halpin and B Troyna (eds): *Researching Education Policy: Ethical and Methodological Issues*. London: Falmer.

Raab, CD (2014): "Privacy as a security value". DW Schartum, L Bygrave and AGB Bekken (eds): *Jon Bing: En hyllest/A Tribute*. Oslo: Gyldendal.

Raeff, M (1983): *The Well-Ordered Police State: Social and Institutional Change through Law in the Germanies and Russia, 1600–1800*. New Haven, CT: Yale University Press.

Rao, AM and S Supphellen (1996): "Power elites and dependent territories". W Reinhard and S Supphellen (eds): *Power Elites and State Building*. Oxford: Clarendon.

Reiner, R (1992): *The Politics of the Police.* New York: Harvester Wheatsheaf.

Rieber-Mohn, GF (1996): "Etterforsking og påtalemyndighet". *Nytt i strafferetten.* 1996 (2), 19–47.

Rijken, C (2006): "Joint investigation teams: Principles, practice, and problems: Lessons learnt from the first efforts to establish a JIT". *Utrecht Law Review.* 2 (1), 99–118.

Rijken, C and G Vermeulen (2006a): *Joint Investigation Teams in the European Union: From Theory to Practice.* The Hague: Asser.

Rijken, C and G Vermeulen (2006b): "The legal and practical implementation of JITs: The bumpy road from EU to member state level". C Rijken and G Vermeulen (eds): *Joint Investigation Teams in the European Union: From Theory to Practice.* The Hague: Asser.

Ringmar, E (1996): "On the ontological status of the state". *European Journal of International Relations.* 2 (4), 439–466.

Robinson, CD, R Scaglion and MJ Olivero (1994): *Police in Contradiction: The Evolution of the Police Function in Society.* Westport, CT: Greenwood Press.

Rousseau, J-J (1958) [1762]: *Om samfunnspakten, eller statsrettens grunnsetninger.* Oslo: Dreyer.

Ruback, TJ (2011): "Sovereignties (once again) in question". *International Studies Review.* 13 (4), 1–6.

Rui, JP (2009): *Forbudet mot gjentatt straffeforfølgning.* Oslo: Universitetsforlaget.

Runhovde, S (2010): *Tillit til politiet.* Oslo: Politihøgskolen.

Ruud, M (2016): *Straffesaker i utlandet: Bistand og samarbeid.* Oslo: Universitetsforlaget.

Saloven, M, E Grant, P Hanel, V Makai, KB Hansen, L Belevicius and A Pohnitzer (2010): *Study on the Status of Information Exchange amongst Law Enforcement Authorities in the Context of Existing EU Instruments.* Vienna: International Centre for Migration Policy Development.

Sand, I-J (2010): "Teoretiske utfordringer for rettssosiologien i globaliseringens tid". BL Kristiansen and A Storgaard (eds): *Nordisk retssociologi: Status, aktuelle udfordringer, visioner.* København: DJØF.

Sarooshi, D (2004): "The essentially contested nature of the concept of sovereignty: Implications for the exercise by international organizations of delegated powers of government." *Michigan Journal of International Law.* (25) 1107, 1108–1109.

Sassen, S (2008): *Territory, Authority, Rights: From Medieval to Global Assemblages.* Princeton, NJ: Princeton University Press.

Schalken, T and M Pronk (2002): "On joint investigation teams, Europol and supervision of their joint actions". *European Journal of Crime, Criminal Law and Criminal Justice.* 10 (1) 70–82.

Schmitt, C (1996): *The Concept of the Political.* Chicago, IL: University of Chicago Press.

Schumacher, T (2011): *EU: "The Law Will Bring Peace": View on the European Gendarmerie Force (EGF).* London: Statewatch.

Schutte, J (1995): "Judicial co-operation under the European Union". R Bieber and J Monar (eds): *Justice and Home Affairs in the European Union: The Development of the Third Pillar.* Brussels: European Interuniversity Press.

Scott, JC (1998): *Seeing Like a State: How Certain Schemes to Improve the Human Condition Have Failed.* New Haven, CT: Yale University Press.

Sejersted, F (2002): *Kontroll og konstitusjon: Statsrettslige studier av Stortingets kontrollvirksomhet.* Oslo: Cappelen.

Sejersted, F (2004): *EØS-rett.* Oslo: Universitetsforlaget.

Sejersted, F (2011): *EØS-rett.* Oslo: Universitetsforlaget.

Sejersted, F (2013): *Sosialdemokratiets tidsalder: Norge og Sverige i det 20. århundre.* Oslo: Pax.

Sheptycki, JWE (1995): "Transnational policing and the makings of a postmodern state". *British Journal of Criminology.* 35 (4), 613–635.

Sheptycki, JWE (2000): *Issues in Transnational Policing.* London & New York: Routledge.

Sheptycki, JWE (1998): "Police cooperation in the English channel region, 1968–1996". *European Journal of Crime, Criminal Law, and Criminal Justice.* 6 (3), 216–235.

Sheptycki, JWE (2002): *In Search of Transnational Policing: Towards a Sociology of Global Policing.* Aldershot: Ashgate.

Silver, A (1967): "The demand for order in the civil society". DJ Bordua (ed.): *The Police: Six Sociological Essays.* New York: Wiley.

Skaflem, I (2014): *Kommentar til straffeprosessloven.* (Available at: http://rettsdata.no/direkte?grlink=gL19810522z2D25z2EzA782 [13.07.2014]).

Skarðhamar, T, LR Thorsen and K Henriksen (2011): *Kriminalitet og straff blant innvandrere og øvrig befolkning.* Oslo: SSB.

Slaughter, A-M (2004): *A New World Order.* Princeton, NJ and Oxford: Princeton University Press.

Snacken, S (2012): "Conclusion: Why and how to resist punitiveness in Europe". S Snacken and E Dumortier (eds): *Resisting Punitiveness in Europe? Welfare, Human Rights and Democracy.* London: Routledge.

Solberg, J-P (2011a): "Nyttig kunnskap og sterke inntrykk." *Norsk politi.* (2), 34–41.

Solberg, J-P (2011b): "Portalen mot verden." *Norsk politi.* (2), 30–32.

Sollund, R (2007): *Tatt for en annen: En feltstudie av relasjonen mellom etniske minoriteter og politiet.* Oslo: Gyldendal.

Spapens, T (2008): "Policing in a European border region: The case of the Meuse-Rhine Euroregion". F Geyer and E Guild (eds): *Security Versus Justice? Police and Judicial Cooperation in the European Union.* Aldershot: Ashgate.

Spapens, T (2010): "Cross-border public order policing in the Dutch border areas". A Verhage et al. (ed.): *Policing in Europe.* Antwerpen: Maklu.

Spapens, T (2011): "Joint investigation teams in the European Union: Article 13 JITS and the Alternatives". *European Journal of Crime, Criminal Law and Criminal Justice.* 19 (3) 239–260.

Spapens, T and C Fijnaut (2005): *De problemen van criminaliteit en rechtshandhaving in de Euregio Maas-Rijn.* Antwerpen & Oxford: Intersentia.

Stefanou, C and H Xanthaki (2008): *Towards a European Criminal Record.* Cambridge: Cambridge University Press.

Stene, RJ (2002): "Politiet er mest avgjørende i rettssystemet". *Samfunnsspeilet.* 16 (3), 2–18.

Stevnsborg, H (2010): *Politi 1682–2007.* Frederiksberg: Samfundslitteratur.

Steyerlynck, S and S Thomaes (2002): *Finding the Best Place for Procecution: European Study on Jurisdiction Criteria.* Antwerpen: Maklu.

Stilz, A (2011): "Nations, States, And Territory". *Ethics.* 121 (3), 572–601.

Stolleis, M (1988): *Geschichte des öffentlichen Rechts in Deutschland.* München: Beck.

Strype, J (2005): "Bevæpning og bruk av våpen i norsk politi". J Knutsson (ed.): *Politiets bruk av skytevåpen i Norden.* Oslo: Politihøgskolen.

Stumpf, J (2006): "The crimmigration crisis: Immigrants, crime and sovereign power". *American University Law Review.* 56 (2), 367–419.

Suominen, A (2008): "The past, present and the future of Eurojust". *Maastricht Journal of European and Comparative Law.* 15 (2), 217–234.

Suominen, A (2010): *The Principle of Mutual Recognition in Cooperation in Criminal Matters – A Study of the Principle in Four Framework Decisions and in the Implementation Legislation in the Nordic Member States.* Cambridge: Intersentia.

Tak, PJP (2000): "Bottlenecks in international police and judicial cooperations in the EU". *European Journal of Crime, Criminal Law and Criminal Justice.* 8 (4), 343–360.

Tamanaha, BZ (2004): *On the Rule of Law.* Cambridge: Cambridge University Press.

Tanil, G (2012): *Why is Norway Outside the European Union? Norwegian National Identity and the Question of European Integration.* Frankfurt am Main: Peter Lang.

Thomassen, G, J Strype and M Egge (2014): "Trust no matter what? Citizens' perception of the police one year after the terror attacks in Norway". *Policing.* 8 (1), 69–78.

Thorburn, M (2010): "Reinventing the nigh-watchman state?" *University of Toronto Law Journal.* 60 (2), 425–443.
Tilly, C (1975): "Reflections on the history of European state-making". C Tilly (ed.): *The Formation of National States in Western Europe.* Princeton, NJ: Princeton University Press.
Timasheff, NS (1937): "What is "sociology of law"?" *American Journal of Sociology.* 43 (2), 225–235.
Torgersen, R (2009): *Ulovlig beviserverv og bevisforbud i straffesaker.* Oslo: Papinian.
Torgersen, R (2011): "Påtalejuristens rolle, hvordan den har forandret seg de siste 50 år og hva som forventes for fremtiden". *Lov og rett.* 50 (1–2), 42–62.
Tuffin, B, J Morris and A Poole (2006): *An Evaluation of the Impact of the National Reassurance Policing Programme.* London: Home Office.
Turner, B (2007): "The enclave society: Towards a sociology of immobility". *European Journal of Social Theory.* 10 (2), 287–303.
Tønnesen, S (1978): "Internasjonal strafferett, herunder internasjonal rettshjelp i strafferettspleie". S Tønnesen (ed.): *Politirett.* Bergen: Institutt for offentlig rett.
Tønnesen, S (1981): *Internasjonal strafferettspleie.* Bergen: Institutt for offentlig rett.
Ugelvik, S (2009): "(Et større antall særdeles) alvorlige straffbare handlinger: Fire ord som forsvant i den nye SIS-loven" Available at: www.kriminalpolitikk.uio.no.
Ugelvik, S (2012): "Mot et harmonisk Europa? Om utviklingen av den strafferettslige kontrollen i EU, og hvordan denne kan føre til et mindre likeverdig fellesskap". *Retfærd.* 136 (1), 36–54.
Ugelvik, S (2013): "En utdatert politilov? Om forholdet mellom 'person', 'borger', 'samfunn' og 'stat' i Norge og Schengen". NB Johansen, T Ugelvik, KF Aas (eds): *Krimmigrasjon? Den nye kontrollen av de fremmede.* Oslo: Universitetsforlaget.
Ugelvik, T (2014): "The incarceration of foreigners in European prisons". S Pickering and J Ham (eds): *Routledge Handbook on Crime and International Migration.* London: Routledge.
Utseth, S (1947): *Trondheimspolitiet gjennom tusen år.* Trondheim: Laget.
Valland, TCBD (2011): *Nordisk politiforskning 2004–2009: En kommentert oversikt.* Oslo: Politihøgskolen.
Valverde, M and MD Dubber (2006): *The New Police Science.* Stanford, CA: Stanford University Press.
van Duyne, P and T Vander Beken (2009): "The incantations of the EU organised crime policy making". *Crime, Law and Social Change.* 51 (2), 261–281.
Vandvik, B (2004): "Asyl og opphold på humanitært grunnlag: Ankomstregistrering". R Bunæs, KO Kvigne and B Vandvik (eds): *Utlendingsrett.* Oslo: Universitetsforlaget.
Verhage, A, J Terpstra, P Deelman, E Muylaert and P Van Parys (2010): "Policing in Europe: An introduction". A Verhage et al. (eds): *Policing in Europe.* Antwerpen: Maklu.
Vries, SA de (2013): "Balancing fundamental rights with economic freedoms according to the European Court of Justice". *Utrecht Law Review.* 9 (1), 169–192.
Wacquant, LJD (2009): *Prisons of Poverty.* Minneapolis: University of Minnesota Press.
Wade, ML (2013): "General principles of transnationalised criminal justice? Exploratory Reflections". *Utrecht Law Review.* 9 (4), 1–11.
Walker, N (1993): "The accountability of European police institutions". *European Journal on Criminal Policy and Research.* 1 (4), 34–52.
Walker, N (2000): *Policing in a Changing Constitutional Order.* London: Sweet & Maxwell.
Walker, N (2002): "Policing and the supranational". *Policing and Society.* 12 (4), 307–321.
Walker, N (2004a): *Europe's Area of Freedom, Security and Justice.* Dordrecht: M. Nijhoff.
Walker, N (2004b): "A constitutional odyssey". N Walker (ed.): *Europe's Area of Freedom, Security and Justice.* Dordrecht: M. Nijhoff.
Wallace, W (1999): "The sharing of sovereignty: the European paradox". *Political Studies.* XLVII, 503–521.
Walter, C (2007): "The history and development of European fundamental rights and fundamental freedoms". D Ehlers (ed.): *European Fundamental Rights and Freedoms.* Berlin: de Gruyter.

Weber, M (1958): "Politics as vocation". HH Gerth and C Wright Mills (ed.): *From Max Weber: Essays in Sociology*. New York: Oxford University Press.
Weiler, JHH (1991): "The transformation of Europe". *The Yale Law Journal*. 100 (8), 2403–2483.
Weiler, JHH. (1998): "Europe: The case against the case for statehood". *European Law Journal*. 4 (1), 43–62.
Weiler, JHH (1999): *The Constitution of Europe: "Do the New Clothes Have an Emperor?" and Other Essays on European Integration*. Cambridge: Cambridge University Press.
Wold, E (2004): *Europol som samarbeidspartner for norsk politi*. Bergen: Fagbokforlaget.
Wæver, O (2002): "Identities, communities and foreign policy: Discourse analysis as foreign policy theory". L Hansen and O Wæver (eds): *European Integration and National Identity: The Challenge of the Nordic States*. London: Routledge.
Xanthaki, A (2008): "The ECR: Human rights considerations" C Stefanou and H Xanthaki (eds): *Towards a European Criminal Record*. Cambridge: Cambridge University Press.
Young, J (1999): *The Exclusive Society: Social Exclusion, Crime and Difference in Late Modernity*. London: SAGE.
Zedner, L (2006): "Policing before and after the police". *British Journal of Criminology*. 46 (1), 78–96.
Zureik, E and MB Salter (2005): *Global Surveillance and Policing*. Cullompton: Willan.

16.1 Norwegian legislation and public documents

16.1.1 Norwegian legislation

Lov av 17. mai 1814 Grunnloven (the Norwegian Constitution).
Lov av 22. mai 1869 om emigrantkontrol (Act on Emigration).
Lov av 6. juni 1891 nr.1 om politivedtægter for rigets herreder (Act on Giving Police Instructions).
Lov av 31. mai 1900 nr.5 om løsgjengeri, betleri og drukkenskap (Vagrancy Act, VA).
Lov av 4. mai 1901 nr.1 [tidligere lov] om utlendingers adgang til riket og deres opphold her (former Immigration Act).
Lov av 22. mai 1902 nr.10 [tidligere lov] almindelig borgerlig straffelov (former straffeloven, General Civil Penal Code).
Lov av 13. mars 1936 nr.3 [tidligere lov] om politiet ((former)1936 Police Act).
Lov av 15. november 1963 nr.1 om fullbyrding av nordiske dommer på straff m.v. (Nordisk straffullbyrdingslov, Act on Enforcing Nordic Criminal Court Verdicts).
Lov av 10. februar 1967 nr.1 om behandlingsmåten i forvaltningssaker (Forvaltningsloven, Public Administration Act).
Lov av 11. juni 1971 nr.52 om strafferegistrering (Strafferegistreringsloven, Criminal Register Act, CRA).
Lov av 13. juni 1975 nr.39 om utlevering av lovbrytere m.v. (Utleveringsloven, Extradition Act).
Lov av 22. mai 1981 nr.25 om rettergangsmåten i straffesaker (Straffeprosessloven, Act Relating to Legal Procedure in Criminal Cases, CPA).
Lov 27. november 1992 nr. 109 om gjennomføring i norsk rett av hoveddelen i avtale om Det europeiske økonomiske samarbeidsområde (EØS) m.v. (EEA Act).
Lov av 8. januar 1993 nr.21 om gjennomføring i norsk rett av Luganokonvensjonen om domsmyndighet og fullbyrdelse av dommer i sivile og kommersielle saker (Lugano Act).
Lov av 4. august 1995 nr.53 om politiet 1995 (the Police Act, PA).
Lov 20.03. 1998 nr. 10. om forebyggende sikkerhetstjeneste (sikkerhetsloven, Security Act).
Lov av 29. mars 1998 nr.11 om etteretningstjenesten (Intelligence Service Act, ISA).

Lov av 21. mai 1999 nr.30 om styrking av menneskerettighetenes stilling i norsk rett (menneskerettighetsloven, Human Rights Act).
Lov av 17. april 2000 nr.31 om behandling av personopplysninger (Personal Data Act).
Lov av 4. juli 2003 nr.81 om endringer i utlendingsloven (Act on Changes in the Immigration Act).
Lov av 15. mai 2008 nr.35 Utlendingsloven (Immigration Act).
Lov av 28. mai 2010 nr.16 om behandling av opplysninger i politiet og påtalemyndigheten (Police Registration Act, PRA).
Lov av 20. januar 2012 nr.4 Arrestordreloven (Arrest Warrant Act).

16.1.2 Norwegian administrative and parliamentary documents

NOU 1981: 35 *Politiets rolle i samfunnet. Delutredning I.*
NOU 1987: 27 *Politiets rolle i samfunnet. Delutredning II.*
NOU 1988: 39 *Politi og påtalemyndighet: Arbeids-og ansvarsfordeling.*
NOU 1993: 3 *Strafferettslige regler i terroristbekjempelsen.*
NOU 1994: 1 *Streikerett for politiet og lensmannsetaten.*
NOU 1994: 13 *Passlov.*
NOU 1997: 15 *Etterforskingsmetoder for bekjempelse av kriminalitet. Delinnstilling II.*
NOU 1999: 10 *En bedre organisert politi- og lensmannsetat.*
NOU 2004: 6 *Mellom effektivitet og personvern: Politimetoder i forebyggende øyemed.*
NOU 2009: 15 *Skjult informasjon – åpen kontroll.*
NOU 2009: 20 *Ny grenselov.*
NOU 2012: 2 *Utenfor og innenfor: Norges avtaler med EU.*
NOU 2012: 14 *Rapport fra 22. juli-kommisjonen.*
NOU 2013: 9 *Ett politi – rustet til å møte fremtidens utfordringer.*
NOU 2016:24 *Ny straffeprosesslov.*
NOU 2017:9 *Politi og bevæpning.*

Ot.prp. nr.59 (1920) *Om lov om politiets ordning m.v.*
Ot.prp. nr.46 (1986–1987) *Om lov om utlendingers adgang til riket og deres opphold her (utlendingsloven).*
Ot.prp. nr.22 (1994–1995) *Om lov om politiet (politiloven).*
Ot.prp. nr.56 (1998–1999) *Om lov om Schengen informasjonssystem (SIS) og lov om endringer i utlendingsloven.*
Ot.prp. nr.64 (1998–1999) *Om lov om endringer i straffeprosessloven og straffeloven mv. (etterforskningsmetoder m.v.).*
Ot.prp. nr.54 (1999–2000) *Om lov om vaktvirksomhet.*
Ot.prp. nr.58 (2001–2002) *Om lov om endringer i straffeloven og politiloven (tiltak mot ulovlig bruk av kniv og skytevåpen).*
Ot.prp. nr.49 (2002–2003) *Om lov om endringer i utlendingsloven.*
Ot.prp. nr.62 (2002–2003) *Om lov om endringer i straffeloven og straffeprosessloven mv.*
Ot.prp. nr.61 (2003–2004) *Om lov om endringer i politiloven.*
Ot.prp. nr.60 (2004–2005) *Om lov om endringer i straffeprosessloven og politiloven.*
Ot. prp. nr.77 (2004–2005) *Om lov om endring av straffeprosessloven.*
Ot.prp. nr.75 (2006–2007) *Om lov om utlendingers adgang til riket og deres opphold her (utlendingsloven).*
Ot.prp. nr.38 (2007–2008) *Om lov om endringer i lov 16. juli 1999 nr.66 om Schengen informasjonssystem (SIS).*
Ot.prp. nr.36 (2008–2009) *Om lov om endringer i utlendingsloven 1988 og utlendingsloven 2008*
Ot.prp. nr.108 (2008–2009) *Om lov om behandling av opplysninger i politiet og påtalemyndigheten.*

Prop. 94 L (2009–2010) *Proposisjon til Stortinget (forslag til lovvedtak) Endring i lov 16. juli 1999 nr.66 om Schengen informasjonssystem (SIS).*

Prop. 1 S (2011–2012) *Proposisjon til Stortinget (forslag til stortingsvedtak). For budsjettåret 2012.*

Prop. 97 LS (2011–2012) *Endringer i utleveringsloven m.m. og samtykke til ratifikasjon av Avtale 19. desember 2003 mellom Den europeiske union og Republikken Island og Kongeriket Norge og Annen tilleggsprotokoll 8. november 2001 til Den europeiske konvensjon om gjensidig hjelp i straffesaker.*

Prop. 114 L (2012–2013) *Endringer i politiregisterloven mv.*

Prop. 147 L (2012–2013) *Endringer i straffeprosessloven mv. (behandling og beskyttelse av informasjon).*

Prop. 152 L (2012–2013) *Endringer i politiloven.*

Prop. 25 S (2013–2014) *Proposisjon til Stortinget (forslag til stortingsvedtak) Samtykke til godtakelse av endring av avtale av 19. januar 2001 mellom Norge og Island og* EF *om kriterier og mekanismer for å avgjøre hvilken stat som er ansvarlig for behandlingen av en asylsøknad som fremlegges i Norge, Island eller en medlemsstat, ved innlemmelse av Dublin III-forordningen og Eurodac-forordningen av 26. juni 2013.*

Prop. 62 L (2014–2015) *Endringer i utlendingsloven (gjennomføring av Eurodac-forordningen 2013).*

Prop. 54 S (2015–2016) *Samtykke til 1) inngåelse av avtale mellom* EU *og Island og Norge om anvendelse av visse bestemmelser i rådsbeslutning 2008/615/JIS og rådsbeslutning 2008/616/JIS av 26. november 2009, 2) inngåelse av avtale mellom Norge og USA om styrket samarbeid om forebygging og bekjempelse av alvorlig kriminalitet av 8. mai 2012.*

Prop.161 L (2016–2017) *Lov om grensetilsyn og grensekontroll av personer (grenseloven).*

Indstilling fra den departementale politilovkomite av 1912 (Politilovinnstilling): Utkast til lov om politiets ordning m.v. Vedlegg til Ot.prp. nr.59 (1920).

Innstilling til den sentrale politiorganisasjon 20. november 1970 (Aulie-innstillingen). Trykket som vedlegg til Ot.prp. nr.60 (1972–1973).

Innst. O. nr.89 (1998–1999) *Innstilling fra justiskomiteen om lov om Schengen informasjons-system (SIS) og lov om endringer i utlendingsloven og i enkelte andre lover som følge av Schengen-samarbeidet.*

Innst. O. I (1936) *Innstilling fra justiskomiteen til lov om politiet.*

Innst. S. nr.192 (1991–1992) *Om bekjempelse av kriminalitet.*

Innst. S. nr.229 (1996–1997) *Innstilling fra utenrikskomiteen om samtykke til ratifikasjon av samarbeidsavtale av 19. desember 1996 mellom partene i Schengen-avtalen og Schengen-konvens-jonen, og Island og Norge om avskaffelse av personkontroll på de felles grenser.*

Innst. S. nr.147 (1998–1999) *Innstilling fra utenrikskomiteen om samtykke til inngåelse av en avtale mellom Rådet for Den europeiske union og Republikken Island og Kongeriket Norge om de sistnevnte statenes tilknyning til gjennomføringen, anvendelsen og videreutviklingen av Schengen-regelverket.*

Innst. 331 S (2011–2012) *Innstilling fra justiskomiteen om samtykke til ratifikasjon av Avtale 19. desember 2003 mellom Den europeiske union og Republikken Island og Kongeriket Norge og Annen tilleggsprotokoll 8. november 2001 til Den europeiske konvensjon om gjensidig hjelp i straffesaker.*

Innst. 48 L (2013–2014) *Innstilling fra kommunal- og forvaltningskomiteen om endringer i utlendingsloven mv. (heving av strafferammen ved brudd på innreiseforbud).* Innst. 225 S (2015–2016) Innstilling fra justiskomiteen om Samtykke til 1) inngåelse av avtale mellom EU og Island og Norge om anvendelse av visse bestemmelser i rådsbeslutning 2008/615/JIS og rådsbeslutning 2008/616/JIS av 26. november 2009, 2) inngåelse av avtale mellom Norge og USA om styrket samarbeid om forebygging og bekjempelse av alvorlig kriminalitet av 8. mai 2012.

St.meld. nr.33 (1998–99) *Om regelverk som avtalen med Den Europeiske Union om institusjonelle løsninger for tilknytning til Schengen-samarbeidet skal anvendes på.*
St. meld. nr. 17 (2001–2002) *Samfunnssikkerhet: Veien til et mindre sårbart samfunn.*
St.meld. nr.18 (1999–2000) *Om Norges deltakelse i internasjonalt politisamarbeid.*
St.meld. nr.22 (2000–2001) *Politireform 2000: Et tryggere samfunn.*
St.meld. nr.42 (2004–2005) *Politiets rolle og oppgaver.*
St.meld. nr.37 (2007–2008) *Straff som virker – mindre kriminalitet – tryggere samfunn (kriminalomsorgsmelding).*
Meld.St. 7 (2010–2011) *Kampen mot organisert kriminalitet – en felles innsats.*
Meld.St. 7 (2011–2012) *Nordområdene: Visjon og virkemidler.*
Meld.St. 21 (2012–2013) *Terrorberedskap. Oppfølging av NOU 2012: 14 Rapport fra 22. juli-kommisjonen.*

St.prp. nr.42 (1996–1997) *Om samtykke til ratifikasjon av samarbeidsavtale av 19 desember 1996 mellom partene i Schengenavatalen og Schengenkonvensjonen, og Island og Norge om avskaffelse av personkontroll på de felles grenser.*
St.prp. nr.50 (1998–1999) *Om samtykke til inngåelse av en avtale mellom Rådet for Den europeiske union og Republikken Island og Kongeriket Norge om de sistnevnte statenes tilknytning til gjennomføringen, anvendelsen og videreutviklingen av Schengen-regelverket.*
St.prp. nr.98 (2000–2001) *Om samtykke til inngåelse av en avtale mellom Kongeriket Norge og Den europeiske politienhet (Europol) mv.*
St.prp. nr.44 (2007–2008) *Om samtykke til godtakelse av vedtak om videreutvikling av Schengen-regelverket mv.*

Høringsnotat 26. mars 2010: Forslag til lovendringer for gjennomføring av avtale 19. desember 2003mellom Den europeiske union og Republikken Island og Kongeriket Norge og annen tilleggsprotokoll 8. november 2001 til den europeiske konvensjon om gjensidig hjelp i straffesaker. (Available at: https://www.regjeringen.no/no/dokumenter/horing-forslag-til-lovendringer-for-gjen/id599445/ [18.12.2017])
Høringsbrev 26. mars 2010: Forslag til lovendringer for gjennomføring avtale 19. desember 2003 mellom EU, Island og Norge, samt annen tilleggsprotokoll til den europeiske konvensjon om gjensidig hjelp i straffesaker.
Høringsbrev 21. mars 2014: Forslag til endring i politiloven § 14 – adgang for kommunene til å forby tigging på offentlig sted. 13/5833.
Høringsbrev 6. juni 2014: Endringer i utlendingsloven og -forskriften (gjennomføring av Eurodac-forordningen av 2013 i norsk rett). 14/2774.
Høringssvar 2013: Fra Riksadvokaten til *Ett politi – rustet til å møte fremtidens utfordringer.*
Høringssvar 2013: Fra Politihøgskolen til *Ett politi – rustet til å møte fremtidens utfordringer.*

16.1.3 Norwegian regulations, directives, circulars, instructions

Forskrift av 12. mars 1963 nr.1 om samarbeid med Danmark, Finland, Island og Sverige om fullbyrding av nordiske dommer på straff m.v. (Directive on Cooperation between Denmark, Finland, Iceland and Sweden on Carrying Out Nordic Criminal Sanctions).
Forskrift av 28. juni 1985 nr.1679 Påtaleinstruksen (The Administrative Regulation of the Prosecution, Prosecution Directive).
Forskrift av 1. august 1989 nr.4872: Politiets våpeninstruks (Våpeninstruksen, The Police Weapons Directive).
Forskrift av 22.06.1990 nr.3963 Politiinstruksen (The Police Directive).
Forskrift av 21. desember 2000 nr.1365 SIS-forskriften (SIS Directive).
Forskrift av 15. desember 2006 nr.1456 til forvaltningsloven (Forvaltningslovforskriften).

Forskrift av 15. oktober 2009 nr.1286 om utlendingers adgang til riket og deres opphold her (Immigration Directive, IMD).
Forskrift av 14. desember 2012 nr.1227 om internasjonalt samarbeid i straffesaker (Directive on International Cooperaiton in Criminal Cases).
Forskrift av 20. september 2013 nr.1097 om behandling av opplysninger i politiet og påtalemyndigheten (Politiregisterforskriften). (PRD Directive).

Instruks 1920: (Tidligere) Instruks for politiet (Politiinstruksen, Former Police Directive).
Intruks 31. august 2001 nr.1012: Instruks om Etterretningstjenesten (E-tjenesteinstruksen, Secret Service Instruction).

Rundskriv av 26. april 2000 (RA 2/2000): Vederlag til politiets kilder og provokasjon som etterforskningsmetode (Circular on Police Provocation, etc.).
Rundskriv av 1. august 2001 (G 19/2001): Internasjonalt rettslig samarbeid i straffesaker: Gjensidig hjelp i straffesaker og utlevering av lovbrytere (Circular on Mutual Cooperation in Criminal Cases, etc.).
Rundskriv av 1. mars 2004 (2004/004): Avtale mellom Finland, Norge og Sverige om den nærmere tillempning av artiklene 40 og 41 i Schengenkonvensjonen (Circular on Articles 40 and 41 in the Schengen Convention Applicable for Finland, Norway and Sweden).
Rundskriv av 21. mai 2010 (2001/021): Politiets utøvelse av utlendingskontroll på territoriet, herunder i grenseområdene (Circular on Police Immigration Control).
Rundskriv (RPOD 2010/005): Ordreinstruks for politiet (Circular on Police Orders).
Rundskriv av 15. oktober 2012 (G 12/2012) om nordisk arrestordre (Circular on Nordic Arrest Warrants).
Rundskriv av 1. februar 2014 (1/2014): Mål og prioriteringer for straffesaksbehandling i 2014: Politiet og Statsadvokatene (Circular on Prioritisations in the Public Prosecution Norway).
Rundskriv av 26. juni 2014 (2014/03683-3502): Direktiv for gjennomføring av straffesaksbehandlingen i Romerike politidistrikt (Circular on Criminal Investigation in Romerike Police District).
Direktoratet for forvaltning og ikt (Difi) (2012): «Noregs nasjonale ekspertar i Kommisjonen – Ein ressurs for Noreg, eller berre for EU?». *Difi rapport* 2012:1. Available at: https://www.difi.no/rapport/2012/03/noregs-nasjonale-ekspertar-i-kommisjonen-ein-ressurs-noreg-eller-berre-eu

16.2 Nordic legislation, agreements and other documents

Law 2000:343 om internationellt polisiärt samarbete (Swedish Act on International Police Cooperation).
Förordning 2010:705 om internationellt polisiärt samarbete (Swedish Directive on International Police Cooperation).
SOU 2011:25 *Utökat polissamarbete i Norden och EU.*

Den nordiske politisamarbeidsavtale 23. mars 1972 (Nordic Agreement on Mutual Legal Assistance). Rev. 02.09.2002 and 22.08.2012.
Aftalen af 6. oktober 1999 mellem Kongeriget Danmarks regering og Kongeriget Sveriges regering om politimæssigt samarbejde i Øresundsregionen (The Øresund Agreement).
Konvensjon av 15 desember 2005 (København) om overføring av domfelte mellom de nordiske land (Nordic Arrest Warrant, NAW).
Avtale av 2. November 2010 mellom Kongeriket Norges regjering og Den Russiske Føderasjons regjering om forenkling av gjensidige reiser for grenseboere i Kongeriket Norge og Den Russiske Føderasjon (Grenseboeravtalen Russland-Norge).

Nordisk samtjänstgöringsrapport 2009: Samtjänstgöring mellan nordisk polispersonal: Rapport från den nordiska arbetsgruppen tillsatt av Nordiska ämbetsmannakommittén för lagstiftningssamarbete.
Prosjektrapport 2014: Utredning om mulighetene for økt Samarbeid mellom norsk og svensk politi i Vaajmaregionen (Vaajma IntReg Report).

16.3 European Union policy and legislative documents

[1992] OJ C 191/1 Treaty on European Union (Maastricht Treaty).
[1997] OJ C 340/1 Treaty of Amsterdam amending the Treaty of the European Union, the Treaties establishing the European Communities and certain related acts (Amsterdam Treaty).
[1995] OJ C 316/1 Council Act of 26 July 1995 drawing up the Convention based on Article K.3 of the Treaty on European Union, on the establishment of a European Police Office (Europol Convention).
[1996] OJ C 299/1 Council Act of 23 July 1996 drawing up, on the basis of Article K.3 of the Treaty on European Union, the Protocol on the interpretation, by way of preliminary rulings, by the Court of Justice of the European Communities of the Convention on the establishment of a European Police Office.
[1997] OJ C 10/1 Council Resolution of 20 December 1996 on individuals who cooperate with the judicial process in the fight against international organized crime.
[1997] OJ C 221/1 Council Act of 19 June 1997 drawing up, on the basis of Article K.3 of the Treaty on European Union and Article 41 (3) of the Europol Convention, the Protocol on the privileges and immunities of Europol, the members of its organs, the Deputy Directors and employees of Europol.
[1998] OJ C 24/1 Council Act of 18 December 1997 drawing up, on the basis of Article K.3 of the Treaty on European Union, the Convention on mutual assistance and cooperation between customs administrations (Naples II) (98/C 24/01). [1998] OJ C 408/1 Council Resolution of 21 December 1998 on the prevention of organised crime with reference to the establishment of a comprehensive strategy for combating it.
[1999] OJ C 26/6 Council Decision of 3 December 1998 instructing Europol to deal with crimes committed or likely to be committed in the course of terrorist activities against life, limb, personal freedom or property.
[1999] OJ C 149/2 Council Decision of 29 April 1999 extending Europol's mandate to deal with forgery of money and means of payment.
[1999] OJ C 162/1 Council Resolution of 27 May 1999 on combating international crime with fuller cover of the routes used.
[2000] OJ C 197/01 Council Act of 29 May 2000 establishing in accordance with Article 34 of the Treaty on European Union the Convention on Mutual Assistance in Criminal Matters between the Member States of the European Union.
[2000] C 197/3 OJ [2000] C 197/3 Council act of 29 May 2000 establishing in accordance with Article 34 of the Treaty on European Union the Convention on Mutual Assistance in Criminal Matters between the Member States of the European Union.
[2000] OJ C 358/1 Council Act of 30 November 2000 drawing up on the basis of Article 43(1) of the Convention on the establishment of a European Police Office (Europol Convention) of a Protocol amending Article 2 and the Annex to that Convention.
[2000] OJ C 379/7 Explanatory report on the Convention of 29 May 2000 on Mutual Assistance in Criminal Matters between the Member States of the European Union (2000/C 379/02).
[2001] OJ C 326/1 Council Act of 16 October 2001 establishing, in accordance with Article 34 of the Treaty on European Union, the Protocol to the Convention on Mutual Assistance in Criminal Matters between the Member States of the European Union.

[2001] OJ C 362/1 Council Decision of 6 December 2001 extending Europol's mandate to deal with the serious forms of international crime listed in the Annex to the Europol Convention.

[2002] OJ C 312/1 Council Act of 28 November 2002 drawing up a Protocol amending the Convention on the establishment of a European Police Office (Europol Convention) and the Protocol on the privileges and immunities of Europol, the members of its organs, the deputy directors and the employees of Europol.

[2004] OJ C 116/20 Council Resolution of 29 April 2004 on a Model Protocol for the establishment in Member States of partnerships between the public and private sectors to reduce the harm from organised crime.

[2006] OJ C 322/1 Council Resolution of 4 December 2006 concerning an updated handbook with recommendations for international police cooperation and measures to prevent and control violence and disturbances in connection with football matches with an international dimension, in which at least one Member State is involved (2006/C 322/01).

[2007] OJ C 255/13 Opinion of the European Data Protection Supervisor on the Proposal for a Council Decision establishing the European Police Office (Europol) — COM(2006) 817 final (2007/C 255/02).

[2007] OJ C 306/01 Treaty of Lisbon amending the Treaty on European Union and the Treaty establishing the European Community, signed at Lisbon, 13 December 2007.

[2010] OJ C 70/1 Council Resolution of 26 February 2010 on a Model Agreement for setting up a Joint Investigation Team (JIT) (2010/C 70/01).

[2010] OJ C 165/22 Initiative of the Kingdom of Belgium, the Republic of Bulgaria, the Republic of Estonia, the Kingdom of Spain, the Republic of Austria, the Republic of Slovenia and the Kingdom of Sweden for a Directive of the European Parliament and of the Council of [. . .] regarding the European Investigation Order in criminal matters (2010/C 165/02).

[2012] OJ C 326/1 Protocol (No 36) on transitional provisions.

[2012] OJ C 326/2 Charter of Fundamental Rights of the European Union (CFREU).

[2017] OJ C 18/1 Council Resolution on a Model Agreement for setting up a Joint Investigation Team (JIT).

[1987] OJ L 169/1 The Single European Act.

[1994] OJ L 344/1, Agreement between the EFTA states on the establishment of a surveillance authority and a court of justice, Oport 2 May 1992.

[1995] OJ L 62/1 Joint Action of 10 March 1995 adopted by the Council on the basis of Article K.3 of the Treaty on European Union concerning the Europol Drugs Unit.

[1995] OJ L 281/31 Directive 95/46/EC Of the European Parliament and of the Council of 24 October 1995 on the protection of individuals with regard to the processing of personal data and on the free movement of such data.

[1996] OJ L 342/2 Joint Action of 29 November 1996 adopted by the Council on the basis of Article K.3 of the Treaty on European Union, concerning the creation and maintenance of a directory of specialized competences, skills and expertise in the fight against international organized crime, in order to facilitate law enforcement cooperation between the Member States of the European Union, 96/747/JHA.

[1996] OJ L 342/4 Joint Action of 16 December 1996 adopted by the Council on the basis of Article K.3 of the Treaty on European Union extending the mandate given to the Europol Drugs Unit.

[1998] OJ L 351 Joint action of 21 December 1998 adopted by the Council on the basis of Article K.3 of the Treaty on European Union, on making it a criminal offence to participate in a criminal organisation in the Member States of the European Union (98/733/JHA).

[2000] OJ L 239/407 Decision of the Schengen Executive Committee of 16 December 1998 on the Handbook on cross-border police cooperation [SCH/Com-ex (98)52].

[2000] OJ L 248/1 Council decision of 28 September 2000 establishing a procedure for amending Articles 40(4) and (5), 41(7) and 65(2) of the Convention implementing the

Schengen Agreement of 14June 1985 on the gradual abolition of checks at common borders (2000/586/JHA).

[2001] OJ L 93/40 Agreement between the European Community and the Republic of Iceland and the Kingdom of Norway concerning the criteria and mechanisms for establishing the State responsible for examining a request for asylum lodged in a Member State or in Iceland or Norway 03/04/2001 (Dublin).

[2001] OJ L 182/1Council Framework Decision 2001/500/JHA of 26 June 2001 on money laundering and confiscation of proceeds of crime.

[2001] OJ L 329/1 Council Decision of 6 December 2001 on the protection of the Euro against counterfeiting.

[2002] OJ L 63/1 2002/187/JHA Council decision of 28 February 2002 setting up Eurojust with a view to reinforcing the fight against serious crime.

[2002] OJ L 121/1 Council Decision of 25 April 2002 concerning security in connection with football matches with an international dimension 2002/348/JHA.

[2002] OJ L 162/1 Council framework decision of 13 June 2002 on joint investigation teams.

[2002] OJ L 164/3 Council Framework Decision 2002/475/JHA of 13 June 2002 on combating terrorism.

[2002] OJ L 190/1 Council Framework Decision of 13 June 2002 on the European arrest warrant and the surrender procedures between Member States (2002/584/JHA).

[2003] OJ L 50/1 Council Regulation (EC) No 343/2003 of 18 February 2003 establishing the criteria and mechanisms for determining the Member State responsible for examining an asylum application lodged in one of the Member States by a third-country national.

[2003] OJ L 67/27 Council Decision 2003/170/JHA of 27 February 2003 on the common use of liaison officers posted abroad by the law enforcement agencies of the Member States.

[2003] OJ L 76/25 Commission Regulation (EC) No 522/2003 of 21 March 2003 concerning applications for export licences for rice and broken rice with advance fixing of the refund.

[2003] OJ L 260/37 Council Decision 2003/725/JHA of 2 October 2003 amending the provisions of Article 40(1) and (7) of the Convention implementing the Schengen Agreement of 14 June 1985 on the gradual abolition of checks at common borders.

[2004] OJ L 26/1 Council Decision of 17 December 2003 on the signing of the Agreement between the European Union and the Republic of Iceland and the Kingdom of Norway on the application of certain provisions of the Convention of 29 May 2000 on Mutual Assistance in Criminal Matters between the Member States of the European Union and the 2001 Protocol thereto.

[2004] OJ L 26/3 Agreement between the European Union and the Republic of Iceland and the Kingdom of Norway on the application of certain provisions of the Convention of 29 may 2000 on Mutual Assistance in Criminal Matters between the Member States of the European Union and the 2001 Protocol thereto.

[2004] OJ L 158/77 Directive 2004/38/EC of 29 April 2004 on the right of citizens of the Union and their family members to move and reside freely within the territory of the Member States amending Regulation (EEC) No 1612/68 and repealing Directives 64/221/EEC, 68/360/EEC, 72/194/EEC, 73/148/EEC, 75/34/EEC, 75/35/EEC, 90/364/EEC, 90/365/EEC and 93/96/EEC (Residence Directive).

[2006] OJ L 105/1 Regulation (EC) No 562/2006 of the European Parliament and of the Council of 15 March 2006 establishing a Community Code on the rules governing the movement of persons across borders (Schengen Borders Code).

[2006] OJ L 105/54 Directive 2006/24/EC of the European Parliament and of the Council of 15 March 2006 on the retention of data generated or processed in connection with the provision of publicly available electronic communications services or of public communications networks and amending Directive 2002/58/EC.

[2006] OJ L 256/18 Council Decision 2006/631/JHA of 24 July 2006 fixing the date of application of certain provisions of Decision 2005/211/JHA concerning the introduction of some new functions for the Schengen Information System, including in the fight against terrorism.

[2006] OJ L 292/1 Council Decision of 27 June 2006 on the signing of the Agreement between the European Union and the Republic of Iceland and the Kingdom of Norway on the surrender procedure between the Member States of the European Union and Iceland and Norway.

[2006] OJ L 381/4 Regulation (EC) No 1987/2006 of the European Parliament and of the Council of 20 December 2006 on the establishment, operation and use of the second generation Schengen Information System (SIS II).

[2006] OJ L 386/89 Council Framework Decision 2006/960/JHA of 18 December 2006 on simplifying the exchange of information and intelligence between law enforcement authorities of the Member States of the European Union ('Swedish initiative').

[2007] OJ L 205/63 Council Decision 2007/533/JHA of 12 June 2007 on the establishment, operation and use of the second generation Schengen Information System (SIS II).

[2008] OJ L 138/14 Council Decision 2002/187/JHA on the strengthening of Eurojust and amending Decision setting up Eurojust with a view to reinforcing the fight against serious crime.

[2008] OJ L 210/1 Council Decision 2008/615/JHA of 23 June 2008 on the stepping up of cross-border cooperation, particularly in combating terrorism and cross-border crime (the Prüm Decision).

[2008] OJ L 210/12 Council Decision 2008/616/JHA of 23 June 2008 on the implementation of Decision 2008/615/JHA on the stepping up of cross-border cooperation, particularly in combating terrorism and cross-border crime.

[2008] OJ L 210/73 Council Decisions 2008/617/JHA of 23 June 2008 on the improvement of cooperation between the special intervention units of the Member States of the European Union in crisis situations.

[2008] OJ L 218/60 Regulation (EC) No 767/2008 of the European Parliament and of the Council of 9 July 2008 concerning the Visa Information System (VIS) and the exchange of data between Member States on short-stay visas (VIS Regulation).

[2008] OJ L 218/129 Council Decision 2008/633/JHA of 23 June 2008 concerning access for consultation of the Visa Information System (VIS) by designated authorities of Member States and by Europol for the purposes of the prevention, detection and investigation of terrorist offences and of other serious criminal offences.

[2008] OJ L 330/23 Council Framework Decision 2008/919/JHA of 28 November 2008 amending Framework Decision 2002/475/JHA on combating terrorism.

[2008] OJ L 350/60 Council Framework Decision 2008/977/JHA of 27 November 2008 on the protection of personal data processed in the framework.

[2008] OJ L 350/72 Council Framework Decision 2008/978/JHA of 18 December 2008 on the European evidence warrant for the purpose of obtaining objects, documents and data for use in proceedings in criminal matters.

[2009] OJ L 93/33 Council Decision 2009/316/JHA of 6 April 2009 on the establishment of the European Criminal Records Information System (ECRIS) in application of Article 11 of Framework Decision (2009/315/JHA).

[2009] OJ L 121/37 Council Decision of 6 April 2009 establishing the European Police Office (Europol) (2009/371/JHA).

[2009] OJ L 138/14 Council Decision 2009/426/JHA of 16 December 2008 on the strengthening of Eurojust and amending Decision 2002/187/JHA setting up Eurojust with a view to reinforcing the fight against serious crime.

[2009] OJ L 283/62 Council Decision 2009/796/JHA of 4 June 2009 amending Decision 2002/956/JHA setting up a European Network for the Protection of Public Figures.

[2009] OJ L 321/44 Council Decision 2009/902/JHA of 30 November 2009 setting up a European Crime Prevention Network (EUCPN) and repealing Decision 2001/427/JHA

[2009] OJ L 325/14 Council Decision 2009/936/JHA of 30 November 2009 adopting the implementing rules for Europol analysis work files.

[2009] OJ L 328 Council Decision 2009/1004/CFSP of 22 December 2009 updating the list of persons, groups and entities subject to Articles 2, 3 and 4 of Common Position 2001/931/CFSP on the application of specific measures to combat terrorism.
[2010] OJ L 52/50 Council Decision of 25 February 2010 on setting up the Standing Committee on operational cooperation on internal security (2010/131/EU).
[2010] OJ L 195/1 Council Decision of 28 June 2010 on the signing, on behalf of the Union, of the Agreement between the European Union and the United States of America on the processing and transfer of financial messaging data from the European Union to the United States for the purposes of the Terrorist Finance Tracking Program.
[2010] OJ L 238/1 Council Decision of 26 July 2010 on the conclusion of the Agreement between the European Union and Iceland and Norway on the application of certain provisions of Council Decision 2008/615/JHA on the stepping up of cross-border cooperation, *etc.*
[2013] OJ L 71/1 SIRENE 2013 Commision Implementing Decision of 26 February 2013 on the Sirene Manual and other implementing measures for the second generation Schengen Information System (SIS II) (notified under document C (2013) 1043) 2013/115/EU.
[2013] OJ L 180/1 Regulation (EU) No 603/2013 of the European Parliament and of the Council of 26 June 2013 on the establishment of 'Eurodac' for the comparison of fingerprints for the effective application of Regulation (EU) No 604/2013 *etc.*
[2013] OJ L 180/31 Regulation (EU) No 604/2013 of the European Parliament and of the Council of 26 June 2013 establishing the criteria and mechanisms for determining the Member State responsible for examining an application *etc.*
[2013] OJ L 180/60 Directive 2013/32/EU of the European Parliament and of the Council of 26 June 2013 on common procedures for granting and withdrawing international protection (recast) [Dublin II, in force 1 January 2014].
[2016] OJ L 135/53 Regulation (EU) No 2016/794 of the European Parliament and of the Council of 11 May 2016 on the European Union Agency for Law Enforcement Cooperation (Europol) and replacing and repealing Council Decisions 2009/371/JHA, 2009/934/JHA, 2009/935/JHA, 2009/936/JHA and 2009/968/JHA.
[2016] OJ L 251/1 Regulation (EU) 2016/1624 of the European Parliament and of the Council of 14 September 2016 on the European Border and Coast Guard and amending Regulation (EU) 2016/399 of the European Parliament and of the Council and repealing Regulation (EC) No 863/2007 of the European Parliament and of the Council, Council Regulation (EC) No 2007/2004 and Council Decision 2005/267/EC.
[2017] OJ L 283/1 Council Regulation (EU) 2017/1939 of 12 October 2017 implementing enhanced cooperation on the establishment of the European Public Prosecutor's Office ('the EPPO').

The Stockholm Programme – An open and secure Europe serving and protecting the citizens, Council document 17024/09, JAI 896, Brussels, 2 December 2009.
Council recommendation of 25. April 2002 for the establishment of multinational ad-hoc teams for gathering and exchanging information on terrorists. (Available at: https://www.consilium.europa.eu/ueDocs/cms_Data/docs/polju/en/EJN278.pdf [10.07.14]).
The Hague programme The Hague programme : strengthening freedom, security and justice in the European Union (16054/04), Brussels, 13 December 2004.
Council doc. 11037/05, 8. July 2005 Document establishing the JITs network.
Council doc. 15801/06 2768th Council Meeting Justice and Home Affairs, Brussels, 4–5 December 2006 (Available at: http://www.consilium.europa.eu/uedocs/cms_data/docs/pressdata/en/jha/91997.pdf [10.07.14]).
Council doc. 10842/09, 16. June 2009 Draft updated Catalogue of Recommendations for the correct application of the Schengen Acquis and Best practices: Police cooperation (Available at: http://register.consilium.europa.eu/doc/srv?l=EN&f=ST%2010842%202009%20INIT [10.70.14]).

Council doc. 13039/11, 30. Aug 2011 2009 Schengen catalogue Recommendations and best practices (revised) SIS (13039/11) (Available at: http://www.consilium.europa.eu/media/1406742/st13039.en11.pdf [10.07.14]).

Council doc. 15785/2/10, 25 January 2011 Schengen catalogue – recommendations and best practices: police cooperation (revised) (Available at: http://register.consilium.europa.eu/doc/srv?l=EN&f=ST%2015785%202010%20REV%202 [10.07.14]).

Council doc. 6128/1/17, 14. February 2017 Joint Investigation Teams Practical Guide (Available at: https://www.europol.europa.eu/publications-documents/jits-practical-guide) [12.12.2017]).

Council conclusions of 6. December 2011 on the fight against crimes committed by mobile (itinerant) criminal groups (Available at: http://register.consilium.europa.eu/doc/srv?l=EN&f=ST%206038%202012%20INIT [10.07.14]).

EU Council Declaration on Combating Terrorism EU Council Declaration on Combating Terrorism (Brussels, 25.03.2004).

COM (2004) 376 Commission's Communication on police cooperation (19 May 2004).

COM (2004) 858 Report from the Commission on national measures taken to comply with the Council Framework Decision of 13 June 2002 on Joint Investigation Teams, Commission of the European Communities (7 January 2005).

COM (2005) 490 final Proposal for a Council Framework Decision on the exchange of information under the principle of availability, (12 October 2005).

COM (2005) 597 final Communication from the Commission to the Council and the European Parliament on improved effectiveness, enhanced interoperability and synergies among European databases in the area of Justice and Home Affairs (Brussels, 24 November 2005).

COM (2010) 673 final The EU Internal Security Strategy in Action: Five steps towards a more secure Europe, COM(2010) 673 final, Brussels, 22 November 2010.

COM (2011) 561 COM (2011) 561 Communication from the Commission ot the European Parliament, the Council, the EUropean Exonomic and Social Committee and the COmmittee of the Regions – Schengen governance – strengthening the area without internal border control.

COM (2012) 230 COM (2012) 230 Communication from the Commission to the European Parliament and the Council – Biannual report on the functioning of the Schengen area 1 November 2011–30 April 2012.

COM(2013) 173 final Proposal for a REGULATION OF THE EUROPEAN PARLIAMENT AND OF THE COUNCIL on the European Union Agency for Law Enforcement Cooperation and Training (Europol) and repealing Decisions 2009/371/JHA and 2005/681/JHA (COD).

COM/2013/0534 final Proposal for a Council Regulation on the establishment of the European Public Prosecutor's Office (COM/2013/0534 final – 2013/0255 [APP]).

16.4 International conventions

Geneva Conventions of 29. April 1958 on the Law of the Sea (UNCLOS).

UN Convention of 1971 on psychotropic substances.

UN Convention of 1972: Single convention on Narcotic Drugs of 1961, as amended by the 1972 Protocol amending the 1961 Single Convention on Narcotic Drugs.

Convention of 28. January 1981 for the protection of individuals with regard to automatic processing of personal data.

UN Convention of 20. December 1988 against illicit traffic in narcotic drugs and psychotropic substances.

UN Convention of 1982 on the law of the sea (UNCLOS III).

UN Convention of 15. November 2000 against transnational organized crime (UNCTOC).

Convention implementing the Schengen Agreement of 14 June 1985 between the Governments of the States of the Benelux Economic Union, the Federal Republic of Germany and the French Republic on the gradual abolition of checks at their common borders. ([2000] OJ L 239/19).

ETS 182 (2001) Council of Europe 1959 Mutual assistance in criminal matters (Second Additional Protocol), 8.XI.2001.

List of declarations made with respect to treaty No. 182 (Available at: http://conventions.coe.int/Treaty/Commun/ListeDeclarations.asp?NT=182&CM=1&DF=&CL=ENG&VL=1 [09.09.13]).

The European Convention for the Protection of Human Rights and Fundamental Freedoms (ECHR).

1957 Eur.Convention on Extradition European Convention on Extradition, Paris, 13.XII.1957.

ETS 30 (1959) European Convention on Mutual Assistance in Criminal Matters, Strasbourg, 20.IV.1959.

1972 Eur.Convention on the Transfer of Proceedings in Criminal Matters European Convention on the Transfer of Proceedings in Criminal Matters CETS No.: 073, Strasbourg, 15.5.1972.

1999 Schengen Association Agreement concluded by the Council of the European Union and the Republic of Iceland and the Kingdom of Norway concerning the latters' association with the implementation, application and development of the Schengen acquis (SAA).

Agreement between the Kingdom of Norway and the European Police Office, 20 June 2001 (Europol – Norway [E/N] Agreement).

Agreement between the Kingdom of Norway and Eurojust, Oslo 28 April 2005 (Eurojust – Norway [EJ/N] Agreement).

Agreement between Eurojust and Europol (revised), the Hague 1 October 2009 (Europol/Eurojust Agreement).

16.5 Court decisions

Norwegian Supreme Court

Rt. 1986.779
Rt. 1992.1088
Rt. 1993.319
Rt. 1993.473
Rt. 1994.319
Rt. 1998.407
Rt. 1999.1269
Rt. 2000.1223
Rt. 2004.1826
Rt. 2005.1524
Rt. 2008.1659
Rt. 2009.567

Lower Courts

RG. 2013.615
LB 2013.112693
LG 2013.25651

EU Court of Justice

C–26/62 Van Gend en Loos v Nederlandse Administratie der Belastingen (1963)
C–436/03 Van Esbroek (2006)
C–137/09 Marc Michel Josemans v Burgemeester van Maastricht (2010)
C–188/10 Aziz Melki (2010)
C–189/10 Sélim Abdeli (2010)
C–278/12 PPU Atiquallah Adil v. Minister voor Immigratie, Inegratie en Asiel (2012)

ECtHR

Handyside v. UK (1976 1 737)
Lüdi v. Switzerland 12433/86 June 15 1992, Series A 238
M and others v Bulgaria 41416/08 26.07.2011
Teixeira de Castro v. Portugal 44/1997/828/1034, 9.6
Saadi v UK 13229/03 Grand Chamber 28 January 2009

16.6 Reports, opinions, policy papers, etc.

Riksadvokatens brev av 20.01.2003 om Rt. 2002.1744.

Dok. 3:10 (2009–2010) Riksrevisjonens undersøkelse av politiets innsats mot organisert kriminalitet.

Mandate letter to the Committee to prepare a Criminal Procedure Act Reform (Available at: http://www.regjeringen.no/upload/JD/Vedlegg/mandat_utvalg_straffeprosesslov.pdf [10.07.2014]).

Arbeidsprogram for EU/EØS-saker 2013 (Working program for EU/EEC matters 2013).

Arbeidsprogram for EU 2017 (Working program for EU matters 2017) (Available at: https://www.regjeringen.no/no/dokumenter/program_eu2017/id2536921/ [18,12,2017]).

European Security Strategy 2003 A secure Europe in a better world: European Security Strategy, Brussels 12 December 2003.

Resolution CMP Ref. 1123117 COMMITTEE OF MEMBERS OF PARLIAMENT OF THE EFTA COUNTRIES (CMP) Adopted pursuant to article 4 of the rules of procedure, 24 June 2013 Resolution of the CMP on Parliamentary scrutiny of Europol and Eurojust; the importance of including the national parliaments of the EFTA countries.

(SCH/Com-ex (98)52) Decision of the Executive Committee of 16 December 1998 on the Handbook on cross-border police cooperation.

Eurojust Annual Report 2007, 2012 and 2016. (Available at: http://eurojust.europa.eu/doclibrary/corporate/Pages/annual-reports.aspx?Page=2 [18.12.2017]).

Europol review 2012: General review of Europol activities 2012.

EU Organised Crime Threat Assessment 2011. (Available at: https://www.europol.europa.eu/newsroom/news/europol-organised-crime-threat-assessment–2011 [18.12.2017]).

SOCTA 2013 EU Serious and Organised Crime Threat Assessment. (Available at: https://www.europol.europa.eu/activities-services/main-reports/eu-serious-and-organised-crime-threat-assessment-socta–2013 [18.12.2017]).

Eurojust Grant Programme for 2014 Grants for financial assistance to Joint Investigation Teams.

AWF 2012 EUROPOL New AWF Concept Guide for MS and Third Parties (O1 – Operational Centre EDOC#525188v14 31/05/2012).

Guide to EU MS JIT legislation Guide on EU Member States' legislation on joint investigation teams (from Europol and Eurojust. (Available at: https://www.europol.europa.eu/activities-services/joint-investigation-teams).

CBO Manual fact sheets (10505/4/09) Manual on cross-border operations – addendum (national fact sheets) (10505/4/09 REV 4 ADD 1 REV 3).

CBO Manual 10505/3/09 (REV 3) Manual on cross-border operations (10505/3/09 REV 3).

EDPS Opinion 29.04.13 Opinion of the European Data Protection Supervisor on the Communication from the Commission to the European Parliament and the Council entitled 'Strengthening law enforcement cooperation in the EU: the European Information Exchange Model (EIXM), 29 April 2013.

Index

Agamben, G 241
Ahnfelt, E 227
alerts 102–4, 106–10, 130–31, 136, 137, 156, 236
Amsterdam Treaty 4n15, 48, 70, 71, 72, 172, 187
Analysis Work Files (AWFs) 119, 123, 124–26, 127, 218
Andenæs, J 9
Anderson, M 61n22, 222, 227
apprehension and detention 31–32; CISA and 135–36, 137–38, 144, 157–58; coercive powers and 156–59; foreign police and 192–94, 204; hot pursuit and 151, 155, 156–59, 169; identity and 33; information exchange and 128, 134, 135–39; private security companies and 41; 'serious crimes' and 115n79, 128
approximation 227–30
Area of Freedom, Security and Justice (AFSJ): Amsterdam Treaty and 187; challenges of 91; establishment of 56, 90; EU as 213, 228, 241; member states and 93; mission and role of 4, 47–49, 69, 94
armed forces, police vs. 3, 5
arrest: citizen's arrest 41, 144, 156, 158, 193, 205; coercive powers and 157–58; covert operations 167; foreign police and 73–74; hot pursuit and 157–58, 160, 161, 162, 163; individual rights and 32, 34; information exchange and 59, 100, 103, 104, 105, 106–7, 110, 121, 124, 127, 130, 134, 135–39; JITs and 177, 183, 193, 195, 200; operational cooperation 142, 144, 145, 147, 150; proximity policing and 215n57, 222; social contract theory and 232; *see also* European Arrest Warrant (EAW); extradition; Nordic Arrest Warrant (NAW)
Aschehoug, TH 247
asylum seekers 32n26, 48, 58, 71, 111, 113–14, 116, 117, 236
Auglend, RL 148, 149, 151, 152–53, 154, 159, 197, 211–12
Aulie report 35–36, 220
Austria 58n8, 142n3, 214
Austria-Hungary 142n3
Automated Fingerprint Identification System (AFIS) 111–12, 114

bail 32
Bartelson, J 15
Bayley, DH 7, 12, 205, 237
Beck, U 214n54, 227
Belgium 171, 193
Benelux Treaty 142n3, 147, 154n64
Bevers, H 151, 157
Bigo, D 94, 140, 141, 207, 216
biometric data 101, 102, 107–8, 111–12, 131; *see also* fingerprints
Block, L 175n25, 176, 185, 207
Bodin, Jean 15
border control 14–16, 58–59, 68, 69, 97–98, 104n32, 112–18, 191; *see also* freedom of movement; immigration control
Boucht, J 153n61, 165, 197, 213
Bowling, B 63, 208, 245
Brodeur, J-P 11, 12
Brown, SD 166
Buzan, B 216

Cameron, I 178, 181
'caught in the act' requirement 41, 144, 148–51
CBO Manual 153n61, 188–90, 191, 194n122
CEPOL (European Police College) 53, 214
CFREU (European Union Charter of Fundamental Rights) 49, 240–41
Chayes, A 243
Chayes, AH 243
Christie, N 35, 223
circulation *see* freedom of movement
citizen rights, origins 11

citizen's arrest 41, 144, 156, 158, 193, 205
citizenship 34, 147, 197, 213, 234, 239n74, 244
civilian responsibility 40–41
coast guard 5, 15, 105n33, 175n26
coercion: covert investigation and 164, 166, 167, 168; defined 30–31; foreign police and 73, 77, 103, 166, 171, 183–85, 192–93; information exchange and 97, 100, 102, 110, 125–27, 134–35, 135–36, 138; JITs and 102–93, 176–77, 179–80, 183, 184, 192–93, 199; liaison officers and 140; measures of 30–33, 37, 54, 64–65, 101, 125, 150, 156–59; nation-states and 2–3, 11, 14, 75, 142, 205, 238; police authority and 2–3, 5, 7, 9–10, 11, 143, 144, 150, 151, 156–58; potential of 64–65; public order and 191, 215n59, 220; surveillance and 134–35, 150, 156–58, 199; Weberian notion of 2–3, 205
collective safety 29
community, concept of 237–40
Connolly, WE 90
controlled deliveries *see* cross-border controlled deliveries
Convention Implementing the Schengen Agreement (CISA): apprehension and detention 135–36, 137–38, 144, 157–58; cross-border controlled deliveries and 161–62, 163; data registration and 132; discrimination in immigration control 235; drug-related crimes 67; EEA agreement and 76–77; external border control and 97–98; foreign police 143, 144, 193; hot pursuit and 145, 147–50, 152–53, 154–56, 157–59, 214; information exchange and 102, 103, 105, 106–7, 108, 109, 130, 185; liaison agreements 140; public order and 220; reporting requirements 159; security deficit arguments 216n67; signing of 58–59; sovereignty and 73, 76–77; surveillance and 134–35, 146; use of force 157; use of service weapons 154
Convention on Mutual Assistance in Criminal Matters (MLA) *see* MLA Convention on Mutual Assistance in Criminal Matters
cooperation *See* cross-border police cooperation
Co-operation Group to Combat Drug Abuse and Illicit Trafficking in Drugs (Pompidou Group) 51
COSI (Standing Committee on Operational Cooperation on Internal Security) 47n8, 218
Council of Europe (CoE) 45, 50–51, 147, 159–60, 162
Court of Justice of the European Union (CJEU) 46, 55, 81–84, 86–87, 89
covert investigation *see* cross-border covert investigation
crime control policies 45–49, 225–47; 'culture of control' 233; effects of 226–37, 244; measuring level of 229–30; sovereignty and 240–45
criminal investigation 12, 18, 29, 33, 37, 87–88, 97, 116, 150; *see also* information exchange; Joint Investigation Teams (JITs); Kripos (National Criminal Investigation Service)
Criminal Procedure Act (CPA): covert investigation and 165, 167; criterion for reasonable grounds 116; definitions 29; JITs and 176, 183, 193, 199; pre-Schengen cooperation 42; reform of 244n103; *see also* specific procedure
Crisis and Hostage Negotiation Service 39n63
cross-border controlled deliveries 21, 128, 135, 140, 160–63, 164, 170, 171, 179
cross-border covert investigation 39, 147, 160, 161n106, 163–69, 171, 184, 185–86; *see also* Joint Investigation Teams (JITs)
cross-border crime 65–69, 128, 146–54, 165, 217–20; *see also* hot pursuit; specific crime
Cross-Border Interventions Teams 188
cross-border police cooperation: impact on Norwegian police 206–24; impact on Norwegian society 225–47; jurisdictional issues 142–43; measuring effectiveness of 62, 217–20; methods for studying 3, 16–21; origins and development of 2, 4–6, 25–26, 45–56; perception of safety and 215–20; reservations to 159–60; 'soft laws' 144–45; special police units and 38–41; types of 97–98; *see also* information exchange; Nordic cooperation; operational cooperation
cross-border surveillance: covert investigation vs. 163–64; cross-border controlled deliveries and 161–62; definitions 134–35, 142–43; duty of reporting 158–59; emergency situations and 193; general rules 152–53, 199; hot pursuit and 143, 144, 145–60, 169–70, 206; JITs and 193, 202, 203; liaison officers and 140; market regulations and 86; notification requirements 153–54; offences for 145–52; public order and 220; sovereignty and 70, 73; use of service weapons 154,

194–95, 213; *see also* information exchange
cultural values 1
customs: covert investigation and 164n125, 166; cross-border controlled deliveries and 161; EU Convention (2000) and 146–47; heroin seizures 60n20; hot pursuit and 152; immigration control and 104n32, 234n54; information exchange and 104n32, 105n33, 108, 136, 141; JITs and 175n26, 187; liaison officers and 140, 141; policing definitions 5; post-passport control 42–43, 58, 59; PTN and 42, 44, 140
Czech Republic 229

Daman, M 146, 155, 156, 159, 169
databases 59, 99, 100, 110–26, 129–39, 188; *see also* specific database
data protection 21, 100, 109, 116, 121–24
Data Retention Directive 86
de Busser, Ed 174, 177
Deflem, M 25, 211
de Moor, Ad 222
den Boer, M 61n22, 210n33, 211, 229
Denmark 7, 8–12; arming of police 195; cross-border controlled deliveries and 161n108, 162, 163; Europol and 126; Holocaust and 226; hot pursuit and 148, 149, 151, 154–55, 160; MLA and 50n2; opting out of police measures 201n153; police education and training 177n38, 228n18; police structure and organisation 37, 127; Schengen *Acquis* and 58n8; sovereignty and 73n52; terrorism and 228n18
detention *see* apprehension and detention
Directive on Police Registers 101
displacement 236
DNA databases 101, 111–12
Doelle, P 61n22, 210n33, 211, 229
DPP (Norwegian Director of Public Prosecution) 165–66, 167, 215
drug-related crime 43, 45, 51, 60, 60n20, 67, 146, 161n109
Dubber, MD 239
Dublin Agreement 113–14, 116, 117, 118

economic cooperation 45–47
ECRIS (European Union Criminal Records Information System) 112
ECSC (Treaty on the European Coal and Steel Community) 45–46
Efjestad, JS 75n61
Elholm, T 228n18
ELYS 103
Emergency Response Unit 39n63
England 12, 229
Enlightenment era 10–11, 15
environmental rights 49
Ericson, RV 206
E-tjenesten 40
EUCPN 188
EU law, research on 20
EU Lisa 112
EURATOM (Treaty on the European Atomic Energy Community) 45–46
Eurodac 59, 111, 112, 114, 118, 130
Eurojust: Europol and 55, 120, 126–27, 128; growth of 94; information exchange and 105–6, 130, 138–39; JITs and 174–75, 178–80, 199–200, 202, 203, 226; liaison officers 140–41; mission and role of 55, 85, 126–29, 163, 179–80; operational powers 75n61, 138–39, 163; SIRENE and 130; threat assessment reports 218
European Arrest Warrant (EAW) 66, 85, 226; extradition and 132, 137–38, 147, 169; information exchange and 102, 108, 109, 115, 120, 126, 128, 132, 136; mission and role of 137–38
European Commission (Commission) 79–81, 82, 84, 86
European Community (EU) 45–47
European Convention of Human Rights (ECHR) 4, 32, 34n35, 45, 49, 50–51, 88, 100, 167
European Council (Council) 79–81, 82, 83–85
European Court of Human Rights (ECtHR) 4, 32n26, 100, 167, 244
European Court of Justice 46, 79
European Data Protection Supervisor (EDPS) 55
European Economic Agreement (EEA): as added legal system 20; external sovereignty and 13, 80, 81, 84, 86, 88, 91; harmonisation and 201; impact of 228, 229–30, 231–32, 235, 237; internal sovereignty and 69–71, 73, 76–77; mission and role of 3–4, 57; sovereignty and 13
European Economic Area (EEA) 57
European Economic Community (EEC) 46, 241
European Evidence Warrant (EEW) 135
European Free Trade Association (EFTA) 57, 70, 77, 81, 84, 85–86, 89
European Free Trade Association Surveillance Authority (ESA) 86
European Information System (EIS) 119, 120, 124–26, 127, 130, 131
European Investigation Order (EIO) 135

European Parliament (EP) 46, 53, 55, 79–80, 82, 83
European Police College (CEPOL) 53, 214
European Police Force 240–41
European Public Prosecutors Office (EPPO) 83, 138–39, 240–41
European Union (EU) 79–95; courts 81–84; legislative procedure post-Lisbon 83–84; mission and role of 228, 231, 241; as nation-state 92–95; political institutions 79–81; post-Schengen 212; sovereignty of 240–45
European Union Charter of Fundamental Rights (CFREU) 49, 240–41
European Union Criminal Records Information System (ECRIS) 112
Europol (European Police Office): accountability 55; affiliation with 64; Analysis Work Files (AWFs) 119, 123, 124–26, 127, 218; autonomy of 55, 211; CBO Manual 188–90, 191; coercive powers of 54, 75n61, 138; comparisons to other systems 129–33; employee statistics 54; Eurojust and 55, 120, 126–27, 128; growth of 94; impact of 227; information exchange and 59, 105–6, 115–28, 129–32, 135, 138–39, 221; JITs and 112, 124, 125, 171, 174–75, 178–80, 188–90, 199–200, 202, 203, 204, 221, 226; liaison officers 52, 54, 127, 135, 140–41; mission and role of 4, 47, 52–54, 85, 120–21, 138–39, 163, 179–80, 217, 218–19, 221, 222; operational powers 75n61; operative analysis projects (OAPs) 123–24; origins of 50–56; public order policing 221; threat assessment reports 217–19
Europol Decision (EPCD) 53, 122, 222
Europol Drugs Unit (EDU) 52
Europol Information System (EIS) 119–20, 124–26, 127, 130, 131
Europol–Norway Agreement (E–N) 129
Europol Regulation (ER) 47, 53, 119, 120, 122, 179, 180
external sovereignty 2, 15, 22, 23, 25, 79–95, 205, 243
extradition 21; CoE and 51; cross-border controlled deliveries and 162; harmonisation and 42; hot pursuit and 145–48, 156–58; information exchange and 104, 106, 109n45, 114, 124, 132; JITs and 97, 174; Nordic Arrest Warrant (NAW) and 65–66, 137–38, 147, 169; Nordic Extradition Act 146, 147–48; rules for 145, 147, 169; SIS Act and 136–38

Fijnaut, C 168, 200n152
fingerprints 102, 107–8, 111–12, 113, 114–15, 117, 128–29, 186, 188
Finland: arming of police 195; hot pursuit and 66, 73n52, 144, 148, 151, 152, 153, 155, 157–58, 160; JITs and 174, 193–94, 195, 197, 202; Schengen *Acquis* and 58n8; terrorism and 228n18; use of firearms in 195n125
firearms 33, 47, 60, 107, 128n136, 154, 194–95, 201, 213
forarbeid, defined 16
foreign police powers 33, 41, 204
Foucault, Michel 9, 232
France 142n3, 146, 176, 193
freedom of movement 42–43, 58–59, 64, 69, 112–14, 187, 230–34, 241–42, 244; *see also* immigration control
From, J 227
Frontex border guard system 15, 127, 218, 241
fundamental rights, human rights vs. 241–42, 246

Gade, I 151
gang-related crime 44, 60, 174, 218–19, 236
Garland, D 226–27, 233
gendarmerie 10, 11
General Civil Penal Code (GCPC) 33–34, 142, 154, 161, 191
Germany 142n3, 146, 151, 176, 193, 214, 229
Gerspacher, N 219n87
globalisation 4, 68, 94–95, 228n16, 230, 245
Great Britain 12, 168, 174
Greece 50n2
guns *see* firearms

Haggerty, KD 206
Hague Programme 47, 110
Halvorsen, V 168
harmonisation 4, 227–30, 238
Henricson, I 126–27, 150
Hobbes, Thomas 15, 63
Høigård, C 228
hot pursuit: internal sovereignty and 73–74; JITs and 171, 193, 194, 197, 202, 203, 206; operational cooperation and 142, 143, 144, 145–63, 169–70; weapons and 194, 213–14
Hufnagel, S 169, 203
human rights: ECHR and 4, 32, 34n35, 45, 49, 50–51, 88, 100, 167; fundamental rights vs. 241–42, 246; police sociology and 18–19; procedural 4, 32, 32n26, 100,

167, 226, 244; *see also* data protection; privacy
human trafficking 60, 146, 171, 177, 208
Huysmans, EF 216

Iceland 58n8, 74, 79, 84, 108, 178, 182, 195
immigration control: customs and 104n32, 234n54; discriminatory aspects 234–35; Europol and 52; impact of 230–37; information exchange and 106–7, 110–19, 129, 130–33; Norwegian Immigrant Register 113; Norwegian Immigration Act 106, 113–14, 116, 118, 208–9, 234n57, 235, 236; passports 42–43, 58–59, 69, 114, 130; pillar system and 48; public order and 187; Visa Information System (VIS) 59, 101, 111, 112, 113–17, 119, 129–33; *see also* border control; freedom of movement
Imsen, S 11
individual freedoms 28–29, 32
infiltration 135, 163–64, 165–68, 196
information exchange 44, 99–139; access and control 103–6, 110, 206, 221; alerts 102–3, 106–10, 130–31, 136, 137, 156, 236; collection and storage 101; criteria for reasonable grounds 116; data protection 21, 100, 109, 116, 121–24; differences and similarities between systems 129–33; interoperability 110–11, 118–19; legal basis for 100–101; privacy 21, 29, 34, 64–65, 100, 106–8, 118, 164, 167; registration data 106–8; transmission of 109–10, 121; *see also* specific database
Integrated Data Management Concept 119
internal security 61
internal sovereignty 2, 15, 22, 23, 62–78, 205, 237, 238, 243
International Criminal Police Commission 211
internationalisation 4, 60–61, 95
Interpol 51, 59, 103, 211, 213, 219
investigation, concept of 29, 97
Italy 50n2, 58n8

Jessop, B 14
Joint Hit Teams (JHT) 193
Joint Investigation Teams (JITs) 171–204; accountability 55; benefits 172; definitions 171–72, 187; establishment of 175; finance and funding 178–79; hot pursuit and 171, 193, 194, 197, 202, 203, 206; initiation of 125, 126; joint operations and patrols vs. 97, 171–72, 173, 186–98; legal changes and 183–85; managing 198–204; members and leadership 176–78, 185, 202; mission and role of 172–73, 174, 176–78, 186–89; Nordic 182–85; OAPs and 124; origin of 172; parallel investigations 185–86; requirements for 173–76; transferring of information and 141, 181–82
joint patrolling 97, 171–72, 173, 186–98
Joubert, C 151, 157
justice agreements 47–49
Justice and Home Affairs Council (JHA) 55

Karanja, SK 18
Krasner, SD 15
Kripos (National Criminal Investigation Service): comparisons to other systems 131, 132; cross-border controlled deliveries and 161; information exchange and 103, 104, 105, 109, 110, 113, 116, 117, 119, 131, 132, 137, 138, 148; JITs and 173, 175, 180; liaison officers and 44, 125, 140–41; Lithuanian gang project 236; mission and role of 44, 103, 104, 221; police cooperation with 36, 38, 39, 142, 143–44; SIRENE and 103, 104, 130–31, 132, 137; threat assessment reports 217, 219
Kvam, B 18, 48, 69n35, 101, 185n78, 221

Lacey, N 229–30, 233
Latvia 229
Lavenex, S 93
lensmen 9, 10, 223
Levi, R 232
liaison officers (LO): Europol and 52, 54, 127, 135, 140–41; information exchange and 97, 105, 115, 125, 127, 128, 129, 131–32, 138; JITs and 179, 185n78, 190, 199n145, 204; Kripos and 43–44, 125, 140–41; mission and role of 141; PTN and 43–44, 140
Lipset, SM 93–94
Lisbon Treaty (LT) 17, 48, 53, 80, 83–84, 85, 187, 240
Lithuania 161n106, 236
Loader, I 238
Locke, John 9, 15, 63
Lorentzen, H 36
Lüdi case 167–68
Lugano Convention 136
Lyon, D 234

Maastricht Treaty 46, 47, 48, 52, 151, 240
Manning, P K 2
Marx, GT 168
mass media 35–36, 208, 213, 218, 233–34
Mathiesen, G 35, 36, 235–36
Mayer, M 175n25, 178

Military Intelligence Service (E-tjenesten) 40
Mitsilegas, V 94, 111, 180, 203
MLA Convention on Mutual Assistance in Criminal Matters: association agreement 159–60; covert investigation and 164, 168; cross-border controlled deliveries and 162, 163; drug searches 161n109; effects of 170; establishment of 50–51, 146n20, 147; JITs and 172–73, 174–75, 177–79, 181, 182, 203; mission and role of 50–51, 147, 206; reservation clauses 160
Mobile Deployment Concept 39n63
mobility *see* freedom of movement
motorcycle gang-related crime 44, 60, 218–19
mutual recognition principle 136
Myhrer, T-G 113

Næshagen, FL 217
Naples II Convention 166
National Authority for Investigation and Prosecution of Economic and Environmental Crime (Økokrim) 38, 110
National Authority for Prosecution of Organised and Other Serious Crime (NAST) 173
National Criminal Investigation Service *see* Kripos (National Criminal Investigation Service)
nation-states: challenges to 3; coercion and 2–3, 11, 14, 75, 142, 205, 238; defined 8, 237–40, 244; EU as nation-state 92–95; evolution of 9, 14–15, 63, 242–45; features 11, 14, 238; obligation of to justify 64–65; policing and 2–3, 5–6, 11, 142, 225; social contract with citizens 92; territorial authority 14–16; Weberian notion of 2, 63, 93, 171, 205, 245
NATO 40, 73
neighborhood watch networks 198
Netherlands: cross-border controlled deliveries and 161; custody escape 151; drug policy 67; JITs and 174, 176, 178, 183, 184, 190, 193, 197, 202n161; prison population in 229
Network of National Experts on Joint Investigative Teams 174
Neumann, IB 69n36
9/11 terrorist attack 172n7
Nordic Agreement on Mutual Legal Assistance 104n31
Nordic Arrest Warrant (NAW) 44, 65–66, 109, 137–38, 147, 169, 199
Nordic Committee of Senior Officials for Legislative Issues (EK-LOV) 196
Nordic cooperation 42–44
Nordic Extradition Act 146, 147–48
Nordic Organized Crime Threat Assessment 43
Nordic Passport Union 42–43, 58, 69
Nordic Police and Customs Cooperation (PTN) 140
Nordic Police Cooperation Agreements 43, 65, 108, 172, 182, 196
Norway: crime statistics 60, 68, 207, 215, 229–30, 233; economic growth in 61; origins of attitude toward Europe 7–8; post-WWII 35–36; prison population in 229–30; referendums 57, 69–70
Norwegian Bar Association 184
Norwegian Bureau for the Investigation of Police Affairs (SEFO) 222
Norwegian Constitution 14, 64, 72–78, 243
Norwegian Data Protection Authority 116
Norwegian Director of Public Prosecution (DPP) 165–66, 167, 215
Norwegian Europol Agreement 55–56
Norwegian Immigrant Register 113
Norwegian Immigration Act 106, 113–14, 116, 118, 208–9, 234n57, 235, 236
Norwegian Parliament *(Stortinget)*: departure control 59n10; Europol and 56; external sovereignty 80, 84; information exchange and 114; internal sovereignty and 67–69, 71, 72–73, 75, 76–78; JITs and 183–84, 188; reports to 246
Norwegian Penal Code *See* General Civil Penal Code (GCPC)
Norwegian police: assessments and reports about 65, 207–8, 209, 246; authority of 206; civilian responsibility 40–41; education and training of 33, 212–14; employee statistics 36–37; foreign court jurisdiction and 85–89; history of 6–13, 35–36; impact of international cooperation on 206–24; mission and role of 1–3, 4, 7, 8–9, 16, 27–33, 38–40, 95, 220–24, 230, 234–35, 237–40, 246; organization and structure of 36–41, 97, 209–12; Oslo Police District 38, 39; 'police culture' and 212–14; reform of 209–12; Romerike Police District 233–34; rules of conduct 29–30, 33–35
Norwegian Police Academy 212–13
Norwegian Police Act of 1927 12, 27
Norwegian Police Act of 1936 27, 34
Norwegian Police Act of 1995 5–6, 21, 23, 25–41; coercive measures 30–32; concepts in 237–40, 246; context of 35–36; JITs and 183–85, 188; mission and role of police 1, 3, 4, 16, 27–33, 95, 220–24, 234–35, 237–40, 246; organization and structure of police 36–41; rules of conduct 29–30, 33–35; Schengen changes to

97–98; service weapons 154, 194–95, 213; *see also* operational cooperation
Norwegian Police Acts, origins 12, 19
Norwegian Police Committee (1912) 12, 66
Norwegian Police Registration Act 102
Norwegian Police's Bomb Squad 39n63
Norwegian Police Security Service (PST) 37, 39–40, 116, 195
Norwegian Police's Helicopter Service 39n63
Norwegian Schengen Affiliation Agreement (SAA) 17, 71–78, 81–82, 114
Norwegian Supreme Court 136, 157, 161, 166
Norwegian Vagrancy Act 231–32
notification 153–54

Office of the Auditor General (Norway) 65
Økokrim 38, 110
OLAF 120, 127, 174
open border development 42–43
operational cooperation 142–70; coercive powers 156–58; duty of reporting 158–59; hot pursuit and 142, 143, 144, 145–63, 169–70; legal basis 143–45; *see also* cross-border police cooperation; cross-border surveillance; hot pursuit
Operation Golf 171
operative analysis projects (OAPs) 123–24
Øresund Agreement 148, 194
organised crime: customs cooperation and 43; emergence of 208; Eurojust and 126; Europol and 54, 56, 130, 218–19; increase in 60, 61; information exchange and 123, 126, 130; JITs and 171, 174; reports on 65, 207–8, 218–19; strategies combatting 210–11, 221, 227–28
Oslo Police District 38, 39, 208, 209, 219

Palombella, G 241
parallel investigations 185–86
passports 42–43, 58–59, 69, 114, 130
Peers, S 168
personal safety 28
pillar system 46–47, 48, 58, 83, 85
Poland 229
police: autonomy of 205; birth of global 25–26; centralisation vs. decentralisation of 35–36, 38; definitions 4, 5, 6, 12, 16, 225; development of 6–13, 35–36, 231; education and training of 8, 33, 52, 53, 177n38, 189–90, 204, 212–14, 219n87, 228n18; as enforcers of state violence 1, 2–3, 93; mission and role of 1, 27–33, 95; policing vs. 6–7, 12–13; Weberian notion of 2–3, 93; *see also* Norwegian police
Police and Customs Cooperation (PTN) 42, 43, 140
police brutality 222
police cooperation *See* cross-border police cooperation
'police culture' 212–14
Police Directive (PD) 42
police infiltration 135, 163–64, 165–68, 196
Police Negotiation Unit 39n63
police provocation 160, 161, 164, 165–67, 196
police reform committees 35
Police Register Directive (PRD) 185–86, 188, 221
Police Role Committee 36
police sociology 18–19
Pompidou Group 51
Portugal 58n8
prisons 3, 60–61, 196–97, 228, 229–31, 233
privacy 21, 29, 34, 64–65, 100, 106–8, 118, 164, 167; *see also* data protection
private policing 3, 4, 6, 33–34, 36, 205
prostitution 60
provocation 160, 161, 164, 165–67, 196
proximity policing 36, 198, 213, 214–24, 245–47
Prüm Decision 4–5; apprehension and 157; information exchange and 94, 97, 101, 102–3, 111–12, 117, 118, 135–36; JITs and 186–98
Prussia 142n3, 214
PST (Norwegian Police Security Service) 37, 39–40, 116, 195
PTN (Nordic Police and Customs Cooperation) 140
Public Administration Act 29
public order policing 13, 85, 130, 157–58, 171, 186–87, 191–95, 215n59, 220–24

qualified majority voting (QMV) 83–84

reciprocity, principle of 136–37
registers *see* databases
Rijken, C 181, 185–86
Romania 171, 172
Romerike Police District 233–34
Rousseau, Jean-Jacques 9, 15, 63
Royal Ministry of Foreign Affairs (MFA) 39n63
Royal Police Escort 39n63
Russia 59, 66, 98, 155, 160, 229n23
Ruud, M 18
Rwanda 229n23

SAA (Norwegian Schengen Affiliation Agreement) 17, 71–78, 81–82, 114
Saadi v UK 32n26
Samordningsorgan 219, 236

Schengen *Acquis:* defined 58n8; EU implementation of 48, 70, 71, 72, 74, 79, 83, 88, 146, 186n90; extradition 137n13, 146; origins 4n15
Schengen Agreement 58–78; decision-making rights 84–85; effects of 3–4, 25–26, 59–61; justifications to join 42–44, 62–69; legislative changes due to 97–98; mission and role of 1, 3–4, 58, 142–43, 206, 228; prior to 42–44, 59–60; *see also* Convention Implementing the Schengen Agreement (CISA)
Schengen Borders Code 87
Schengen Convention 4–5, 13
Schengen Implementation Convention 58n8
Schengen Information System (SIS): access and control 84, 101–6, 113; comparisons to other systems 129–33; contents and rules 103–4; data registration 106–8; discrimination and 235–36; enactment of 98; impact of 206, 220, 235–36; information transmission 109–10; interlinking alerts 108–9; interoperability 110–11, 118–19; PST and 40; target areas 47–48
Schengen Information System II (SISII) 47–48, 59, 101–11, 119, 132, 134–39, 141
search and seizure: assessments of 65, 207; authority for 21, 39–40, 41, 101, 156n82, 157, 161, 163, 193; defined 32–33; information exchange and 101, 104, 107, 110, 112, 117n95, 118, 124, 134–35; JITs and 171, 178, 187
search registers *see* databases; specific register
secondment measures 140–41
securitisation 216–17
Security Act 40
security agreements 47–49
security criminology 19
security guards 3, 4, 6, 205
SEFO (Norwegian Bureau for the Investigation of Police Affairs) 222
Serious and Organised Crime Threat Assessments (SOCTA) 218
service weapons 154, 194–95, 213
Sheptycki, J 53n23, 63, 203, 206, 208, 222, 245
SIENA (Secure Information Exchange Network Application) 125
Single European Act (SEA) 46, 52, 60, 240
SIRENE 103, 104, 130–31, 132, 137
social rights 28–29; *see also* human rights
sovereign states, origins of 9
sovereignty 13–16, 62–95; border control as 15; challenges to 1–2, 3, 206, 237; definitions 2, 14, 22; EU and 240–45; external sovereignty 2, 15, 22, 23, 25, 79–95, 205, 243; facets of 15, 22, 23, 203, 225; infringements of 71–78; internal sovereignty 2, 15, 22, 23, 62–78, 205, 237, 238, 243
Spain 58n8, 171, 176, 181, 202n161
Spapens, T 185, 193
Standing Committee on Operational Cooperation on Internal Security (COSI) 47n8, 218
Stevnsborg, H 8
Stockholm Programme 47
Stortinget see Norwegian Parliament (*Stortinget*)
surveillance 40, 86, 101, 134–35, 142–43, 146, 199; *see also* cross-border surveillance
'surveillance assemblage' 206
surveillance studies 19
Sweden 7; arming of police officers 195; hot pursuit and 144, 145, 148, 151, 152, 153, 155, 157n84, 160; information exchange and 94, 112; JITs and 169, 174, 175, 178, 183, 184, 193–94, 195, 197, 198; MLA and 50n2; police structure and organisation 37; prison population in 196, 229–30; Schengen *Acquis* and 58n8; sovereignty and 65, 66, 73n52, 94; terrorism and 228n18
Swedish Initiative Decision 102
Swedish International Police Cooperation Act 178
Switzerland 58n8, 142n3, 167–68

Tak, PJP 203
Tampere Programme 47
technology 4, 44, 102, 206
terrorism: European Agenda on Security and 47–48; Europol and 54, 120–21, 123; as form of non-state war 90–91; globalisation and 246; information exchange and 110–11, 114–15, 117–18, 123, 128; JITs and 174, 187, 195, 202n161; level of punishment and 228–29; military and 39; 9/11 attack 172n7; origin of police cooperation and 25, 39, 240; police service weapons and 195; temporary border controls and 58n6; terrorist lists 91; TREVI and 51–52; 22/7 attacks 58n6, 128, 187, 215, 245; Utøya 209, 215
TETRA network 153
threat assessments 40, 43, 54, 217–20, 224

threshold of suspicion 108, 147, 148–52, 157, 169, 180
Tilly, C. 7
trade agreements 45–46, 57
treaties 45–49, 52, 135, 240–41; *see also* specific treaty
Treaty on European Union (TEU) 46, 88, 138
Treaty on the European Atomic Energy Community (EURATOM) 45–46
Treaty on the European Coal and Steel Community (ECSC) 45–46
Treaty on the European Economic Community (TEC) 45–46, 119–20
TREVI cooperation 50–56
22/7 terrorist attacks 58n6, 128, 187, 215, 245

UK Metropolitan Police (MET) 171
uniforms 10, 58, 152, 194, 196
Union Treaty (1993) 52
United Kingdom 32n26, 53, 154n65, 171, 174, 202n161
United Nations 45, 67
Utøya 209, 215

vehicle registration authorities (VRA) 105, 107, 108–9, 111–12, 134, 186
vehicles/vehicle trafficking 52, 60, 100, 104, 152, 157
Vermeulen, G 181, 222
Visa Information System (VIS) 59, 101, 111, 112, 113–17, 119, 129–33

Wales 229
Walker, N 215, 238
weapons 33, 44, 154, 194–95, 201, 213; *see also* firearms
Weber, Max 2–3, 63, 93, 171, 205, 245
welfare state 9, 216, 227, 228, 230, 234–35, 237
wire-tapping 21, 30n21, 134, 136, 164, 167, 181
Working Program 91
World War II 4, 35, 45, 226

For Product Safety Concerns and Information please contact our EU representative GPSR@taylorandfrancis.com Taylor & Francis Verlag GmbH, Kaufingerstraße 24, 80331 München, Germany

Batch number: 10726294

Printed by Printforce, the Netherlands